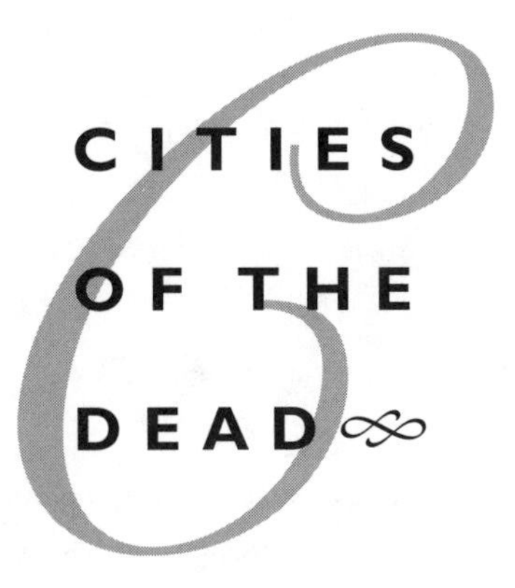

The Social Foundations of Aesthetic Forms

JONATHAN ARAC, EDITOR

The Social Foundations of Aesthetic Forms

A series of Columbia University Press

JONATHAN ARAC, EDITOR

Critical Genealogies: Historical Situations for Postmodern Literary Studies
Jonathan Arac

Advertising Fiction: Literature, Advertisement, and Social Reading
Jennifer Wicke

Masks of Conquest: Literary Study and British Rule in India
Gauri Viswanathan

Left Politics and the Literary Profession
Leonard J. Davis and M. Bella Mirabella, editors

The Vietnam War and American Culture
John Carlos Rowe and Rick Berg, editors

Authors and Authority: English and American Criticism, 1750–1990
Patrick Parrinder

Reaches of Empire: The English Novel from Edgeworth to Dickens
Suvendrini Perera

Radical Parody: American Culture and Critical Agency After Foucault
Daniel T. O'Hara

Narrating Discovery: The Romantic Explorer in American Literature, 1790–1855
Bruce Greenfield

The Author, Art, and the Market: Rereading the History of Aesthetics
Martha Woodmansee

Rethinking Class: Literary Studies and Social Formations
Wai Chee Dimock and Michael T. Gilmore, editors

CITIES OF THE DEAD

Circum-Atlantic Performance

JOSEPH ROACH

COLUMBIA UNIVERSITY PRESS NEW YORK

Columbia University Press
New York Chichester, West Sussex

Library of Congress Cataloging-in-Publication Data
Roach, Joseph R.
Cities of the dead : circum-Atlantic performance / Joseph Roach.
p. cm. — (The social foundations of aesthetic forms)
Includes bibliographical references and index.
ISBN 0–231–10460–X
ISBN 0–231–10461–8 (pbk.)
1. Carnival—Louisiana—New Orleans—History. 2. Folklore—Louisiana—New Orleans—Performance. 3. Theater and society—Louisiana—New Orleans—History. 4. Folklore—England—London—Performance. 5. Theater and society—England—London—History. 6. Communication and culture. 7. Memory—Social aspects. 8. New Orleans (La.)—History. 9. London (England)—History. I. Title. II. Series: Social foundations of aesthetic forms series.
GT4211.N4R63 1996
791—dc20 95–33447
CIP

Casebound editions of Columbia University Press books are printed on permanent and durable acid-free paper.

Printed in the United States of America

c 10 9 8 7 6 5 4 3 2 1
p 10 9 8 7 6 5 4 3

The Discovery of America, and that of a passage to the East Indies by the Cape of Good Hope, are the two greatest and most important events recorded in the history of mankind.

~ADAM SMITH

Before Elvis there was nothing.

~JOHN LENNON

CONTENTS

PREFACE

CITIES OF THE DEAD ARE PRIMARILY FOR THE LIVING. THEY EXIST NOT ONLY AS artifacts, such as cemeteries and commemorative landmarks, but also as behaviors. They endure, in other words, as occasions for memory and invention. This book shows how the memories of some particular times and places have become embodied in and through performances. But it also suggests how memories torture themselves into forgetting by disguising their collaborative interdependence across imaginary borders of race, nation, and origin. The social processes of memory and forgetting, familiarly known as culture, may be carried out by a variety of performance events, from stage plays to sacred rites, from carnivals to the invisible rituals of everyday life. To perform in this sense means to bring forth, to make manifest, and to transmit. To perform also means, though often more secretly, to reinvent. This claim is especially relevant to the performances that flourish within the geohistorical matrix of the circum-Atlantic world. Bounded by Europe, Africa, and the Americas, North and South, this economic and cultural system entailed vast movements of people and commodities to experimental destinations, the consequences of which continue to visit themselves upon the material and human fabric of the cities inhabited by their successors. As the most visible evidence of an oceanic interculture only now beginning to be reclaimed on its own terms, performances reveal what it means to live through memory in cities of the dead.

In recognition of the dynamism of circum-Atlantic performances, the form of this book follows its subject matter. Although mostly limited to events and traditions in only two cities, fixed points along the Atlantic rim, the presentation of the materials that follow emulates the restless migrations by which those cities, London and New Orleans, have been continuously recreated. Since the late seventeenth and early eighteenth centuries, local cultural productions have been hybridized routinely by the hemispheric circulation of collectively created forms. The following chapters thus plot the changing position of identities that have endured—and can continue to endure—only as relationships.

This approach necessarily requires movement across conventional disciplinary categories and sometimes against their grain. My own specialty, theatrical history and dramatic literature, has, of course, limited the choices that I have made from an array of possible periods, genres, and traditions. Increasingly, however, the principles underlying my choices have been redefined by the expansive interdisciplinary or postdisciplinary agenda of performance studies. A reader curious about the scope of that agenda will find that, in addition to the other expositional work that chapter 1 and the first section of chapter 2 must do, they also function as a kind of extended bibliographic essay on a key issue in the field of performance studies as I see it now: the relationship between memory and history.

The pursuit of performance does not require historians to abandon the archive, but it does encourage them to spend more time in the streets. When students ask about the problems of reconstructing historic performances—tasks I have shared in producing such works as Henry Purcell and Nahum Tate's *Dido and Aeneas* with period instruments and dance styles—I now ask them: What evidence do we have that they ever died out? This question follows logically from joining Second Line parades in New Orleans in recent years, parades that have a continuous history since the eighteenth century in the celebrations of the African-American social clubs and burial societies. In a related sense, it also follows logically from the experience of a determined pedestrian in a city where the dead remain more gregariously present to the living, materially and spiritually, than they do anywhere else I have walked, with the possible exception of Westminster Abbey.

The topoi of memory as performance that recur below—in death and surrogation (chapters 2 and 3), in law and popular culture (chapters 2 and

6), in sacrificial expenditure and commodification (chapters 4 and 5), and in myths of origin (throughout)—share a common inspiration derived from the aesthetic tangibility of live performances. I use the word *aesthetic* in what I understand to be its eighteenth-century meaning: the vitality and sensuous presence of material forms. In the name of memory, I hope that I may be forgiven this nostalgia for presence on the plea that, as a practical matter, the voices of the dead may speak freely now only through the bodies of the living.

ACKNOWLEDGMENTS

THIS PROJECT WAS SUPPORTED BY A SENIOR RESEARCH FELLOWSHIP FROM THE National Endowment for the Humanities for 1992–93. At crucial stages of the research, I received valuable assistance from staff members at several libraries and archives: Fred Hoxie at the D'Arcy McNickle Center for the History of the American Indian at the Newberry Library; Russell Maylone at Northwestern University Special Collections; Jude Solomon at the Historic New Orleans Collection; and the staff of the Amistad Research Center at Tulane University, including Fred Stielow and Brenda B. Square. At Tulane's Howard-Tilton Memorial Library, Bill Meneray and Courtney Page of Special Collections, Leon Miller, Helen Burkes, and Mary Leblanc of Manuscripts, Sylvia Metzinger of Rare Books, Joan Caldwell and Richard Campbell of the Louisiana Collection, and Bruce Raeburn, Alma Williams, and Diane Rose of the William Ransom Hogan Jazz Archive provided many hours of expert guidance. They did so with unfailing professionalism, even though the range of materials that I requested must have seemed eccentric at the very least.

Several colleagues with a special interest in the project—Marvin Carlson, Errol Hill, Richard Wendorf, Bruce McConachie, Thomas Postlewait, and Richard Rambuss—agreed to read and comment on the manuscript in various stages and sections, while Judith Milhous, Joseph Cohen, Lawrence Powell, and Joseph Logsdon offered valuable information from the perspective of their specialties. Michael P. Smith willingly shared his unique knowledge of New Orleans with me, offering both insight and inspiration. All these contributions proved timely and helpful, but I am responsible for the conclusions presented here as well as any residual errors or infelicities.

To the faculty and students at 1979 Sheridan Road, Evanston, Illinois, including Dwight Conquergood and Margaret Thompson Drewal, and at 721 Broadway, New York City, particularly Richard Schechner, Barbara Kirshenblatt-Gimblett, Brooks MacNamara, and Peggy Phelan, my debt is various, general, and profound. They continue to reinvent the field of performance studies, which is limited in scope only by what people actually do, on the cusp of the arts and human sciences.

Earlier versions of some of the materials in chapters 5 and 6 first appeared in *Theatre Journal*, *Theatre Survey*, and *The Drama Review*.

During the past year I have been grateful to Jennifer Crewe at Columbia University Press for bringing together a team of readers and editors, especially Anne McCoy and Sarah St. Onge, who were able first to see this manuscript as a book and then to see it through the process of becoming one. Over the years Jonathan Arac and Carol Kay have seen my work before anyone else, except for Janice Carlisle, who somehow sees it before I do.

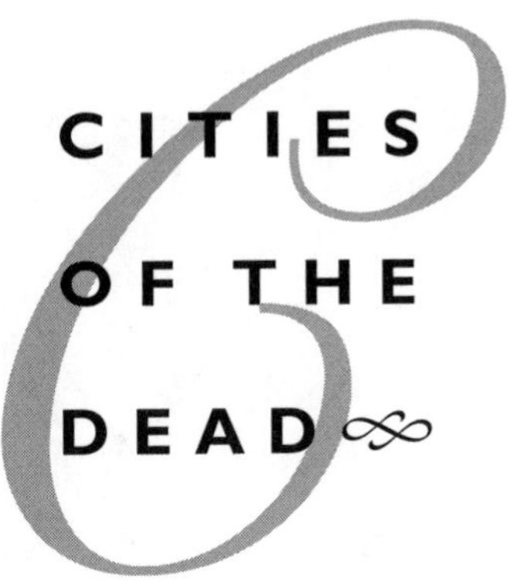
CITIES
OF THE
DEAD

1 INTRODUCTION: HISTORY, MEMORY, AND PERFORMANCE

Today documents include
the spoken word, the image, gestures.

-JACQUES LEGOFF

WHEN BENEVOLENT MANAGERS SPEAK NOW OF BALANCING BUDGETS BY "NATURAL attrition," they propose to harvest the actuarial fruits of retirement, resignation, and death. But more often than not, they also propose to replace the recently departed by asking those remaining behind to enhance their performances. These performances then constitute rites of memory in honor of the artificially superannuated. Into the professional and social places they once occupied step the anxious survivors, who now feel obliged more or less to reinvent themselves, taking into account the roles played by their predecessors. As a lifelong theater person, I take a keen interest in the imposition of such histrionics on civilian life. They bring to mind theatrical terms such as casting and miscasting, script and improvisation, memory and imagination. In addition to the ample opportunities for overwork that such policies often provide, they may also entail the demanding psychological obligations of double consciousness, the self-reflexive interaction of identity and role.

The all-too-familiar practice of downsizing by attrition, however, takes advantage of a much more powerful underlying phenomenon. Even when financial exigencies do not dictate retrenchment, a process goes on normally that is very much like the one that administrations impose in a pinch. Here too the dramaturgy of doubling in a role governs the functions of cultural transmission in the service of institutional memory. I have noticed, for instance, that when death or retirement removes a colleague from a community as interdependent as an academic department, despite the conventional panegyrics attesting to the fact that he or she can never be replaced, one or more of the survivors will move in to take over, overtly or covertly, the positions vacated by the decedent. These positions will more often prove to be the emotional and psychological nodal points within the human dynamics of the community, though they may encompass the intellectual ones as well. Consciously or unconsciously, even the big shoes will get filled, but rarely by the new person hired as a replacement. I am not the only one among my acquaintances to have remarked on this phenomenon. The speed at which roles can change hands prompted a recent retiree I know to define the status of professor emeritus as "forgotten but not gone." While savoring this witty inversion of the spurious immortality routinely granted by eulogists, I have also been pondering its double meaning, the real functions of social continuity and cultural preservation that it suggests. As he was fading away, my retiring colleague stumbled over the paradox of collective perpetuation: memory is a process that depends crucially on forgetting.

This book, in fact, takes up the three-sided relationship of memory, performance, and substitution. In it I propose to examine how culture reproduces and re-creates itself by a process that can be best described by the word *surrogation*. In the life of a community, the process of surrogation does not begin or end but continues as actual or perceived vacancies occur in the network of relations that constitutes the social fabric. Into the cavities created by loss through death or other forms of departure, I hypothesize, survivors attempt to fit satisfactory alternates. Because collective memory works selectively, imaginatively, and often perversely, surrogation rarely if ever succeeds. The process requires many trials and at least as many errors. The fit cannot be exact. The intended substitute either cannot fulfill expectations, creating a deficit, or actually exceeds them, creating a surplus. Then too the surrogate-elect may prove to be a divisive choice, one around whom factions polarize, or the prospective nominee may tap deep motives of prejudice and fear, so that even before the fact the unspoken possibility of his or her candidacy incites phobic anxiety. Finally, the very uncanniness of the process of surrogation, which tends to disturb the complacency of all thoughtful incumbents, may provoke many unbidden emotions, ranging from mildly incontinent sentimentalism to raging paranoia. As ambivalence deepens before the specter of inexorable antiquation, even the necessary preparations of the likely successors may alienate the affections of the officeholders—all the more powerfully when social or cultural differences exacerbate generational ones. At these times, improvised narratives of authenticity and priority may congeal into full-blown myths of legitimacy and origin.

In the likely event that one or more of the above calamities occurs, selective memory requires public enactments of forgetting, either to blur the obvious discontinuities, misalliances, and ruptures or, more desperately, to exaggerate them in order to mystify a previous Golden Age, now lapsed. In such dramas of sacrificial substitution, the derivation of the word *personality* from *mask* eerily doubles that of *tragedy* from *goat*. I believe that the process of trying out various candidates in different situations—the doomed search for originals by continuously auditioning stand-ins—is the most important of the many meanings that users intend when they say the word *performance*.

Competing definitions do proliferate. In his etymological account, anthropologist Victor Turner traces *performance* to the Old French word *parfournir*, meaning "to furnish forth," "to complete," or "to carry out thoroughly" (*From Ritual to Theatre*, 13). Ethnolinguist Richard Bauman, in his concise entry in the *International Encyclopedia of Communications*, locates the meaning of *performance* in the actual execution of an action as opposed to its potential (3:262–66), a meaning that operates in the theatrical performance of a script, in an automobile's performance on the test track, or in *parole*'s performance of *langue*. Theorist and director Richard Schechner, who has advanced the most focused and at the same time the most widely applicable definition of *performance*, calls it "restored behavior" or "twice-behaved behavior," by which he actually means behavior that "is always subject to revision," behavior that must be reinvented the second time or "the nth time" because it cannot happen exactly the same way twice, even though in some instances the "constancy of transmission" across many generations may be "astonishing" (*Between Theater and Anthropology*, 36–37; cf. Bauman and Briggs; Hymes). These three definitions of performance—that it carries out purposes thoroughly, that it actualizes a potential, or that it restores a behavior—commonly assume that performance offers a substitute for something else that preexists it. Performance, in other words, stands in for an elusive entity that it is not but that it must vainly aspire both to embody and to replace. Hence flourish the abiding yet vexed affinities between performance and memory, out of which blossom the most florid nostalgias for authenticity and origin. "Where memory is," notes theorist-director Herbert Blau, "theatre is" (382).

This book, however, is not about surrogation (or performance) as a universal, transhistorical structure. I want to contextualize its processes within a specific though very extensive historic and material continuum. The research strategies I favor emphasize the comparative approach to the theatrical, musical, and ritual traditions of many cultures. To that agenda, however, I would add the qualification of historical contingency: first, the intercultural communication that certain performances enabled at specific times and places; and second, the internal cultural self-definition that these and other performances produced by making visible the play of difference and identity within the larger ensemble of relations.

Circum-Atlantic Memory

Both intercultural and internally self-referential occasions of performance mark the connected places and times that constitute what I am calling, as the geohistorical locale for my thesis about memory as substitution, the circum-Atlantic world. As it emerged from the revolutionized economies of the late seventeenth century, this world resembled a vortex in which commodities and cultural practices changed hands many times. The most revolutionary commodity in this economy was human flesh, and not only because slave labor produced huge quantities of the addictive substances (sugar, coffee, tobacco, and—most insidiously—sugar and chocolate in combination) that transformed the world economy and financed the industrial revolution (Mintz). The concept of a circum-Atlantic world (as opposed to a transatlantic one) insists on the centrality of the diasporic and genocidal histories of Africa and the Americas, North and South, in the creation of the culture of modernity. In this sense, a New World was not discovered in the Caribbean, but one was truly invented there. Newness enacts a kind of surrogation—in the invention of a new England or a new France out of the memories of the old—but it also conceptually erases indigenous populations, contributing to a mentality conducive to the practical implementation of the American Holocaust (Stannard). While a great deal of the unspeakable violence instrumental to this creation may have been officially forgotten, circum-Atlantic memory retains its consequences, one of which is that the unspeakable cannot be rendered forever inexpressible: the most persistent mode of forgetting is memory imperfectly deferred.

For this region-centered conception, which locates the peoples of the Caribbean rim at the heart of an oceanic interculture embodied through performance, I am indebted to Paul Gilroy's formulation of the "Black Atlantic." In three prescient books, *"There Ain't No Black in the Union Jack": The Cultural Politics of Race and Nation* (1987), *The Black Atlantic: Modernity and Double Consciousness* (1993), and *Small Acts: Thoughts on the Politics of Black Cultures* (1993), Gilroy expands the cultural horizons of modern history in a way that does not begin and end at national borders but charts its course along the dark currents of a world economy that slavery once propelled: "A new structure of cultural exchange," he writes, "has been built up across the imperial networks which once played host to the triangular trade of sugar, slaves and capital" (*Union Jack*, 157). The idea of circum-Atlantic cultural exchange does not deny Eurocolonial initiatives their place in this history—indeed, it must newly reconsider and interrogate them—but it regards the results of those initiatives as the insufficiently acknowledged cocreations of an oceanic interculture. This interculture shares in the contributions of many peoples along the Atlantic rim—for example, Bambara, Iroquois, Spanish, English, Aztec, Yoruba, and French. I argue in this book that the scope of the circum-Atlantic interculture may be discerned most vividly by means of the performances, performance traditions, and the representations of performance that it engendered. This is true, I think, because performances so often carry within them the memory of otherwise forgotten substitutions—those that were rejected and, even more invisibly, those that have succeeded.

The key to understanding how performances worked *within* a culture, recognizing that a fixed and unified culture exists only as a convenient but dangerous fiction, is to illuminate the process of surrogation as it operated *between* the participating cultures. The key, in other words, is to understand how circum-Atlantic societies, confronted with revolutionary circumstances for which few precedents existed, have invented themselves by performing their pasts in the presence of others. They could not perform themselves, however, unless they also performed what and who they thought they were not. By defining themselves in opposition to others, they produced mutual representations from encomiums to caricatures, sometimes in each another's presence, at other times behind each other's backs. In the very form of minstrelsy, for example, as Eric Lott suggests in *Love and Theft: Blackface Minstrelsy and the American Working Class* (1993), there resides the deeply seated and potentially threatening possibility of involuntary surrogation through the act of performance. "Mimicry," writes Homi K. Bhabha, "is at once resemblance and menace" (86). This is so because, even as parody, performances propose possible candidates for succession. They raise the possibility of the replacement of the authors of the representations by those whom they imagined into existence as their definitive opposites.

A number of important consequences ensue from this custom of self-definition by staging contrasts with other races, cultures, and ethnicities. Identity and difference come into play (and into question) simultaneously and coextensively. The process of surrogation continues, but it does so in a climate of heightened anxiety that outsiders will somehow succeed in replacing the original peoples, or autochthons. This process is unstoppable because candidates for surrogation must be tested at the margins of a culture to bolster the fiction that it has a core. That is why the surrogated double so often appears as alien to the culture that reproduces it and that it reproduces. That is why the relentless search for the purity of origins is a voyage not of discovery but of erasure.

The anxiety generated by the process of substitution justifies the complicity of memory and forgetting. In the face of this anxiety—a momentary self-consciousness about surrogation that constitutes what might pass for reflexivity—the alien double may appear in memory only to disappear. That disappearance does not diminish its contributions to cultural definition and preservation; rather, it enables them. Without failures of memory to obscure the mixtures, blends, and provisional antitypes necessary to its production, for example, "whiteness," one of the major scenic elements of several circum-Atlantic performance traditions, could not exist even as perjury, nor could there flourish more narrowly defined, subordinate designs such as "Anglo-Saxon Liberty." Even the immaculate "guardian angels" who sing the chorus of divine origin in James Thompson's "Rule Britannia," for example, must have recourse to a concept charged with high antithetical seriousness to rhyme with "waves." In *Playing in the Dark: Whiteness and the Literary Imagination* (1992), Toni Morrison interprets the angelic chorus exactly: "The concept of freedom did not emerge in a vacuum. Nothing highlighted freedom—if it did not in fact create it—like slavery" (38).

On the one hand, forgetting, like miscegenation, is an opportunistic tactic of whiteness. As a Yoruba proverb puts it: "The white man who made the pencil also made the eraser." On the other hand, the vast scale of the project of whiteness—and the scope of the contacts among cultures it required—

limited the degree to which its foils could be eradicated from the memory of those who had the deepest motivation and the surest means to forget them. At the same time, however, it fostered complex and ingenious schemes to displace, refashion, and transfer those persistent memories into representations more amenable to those who most frequently wielded the pencil and the eraser. In that sense, circum-Atlantic performance is a monumental study in the pleasures and torments of incomplete forgetting. But more obdurate questions persist: Whose forgetting? Whose memory? Whose history?

Locations and Bearings

Because anything like what might be called coverage of the possible inclusions under the rubric of circum-Atlantic performance would be beyond the imaginable scope of this volume (or many), I have settled here on the exploration of particular historical formations at specific times at two sites, London and New Orleans. Though remote from one another in obvious respects—antiquity, climate, and cuisine spring quickly to mind—these places are not arbitrarily selected. As river-sited ports of entry linking interior lines of communication to sea lanes, London and New Orleans have histories joined at a pivotal moment in the colonial rivalry of francophone and anglophone interests as they collided in the late seventeenth and eighteenth centuries in North America and the West Indies. Historians have stressed the importance of the conflict between Great Britain and France on sea and land—the "whale" against the "elephant"—in the forging of modern nation-states and "Great Powers" (Colley, 1, quoting Kennedy, 160). These European interests, however, were intimately connected with Amerindian and African ones. A significant body of recent historical and ethnohistorical research has reexamined those latter interests as dynamic and inventive (rather than inert) in the face of Eurocolonial expansion. My selective history of circum-Atlantic performance draws heavily on this renovated scholarship of encounter and exchange.

The great Iroquois Confederacy, for instance—a creation of centuries of Forest Diplomacy—negotiated through brilliant intercultural performances the Covenant Chain of trade and military alliances that linked the fur-producing hinterlands of the vast Great Lakes region to the thinly held European enclaves of the eastern seaboard (Axtell; Dennis; Jennings, *Iroquois Diplomacy*; Richter). In "Culture Theory in Contemporary Ethnohistory" (1988), William S. Simmons describes these diplomatic and trade relations as "an interaction and confrontation between autonomous social entities, rather than as a one-sided playing out of Eurocolonial myths of manifest destiny" (6). Iroquois played a significant and self-promoting role in the geometric proliferation of wealth centered in the triangular trade: carrying a different cargo along each leg of the Atlantic triangle comprising the Americas (raw materials), Europe (manufactured goods), and Africa (human beings), the holds of merchant ships never had to cross blue water empty. The consequences of the ensuing material productions are incalculable; the mother of hemispheric superstructural invention, they provide a common matrix for the diversified performance genres to which this book is devoted.

Even for the largest system, however, heuristic opportunity, like God or the Devil, is in the details. One site of circum-Atlantic memory that I propose to excavate is located in London in 1710, during the performance-rich state visit to Queen Anne's court by four Iroquois "Kings." Among other public exhibitions and entertainments, a staging of Sir William Davenant's operatic version of Shakespeare's *Macbeth* honored their embassy, a performance during which their hosts insisted that the Native Americans be placed in full view onstage (Bond, 3–4). Such an imposition need not have been as alien or as intimidating as might be supposed. Experienced in staging Condolence Councils, those great intersocietal mourning and peace rituals that mediated among Dutch, French, English, and diverse Algonquian and Iroquoian interests, the Mohawks referred to themselves as *onckwe*, "the Real People." As such, they believed themselves descended from Deganawidah, the semidivine peacemaker who, with the aid of Hiawatha, overcame witchcraft and the cyclical violence of feuding clans to establish the Great League of Peace and Power. Thereafter the league existed to settle grievances, condole losses, and negotiate alliances through gift exchange and ritual performance of speeches, songs, and dances (Richter, 30–49). The Kings came to London to promote the Anglo-Iroquois invasion of French Canada in the interests of the fur trade, and they arrived at a decisive moment during the War of the Spanish Succession, when events were leading up to the Treaties of Utrecht in 1713–14.

According to *The New Cambridge Modern History*, the watershed Peace of Utrecht—whereby Great Britain acquired the coveted *Asiento*, the monopoly on the slave trade in the Spanish West Indies—"marks the passing of the Mediterranean as the centre of world trade and power rivalries

[when] attention shifted to the Atlantic" (Bromley, 571). Alfred Thayer Mahan, summarizing the War of the Spanish Succession in *The Influence of Sea Power Upon History* (1890), the most materially influential work of academic theory written in the past century, describes its consequences: "Before that war England was one of the sea powers; after it she was *the* sea power, without any second" (225). In the festival panegyric *Windsor-Forest* (1713), a poetical celebration of the Peace of Utrecht, Alexander Pope imagined the glorious deforestation of rural England in the cause of maritime empire:

> Thy Trees, fair *Windsor*! now shall leave their Woods,
> And Half thy Forests rush into my Floods,
> Bear *Britain*'s Thunder, and her Cross display,
> To the bright Regions of the rising Day.
>
> (*Poems* 1:189)

To the dancelike numbers of *Windsor-Forest*, which record the embassy of the "Feather'd People," I will return in a later chapter on the representation of performances of encounter at the time of the Treaties of Utrecht. The geopolitical advantages won by Great Britain in this general peace and the supremacy that the Royal Navy had attained motivated the French to attempt to consolidate their position in North America, including strategic development of the territory bearing the name of Louis XIV. They did this in part by situating a fortified city in Louisiana near the mouth of the Mississippi River, roughly equidistant along water routes between Canada and their island possessions in the West Indies, demarcating a great arc of Gallic entitlement arrayed to contest further trans-Appalachian expansion by the Anglo-Americans and the Real People.

We now know that success did not ultimately crown the French grand strategy. But in the meantime, contemporaneously with the apogee of the North American Covenant Chain, the French in colonial Louisiana relocated significant numbers of West Africans, principally Bambara, from one African regional interculture, Senegambia, into an area already possessing highly developed Amerindian performance cultures. Circumstances favored the reciprocal acculturation of Creoles of various lineages within a unique network of African, American, and European practices. These included mortuary rituals, carnival festivities, and a multitude of musical and dance forms that others would eventually describe (and appropriate) under the rubric of jazz. At the same time, the Africans brought with them vital necessities such as skilled agriculture: "The survival of French Louisiana," writes Gwendolyn Midlo Hall in her magisterial *Africans in Colonial Louisiana: The Development of Afro-Creole Culture in the Eighteenth Century* (1992), "was due not only to African labor but also to African technology" (121). Under the superimpositions of slavery, as well as around its fringes beyond the margins of the *ciprière* (swamp), there flourished a powerful culture that reinvented Africa—and ultimately America—within the only apparently impermeable interstices of European forms. In that respect, Louisiana participated in the formation of the complex identities of the circum-Caribbean rim (Fiehrer), even as it negotiated its incremental assimilation into the hypothetical monoculture of Anglo North America.

The other main site that I explore, then, is located in the records of the long "Americanization" (that is, Anglification and Africanization) of Latin New Orleans, a process that begins before the Louisiana Purchase in 1803 and continues to be reenacted in the streets of this performance-saturated city today (Carter; Hirsch and Logsdon). A principal public instrument of this reenactment remains Mardi Gras, nominally a French cultural residue, which long ago was appropriated by so many competing interests of ethnicity, nationality, class, race, religion, gender, and caste that its meaning can be assessed appropriately only in relationship to other genres of circum-Atlantic and Caribbean performance (Kinser; Mitchell; M. Smith, *Mardi Gras Indians*). Through its complex hierarchy of ritualized memory, Mardi Gras stages an annual spectacle of cultural surrogations, including the multilayered imbrication of carnivalesque license, symbolic freedom marches by descendants of Afro-Amerindian Maroons, and the discursive claims of "Anglo-Saxon Liberty" as realized in float parades and debutante balls. The history of performance in New Orleans supports the wisdom of the exhortation that opens Hall's account of African Louisiana: " 'National history' must be transcended, and colonial history treated within a global context" (xii).

Materials and Methods

The various contributors to *Questions of Evidence: Proof, Practice, and Persuasion Across the Disciplines* (1991), a compendium of essays originally published in *Critical Inquiry*, explore the interdisciplinary dimensions of the issues set forth in the editors' introduction: "the configuration of the fact-evidence distinction in different disciplines and historical moments"

(Chandler, Davidson, and Harootunian, 2). By creating a category called "circum-Atlantic performance" that intentionally cuts across disciplinary boundaries and the conventional subcategories and periodizations within them, I have incurred an obligation to be explicit about the materials and methods—the evidence—I have used to imagine what that category entails.

One important strategy of performance research today is to juxtapose living memory as restored behavior against a historical archive of scripted records (Balme). In the epigraph at the head of this chapter from his *History and Memory* (1992), Jacques Le Goff sets out the variety of mnemonic materials—speech, images, gestures—that supplement or contest the authority of "documents" in the historiographic tradition of the French *annalistes* (xvii). Their vast projects—for instance, histories of private life, histories of death, or histories of memory itself—attend especially to those performative practices that maintain (and invent) human continuities, leaving their traces in diversified media, including the living bodies of the successive generations that sustain different social and cultural identities (Ariès; Nora).

Summarizing the fruits of research into the transmission of culture in societies distinguished by different modalities of communication, Le Goff identifies "three major interests" of those "without writing": (1) myth, particularly myths of origin; (2) genealogies, particularly of leading families; and (3) practical formulas of daily living and special observances, particularly those "deeply imbued with religious magic" (58). While acknowledging the preliminary usefulness of such formulations, typically organized under the portmanteau concept of orality, performance studies goes on to question the assumption that the "interests" Le Goff defines do not also manifest themselves in societies "with writing"—and, for that matter, in those with print, electronic media, and mass communications (Conquergood; Schechner, *The Future of Ritual*; Taussig). Performance studies complicates the familiar dichotomy between speech and writing with what Kenyan novelist and director Ngugi wa Thiong'o calls "orature." Orature comprises a range of forms, which, though they may invest themselves variously in gesture, song, dance, processions, storytelling, proverbs, gossip, customs, rites, and rituals, are nevertheless produced alongside or within mediated literacies of various kinds and degrees. In other words, orature goes beyond a schematized opposition of literacy and orality as transcendent categories; rather, it acknowledges that these modes of communication have produced one another interactively over time and that their historic operations may be usefully examined under the rubric of performance. Ngugi defines the power of orature in collective memory aphoristically: "He is a sweet singer when everybody joins in. The sweet songs last longer, too" (61; cf. Finnegan; Okpewho; Zumthor).

The historical implications of the concept of orature, though not necessarily under that name, have engaged the attention of scholars in a number of disciplines. In a recent study of the role of theatricality in the early cultural history of the United States, for instance, *Declaring Independence: Jefferson, Natural Language, and the Culture of Performance* (1993), Jay Fliegelman begins with the significant but long-neglected fact that the Declaration of Independence was just that—a script written to be spoken aloud as oratory. He goes on to document the elocutionary dimension of Anglo-American self-invention, which Thomas Jefferson himself defined in comparison to the expressive speech of Native Americans, on the one hand, and Africans, on the other (98, 192). Under the close scrutiny of circum-Atlantic memory, no material event, spoken or written, can remain "pure," despite Jefferson's special pleading for the revival of Anglo-Saxon as the primal tongue of essential law and liberty (Frantzen, 203–7).

That the chant of the Declaration of Independence calls on the spirits of Jefferson's Anglo-Saxon ancestors to authorize his claims—to inalienable rights, including the right to revolt against tyranny—recalls the ritual of freedom described by C. L. R. James in *The Black Jacobins: Toussaint L'Ouverture and the San Domingo Revolution* (1938):

> Carrying torches to light their way, the leaders of the revolt met in an open space in the thick forests of the Morne Rouge, a mountain overlooking Le Cap. There Boukman gave the last instructions and, after Voodoo incantations and the sucking of the blood of a stuck pig, he stimulated his followers by a prayer spoken in creole, which, like so much spoken on such occasions, has remained. "The god who created the sun which gives us light . . . orders us to revenge our wrongs. He will direct our arms and aid us. Throw away the symbol of the god of the whites who has so often caused us to weep, and listen to the voice of liberty, which speaks in the hearts of us all." (87)

Endowed by their Creator with liberty, whose voice spoke through them, the Haitians set about the task of altering and abolishing their government with spoken words, which they then took the trouble to write down.

Taking cognizance of the interdependence of orature and literature, the materials of the present study are thematized under categories of those restored behaviors that function as vehicles of cultural transmission. Each category pairs a form of collective memory with the enactments that embody it through performance: death and burials, violence and sacrifices, laws and (dis)obedience, commodification and auctions, origins and segregation. All of these may be written about, of course, but even the laws need not have been written down. They remain partially recorded in the literature, but they are actually remembered and put into practice through orature, a practice that may be prolonged, supplemented, or revised by printed and photographic representations of the performance events.

Although these thematic materials are broadly conceived in the amplitude of circum-Atlantic relations, my method is to study them at narrowly delimited sites. My observations of the street performances of Mardi Gras in New Orleans, for instance, have been accumulating since 1991. That was the last year in which the most traditional of the old-line carnival "krewes" paraded: the passage of a new civil rights ordinance by the New Orleans City Council in December of that year gave the century-and-a-half-old men's clubs the choice of desegregating their membership or staying home (Flake; Vennman, "Boundary Face-Off"). The assertion of legal control over carnival by the City of New Orleans revived memories of the carnival krewes' central role in planning and executing the armed overthrow of the racially integrated government of William Pitt Kellogg in 1874. Known to historians as "the Battle of Liberty Place," this was in fact a bloody riot incited by a race-baiting elite. The ordinance controversy, played out for three years in the council chambers and the media as well as in the streets and running concurrently with the sudden political rise of Klansman David Duke, burst open a deep, suppurating sore that festers in local memory more poisonously than history can write.

The method of observation that I employ takes its cue from "Walking in the City," an essay included in the "Spatial Practices" section of Michel de Certeau's *Practice of Everyday Life* (1984). "To walk," de Certeau notes, "is to lack a place" (103). But to walk is also to gain an experience of the cityscape that is conducive to mapping the emphases and contradictions of its special memory (Boyer; Kirshenblatt-Gimblett). De Certeau looks for key points of articulation between human behavior and the built environment, noting the "pedestrian speech acts" uttered by authors "whose bodies follow the thicks and thins of an urban 'text' they write without being able to read it" (93). Quotidian "speech acts" offer a rich assortment of year-round performances, particularly in a polyglot entrepot and tourist mecca like New Orleans, but festivals—"time out of time"—intensify and enlarge them to Gargantuan proportions (Falassi). As the Mardi Gras revelers take over the streets, canalized by police barricades and conditioned reflexes, their traditional gestures and masked excesses activate the spatial logic of a city built to make certain powers and privileges not only seasonally visible but perpetually reproducible. The crowded spaces become a performance machine for celebrating the occult origin of their exclusions. Walking in the city makes this visible.

Meanwhile, around the public housing projects and under the highway overpasses, the Mardi Gras Indians—"gangs" of African-Americans who identify with Native American tribes and parade on unannounced routes costumed in heart-stoppingly beautiful hand-sewn "suits"—proudly transform their neighborhoods into autonomous places of embodied memory. More intensely than any of the float parades or promiscuous masquerades of Mardi Gras, the Indians restage events of circum-Atlantic encounter and surrogation in which European experience remains only obliquely acknowledged, if at all. Their bodies document those doublings through musical speech, images, and gestures (figure 1.1). As George Lipsitz points out in *Time Passages: Collective Memory and American Popular Culture* (1990), "the Mardi Gras Indians of New Orleans offer an important illustration of the persistence of popular narratives in the modern world" (234; see also Lipsitz, *Dangerous Crossroads*). Their spectacular appearances at Mardi Gras season (which nonetheless remain aloof from it) are only one genre of performance in the year-round cornucopia of Afrocentric forms, among them, the Second Line parades staged by numerous social aid and pleasure clubs and ritual celebrations of death "with music," popularly known as jazz funerals.

The three-sided relationship of memory, performance, and substitution becomes most acutely visible in mortuary ritual. This study closely attends to those epiphanies. In any funeral, the body of the deceased performs the limits of the community called into being by the need to mark its passing. United around a corpse that is no longer inside but not yet outside of its boundaries, the members of a community may reflect on its symbolic embodiment of loss and renewal. In a jazz funeral, the deceased is generally accompanied at least part of the way to the cemetery by a brass band and a crowd of mourners who follow an elegant grand marshall (or "Nelson").

After the body is "cut loose"—sent on its way in the company of family

1.1 Hercules' funeral, 1979.
Chief Bo Dollis, Wild Magnolias, carries the gang flag.
Photo: Michael P. Smith

members—a popular celebration commences, less like a forgetting than a replenishment. As Willie Pajaud, longtime trumpeter for the Eureka Brass Band, once put it: "I'd rather play a funeral than eat a turkey dinner." Animated by a "joyful noise," supported in many instances by the testimony of deep, spirit-world faith, the dead seem to remain more closely present to the living in New Orleans than they do elsewhere—and not only because they are traditionally interred in tombs above ground. Walking in the city makes this audible.

Read in the context created by the sounds and sights of these restored behaviors, then, the documents concerning the London visit of the Iroquois Kings take on a new and different kind of life. In addition to the various performances they attended while in London—a puppet show, a cockfight, a military review, a concert, a Shakespearean tragedy—the Native Americans created other events by their spectacular passages through the streets (Altick). They swept up those walking through the city in impromptu festivals: "When the four *Indian Kings* were in this Country about a Twelve-month ago," Joseph Addison recalled, speaking through the persona of Mr. Spectator, "I often mix'd with the Rabble and followed them a whole Day together, being wonderfully struck with the Sight of every thing that is new or uncommon" (1:211). Addison's ambiguous modifier—who is being struck with new sights here? The Kings? The Rabble? Mr. Spectator?—stages what might be termed the "ethnographic surrealism" of this circum-Atlantic event (Clifford). One important reason why popular performance events entered into the records at this time in greater detail than is usual for such ephemera is that the Kings attended a number of them, while their invited presence at others was heavily advertised to boost attendance.

The daily repertoires of the two official theaters, Drury Lane and the Queen's Theatre, Haymarket, are particularly worthy of attention in this regard. In addition to the performance of *Macbeth* at which the Kings were present, two other revivals held pointed circum-Atlantic interest: John Dryden's *The Indian Emperour; or, The Conquest of Mexico by the Spaniards* (1665) and Thomas Southerne's *Oroonoko; or, The Royal Slave* (1694). At a time of institutional canonization of Shakespeare as the national poet, however, not all the relevant high-culture performances took place onstage (G. Taylor; Dobson). On the same day that the Native Americans departed from England, the great Shakespearean actor Thomas Betterton was buried in Westminster Abbey. His passing held an epoch-marking meaning for many, including Richard Steele, who published a eulogy in *The Tatler*. Betterton's fifty-year career spanned the reigns of Charles II, James II, William and Mary, and Queen Anne; and Steele remarks on the edifying spectacle of attending this "last Office" (2:422). The breadth of the address of this eulogy, which begins with "Men of Letters and Education" and then quickly enlarges to embrace all "Free-born People" (2:423), highlights the powers Steele once attributed to Betterton's moving, speaking body in life but now invests in the stillness of his corpse. That is the power of summoning an imagined community into being. The hailing of the "Free-born," in their role as enthusiasts for enactments of "what is great and noble in Human Nature" by those who "speak justly, and move gracefully" (2:422–23), is piquantly juxtaposed to the critique of social and musical cacophony in the immediately preceding number of *The Tatler*, which ends with an unfavorable allusion to "the Stamping Dances of the *West Indians* or *Hottentots*" (2:421).

Steele's account of Betterton's funeral demonstrates the importance of

The Tatler and *Spectator* to the way in which I am trying to understand the role of performance in circum-Atlantic memory. In *Imagined Communities: Reflections on the Origin and Spread of Nationalism* (1983; rev. 1991), Benedict Anderson stresses the role of printed media in the vernacular, particularly the newspaper, in the formation of modern national consciousness out of dynastic, feudal, and sacred communities (33–36). Like the obsequies performed at tombs of the Unknown Soldier, which Anderson also highlights (9), the burial of an actor, a practitioner of a despised profession, in the cathedral of English dynastic memory suggests a cultural use of marginal identities to imagine a new kind of community. Attending such a ritual performance as a friend of the deceased, Steele the pioneering journalist grasped—or created—its significance as national news.

Steele and Addison characteristically turned local performances into print, for circulation among an expanding audience of readers, and then print into performances, for the edification of many more listeners who heard the papers read aloud in public places. The innovative effects of this form of orature have been convincingly demonstrated on one side of the Atlantic by Michael G. Ketcham in *Transparent Designs: Reading, Performance, and Form in the Spectator Papers* (1985) and on the other by Michael Warner in *The Letters of the Republic: Publication and the Public Sphere in Eighteenth-Century America* (1990). Reports of the authorial deaths of Addison and Steele would seem to have been exaggerated (McCrea). Theater historians, however, attempting to reconstruct the acting of Betterton and others from accounts in *The Tatler* and *The Spectator*, have excerpted and anthologized only the choice descriptive passages concerning the stage. To a historian who views theater in the context of many kinds of performance, such passages take on a more robust life when they are returned to their original place among the wonderful peripatetic observations of the various restored behaviors of Augustan London.

The Everlasting Club

Addison and Steele report on walking in the city. By way of preliminary demonstration of my method, I will attempt here to make a similar kind of report on New Orleans. Fortunately for me, no one will ever be able to say for sure which of our hallucinations, theirs or mine, does the greatest injustice to the fabulous object of its incitement.

In his paper for Wednesday, May 23, 1711 (No. 72), Mr. Spectator continues his account of clubs, ancient and modern. Clubs, with their continuously renegotiated boundaries of exclusion, exemplify the smaller atoms of affiliation through which larger societies may be constructed. Mr. Spectator reports on the "surprising" constitution of one London club in particular, "the EVERLASTING CLUB." This venerable association never ceases to function, day or night, weekdays or holidays, all the days of the year, "no Party presuming to rise till they are relieved by those who are in course to succeed them" (1:308–9). By this regimen no club member ever need be without company at any hour, and the fire, tended by a trusty vestal, "burns from Generation to Generation" (1:310). Continuity, the genial despot, reigns: "It is a Maxim in this Club that the Steward never dies; for as they succeed one another by way of Rotation, no Man is to quit the great Elbow-chair which stands at the upper End of the Table till his Successor is in a Readiness to fill it; insomuch that there has not been a *Sede vacante* in the Memory of Man (1:309)." Individuals come and go, but the templatelike role of steward carries forward through time the implacable integrity of the Everlasting Club: only the Great Fire of London caused a vacancy to occur in the Elbow-chair, when Samaritans intervened to carry the protesting incumbent to safety.

Mardi Gras krewes and other New Orleanian social clubs operate along similar lines of self-perpetuating descent. Like carnival itself, they promote a sense of timelessness based on the apparently seamless repetition of traditional roles. Walking in the city on Mardi Gras day in 1991 afforded a spectacle of the convergence of two such roles: Rex, King of Carnival, and his nemesis on that day, King Zulu, reigning monarch of the Zulu Social Aid and Pleasure Club. Since 1872, interrupted only by war and police strikes, Rex has reigned annually over Mardi Gras as its perpetually smiling Lord of Misrule. Traditionally chosen from the ranks of the city's business elite centered around the exclusive Boston Club, Rex shares power on his day of days with a queen selected annually from among society's leading debutantes. The symbolic mating of a nubile young girl with a middle-aged man wearing gold lamé, rouge, and a false beard, who, as it is always redundantly pointed out, is "old enough to be her father," sets the tone for the intensely endogamous fertility rites to follow (figure 1.2). These include an eye-filling float parade with masked riders showering plastic beads on rapturous crowds of "subjects" and an elegant private ball for the inner circle of worthies.

Since 1909 members of the Zulu Social Aid and Pleasure Club have like-

1.2 Rex, king of carnival, on his float, 1991.
Photo: Michael P. Smith

wise staged an annual float parade, featuring stereotypes of "Africans." In addition to "King Zulu," high officials in the organization take on such personas as "The Big Shot of Africa," "The Witch Doctor," "Governor," "Province Prince," and "Ambassador" (figure 1.3). Originally known as the "The Tramps," the working-class African Americans who founded Zulu took their inspiration from a staged minstrel number, "There Never Was and Never Will Be a King Like Me" (Kinser, 233). They parade on Mardi Gras morning, using the same route along St. Charles Avenue that Rex follows an hour or so later. They wear grass skirts and blackface laid on thick over an underlying layer of clown white circling the eyes and mouth. In addition to plastic beads, Zulu members throw decorated coconuts, for many parade goers the most highly prized "throw" of Mardi Gras. Every year there is a new Rex and a new King Zulu, and every year they are supposed to look and act as they always have.

On Mardi Gras morning in 1991, however, King Zulu got a very late start, Rex refused to wait, and the two parades collided. As a few of the

1.3 King Zulu.
Photo: Courtesy Amistad Research Center, Christopher West Collection

floats ran parallel to each other along either side of St. Charles Avenue, in defiance of the carefully planned and well-policed route schedule, the maskers I watched ignored each other, creating a gulf of silence between two everlasting clubs, each the product of generations of de jure surrogation. Their silence intensified the imagery whereby they performed their pasts in one another's faces, a cruel hyperbolic mirror, but polarity did not constitute symmetry. Behind the gestic speech acts of Rex stood the ambiguous tradition of the European carnivalesque, which might at least appear to overthrow social authority momentarily (Bakhtin, *Rabelais and His World*) but which also might just as well serve to conceal its ever more powerful reassertion under the mask of festivity (Le Roy Ladurie, *Carnival in Romans*). Also behind Rex stood more than a century of white supremacist entitlement, the residue of what I will be calling a genealogy of performance. Behind King Zulu there stood something much more complicated: a deconstruction of that white genealogy and the veiled assertion of a clandestine countermemory in its stead.

To see how this semiotic tour de force works, the beholder must first understand that the members of both everlasting clubs, Rex *and* Zulu, represent whiteness and perform whiteface minstrelsy. Rex speaks for himself: of his 1992 parade, entitled "Voyages of Discovery" in honor of the quincentennial year, the King of Carnival stated, "We would have had a black explorer, but we couldn't find any" (quoted in Vennman, "Boundary Face-Off," 76). Thus did Rex in his own way—by performing a demeaning comic stereotype of the white amnesiac—honor the memory of the Haitian creole explorer, Jean-Baptiste Point Du Sable, in the city from which he most probably departed to found Chicago (Bennett, 96–101). But the question remains as to why Zulu has walked such a thin line between ridiculing and reinforcing the race-conscious imagery that Mardi Gras festivities perpetually reinvoke. Walking between the two parades along the "neutral ground" of St. Charles Avenue, I thought the answer seemed plainly visible in the performance: Zulu seizes on the annual occasion of the great festive holiday of Eurocentric tradition to make ribald fun of white folks and the stupidity of their jury-rigged constructions of race (figures 1.4 and 1.5).

As the parades collided, Zulu's bone-wielding "Witch Doctor" evoked the legends of cannibalism that permeate accounts of circum-Atlantic encounters (Hulme, Jehlen), especially as they relate to the invention of Africa (Mudimbe). This Africa is the dystopia of racist fantasy, valuable as an antitype to help the xenophobic European tribes exaggerate distinctions among themselves: "Africa," runs the tired old British slur on the French, "begins at Calais." Introduced in the decade after *Plessy v. Ferguson*, amid the triumph of Southern Redemption and its explosive mania about race, King Zulu turns Rex not so much upside down as inside out. The white greasepaint under his blackface discloses an acute reflexivity in the way that Zulu, laughing behind the mask of apparent self-deprecation, reproduces a kind of Africa by mocking absurd Eurocentric stereotypes of divine kingship.

As whiteface minstrelsy, however, Zulu has layers within layers, and behind the visible mask of carnivalesque satire there is a practice of disruptive humor that introduces another circum-Atlantic version of Africa. As a New Orleans social aid and pleasure club, Zulu participates in the tradition of Afrocentric mutual aid and burial societies dating from the colonial period, when people of African descent constituted the majority in New Orleans (as they do again today) and when, as slaves and free people

1.4 Rex and his court, 1971.
Courtesy The Historic New Orleans Collection, Museum/Research Center, acc. no. 1974.25.19.332

of color, they had developed resilient solidarities within their own castes and kinship networks. "New Orleans," according to Gwendolyn Midlo Hall in *Africans in Colonial Louisiana*, "was overwhelmingly black," one factor among several that made "Louisiana creole culture the most significant source of Africanization of the entire culture of the United States" (176, 157).

In the "Retentions and Survivals" chapter of their rigorous *Birth of African-American Culture* (1976), Sidney Mintz and Richard Price caution that historical research has "reduced the number of convincing cases" of exact formal retentions between Africa and the cultures of the New World. They also allow, however, that more general continuities may be discerned by "the analysis of systems or patterns in their social contexts" (52). Since the famous debate between Melville Herskovits and E. Franklin Frazier, the nature and extent of Africanisms in American culture have defied settled

1.5 King Zulu and his court, 1940.
Courtesy The Historic New Orleans Collection,
Museum/Research Center, acc. no. 19 0.54

conclusions, but the area of performance has produced some of the most compelling research. In *After Africa* (1983), for example, Roger Abrahams and John Szwed discuss the African derivation of such popular performance genres as cheerleading, baton twirling, and broken-field running in football, and in Abrahams's classic *Man-of-Words in the West Indies: Performance and the Emergence of Creole Culture* (1983), there is a persuasive account of the diasporic genesis of a particular kind of eloquence not unknown to Zulu maskers: "talking broad," "talking sweet," and "talking nonsense." It is widely accepted that in New Orleans concentrated forms of African music and dance remained in the celebrated bamboulas of Congo Square and elsewhere until very late, with powerful, though undocumentable, consequences for the development of jazz (Kmen). Comparative studies such as John Nunley and Judith Bettelheim's *Caribbean Festival Arts: Each and Every Bit of Difference* (1988) locate the festive traditions of New Orleans in a network of circum-Caribbean forms. Scholarship along these lines tends to support my impression that in the sardonic laughter of King Zulu there resonates a voice that cannot be accounted for by the comparatively crude inversions of the European carnivalesque.

I believe that through the sophisticated disguises of diasporic memory, the Janus-faced Trickster figure erupts at Mardi Gras in the Zulu parade, reinventing an African cultural pattern in its New Orleanian social context. Embodying the deconstructive spirit of Esu (Gates, *The Signifying Monkey*, 31–42), the Trickster turns the tables on the powerful and emerges unscathed from the ensuing contretemps, confounding his adversary by dint of the dexterity with which he can reverse polarities: bad is good and white is black. In *Domination and the Arts of Resistance* (1990), James C. Scott identifies such a "hidden transcript" as one of the "Arts of Political Disguise" exemplified by the Jamaican slave saying "Hitting a straight lick with a crooked stick" (136–82). The Trickster in his New Orleanian manifestation did not exist as such in Africa, but neither did "The Tramps" invent their traditions solely out of "There Never Was and Never Will Be a King Like Me." On the scene of the colliding parades in 1991, no one who looked to be in the know seemed to think that Zulu's late departure was really an accident. Living on the tips of many tongues, performance tradition, not scripted records, incorporates these supple ironies in the dignity and cunning of resistant memory. Arriving at direction through indirection, talking big and smiling back, King Zulu lets Rex drink with gusto from the deep bowl of racist laughter, but only after the Trickster has pissed in the soup.

Before going on to address the theoretical basis for what I am calling genealogies of performance, I want to reemphasize an important conclusion drawn from walking in the city, listening to the orature, and reading the literature: Trickster-Zulu is not an African retention but a circum-Atlantic reinvention. In his formation out of the linked surrogations of a densely concentrated interculture, Zulu might very well have taken his present form without Esu per se, but he certainly could not exist in the same way today without Rex, nor, it must be emphasized, could Rex exist in the same way without Zulu.

The meaning of the comic effect that Addison achieves in his account of the Everlasting Club now comes into sharper focus. Mr. Spectator takes his learned epigraph from the *Georgics* of Virgil; they emerge from John Dryden's translation thus:

> Th' immortal Line in sure Succession reigns,
> The Fortune of the Family remains:
> And Grandsires Grandsons the long List contains.
> (quoted in *Spectator*, 1:308n)

Addison knows—and the white circles around the eyes and lips of King Zulu and his merry krewe playfully confirm—that pristine descent in "sure Succession" is no more plausible a fiction than that of the steward who never dies or, it might be added, that of the purportedly foolproof lineages of European dynasties. Yet the illusion created by this fiction is so powerful and evidently so enduringly persuasive that specialists of each intellectual generation since the publication of *Genealogy of Morals* have had to reinvent Friedrich Nietzsche's caustic demolition of origins in order to make it their own.

Genealogies of Performance

As I hope my account of the impromptu concatenation of Rex and Zulu has suggested, genealogies of performance document—and suspect—the historical transmission and dissemination of cultural practices through collective representations. For this formulation, I am indebted to Jonathan Arac's definition, applying Nietzsche and Foucault, of a "critical genealogy" that "aims to excavate the past that is necessary to account for how we got here and the past that is useful for conceiving alternatives to our present condition" (2). Genealogies of performance take from Foucault's seminal essay in *Hommage à Jean Hyppolite* (1971) the assurance that discontinuities rudely interrupt the succession of surrogates, who are themselves the scions of a dubious bloodline that leads the genealogist back to the moment of apparent origin in order to discover what is and is not "behind things": "not a timeless and essential secret, but the secret that they have no essence or that their essence was fabricated in a piecemeal fashion from alien forms. . . . What is found at the historical beginning of things is not the inviolable identity of their origin; it is the dissension of other things. It is disparity" (Foucault, "Nietzsche, Genealogy, History," 142). The practical experience of applying this principle suggests that it is far more hortatory than nihilistic.

Genealogies of performance attend not only to "the body," as Foucault suggests, but also to bodies—to the reciprocal reflections they make on one another's surfaces as they foreground their capacities for interaction.

Genealogies of performance also attend to "counter-memories," or the disparities between history as it is discursively transmitted and memory as it is publicly enacted by the bodies that bear its consequences. In the chapters that follow I will be applying three principles that govern the practices of memory and show how genealogies of performance may be analyzed: kinesthetic imagination, vortices of behavior, and displaced transmission.

Performance genealogies draw on the idea of expressive movements as mnemonic reserves, including patterned movements made and remembered by bodies, residual movements retained implicitly in images or words (or in the silences between them), and imaginary movements dreamed in minds, not prior to language but constitutive of it, a psychic rehearsal for physical actions drawn from a repertoire that culture provides. This repertoire has been defined by the French historian Pierre Nora as "true memory," which he finds in "gestures and habits, in skills passed down by unspoken traditions, in the body's inherent self-knowledge, in unstudied reflexes and ingrained memories" (13). Nora develops the idea of "places of memory" (*lieux de mémoire*), the artificial sites of the modern production of national and ethnic memory, in contrast to "environments of memory" (*mileux de mémoire*), the largely oral and corporeal retentions of traditional cultures. Modernity is characterized as the replacement of environments of memory by places of memory, such as archives, monuments, and theme parks: "moments of history torn away from the movement of history, then returned; no longer quite life, not yet death, like shells on the shore when the sea of living memory has receded" (12). "Living memory" remains variously resistant to this form of forgetting, however, through the transmission of gestures, habits, and skills.

What Nora talks about here overlaps to a considerable degree with what Paul Connerton, in his suggestive book *How Societies Remember* (1989), describes as the "incorporating practice" of memory, which "is sedimented, or amassed, in the body" (72). Human agents draw on these resources of memory stored up (but also reinvented) in what I will call, stretching an old term to fit my purpose, the kinesthetic imagination. In this I am inspired by the work of dance historians on the transmission (and transformation) of memory through movement. Taking together the important work of Mark Franko in *Dance as Text: Ideologies of the Baroque Body* (1993) and Susan Foster in *Storying Bodies: The Choreography of Narrative and Gender in the French Action Ballet* (forthcoming), for instance, shows how ballet has disseminated, transmitted, and contested social and even political attitudes from the seventeenth century onward. Foster particularly demonstrates how the dance can indeed be separated from the dancers as a transmittable form, a kinesthetic vocabulary, one that can move up and down the social scale as well as from one generation to the next. She discloses the size of the stakes in such *mileux de mémoire* when she asks: "Do not all records of human accomplishment document the motions of bodies?" The essays collected in Jan Bremmer and Herman Roodenburg's *Cultural History of Gesture* (1992) tend to answer Foster in the affirmative.

As a faculty of memory, the kinesthetic imagination exists interdependently but by no means coextensively with other phenomena of social memory: written records, spoken narratives, architectural monuments, built environments. Along with culturally specific affiliations such as family, religion, and class, these forms constitute what Maurice Halbwachs calls "the social frameworks of memory" (38). The kinesthetic imagination, however, inhabits the realm of the virtual. Its truth is the truth of simulation, of fantasy, or of daydreams, but its effect on human action may have material consequences of the most tangible sort and of the widest scope. This faculty, which flourishes in that mental space where imagination and memory converge, is a way of thinking through movements—at once remembered and reinvented—the otherwise unthinkable, just as dance is often said to be a way of expressing the unspeakable. The kinesthetic imagination exists to a high degree of concentration in performers, and its effects will be obvious in my account of the public reception of exemplary histrionics, such as the mourning woman's leap into the grave at her grandmother's funeral in Benjamin Henry Latrobe's account of a creole funeral (chapter 2), Thomas Betterton's acting of Shakespeare (chapter 3), the Mohawk Kiotseaeton's handling of wampum strings at the Three Rivers treaty (chapter 4), Agnes Robertson's transformative embodiment of the title role of Dion Boucicault's *The Octoroon* (chapter 5), or the carnival tableaux of the Mistick Krewe of Comus (chapter 6). But it also operates in the performance of everyday life, consolidated by deeply ingrained habits and reinforced by paradigmatic systems of behavioral memory such as law and custom. Kinesthetic imagination is not only an impetus and method for the restoration of behavior but also a means of its imaginative expansion through those extensions of the range of bodily movements and puissances that technological invention and specialized social organization can provide.

Technological invention (architectural innovation particularly) and social organization create what Nora calls "places" or sites of memory—

what I call vortices of behavior. Their function is to canalize specified needs, desires, and habits in order to reproduce them. They frequently provide the crux in the semiotext of the circum-Atlantic cityscape—the grand boulevard, the marketplace, the theater district, the square, the burial ground—where the gravitational pull of social necessity brings audiences together and produces performers (candidates for surrogation) from their midst. As Marvin Carlson has documented in *Places of Performance: The Semiotics of Theatre Architecture* (1989), the urban confluence of pathways, borders, nodes, and landmarks favors the theatrical and the performative (10–11). The behavioral vortex of the cityscape, the "ludic space" in Roland Barthes's propitious term, constitutes the collective, social version of the psychological paradox that masquerade is the most powerful form of self-expression. The vortex is a kind of spatially induced carnival, a center of cultural self-invention through the restoration of behavior. Into such maelstroms, the magnetic forces of commerce and pleasure suck the willing and unwilling alike. Although such a zone or district seems to offer a place for transgression, for things that couldn't happen otherwise or elsewhere, in fact what it provides is far more official: a place in which everyday practices and attitudes may be legitimated, "brought out into the open," reinforced, celebrated, or intensified. When this happens, what I will be calling condensational events result. The principal characteristic of such events is that they gain a powerful enough hold on collective memory that they will survive the transformation or the relocation of the spaces in which they first flourished.

In the circum-Atlantic cities of New Orleans and early eighteenth-century London, the behavioral vortices of which I speak developed in marketplaces (the Royal Exchange, the St. Louis Exchange), in the unofficially designated auditoria of cultural self-enunciation (coffee and chocolate houses, opera boxes, Congo Square), in combined theater and red-light districts (Drury Lane, Storyville), and in the newly invented urban cemeteries, which seem less surprising as nominees for the category of "ludic space" when one takes into account that the performances marking the rites of passage from life to death represent some of the most elaborately staged occasions on which fictions of identity, difference, and community come into play.

Displaced transmission constitutes the adaptation of historic practices to changing conditions, in which popular behaviors are resituated in new locales. Much more happens through transmission by surrogacy than the reproduction of tradition. New traditions may also be invented and others overturned. The paradox of the restoration of behavior resides in the phenomenon of repetition itself: no action or sequence of actions may be performed exactly the same way twice; they must be reinvented or recreated at each appearance. In this improvisatorial behavioral space, memory reveals itself as imagination. The African-American tradition of "signifyin(g)," for instance, as explained by Henry Louis Gates, Jr., with reference to Jelly Roll Morton's stomp variation on Scott Joplin's rag (63–88), and applied as "repetition with revision" to Yoruba ritual by Margaret Thompson Drewal (4–5), illuminates the theoretical and practical possibilities of restored behavior not merely as the recapitulation but as the transformation of experience through the displacement of its cultural forms.

Improvisation may even erupt into forms as ostensibly conservative as ritual. In her study of the dynamism, play, and agency of Yoruba *etutu*, Drewal contests what she terms "the dominant notion in scholarly discourse that ritual repetition is rigid, stereotypic, conventional, conservative, invariant, uniform, redundant, predictable, and structurally static" (xiv). What she describes in the dynamic performance practices of Yorubaland complements Renato Rosaldo's general assertion in *Culture and Truth: The Remaking of Social Analysis* (1989; rev. 1993) that ritual most often resembles "a busy intersection" in which unanticipated or novel junctures may occur. "In contrast with the classic view," Rosaldo writes, "which posits culture as a self-contained whole made up of coherent patterns, culture can arguably be conceived as a more porous array of intersections where distinct processes crisscross from within and beyond its borders" (20). The characteristically performative circum-Atlantic image of the busy intersection evokes what I am calling the behavioral vortex where cultural transmission may be detoured, deflected, or displaced. The arc of memory suggested here, a trajectory launched by sustained contact and exchange among the peoples of the Atlantic world, is charted by accounts of improvisation ranging from Stephen Greenblatt's in *Renaissance Self-Fashioning: From More to Shakespeare* (1980) to Paul Berliner's in *Thinking in Jazz: The Infinite Art of Improvisation* (1994). The spirit of syncretism and bricolage inherent in such inventive displacements finds an elegant summation in Franz Kafka's parable, a vivid instance of the derivation of essence from the serendipitous copulation of alien forms: "Leopards break into the temple and drink the sacrificial chalices dry; this occurs repeatedly, again and again: finally it can be reckoned on beforehand and becomes part of the ceremony" (quoted in

States, 40; cf. Kertzer). Describing the subversive paradox of memory as performance—that repetition is change—Peggy Phelan, in *Unmarked: The Politics of Performance* (1993), speaks of the possibility of "representation without reproduction" (3; cf. Michie). I argue in the following chapters that this possibility becomes an inevitability under historic conditions of wholesale surrogation: careless acolytes leave the temple gates ajar; leopards work up powerful thirsts; and, for good or ill, the befuddled celebrants come to embrace desperate contingencies as timeless essentials.

A genealogy of performance for the circum-Atlantic world is, therefore, an intricate unraveling of the putative seamlessness of origins. It is at once a map of diasporic diffusions in space and a speculation on the synthesis and mutation of traditions through time (Boyarin). Behind this notion of specific continuities and ruptures operates a more general conception (if any conception can be more general than a performance genealogy for an oceanic interculture). That generality, if I may be allowed it, goes something like this: what I am calling the circum-Atlantic world was itself a vast behavioral vortex, the forces of which created certain characteristic patterns that continue to influence values and practices still extant today. Admittedly, another body of evidence, drawn from different sites or from the same sites at different times, would have yielded other priorities—very different ones, perhaps, but I suspect not wholly different. That is so, I am arguing, because the mutually interdependent performances of circum-Atlantic memory remain visible, audible, and kinesthetically palpable to those who walk in the cities along its historic rim.

The status of the evidence required to reconstruct performances depends on the success of two necessarily problematic procedures—spectating and tattling. This is not a disclaimer. Often the best hedge against amnesia is gossip, a claim that the following juicy tidbit might serve to clarify. In *The Spectator*, no. 80 (Friday, June 1, 1711), obviously a slow news day, Addison recounts the tale of Phillis and Brunetta, "two Rivals for the Reputation of Beauty" (1:343). Vying with one another for the attentions of the marriageable bachelors in London, both succeed after an intense campaign, waged with beautiful gowns and strategic flirtations, in marrying wealthy West Indian sugar planters, next-door neighbors in Barbados, whither the newlyweds sail. Once there, the jealousy of Phillis and Brunetta escalates with every provincial ball. The former seems to steal a march on the latter, Addison relates, when a ship from London arrives carrying "a Brocade more gorgeous and costly than had ever before appeared in that Latitude." Phillis, the consignee, gloats and preens. Brunetta fumes and rages until a remnant of the dreaded brocade falls into her hands: she then appears at the "publick Ball in a plain black Silk Mantua, attended by a beautiful Negro Girl in a Petticoat of the same Brocade with which *Phillis* was attired." Phillis swoons. She then flees the ball in chagrined despair, to depart the West Indies forever on the next ship home (1:344).

Many things could be said about Addison's misogynistic anecdote: that its semiosis of conspicuous consumption recapitulates the triangular trade in material goods and human flesh, for instance, or that women and their erotic ornaments come to symbolize and embody the astonishing superabundance created (and then maldistributed) by such circum-Atlantic argosies. These possibilities, including the role of women's clothed and unclothed bodies as commodified signifiers of abundance and fecundity, will be taken up elsewhere. For the moment, however, there is one salient point to consider: the tale's meaning as gossip can flourish only in a particular kind of world, one in which racial surrogation operates as a potent social threat. In their performance of everyday life, the transoceanic micropolitics of rival pulchritudes, Phillis and Brunetta require the strategic availability of "a beautiful Negro Girl." They need a cameo appearance from her to tip the balance and bring their hateful little revenge comedy to its mock-catastrophic end. To perform as protagonists of gendered whiteness they must rely on an unnamed black antagonist, who, like millions of indispensable actors in the dramas of the circum-Atlantic world, remains forgotten but not gone.

ECHOES IN THE BONE

That which we remember is, more often than not,
that which we would like to have been; or that which we hope to be.

- RALPH ELLISON

THE POIGNANCY OF RALPH ELLISON'S ACCOUNT OF MEMORY RESIDES IN ITS identification of amnesia as the inspiration to imagine the future. Like performance, memory operates as both quotation and invention, an improvisation on borrowed themes, with claims on the future as well as the past. Where time is sculpted as cogently as it is through performance, a longing for clear beginnings (cognate to origins) accompanies an even more pronounced desire for the telos of perfect closure. From the heritage of tragic drama in the West, I believe, circum-Atlantic closures especially favor catastrophe, a word rife with kinesthetic imagination, which carries forward through time the memory of a movement, a "downward turning," redolent of violence and fatality but also of agency and decision. Like catastrophe, with which it often coincides, the illusory scene of closure that Eurocentrists call memory ("what's done is done") incites emotions that turn toward the future, in aspiration no less than in dread ("God's will be done"). The choreography of catastrophic closure—Fortinbras arrives, Aeneas departs, Creon remains—offers a way of imagining what must come next as well as what has already happened. Under the seductive linearity of its influence, memory operates as an alternation between retrospection and anticipation that is itself, for better or worse, a work of art.

This chapter borrows its title from *An Echo in the Bone* (1974), a play by the late Jamaican dramatist Dennis Scott. Scott uses the structure of the Nine-Night Ceremony, which, through the ritual magic of the Jamaican practice of obeah, welcomes the spirit of a deceased person back into his or her home on the ninth night after death has occurred. Restoring the behaviors pertaining to spirit-world trance and possession, the playwright shows how the voices of the dead may speak through the bodies of the living. He enlarges on the Ninth Night return of one recently departed soul in order to populate the stage with spirits resurrected from the depths of circum-Atlantic memory, including masters and their human chattel on a slave ship off the coast of Africa in 1792, the traders and the traded in a slave auctioneer's office in 1820, a defiant band of Maroons, and the white and black inhabitants of a Jamaican sugar plantation, past and present. Errol Hill, in the epilogue to his path-breaking *Jamaican Stage, 1655–1900: Profile of a Colonial Theatre* (1992), places *An Echo in the Bone* in the complex historical context of Caribbean performance traditions, including amateur and professional productions of Shakespeare in colonial Kingston and Afrocentric spirit-world rituals such as Nine Night. Like *Hamlet*, a particular favorite of Kingston audiences since the eighteenth century (Hill, passim), *An Echo in the Bone* dramatizes the cultural politics of memory, particularly as they are realized through communications between the living and the dead.

It is precisely the politics of communicating with the dead that concern me generally in the following chapters and most urgently in the present one. Echoes in the bone refer not only to a history of forgetting but to a strategy of empowering the living through the performance of memory. In *Making History: Social Revolution in the Novels of George Lamming* (forthcoming), Supriya Nair stresses the importance of obeah and vodun as resistant practices in the Caribbean: Haiti provides the obvious but far from the sole example of an imagined diasporic community coalescing around spirit-world memories and performances (James); similar claims have been made for voodoo and hoodoo in New Orleans (Mulira), claims that recognize the Ceremony of Souls not as nostalgia but as hidden agenda. If Frantz Fanon remained skeptical about the political edge of vodun (*Wretched of the Earth*, 55–58), Lamming himself, in a passage illustrative of the circulation of circum-Atlantic performance genres, evokes Shakespeare's *Hamlet* to describe the revolutionary potential of the spirit-world presence: "If that presence be no more than a ghost, then it is like the ghost that haunted Hamlet, ordering memory and imagination to define and do their duty" (125).

In contrast to the linear narrative of catastrophe so powerfully present in Western tragic drama, however, spirit-world ceremonies, celebrations of the cycle of death and life, tend to place catastrophe in the past, as a grief to be expiated, and not necessarily in the future, as a singular fate yet to be endured. In this they closely resemble the great Condolence Councils of the Iroquois, the action of which culminates in a "Lifting Up of Minds," transforming "dysphoria" into "euphoria" (Fenton, 19; Myerhoff; Radcliffe-Brown). *An Echo in the Bone* ends not in the obligatory fifth-act carnage of revenge tragedy—the die is cast, the cast must die—but in celebration: "Play," a devotee tells the drummer, "for what [we] leave behind. Play for the rest of us." The playwright brings down the curtain only "*When the stage is full of their celebration, somewhere in the ritual*" (136–37). This affirmation contests the closure of investing the future with the fatality of the past, a position more easily maintained by those whose communication with their ancestors was continuous, dynamic, and intimate. However strange such relations may appear to some, in world-historical terms they are actually quite normal. To educate the reader of *Things Fall Apart* (1958) to this fact, Chinua Achebe dramatizes the regularity of the ancestors' return, not as supernumeraries to the apocalypse but as an annual board of visitors (62–66). In such circumstances, memory circulates and migrates like gossip from location to location as well as from generation to generation, growing or attenuating as it passes through the hands of those who possess it and those whom it possesses. As Achebe expresses the commonsense negotiation of propinquity and difference: "Spirits always addressed humans as 'bodies' " (64).

In the vortex of the circum-Atlantic world since the late seventeenth century, the peculiarity of the development of European memory with regard to ancestral spirits is conspicuous. Later on in this chapter, I examine the nature of that peculiarity by reconstructing memorial performances of different kinds at several apparently unconnected sites: the mythic evocation of England's Mediterranean origins in Henry Purcell's opera *Dido and Aeneas* (1689), the segregation of the dead from the living as promulgated by urban planners in London (1711) and New Orleans (1721), the interactive adaptation of African burial practices under the French *Code noir* in Louisiana (after 1724), the "slave dances" of Congo Square (ca. 1820), and, briefly, the emergent secular sainthood of a gifted but derivative rhythm-and-blues singer (ca. 1954). Before those performances can be addressed as if they do somehow in fact belong to the same world, however, I need to define a general phenomenon of collective memory that functions in all of them: the effigy. The effigy is a contrivance that enables the processes regulating performance—kinesthetic imagination, vortices of behavior, and displaced transmission—to produce memory through surrogation. Moreover, the effigy operates in all the cultural constructions of events and institutions that I define as central to circum-Atlantic memory: death and burials, violence and sacrifices, commodification and auctions, laws and (dis)obedience, origins and segregation.

The Effigy

Normal usage employs the word *effigy* as a noun meaning a sculpted or pictured likeness. More particularly it can suggest a crudely fabricated image of a person, commonly one that is destroyed in his or her stead, as in hanging or burning *in effigy*. When *effigy* appears as a verb, though that usage is rare, it means to evoke an absence, to body something forth, especially something from a distant past (*OED*). *Effigy* is cognate to *efficiency*, *efficacy*, *effervescence*, and *effeminacy* through their mutual connection to ideas of producing, bringing forth, bringing out, and making. *Effigy*'s similarity to *performance* should be clear enough: it fills by means of surrogation a vacancy created by the absence of an original. Beyond ostensibly inanimate effigies fashioned from wood or cloth, there are more elusive but more powerful effigies fashioned from flesh. Such effigies are made by performances. They consist of a set of actions that hold open a place in memory into which many different people may step according to circumstances and occasions. I argue that performed effigies—those fabricated from human bodies and the associations they evoke—provide communities with a method of perpetuating themselves through specially nominated mediums or surrogates: among them, actors, dancers, priests, street maskers, statesmen, celebrities, freaks, children, and especially, by virtue of an intense but unsurprising paradox, corpses. No doubt that is why effigies figure so frequently in the performance of death through mortuary rituals—and why the ambivalence associated with the dead must enter into any discussion of the relationship between memory, performance, and substitution.

From the work of Emile Durkheim and Sir James Frazer on, the anthropological classics have given great weight to the revelatory meanings of funerary ceremonies and practices among diverse cultures. In his retrospective preface to the 1922 edition of *The Golden Bough*, Frazer summarized the importance of this subject to his entire project: "the fear of the human dead," he wrote, not vegetation worship, was "the most powerful force in the making of primitive religion" (vii). In Arnold van Gennep's seminal formulation of death as a rite of passage, the binary distinction that creates two categories, dead and alive, simultaneously creates in its interstices a threefold process of living, dying, and being dead. The middle state (dying, or more expressively, "passing") is the less stable stage of transition between more clearly defined conditions: it is called the "liminal" (literally, "threshold") stage, and it tends to generate the most intense experiences of ritual expectancy, activity, and meaning. As further developed by Victor Turner, the concept of liminality—a state of betwixt-and-betweenness, a "subjunctive mood" in the grammar of communal activity—characterizes as "social dramas" those behaviors in which normative categories are transgressed or suspended only to be reaffirmed by ritual processes of reincorporation (*Forest of Symbols*, 94).

Turner and others have hypothesized that celebrations of death function as rites of social renewal, especially when the decedents occupy positions to which intense collective attention is due, such as those of leaders or kings. Digressing on the power of royal corpses in their survey of the anthropology of death, Richard Huntington and Peter Metcalf (to whom I am much indebted for the materials relating to mortuary ritual in this section) explain: "It seems that the most powerful natural symbol for the continuity of any community, large or small, simple or complex, is, by a strange and dynamic paradox, to be found in the death of its leader, and in the representation of that striking event" (182). It is also in connection with the death of its leader or another similarly august luminary that a community is likely to construct an effigy, animate or inanimate. As the Mande proverb elegantly sums up: "It takes more than death to make an ancestor."

The rich anthropological literature on this subject includes such classics as Frazer's account, revised by E. E. Evans-Pritchard, of ritual regicide among the Shilluk people of the Upper Nile (the Shilluks replaced the failing body of their king with a wooden effigy until a successor could be named). It likewise includes parallel studies of the Dinkas of southern Sudan, who buried their chieftain alive during what they took to be his final illness (Deng). These practices, which define as intolerable the decay of the body of the leader, resemble in certain respects the tribal customs of the French and the English, including the British policy of early recall of colonial civil servants (before they reached the age of fifty-five) so that the locals would never see their European governors falling into illness or decrepitude (Said, 42). Such practices derive from the venerable principle of divine kingship. They answer the need to symbolize the inviolate continuity of the body politic (Huntington and Metcalf, 121–83). They do so by dramatizing a duality, a core of preternatural durability invested within a shell of human vulnerability (Soyinka). This paradox of immortality amid physical decay symbolically asserts the divinely authorized continuity of human institutions while recognizing their inherent fragility. It also discovers the profoundly ambivalent emotions human beings harbor for the dead, who once belonged among the living but who now inhabit some alien country whose citizens putrefy yet somehow endure.

In English and French history particularly, this paradox finds expression in the strange doctrine of the "king's two bodies." As documented and explicated by Ernst Kantorowicz, the legal fiction that the king had not one but two bodies—the *body natural* and the *body politic*—developed out of medieval Christology (the corporeal duality of Man and God) and into an increasingly pragmatic and secular principle of sovereign succession and legal continuity (Giesey; Kantorowicz). Tudor lawyers found it a particularly useful way of holding Queen Elizabeth, for instance, to the grants of property made by Edward VI during his minority. They argued that while the boy-king's "body natural" may have been subject to the infirmities and even imbecilities of age, his "body politic" was always both adult and immortal.

By means of explicit enactments through the disposition of royal remains, the doctrine of the king's two bodies materialized into a spectacular stagecraft: beginning with the funeral of Edward II in 1327, the body of the dead king was represented by a wooden effigy; with interruptions occasioned by the turbulence of the Wars of Roses, this practice, juxtaposing an image of the indestructibility of the king's sovereign body with the display of his rotting human corpse, lasted until Charles II in England and the reign of Louis XIV in France. In the protocols of royal funerals, this venerable contradiction added to the ritualized public announcement, "The king is dead," an only apparently inapposite salutation addressed to the deceased incumbent: "Long live the king." The supposed legacy of such symbolic immutability—its living effigy—is the concept of a constitutional diffusion and continuity of governmental power, an enduring "body politic" under the rule of law.

The principle of surrogation clearly operates here, as a mysterious but powerful sense of affiliation pervades the community on the occasion of its most consequential single loss. That sense of affiliation holds open a place into which tradition injects the rituals of ultimate reincorporation, the crowning of a successor. But in the place that is being held open there also exists an invisible network of allegiances, interests, and resistances that constitutes the imagined community. In that place also is a breeding ground of anxieties and uncertainties about what that community should be—contradictory emotions that focus a range of potentially phobic responses on the body of the deceased. Such contradictory responses do not unfold all at once. Death, as it is culturally constructed by surrogacy, cannot be understood as a moment, a point in time: it is a process.

One crucial aspect of death as a process resides in the conception of marginality itself. In the creative scope of liminal categories, periphery and center may seem to change places. Peter Stallybrass and Allon White, in their excursus beyond Hegel's master-slave dyad, accurately describe this reversal not only of dependency but of contested and appropriated location: "The result is a mobile, conflictual fusion of power, fear and desire in the construction of subjectivity: a psychological dependence upon precisely those Others which are being rigorously opposed and excluded at the social level. It is for this reason that what is *socially* peripheral is so frequently *symbolically* central" (5). This phenomenon operates in many different ways, but one pattern tends to recur: a contradictory push and pull develops as communities construct themselves by both expanding their boundaries and working back in from them. They pull back by excluding or subordinating the peoples those larger boundaries ostensibly embrace. Such contradictory intentions remain tolerable because the myth of coherence at the center requires a constantly visible yet constantly receding perimeter of difference. Sometimes this perimeter is a horizon; more often it is a mirage. Its mythic and potentially bloody frontiers must be continuously negotiated and reinvented, even as its most alarmist defenders panic before the specter of its permeability.

That is why performances in general and funerals in particular are so rich in revealing contradictions: because they make publicly visible through symbolic action both the tangible existence of social boundaries and, at the same time, the contingency of those boundaries on fictions of identity, their shoddy construction out of inchoate otherness, and, consequently, their anxiety-inducing instability. From this perspective, the funerals of performers provide particularly promising sites for investigation because they involve figures whose very profession, itself alternately ostracized and overvalued, entails frequent transitions between states and categories. Performers are routinely pressed into service as effigies, their bodies alternately adored and despised but always offered up on the altar of surrogacy.

The history of what happens at troubled borders needs no reiteration, but the theory of the effigy can clarify the nature of the violence they both provoke and exculpate. In *Violence and the Sacred* (1972), René Girard explores the propensity for violence in human societies through an examination of what he calls the "monstrous double" in rituals of sacrifice. The double displaces violent desire to an agenda of disguises. Girard delineates the contradictory impulses that create the "monstrous double": the sacrificial victim must be neither divisive nor trivial, neither fully part of the community nor fully outside of it; rather, he or she must be distanced by a special identity that specifies isolation while simultaneously allowing plausible surrogation for a member of the community. This occurs in a two-staged process: the community finds a surrogate victim for itself from within itself; then it finds an alien substitute, like an effigy, for the surrogate. This is the "monstrous double" (160–64).

Behind Girard's formulation of the deflection of ritual violence from the heart of the community to the "sacrificeable" double and its critique (Bloch; Burkert; Detienne and Vernaht) lies the tradition defined by Marcel Mauss's account of potlatch in *The Gift: Forms and Functions of Exchange in Archaic Societies* (1924), redefined by Georges Bataille in *The Accursed Share: An Essay on General Economy* (1967), and reopened in a different register by Jacques Derrida in *Given Time* (1992). Although he cites Bataille only in passing (222), Girard's idea that sacrificial violence operates as a kind of expenditure through which society prolongs its sense of coherence in face of a threat of divisive substitutions owes its understanding of excess to him. In an economy where products accumulate more rapidly than they can be consumed, Bataille observed, people take an interest in relieving the consequent pressure by excess or "unproductive" expenditure. In a gift economy, however, unproductive expenditure is hardly purposeless. Where cultural values such as prestige are exchanged as well as goods, as Arjun Appadurai explains his introduction to *The Social Life of Things: Commodities in Cultural Perspective* (1986), reciprocity ensures that "one's desire for an object is fulfilled by the sacrifice of some other object, which is the focus of desire of another" (3). Lewis Hyde, in *The Gift: Imagination and the Erotic Life of*

Property (1979), reiterates the venerable comparison of the economy of sacrifice to the circulation of blood, which, like a gift, "is neither bought nor sold and it comes back forever" (138). This chapter and those that follow explore the ways in which the restored behavior of sacrificial expenditure functions in an expanding circum-Atlantic marketplace filled with commodities of all kinds. These include the sale of human flesh at public auction and the concomitant commerce in images and representations of such exchanges that complicate the meaning of *effigy* with that of *fetish*.

For my purposes here, however, a stark definition emerges from Bataille's meditations on "catastrophic expenditure": violence is the performance of waste. To that definition I offer three corollaries: first, that violence is never senseless but always meaningful, because violence in human culture always serves, one way or the other, to make a point; second, that all violence is excessive, because to be fully demonstrative, to make its point, it must *spend* things—material objects, blood, environments—in acts of Bataillian "unproductive expenditure" (or Veblenian "conspicuous consumption"); and third, that all violence is performative, for the simple reason that it must have an audience—even if that audience is only the victim, even if that audience is only God.

In the circum-Atlantic economy of superabundance, violence occupies a portion of the cultural category that includes the aesthetic. Both represent a form of excess production and expenditure of social energy; that is, outside the relatively rare instances of spontaneous self-defense, violence and the preparations for violence, like the aesthetic, exist as a form of cultural expression that goes beyond the utilitarian practices necessary to physical survival. Whether this excess expenditure is itself an absolute necessity in the establishment of what we call culture is another question, but it incorporates the production of any ornament of culture—from Iroquois face and body painting to a couplet by Alexander Pope—into a symbolic economy of performance that mobilizes the beautiful in the cause of the only apparently disinterested. Here the common usage of *effigy* as the surrogate for violence perpetrated on an absent victim brings together Girard's notions of sacrifice with the idea of the functional similarity of violence and the aesthetic: "burning in effigy" is a performance of waste, the elimination of a monstrous double, but one fashioned by artifice as a stand-in, an "unproductive expenditure" that both sustains the community with the comforting fiction that real borders exist and troubles it with the spectacle of their immolation.

Performing Origins

Wistfully portrayed by musicologists as sui generis, Henry Purcell's *Dido and Aeneas* descends as the masterpiece without progeny in the abortive history of English national opera. Whatever its status as an atypical work in the theatrical and musical history of England, I interpret it, like the Zulu parade in New Orleans, as a representative event in the genealogy of circum-Atlantic performance. This enactment of encounter, rupture, and dynastic establishment premiered in an amateur production "By Young Gentlewomen" at Josias Priest's school in Chelsea in 1689 (Purcell and Tate, 3). With the education of girls then something of a luxury expenditure in any case, the production of an opera for their improvement and exhibition evokes Veblen if not Bataille. But the performance of waste is never "senseless." In an economy of slave-produced abundance, expensive young women may come to signify the importance of excess itself, the symbolic crossing point of material production/consumption and reproductive fecundity. *Dido and Aeneas* opened the same year that James II involuntarily turned his interest in the Royal Africa Company, founded by his brother Charles in 1672, over to its ambitious investors and sailed away (Calder, 347). There has been informed speculation about the local political allegory of *Dido and Aeneas* relating to the royal succession and Williamite policy (Buttrey; Price, introduction to Purcell and Tate, 6–12), but my genealogical reading resituates the opera, like King Zulu's procession, as a performance of cultural memory amid conflicting performances of origin.

By performance of origin I mean the reenactment of foundation myths along two general axes of possibility: the diasporic, which features migration, and the autochthonous, which claims indigenous roots deeper than memory itself. These myths may coexist or compete within the same tradition; indeed, they often do. In *Racial Myth in English History: Trojans, Teutons, and Anglo-Saxons* (1982), Hugh A. MacDougall explains how two contradictory theories of national origin shaped the ethnic fiction of Englishness. The first, which attributed the founding of Britain (and indeed its name) to the Trojan prince Brute (or Brutus), dominated medieval historiographies of origin. The Trojan myth began with Brute's odyssey by a circuitous circum-Atlantic route to Albion. It then ascended through the Arthurian legends of Celtic Britain to support the historic claims of British monarchs to an epic-born legitimacy rivaling that of Rome. Though it had lost ground to modernizing historical research in the sixteenth and seventeenth centuries, the Trojan-Arthurian myth still resonated in the efforts of

John Dryden, Henry Purcell, Nahum Tate, and others to create an English national opera, including the semiopera *King Arthur* as well as the through-composed *Dido and Aeneas*.

The second narrative of national origin, to which I will return in the next chapter, claims greater historicity and yet remains at heart no less a myth. It traces the origins of Britain to Germanic peoples, namely the Anglo-Saxons, and it attributes the supposedly unique "Liberty" of Englishmen and English institutions to the fierce independence and ethnic purity of the Teutonic races (MacDougall). Perhaps the most virulent expression of this version of Anglo-Saxon revisionism came from Richard Verstegen in the *Restitution of Decayed Intelligence in Antiquities Concerning the Most Noble and Renowned English Nation* (1605), the very title of which asserts the reclamation of an indigenous heritage.

As evocations of the past, both myths of origin—the diasporic and the autochthonous—also suggest alternatives for the future. These alternatives inevitably raise the question of surrogation: diaspora tends to put pressure on autochthony, threatening its imputed purity, both antecedent and successive, because it appears to make available a human superabundance for mutual assimilation. At this promising yet dangerous juncture, catastrophe may reemerge from memory in the shape of a wish.

The libretto of *Dido* is by Nahum Tate, better remembered for his neoclassical improvements to *King Lear* and his consummately tactless revival of *Richard II* in 1681 at a particularly tense moment of the Exclusion Crisis. In fact, several of Tate's works for the stage derive directly or indirectly from the materials in Geoffrey of Monmouth's *History of the Kings of Britain* (ca. 1136), a narrative from which he grafted some details onto the fourth book of Virgil's *Aeneid* to produce the *Dido* libretto. In the 1670s Tate had begun a play based on the Dido and Aeneas story, but he decided instead to adapt the plot to fit the epic voyages of the legendary Brute, Aeneas's grandson (or great-grandson in some versions). In this play, called *Brutus of Alba; or, The Enchanted Lovers* (1678), the hero loves and leaves the queen of Syracuse in the same way that Aeneas abandons the queen of Carthage: the grandfather sails away to found Rome; the grandson, according to Tate's dramatization of Geoffrey of Monmouth's account of the oral tradition, sails away to found Britain. Tate then returned to the Aeneas-version when he provided Purcell with a libretto a decade later, but the two stories echo one another as hauntingly as the echo-chorus in the witches' scene, which itself doubles the actions of the Carthaginian court (Savage, 263–66), culminated by an "Eccho Dance of Furies." As each end phrase repeats in the dematerialized voices of an off-stage chorus, lithe spirits choreograph the fated catastrophe:

> In our deep-vaulted cell the charm we'll prepare,
> Too dreadful a practice for this open air.
>
> (Purcell and Tate, 70)

Operas of the time, in addition functioning as allegories of national or dynastic origin, typically employed witches: Davenant's musical version of Shakespeare's *Macbeth*, for instance, qualified to contemporaries as "being in the nature of an Opera" by this reckoning (Downes, 71; see Plank). As in the West Indian deployment of obeah and vodun, works of the political occult like *Dido and Aeneas* and *Macbeth* thus appropriated the echoing spirit world to the secular allegory of imagined community. Witches, like the spirits of the dead, allowed those among the living to speak of (and yet disavow) the hidden transcript of succession: in 1689 the Exclusion Crisis, to which Tate had contributed nine years before, was finally resolved by means of revolution. A crisis of royal succession is perforce a crisis of cultural surrogation, necessarily rich in performative occasions and allegories of origin and segregation.

The epic account of the Trojan Brute, with its echoes of Virgil, narrates the transoceanic movement of empire out of the Mediterranean and into the Atlantic. From Geoffrey of Monmouth's version, it may be inferred that this story lived in an oral memory, as an epic of diasporic origin. Just as Homer and the tragic dramatists recorded and celebrated what they saw as the enormous, epochal shift of cultural and political gravity away from the Asiatic world to the Mycenaean, and just as Virgil immortalized the similar movement out from the Aegean into the larger world of mare nostrum, so the poets, dramatists, and storytellers of the early modern period could once again poetically witness a transfer of the imperial vortex from its historic locus. "Old King Brute" of the chronicles made himself useful to this allegory of Atlantic destiny.

One vision of the role of Great Britain in the diasporic scheme of hemispheric memory took the form of an Augustan ascendancy to the Roman imperium, which would, in the fullness of time, itself be replaced by new and vital cultures. As Horace Walpole wrote: "The next Augustan age will dawn on the other side of the Atlantic. There will perhaps be a Thucydides at Boston, a Xenophon at New York, and in time, a Virgil in Mexico, and a Newton at Peru. At last some curious traveller from Lima will visit England and give a description of the ruins of St. Paul's" (Walpole, 24:61–62). The conception of history as a vast performance of diaspora and surrogation haunts intercultural musings such as Walpole's, which transform invented pasts into gloriously catastrophic futures. Such a conception looks ahead to those who will someday prove worthy to become an audience for the spectacle of our ruin, as we have proven ourselves worthy spectators of the ruins of Troy, Rome, or Carthage. Just as Brute stands in for Aeneas at Britain's founding, so the transatlantic colonists stand in for Brute. The imperial measurement of human time by millennia in evidence here requires a moment of contemplation: Charles II chartered the Royal Africa Company, which operated the slave-taking forts on the Guinea Coast, for one thousand years, its patent to expire in A.D. 2672. The imperial measurement of identity in evidence here requires another moment: even more ethnocentric than the desire to replace others or the fear of being replaced by them is the assumption that their desire is to become what we are.

Although Africa in fact plays a hinge role in turning the Mediterranean-centered consciousness of European memory into an Atlantic-centered one, the scope of that role largely disappears. Yet it leaves its historic traces amid the incomplete erasures, beneath the superscriptions, and within the layered palimpsests of more or less systematic cultural misrecognition. This epic *Dido*, no less than King Zulu, performs, though in a different way. Moving from the Mediterranean world to the Atlantic in its doubled narrative of Trojan heroes, Tate's mythic reiteration of origins, an evocation of collective memory, hinges on the narrative of abandonment, a public performance of forgetting.

In the score's most stunning moment of musical declamation, which prepares for the death of the forsaken Afro-Phoenician queen and the observances performed over her body, Tate gave Purcell a deceptively simple line to set. As Aeneas sets sail for Rome and empire, Dido's last words seem to speak for the victims of transoceanic ambitions: "Remember me, but ah! forget my fate" (Purcell and Tate, 75). Dido pleads that she may be remembered as a woman even as the most pertinent events of her story are erased, a sentiment that more appositely expresses the agenda of the departing Trojans. Dryden's translation of Virgil catches the drama of this moment of decision and catastrophe, an evocation of memory with designs on an apocalyptic future:

Dire auguries from hence the Trojans draw;
Till neither fires nor shining shores they saw.
Now seas and skies their prospect only bound;
An empty space above, a floating field around.
(Dryden, *Virgil*, 126)

As Aeneas casts a parting look back to the rising pillar of smoke, his ambivalence fuses memory and forgetting into one gesture. In that gesture, he enacts the historic tendency of Europeans, when reminded, to recall only emotions of deep love for the peoples whose cultures they have left in flames, emotions predicated on the sublime vanity that their early departure would not have been celebrated locally as deliverance.

The lush, feminized abundance of the Carthaginian court, the lavish exchange of gifts performed there, the bloody sacrifice of the hunt, and the liminal status of the diasporic queen produce tremors of ritual expectancy. Tate knows what effect must be delivered: in the laws of hospitality that govern the visit of death to drama, a suicide offers up the fatted calf, the gift of closure, the performance of waste:

Thy hand Belinda, darkness shades me,
On thy bosom let me rest.
Cupids *appear in the clouds o'er her tomb.*
More I would but death invades me,
Death is now a welcome guest.
(Purcell and Tate, 75)

The eerie effect of lines of such gravity resonating in the slender vocal chords of a schoolgirl (though quite possibly a schoolgirl of freakish musical and dramatic talent—Purcell knew how to compose for exceptional voices) suggests that the opera produces the child as an effigy. Her nubile body, impersonating the Carthaginian queen's, might then activate a signifying chain of substitutions that culminate allegorically in the origin of imperial superabundance on the sacrificial expenditure of Africa.

The key to the genealogy of performance derived from this moment in a Restoration opera, however, rests on the musical setting for the text. The ground bass accompaniment for the vocal line of Dido's lament, "Remember me," which immediately follows the recitative quoted above, is a chaconne (Mellers, 213). This form became widely popular in Europe at the beginning of the seventeenth century, first in Spain as a dance in triple meter with erotic connotations, then in France as a more stately court dance, associated especially with weddings. The only agreement about the origin of what the Spanish call the *chacona* and the Italians *ciaccona*, however, is that it wasn't European and that it drove women crazy. Spaniards attributed it to the Indians of Peru or perhaps the West Indies, where it gave its name to a mythical island, a utopia also called Cucaña (or, in English, Cockaigne). Beauchamp, the French dancing master, confidently traced the chaconne to Africa (Walker, 303; McClary, 87).

Whatever the precise history of the chaconne across four continents, the very confusions about its points of origin suggest its emergence out of the diasporic *métissage* of the Caribbean. Its assimilation into the musical life of a finishing school for daughters of English merchants suggests the invisible domestication and consumption of the Atlantic triangle's vast cultural produce, which, like sugar, its textures effaced, metamorphosed from brown syrup into white powder, until only the sweetness remained. That Dido's final lament, stately threnody that it is, derives its cadences and musical style from a forgotten Native American or African form lends an eerily doubled meaning to the queen's invocation of memory as her lover sails boldly away from the coast of Africa bound for amnesia.

The Segregation of the Dead

"I trade both with the living and the dead," Dryden explains in the introduction to his translation of *The Aeneid* (lxiv). The argument to book six further promises the reader that the sibyl will prophesy the hero's future by returning him to the past via a detour to the afterlife. This promise the poem keeps. Attending Aeneas on a journey into hell, the sibyl introduces him to many of the shades who dwell there, including the ghost of his father, Anchises, "who instructs him in those sublime mysteries of the soul of the world, and the transmigration; and shews him that glorious race of heroes which was to descend from him, and his posterity" (*Aeneid*, 157). But into the exalted prospect of this dynastic scene, fate or guilty conscience introduces an unbidden memory. As Aeneas and his guide pass by the Mournful Fields where the shades of tragic lovers dwell but find no rest, the specter of Dido of Carthage, "fresh from her wound, her bosom bath'd in blood," appears. Aeneas doubts his eyes but readily credits local gossip:

> (Doubtful as he who sees, thro' dusky night,
> Or thinks he sees, the moon's uncertain light,)
> With tears he first approach'd the sullen shade;

> And, as his love inspir'd him, thus he said:
> "Unhappy queen! then is the common breath
> Of rumor true, in your reported death,
> And I, alas, the cause?"
>
> (Dryden, *Aeneid*, 173)

Dido replies with stony silence, which no entreaties can induce her to break, until at last, still speechless, she fades away, "Hid in the forest and the shades of night" (174). Aeneas seems to find this silence troubling but convenient; he is quickly on his way again, while Dido, like the repressed, reenters the Stygian realms from which she staged her silent and brief return.

Citing Virgil's account of hell in a *Tatler* number devoted to the "Empire of Death," Joseph Addison shows how the boundaries that separate life from the afterlife provide a melancholy but not unpleasing occasion to contemplate the idea of boundaries themselves. Addison calls these carefully defined perimeters "the Confines of the Dead" (2:363). As the myths and beliefs of Mediterranean memory play themselves out in the circum-Atlantic world, these obscure, symbolic boundaries, living memories in the minds of Addison and his readers, could be silently reinvented and imposed through the literal construction of the most tangible forms of material culture. I am thinking particularly of that characteristic invention of modern architecture, the behavioral vortices of death: cemeteries.

In a consequential but as yet only partially understood usurpation of popular custom, Europeans attempted to impose on themselves (and on the peoples they colonized) a revolutionary spatial paradigm: the segregation of the dead from the living. Although precedents may be cited in the great thanatological projects of antiquity, from Egypt to Etruria, the ambition of the modern displacement of medieval tradition should be carefully considered (figure 2.1). In this light, modernity itself might be understood as a new way of handling (and thinking about) the dead.

At one time in European tradition, as in many other traditions worldwide, the dead were omnipresent: first, in the mysterious sense that their spirits continued to occupy places among the quick; second, in the material sense that medieval burial custom crowded decomposing corpses into hopelessly overfilled churchyards and crypts, whence they literally overflowed into the space of the living. Though jumbled remains from generations of reburials in the same graves saturated the earth, the burial ground often provided the most convenient public spaces available to merchants, mountebanks, jugglers, and their mixed audiences, who shared in this popular inter-

2.1 St. Louis Cemetery, No. 1. *Harper's Weekly*, March 9, 1867.
Louisiana Collection, Howard-Tilton Memorial Library, Tulane University

mingling of life and death, carnival and Lent (Burke). Hamlet's hands-on eulogy of Yorick takes place in just such an overbooked boneyard, and historians of social custom have noted the uncanny effects produced by the continuous intersection of intimacy and dispossession.

In *Montaillou: The Promised Land of Error* (1979), for example, Le Roy Ladurie speaks of the obtrusive familiarity of the dead: "They had no houses of their own. . . . They might go every Saturday and visit the *ostal* where their widow or widower still lived with their children. They might temporarily occupy their old bedroom" (348–49). As in many traditional African societies, the spaces of the living and the dead in the medieval comté de Foix were not discrete: "Before the harvest, Gélis joined in veritable drinking bouts with the dead, in parties of over a hundred" (347). Indeed, one of the important elements that gave meaning to a particular place—that made it a particular place—was the gregarious presence of the dead.

The rationalizing projects of the European Enlightenment, however, attempted to reform this scandalous propinquity. Under a regime of newly segregationist taxonomies of behavior in several related fields of manners and bodily administration, the dead were compelled to withdraw from the spaces of the living: their ghosts were exorcised even from the stage; their bodies were removed to newly dedicated and isolated cemeteries, which in New Orleans came to be called "Cities of the Dead." As custom increasingly defined human remains as unhygienic, new practices of interment evolved, eventually including cremation, to ensure the perpetual separation of the dead and to reduce or more strictly circumscribe the spaces they occupied. As the place of burial was removed from local churchyard to distant park, the dead were more likely to be remembered (and forgotten) by monuments than by continued observances in which their spirits were invoked. Like the ghost of Dido, the enlightened dead were more likely now to observe the strict silence of the tomb.

As a vast anthropological topic, which I can only begin to outline here, the segregation of the dead has some precise historical dates. When Adrien DePauger laid out the tidy grid of streets and public spaces for the French colonial city of New Orleans in 1721, for instance, a bounded square marked "*cimetière*" appeared, not in the churchyard at the center of the plan but outside the walls of the fortifications at its perimeter (Huber, 3; figure 2.2). By 1819, when the architect Benjamin Henry Latrobe visited St. Louis Cemetery No. 1, a somewhat enlarged but not far distant version of DePauger's detached City of the Dead, it had been further segregated into neighborhoods—Catholic and Protestant—and subdivided into apartment buildings and single-family residences: "[The tombs] are of bricks, much larger than necessary to enclose a coffin, and plaistered over, so as to have a very solid and permanent appearance" (Latrobe, 241).

As metropolitan theory responded to colonial practice, the philosophes had launched attacks on the church and its monuments to superstition by attacking the ubiquity of the dead. In 1764 Voltaire denounced the unhealthy conditions of the churches and charnel houses of Paris, where dogs rooted among the cadavers, and in 1776 Louis XVI forbade further burials within churches except for high officials, dignitaries, and donors (Ragon, 199–200). First by royal decree and then by acts of the Revolutionary Convention, the charnel house in the Church of the Innocents in

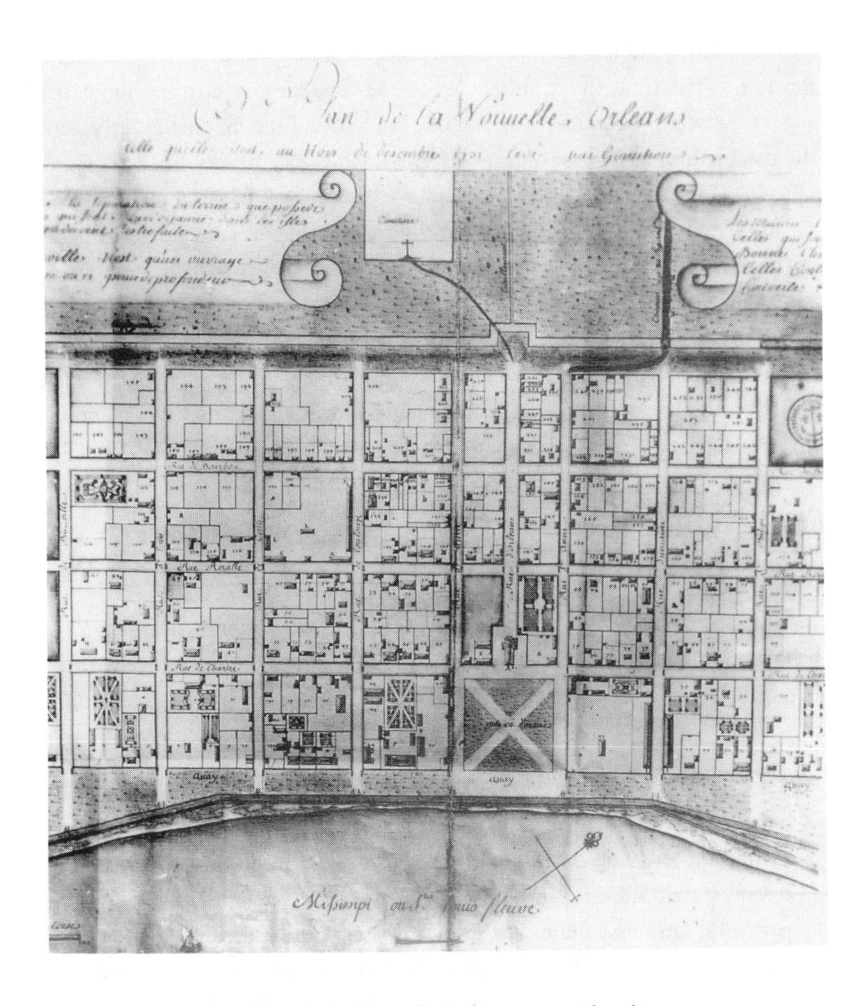

2.2 Plan de la Nouvelle Orleans, 1731 (detail).
Louisiana Collection, Howard-Tilton Memorial Library, Tulane University

rue St. Denis, which contained an estimated four million corpses accumulated over five centuries, was evacuated. The architect-engineer Latrobe, musing on the enormity of this public works project as he strolled through St. Louis Cemetery No. 1 in New Orleans, observed: "The great operation at Paris in removing the dead from the cemetery of St. Innocent, is an astonishing instance of the expensive efforts that have been found necessary to get rid of them—an operation that none but Frenchmen could have conceived or executed" (Latrobe, 245). Latrobe's New Orleanian perspective, however, did not do justice to the conceptual boldness of Londoners, though at the time the architect wrote he was largely correct about the superior state of practical implementation by the French, particularly with the establishment by Napoleon of Père-Lachaise cemetery in 1804 (Curl, 154–67).

The emerging practice of segregating the dead received powerful support in England as a consequence of the rebuilding of London following the Great Fire of 1666. In *Windsor-Forest* (1713), Alexander Pope captures the ambition of this enormous public works project, Augustan in scale, particularly the construction of fifty new parish churches to replace those lost in the fire (and to supply the demands newly created by a rapidly expanding imperial metropolis):

> Behold! *Augusta*'s glitt'ring Spires increase,
> And Temples rise, the beauteous Works of Peace.
> (*Poems*, 1:187)

In his "Proposals" of 1711 for constructing the churches, Sir John Vanbrugh, architect, dramatist, and comptroller of works under Queen Anne, laid out the Enlightenment's case for reorganizing urban space to ghettoize the dead:

> That [the new churches] be free'd from that Inhuman custome of being made Burial Places for the Dead, a Custome in which there is something so very barbarous in itself besides the many ill consequences that attend it; that one cannot enough wonder how it ever prevail'd amongst the civiliz'd part of mankind. But there is now a sort of happy necessity on this Occasion of breaking through it; Since there can be no thought of purchasing ground for Church Yards, where the Churches will probably be plac'd. And since there must therefore be Cemitarys provided in the Skirts of Towne, if they are ordered with that decency they ought to be, there can be no doubt but the Rich as well as the Poor, will be content to ly there. (251)

In Vanbrugh's proposal the scheme of separating the living from the dead offers the city planner an occasion to discriminate between the rich and the poor as well as between the civilized and barbarous. Unlike his senior colleague Sir Christopher Wren, whose proposals envisioned the common interment of rich and poor in the new necropolis, Vanbrugh refined the spatial differentiation to reflect differences among the dead themselves. In so doing he provided one of the earliest descriptions of what would become a commonplace of the well-planned modern urbanscape:

> If these Cemitarys be consecrated, Handsomely and regularly wall'd in, and planted with Trees in such form as to make a Solemn Distinction between one Part and another; there is no doubt, but the Richer sort of People, will think their Friends and Relations more decently inter'd in those distinguish'd Places, than they commonly are in the Ailes and under Pews in Churches; And will think them more honorably remember'd by Lofty and Noble Mausoleums erected over them in Freestone (which no doubt will soon come into practice) then by little Tawdry Monuments of Marble stuck up against Walls and Pillars. (251)

The cemetery grows on the margins to define the social distinction of the fictive center: the dead will dwell in separate houses suitable to their status. The bodies of the indigent, Vanbrugh does not go on to say, were stacked like cordwood in open yards until a sufficient number of corpses accumulated to make digging a common grave worthwhile.

To the accompanying sketch (figure 2.3), the comptroller appends a most significant explanatory note. In it he credits the idea for the segregation of the dead to the colonials in Surat, the East India Company's concession near the coast between Ahmadabad and Bombay: "This manner of Interment has been practic'd by the English at Suratt and is come at last to have this kind of effect" (Vanbrugh, 251). Surat first developed as a trading port in the reign of James I. By 1711 it had been active for nearly a century, and the high death rate among the British factors in residence there created a constant demand for burial places in which the colonials could both visibly separate themselves from and publicly compete with the magnificent entombments of the local moguls (Calder, 158). In their enormous freestanding tombs, for instance, the brothers Sir George and Sir Christopher Oxinden (d. 1659 and 1669, respectively) built mausolea to rival the Taj Mahal (Curl, 136–45). They planted at Surat palaces for the dead that anticipated the massy pretentions of Vanbrugh and Nicholas Hawksmoor's baroque country houses for the living at Blenheim and Castle Howard. (As if to insist on this connection, a stately and hugely expensive mausoleum graced the picturesque landscape garden of the latter palace, a kind of grand finale to its magnificent performance of waste.) Vanbrugh's "Proposals" of 1711 thus appropriate the discriminatory practices developed at the colonial margin for use

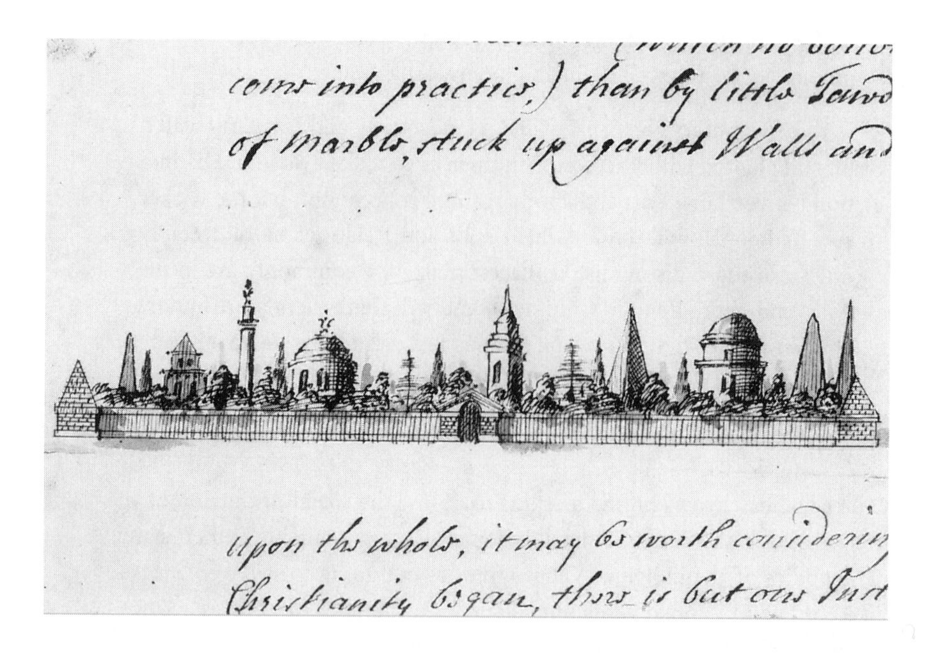

2.3 Sir John Vanbrugh, sketch for an ideal cemetery, as "practic'd by the English at Suratt," from "Proposals for the Fifty Churches," 1711.
Bodleian Library, Oxford University, Ms. Rawl. B. 376, fol. 352r (detail)

in rebuilding the metropolitan center. Although the actual implementation of his ideas for the London cemeteries awaited the founding of Kensal Green by act of Parliament in 1832 (Meller, 6–11), Vanbrugh's scheme serves as one instance among many in which Enlightened Cities of the Dead offered themselves up as conceptual prototypes for the cities in which posterity now lives.

Indeed, London and New Orleans were not the only cities in which emerged architectural spaces that effectively masked the dead (and later the dying) from the daily experience of the living: "The modern West," argues Michel Ragon, "has tended to evacuate death" (14). Many consequences have no doubt ensued from this immense project, this radical rationalization of space, this creation of a necropolis of exiles in the "[out]Skirts of Towne." The most persistently segregationist of these might easily have been the invention of the suburb, that bourgeois simulacrum of heaven, where decency allots to every proper person an inviolable place, detached or semidetached, and where ownership is individually privatized for eternity along its silent, leafy avenues. The most poignant of them must have been the slave ship, the triangular trade's simulacrum of hell, where each of the living dead occupied no more space than a coffin, and the daily wastage disappeared over the side to a grave unmarked except by the sea. The most pervasive of them surely must be the weird silences and circumlocutions that wall off death from life in modern mortuary etiquette, especially in the United States (Mitford). Perhaps a more general consequence resonates in a simple question at the heart of circum-Atlantic modernity: If the dead are forever segregated, how are the living supposed to remember who they are?

Bodies of Law

The complementary projects of Norbert Elias and Michel Foucault suggest that "civilization" or the "carceral society" of the panopticon might best be defined as the concentration of violence in the hands of the state (Elias, *The Civilizing Process*) or its diffusion to the "capillary level" in the micropolitics of daily life (Foucault, *Discipline and Punish*). In my discussion of collective memory and countermemory, I want to extend the concept of restored behaviors, including violence, to include the law. The tradition of retributive justice, of course, is intimately tied to violence as the performance of waste, but I am especially concerned with the legal dimensions of memory in the creation of the body politic. Imagined communities perpetuate themselves through the transmission of their prohibitions and entitlements. As a cultural system dedicated to the production of certain kinds of behaviors and the regulation or proscription of others, law functions as a repository of social performances, past and present. As such, it has been called "Second Nature" (Kelly). It typically bases its legitimacy on precedents, mysteriously reconstructed performances whereby the dead, as in the Ceremony of Souls, may pass judgment on the living: through the operation of law, the state appropriates to itself not only violence but memory. In such a circum-Atlantic resituation of Foucault, the law works like voodoo. It is certainly true that through the magical sway of legal fictions such as "the reasonable man," law transmits effigies—constructed figures that provide templates of sanctioned behavior—across generations. Indispensably, performance infuses the artifacts of written law with bodily action, a meaning that obtains when it is said that a party to a contract "performs."

Legal scholar Bernard J. Hibbitts, in " 'Coming to Our Senses': Communication and Legal Expression in Performance Cultures" (1992), specifies the corporeal nature of performance in his reexamination of comparative legal theory:

> The dynamism of performance is arguably reflected in the performative inclination to think of law not as things but as acts, not as rules or agreements but as processes constituting rule or agreement. A performative contract, for instance, is not an object, but a routine of words and gestures. A witness to a contract testifies not to the identity or correctness of a piece of paper, but to phenomena seen and heard. Likewise, members of performance cultures tend to think of justice not as something that simply is, but rather something that is done. (959)

Attempting to distinguish between the effects of predominantly literate and oral cultures on legal processes, Hibbitts articulates a function of law as performance that appears to operate in almost any culture: regulatory acts and ordinances produce "a routine of words and gestures" to fit the myriad of protocols and customs remembered within the law or evoked by it. These play a significant role in the collective memory of a society, what Connerton calls "incorporation" of "habitual memory" (72) and Nora "true memory" (13).

However, the effect of law on corporeal performance, and hence on collective memory, is never wholly negative (or, if Foucault's view prevails, even predominantly so). Even acts of rigorous prohibition produce alternative, displaced versions of the proscribed behaviors when performers test the limits of the law, incorporating innovations that would not have existed otherwise, creating routines of words and gestures on the margins of legal sanction. Because a law is written and officially enacted does not necessarily mean that it will be obeyed or even enforced; because it is disobeyed or circumvented, however, does not mean that it is without consequences. In his suggestive idea of "hidden transcripts" as records of secret or displaced transgression, James C. Scott illuminates an array of restored behaviors flourishing in the penumbra of the law. "Hidden transcripts" multiply in the interstices of the dominant or official culture's public discourse of legitimacy and legality. "The practice of domination, then, *creates* the hidden transcript," Scott writes; "If domination is particularly severe, it is likely to produce a hidden transcript of corresponding richness" (27). The circum-Atlantic world provides many sites where this hypothesis can be tested.

For instance, in 1685 Louis XIV signed into law the sixty articles of the *Code noir*, its full title translated as the "Black Code; or, Collection of Edicts,

Declarations, and Decrees Concerning the Discipline and the Commerce of Negro Slaves of the Islands of French America." The preamble, addressed to the king's colonial subjects now and in the future, requires him to be in more than one place at the same time: "Although they inhabit countries infinitely far from our land, we are always near them" (*CN* 1685). By the terms of the *Code*, which was adopted with some refinements in Louisiana in 1724, hundreds of thousands and eventually millions of Africans from diverse cultures were incorporated into the king's body politic. Under the aegis of Colbert's assimilationist doctrine of "One Blood," which had encouraged miscegenation in Canada (Johnson, "Colonial New Orleans," 23), the original *Code noir* provided for the manumission of the slaves (*CN* 1685, articles 4, 55, 56), the emergence of a free black population (article 59), and intermarriage between slaves and slaveholders, black or white (article 9). These liberal provisions were struck from the Louisiana edition, most conspicuously the article on miscegenation, which was forbidden between Negroes and whites, and, revealingly, between mulattoes and Negroes (*CN* 1724, article 6). When France briefly reacquired Louisiana in 1803, the newly appointed governor reinstated the *Code noir* of 1724, sweeping away the more liberal Spanish slave codes, including the right of self-manumission (Schafer 2–3, 6–9). Article 6 never explained the presence of the mixed-blood subjects whose existence it both forbade and recognized, but clearly enough, the intimate liaisons once legitimated by Colbert's One Blood and the *Code noir* of 1685 continued to enjoy a degree of popularity in custom long after they had been stigmatized by law. In all editions of the *Code noir*, owners were required to see to the Catholic baptism, instruction, and burial of their slaves (*CN* 1685, articles 2 and 14), incorporating them as "souls" into the heavenly kingdom of "the Catholic, Apostolic and Roman religion" (*CN* 1685, article 6). Owners were also enjoined from making their slaves work on the Sabbath or on feast days (*CN* 1685, article 6).

"Soul" notwithstanding, the incorporated status of the slave's body was inscribed in the *Code noir*'s draconian provisions for the punishment of runaways. The slave absent without leave for one month "will have his ears cut off and [will be] branded on one shoulder with the fleur-de-lys; if he is guilty of a second offense . . . , he shall be hamstrung and also branded with the fleur-de-lys on the other shoulder, and a third time, he will be put to death" (*CN* 1685, article 38; *CN* 1724, article 32). Branding with the lily of France, the time-honored emblem of her monarchial continuity and collective identity, subjects the slave who rejects the king's legal incorporation (by voting with his or her feet) to a most rigorous reminder of the long arm of his law. The body so marked becomes an effigy by way of example, performing the law, so to speak, enacting the body politic in the materiality of the natural body, wearing on his or her person the ineffaceable insignia of national memory.

Yet the *Code noir* contained a more subtle technique of marking—of identity, of continuity, of community—one hallowed in African law and custom as well as in European. The legal status of the subject followed the condition of the mother: the children of a slave father and a free mother are born free; those of a free father and a slave mother are enslaved (*CN* 1685, article 13; *CN* 1724, article 10). This harmonized with the Bambaran principle of *badenya*, or "mother-childness," which, as Gwendolyn Midlo Hall has demonstrated in her history of Africans in Louisiana, "is also the term for the family compound, [and] represents the principle of order, stability, and social conformity centered around obligations to home, village, and kinsmen" (55). It exists in opposition to the principle of *fadenya*, or "father-childness," which honors those who renovate social bonds through dissent or even disobedience. Whereas the Bambaran juridical idea is that any community needs both *badenya* and *fadenya*, the *Code noir* encouraged the former but stipulated exemplary punishments for the latter. The salient point is that Mandekan-speaking Senegambians like the Bambara arrived in Louisiana possessed of prolific arts of law and memory of their own, which, like those of the Europeans, had to be adapted to fit radically transformed circumstances. Unlike the Europeans, however, the Africans did not have the opportunity to publish these revisions and amendments; their most readily available medium of cultural recollection and innovation was performance.

For the historian of unauthorized performances, those that take place in the penumbra of the law, the most poignant written legal record of African retentions and adaptations resides in the *Code noir*'s prohibition of slave assemblies and rituals. Article 3 of the original code forbids the public exercise of any religion other than Catholicism, and it especially enjoins "all gatherings for this purpose." Article 16 reads: "We also forbid slaves belonging to different masters, to gather together, day or night, under pretext of weddings or otherwise, whether on the premises of the masters or elsewhere, and especially along the highways or remote places, under penalty of corporal punishment which must not be less than the lash or fleur-de-lys; and in case of frequent repetition and other aggravating conditions, they may be punished by death" (*CN* 1685, article 16; *CN* 1724, article 13). The obvious motive behind this prohibition is a fear of slave revolts. The rootedness of that fear, however, derives from an informed understanding on the part of the French about the power of public performances to consolidate a sense of community, inside or outside of the law.

The Africanization of Louisiana included the powerful forms of musical celebration, dance, storytelling, and ritual that developed in the interstices of European laws and religious institutions, creolizing them, as they creolized the African ones in turn. Adaptations of African belief systems and spirit-world practices to the forms of Catholicism produced syncretisms in Louisiana similar, though not identical to those found elsewhere in the French and Spanish Caribbean. Immigration from St. Domingue following the French and Haitian revolutions reinforced these invented traditions, though in contrast to Haitian practice, women dominated spirit-world religion in Louisiana (Hall, 302). Death often provided the occasion for the public performance of semisecret memories, for the Catholic rites in and through which they could emerge demonstrated their own adaptive capacity to accommodate as well as to transform African retentions. Into the *Code noir*'s requirements for the proper observance of holy days, feast days, and the rites of Christian burial, for instance, which contradict the proscription of assemblies, restored behavior inserts the living memory of African mortuary ritual. And into the unenforceable spaces between the words of imposed litanies, reinvented communities substitute themselves for living memories. Such displaced transmissions include celebrations of death inspired by apparently orthodox belief in the participation of ancestral spirits—call them "saints"—in the world of the present.

Death has so many uses. After the suppression of the Pointe Coupée slave revolt of 1795, for instance, "festivals of the dead," in defiance of the authorities and the *Code noir*, honored the executed freedom fighters (Hall, 372). Translating James C. Scott's "hidden transcripts" into the funeral rites of creole Louisiana, such "festivals" permit the unauthorized expression of solidarity masked by permissible, indeed obligatory observances. The fact of broad participation itself silently subverts or transgresses the dominant public transcript. When the French naturalist C. C. Robin visited New Orleans at the time of the sale of Louisiana to the United States, when the restrictions on slave assembly had been intensified, not relaxed, he remarked: "I have noticed especially in the city that the funerals of white people are only attended by a few, those of colored people are attended by a great crowd, and mulattoes, quadroons married to white people, do not disdain attending the funeral of a black" (248). The occasion created by death offered this community an opportunity to affirm its semiautonomous but discreetly submerged existence within or against the obligatory rituals of the better publicized fiction called the dominant culture.

A decade after Robin's visit, Benjamin Henry Latrobe recorded in his journal the frequency and distinctiveness of Afro-Catholic burials. His entry for May 4, 1819, for instance, describes a procession at twilight of "at least 200 Negroes men and women who were following a corpse to the cemetery." Unlike the broad range of skin colors observed by Robin, Latrobe sees uniformity: "There were none that I observed, but pitch black faces." The women and many of the men "were dressed in pure White," and half the women carried candles, following the priests and acolytes bearing "urns and Crucifix on silver staves as they began their chant" (301). Latrobe, like Aeneas passing through the Mournful Fields, followed the procession to its destination. While children played among the human bones turned up by the gravedigger's shovel, the pallbearers lowered the coffin into the shallow, water-filled grave, and the candle-bearing women "pressed close to the grave making very loud lamentations." When the first shovel of dirt was thrown in, "at the same instant one of the Negro women who seemed more particularly affected threw herself into the grave upon the Coffin and partly fell into the Water as the Coffin swam to one side" (301–2). The gravedigger, assisted by other mourners, pulled the keening woman forcibly out of the grave and carried her away, hand and foot.

Latrobe inquired after the identity of the dead person who had brought so many together on the occasion and inspired such grief. His informant, one of the women dressed in white, answered that the deceased was a hundred-year-old "African (Congo) Negress belonging to Madam Fitzgerald" (302) and that the woman who had thrown herself in the grave was her granddaughter. In fact, many of those at the burial site were the children, grandchildren, and great-grandchildren of the matriarch. Curious about the meaning of this passing to the mourners, Latrobe persisted: "I asked if her Grand daughter who threw herself into the grave could possibly have felt such excessive distress at the death of an old woman who before her death was almost childish and was supposed to be above 100 Years old—as to be tired of her own life. She shrugged her shoulders two or three times, and then said, '*Je n'en sçais rien, cela est une maniere*' [I don't know about that, that's the way it's done]" (302).

As Latrobe retired from the scene, rowdy boys among the mourners began playing catch with the old bones, pelting each other with them, throwing skulls in the grave, laughing at the loud report they made as they struck the wooden lid of the coffin, adding their din to the "noise and laughter," which had become "general by the time the service was over." Before they joined the festive crowd departing the burial ground, the women picked blades of grass from around the grave site (302).

From the granddaughter's performance of grief and the informant's explanation of it there emerge several assumptions that link law to memory without the necessity of writing. It is not enough to say that the informant's answer simply refers the questioner to custom or tradition, a ploy so often useful for brushing off the tourists, though something like that could very well have been going on, particularly in the answers produced by a French-speaking female slave for the edification of an important Anglo male. Her claim of knowing nothing pertinent, "I don't know about that," cannot disguise the obvious competence of the graveside performance and the certainty of her summation of it, "that's the way it's done." The normalizing authority behind her claim manifests itself in the organization of the funeral itself. Nearly all the mourners are wearing "pure White," the color associated with death and mourning in the semiotics of African, but not European, mortuary ritual. The candle-lit cortege processes solemnly into the cemetery, following the white creole clergy, who carry their Christian liturgical impedimenta and chant the ancient Latin words of the burial rites required for all slaves under the articles of the *Code noir* of Louis XIV, the preamble of which addressed itself, in the conventional legal language of royal imperishability, "to all present and to come." But within the pomp and splendor of the Latin obsequies, required by the timeless majesty of French law and custom, founded on the persuasive fiction of the king's two bodies, Latrobe cannot imagine where all the rude noises are coming from.

Even before the graveside service ends, festivity has broken out. In the momentarily privileged spaces of public assembly opened up amid the formal requirements of Eurocentric memory, there erupts a countermemory in which the living celebrate among the spirits of the dead. The living defy the segregation of the dead. Their celebration begins at a point along the trajectory of mourning that must be sensed collectively by those present on the occasion, a moment in which the community joyously affirms its renewal in the very act of marking the passing of one of its own. In the traditional African-American jazz funerals, still performed in New Orleans to this day,

2.4 Hercules' funeral, 1979. "Cutting the body loose."
Photo: Michael P. Smith

the moment of transformation is called "cutting the body loose." It initiates a burst of joyous music, dance, and humor, often ribald, in which there is no impiety, though there may be some quite pointed irreverence (figure 2.4). There is no impiety because in these sacred rites of memory, death is not so clearly separated from life as it was for Eurocentric observers like Benjamin Latrobe, the architect whose city planner's eye could approve only a much more stringent segregation of the dead. His understanding of memory favored monuments wherein ancestors could be safely confined rather than noisy behaviors whereby they could be turned loose.

Latrobe's puzzlement at the juxtaposition of what he called "excessive distress" and the revelries that he apparently thought of as merely excessive reflects the pronounced tendency of the literate observer to misrecognize incorporated memory as spontaneous emotion. It is important to note that the caretakers of memory in the scene he recounts are the women. The *Code noir* gave recognition and impetus to women's responsibility for memory by predicating the legal status of its subjects on the condition of the mother. As if in symbolic observance of this burden, which may equally or alternatively honor the principle of *badenya* or "mother-childness," it is the women who carry the candles to the edge of the grave, as it is the women who gather the blades of grass and bear the mementoes away. Either the French *Code noir* or West African *badenya*, then, could be cited as the law that deputizes the granddaughter to leap into the grave. Her action may signify not only a willingness to accompany or even change places with the deceased but also a bid to succeed her in the reborn community of the living.

The great age of the matriarch intensifies (not diminishes, as Latrobe supposed) what was at stake in her burial: the unscriptable performance of memory under the gaze of other peoples at a time of acute cultural displacement. Her funeral took place at the extreme limits of what might be called epochal memory and under the localized pressure of larger circum-Atlantic dislocations. The United States suspended the importation of slaves from Africa and the Caribbean soon after the Louisiana Purchase, although the trade was continued illicitly through smuggling. By 1819 the last of the elders from the French era who still possessed firsthand memories of Africa and could transmit those memories to their progeny were passing away. As New Orleans filled with English-speaking Americans, black and white, the francophone Creoles—black, white, and many tints in between—continued to assert their interdependent traditions through various media of public performance. According to popular memory and recent historical research, they persisted even after it was clear to everyone that their inevitable replacements had arrived. As the Anglo-Americans set about the task of dismantling what they saw as dangerous leniencies in creole law and custom, beginning with harsh amendments to the *Code noir* as early as 1806 (Schafer, 6–9), the imagined community still organized by spirit-world memories discreetly differentiated itself through its hallowed rites of death and surrogation. One of those resistant performances, a small but piquant demonstration, took place when the black woman in the pure white robes shrugged and countered Benjamin Latrobe's bemused interrogation with an authority only partially masked by her apparently deferential reply. Kinesthetically punctuated with appropriate gestures, her speech was in its way as obdurate as Dido's stony silence: "That's the way it's done."

Congo Square

"The most intense and productive life of culture," wrote Mikhail Bakhtin, "takes place on the boundaries" (*Speech Genres*, 2). For any genealogy of New Orleanian performance, Bakhtin's argument contains a literal as well as a figurative truth. Outside the original city walls and adjacent to the *cimetière* laid out by DePauger, was an unofficial public marketplace, once a site for the corn feasts of the Poucha-Houmma Indians (Kendall, *History*, 2:679). Here African slaves, free persons of color, and Native Americans could mingle with relative freedom and sell their goods. The provision in the *Code noir* that made the Sabbath a day free from work was interpreted (or ignored) to allow the slaves to work part-time for themselves, which might include the marketing of their own produce on Sunday. To serve this purpose, creole custom set aside a portion of the wasteland between the fortified city wall and the swampy ground leading away to the Bayou St. John. Nearby stood the death house for the indigent sick and the cemetery, a cultural borderland by Bakhtin's definition and many others as well. Any public market becomes a site of cultural self-invention, exchange, and performance, but this patch of ground on the boundary of the colonial city of New Orleans, now generally known to historians of dance and music as Congo Square, witnessed a particularly intense series of transformations and surrogations in its function as a behavioral vortex.

Vortices of behavior tend to occupy liminal ground, situated in the penumbra of the law, open to appropriation by both official texts and hidden transcripts: Congo Square, like the Liberties of London of an earlier date (Mullaney), provides a detailed case in point. As Jerah Johnson has shown, the different names by which the square was known recount its rich and contested history: site of the *fête du blé* or Indian corn feast, Place des Nègres, Place du Cirque, Place Congo, Congo Circus, La Place Publique, Circus Public Square, Congo Plains, Place d'Armes (when the original of that name became Jackson Square), P. G. T. Beauregard Park (after the Confederate general), and finally Louis "Satchmo" Armstrong Park. As the city expanded outward, Congo Square, like the nearby cemetery, was incorporated within its limits, but the liminal character of the old market remained. Although Signor Gaetano's Congo Circus set up in the square during the early years of the American period, the Cuban impresario's animal acts and rope dancers capitalized on what locals and visitors had already come to know as a unique holiday spectacle (Johnson, "New Orleans's Congo Square"; figure 2.5). For a time voodoo rites were practiced there, until they were driven further underground. Liliane Crété's reconstruction evokes the scene:

> In New Orleans, Sunday was a day of relaxation, even for the slaves. Dressed in their finest, they gathered by the hundreds under the sycamores in Congo Place, and from early afternoon until nightfall they danced to the rhythm of tom-toms and crude stringed instruments. The dances were lively and fast paced, with quick steps and many pirouettes. There were sensual, even blatantly erotic dances, in

2.5 Dancing the bamboula, Congo Square, New Orleans, antebellum period. Reconstruction by Edward M. Kemble for George Washington Cable's "Creole Slave Songs," *Century Magazine*, April 1886.
Courtesy The Historic New Orleans Collection, Museum/Research Center, acc. no. 1974.25.53

which the dancers mimicked the motions of lovemaking. There were bright, joyful dances that reflected the influence of European music; dances that were little more than the stamping of feet; dances with sacred undertones, such as the calinda; dances like the carabine, in which the man spun his partner like a top; frenetic dances like the bamboula and the coujaille; and mysterious dances like the pilé chactas, in which the man first circles his partner, then sinks to his knees before her and writhes like a serpent. The slaves danced barefoot on the grass, as the civic guard looked on from a discreet distance and a horde of white spectators pressed round the gates of the square, their faces registering a mixture of amusement, astonishment, shock, scorn, and indulgence. The African rhythms and dances were obviously not to everyone's taste, and some of the Americans in the crowd must have looked on the scene as a display of savagery that no one but a black or a Creole could savor or condone. (226)

One of the easily overlooked insights in Crété's account of this circum-

Atlantic event is the carefully constructed performance of whiteness enacted by the onlookers, most particularly by the "shocked" Anglo-Americans among them.

Helpfully, Benjamin Henry Latrobe corroborates the attribution of fastidiousness and fascination to the newly arrived Anglophones. While walking up St. Peter's Street past the cemetery "in the rear of the city" one Sunday afternoon, he "heard a most extraordinary noise." Latrobe then noted that the crowd of five or six hundred "*blacks*" (his emphasis—he saw only a handful of mulattoes) had divided itself into many smaller groups of dancers, who had gathered around musical ensembles consisting of "African" stringed and percussion instruments, of which the architect made some valuable sketches. One man sang in "some African language, for it was not French" (203–4). The sounds filled the neighborhood around Congo Square for blocks, reminding Latrobe of "horses trampling on a wooden floor" (203). Trying without success to find a comparable experience in his travels and observations, he concluded: "I have never seen anything more brutally savage" (204). Coming from the architect who had overseen repairs to the devastated White House after the remorseless sack and burning of Washington by the British, this critique is an extraordinary piece of Americana indeed.

What he had seen and heard was a convergence of dance and musical forms, clustered feats of daring and invention, which were deeply indebted to Africa yet no longer of it—living proofs of its impermanence and unforgettability. They emerged from the margins of circum-Atlantic performance culture, from "in back of the town," a displaced transmission, rising, Phoenix-like, from the ashes of diaspora and genocide on wings of song. Latrobe, through the meticulous words and images of his journal entries in 1819, responded as if he realized that he was, willingly or otherwise, listening to the future as well as to the past. He had high praise for the liturgical music in the new Episcopal Church in New Orleans, which he attended with his wife every Sunday (258), and he once translated the libretto for the Metastasian opera *Astrea Placata* (106), but he presciently devoted a much longer entry in his journal to the sounds and movements that almost everybody in the world now remembers as jazz.

Louis Armstrong, whose stone effigy smiles down on the site of Congo Square today (figure 2.6), described growing up in New Orleans succinctly: "Yeah, music all around you" (26). What poet Tom Dent calls the Armstrong statue's "shit-eating grin," however, faces the huge Municipal Audi-

2.6 Louis Armstrong Memorial, Armstrong Park, New Orleans.
William Ransom Hogan Jazz Archive, Tulane University

torium, built next to the site of Congo Square, largely for the whites-only use of the carnival krewes. In the 1940s and 1950s, the auditorium became the object of a number of unevenly successful attempts at desegregation (Hirsch and Logsdon, 270, 280, 284; Rogers, 37–38). It is a fortress built by whiteness astride the site of the only plot of ground where slaves could act as if they were free to remember who they were. In "For Lil Louis," Tom Dent puts the obvious question to Satchmo's stone effigy:

> did the moon-blood intrude
> the sleep of your nights
> even sleep of your days
> did you carry moon-blood
> memories to the grave?
>
> (68)

The association of Louis Armstrong with the city of his childhood is strong in popular memory, and few listeners fail to respond to the raspy longing expressed in his version of "Home." But locals cannot pass his statue in Congo Square, that *lieu de mémoire* of ghost notes, without remembering his emphatic instructions regarding the final disposition of his remains: "Don't bury me in New Orleans."

The King Is Dead—Long Live the King!

In circum-Atlantic terms, canon formation in Eurocentric culture parallels the spiritual principle to which bell hooks, in her essay on "Black Indians," attributes the deep affinity of African and Native American peoples: "that the dead stay among us so that we will not forget" (180). The perseverance of memory must cross the threshold of performance, the only scene in which surrogated doubles stand in for absent originals. Dennis Scott's *An Echo in the Bone*, for instance, begins with Rachel, the widow, making obeah by announcing to the mourners, "Tonight I belong to the dead" (76). Obeah, the once-outlawed practice of the Kumina and Pukumina religions of Jamaica, requires a medium to assist the dead in their various journeys, visitations, and returns (Hill, *Jamaican Stage*, 227–29). On the duly appointed Ninth Night, Rachel, as the caretaker of memory, succeeds in bringing back her husband's spirit to possess the bereaved, one by one. Into the bodies of those possessed flow images of the past, bidden and unbidden.

At each moment of possession, the suddenly penetrated body becomes a magical thing, an animate effigy.

In the syncretism of Atlantic spirit-world memory, Scott's subtle dramaturgy prepares for the climactic possession of the dead man's son, diminutively known as Sonson, by Rachel's earlier revelation of his given name: Isaac. As his dead father's voice speaks through him, he is identified as the son whose blood does not have to be shed, in this case because his father has already enacted the sacrifice for him. Thus, as the sacrificeable double is redeemed by his father's gift, the linear telos of catastrophe can be reimagined into a cycle. Today such intimate strategies of memorial performance need not be circumscribed. They animate, for instance, the deeply moving account by Kwame Anthony Appiah of the public dimensions of the funeral of his Ghanaian father, in whose house, we are made to understand, are many mansions: "Only something so particular as a single life—as my father's life, encapsulated in the complex pattern of social and personal relations around his coffin—could capture the multiplicity of our lives in the postcolonial world" (191). Around the Atlantic rim today, this principle of memory and identity still provokes intercultural struggles over the possession of the dead by the living. These struggles take many forms, of which the most remarkable are those in which the participatory techniques of orature—people speaking in one another's voices—predominate.

This form of reversed ventriloquism permeates circum-Atlantic performance, of which American popular culture is now the most ubiquitous ambassador. The voice of African-American rhythm and blues carries awesomely over time and distance, through its cadences, its intonations, its accompaniment, and even its gestures. Elvis Presley inverted the doubling pattern of minstrelsy—black music pours from a white face—and this surrogation has begotten others. It seems to me that the degree to which this voice haunts American memory, the degree to which it promotes obsessive attempts at simulation and impersonation, derives from its ghostly power to insinuate memory between the lines, in the spaces between the words, in the intonation and placements by which they are shaped, in the silences by which they are deepened or contradicted. By such means, the dead remain among the living. This is the purview of orature, where poetry travels on the tips of many tongues and memory flourishes as the opportunity to participate.

In the tabloid instruments of popular memory, the *Tatlers* and *Spectators* of the quickstop checkouts, The King remains every inch an effigy. The official constitution of imagined community, however, requires legitimating monuments of even more imposing gravity. When the United States Postal Service issued a commemorative stamp honoring Elvis a few years ago, it sponsored a contest between two designs. One featured the young crooner holding a microphone. The other showed the aging star, corpulent in his white, Las Vegas–style suit. Offered its choice between The King's two bodies, the American electorate voted its preference in a special election. By a landslide of 75 percent of the ballots cast in fifty states, the people chose to remember Elvis in the immortality of his youth. The number of reported sightings in this form suggests his secure place in the incorruptible body politic of imagined community. From Tupelo to Memphis, from birthplace to final resting place, his homes are sacred shrines.

In my exhaustive but futile attempt to get the rights to reproduce in this book the cover of the U.S. Postal Service's catalog featuring the Elvis Presley stamp, I experienced through a revealing set of exchanges a practical confirmation of my theory of the production of national effigies. Although the U.S. Postal Service maintains a most courteously staffed licensing department to deal with requests to reproduce philatelic images, the actual negotiations concerning celebrity stamps are conducted through an agent, Hamilton Projects, Inc., a unit of Spelling Entertainment Group, Inc. Before it would issue a contract, Hamilton Projects required me to submit my request along with a copy of the manuscript for approval by the licensing department of Graceland, a Division of Elvis Presley Enterprises, Inc. The spokesperson for Hamilton Projects explained that while the U.S. Postal Service holds copyright on the particular image of Elvis on the stamp, Graceland has a fiduciary interest in the image of Elvis "in general." Struck by the implicit claim of inalienability of rights of property in one's own person or persona, transcending even death itself, I rang Memphis. As if in performative confirmation of the immortality of the body politic, the phone at Graceland was answered by Elvis's voice, on that day singing "Tutti Frutti."

The Graceland licensing agent was most accommodating and agreed to review the relevant passages of my manuscript. Her promptly delivered approval contained a bracing assurance: "Since books do fall under your rights of first amendment, clearance from the copyright owner may be all that you need." Despite Graceland's defense of the U.S. Constitution, however, the promised clearance ultimately proved impractical to obtain: in addition to a licensing fee, Hamilton Projects required that I personally obtain a certificate of insurance for one million dollars to be maintained in force for ten years, indemnifying and holding harmless the U.S. Postal Service from any actions or damages, including attorney's fees, arising out of the publication of Elvis's image in this space. These stringent refinements of copyright law were of course generally unavailable to Elvis Presley's circum-Atlantic predecessors. They were applied in this case, I believe, to protect not intellectual property per se but the effigy's power of selection over what is remembered inviolately and by whom.

"The King lives on," the United States Postal Service concludes, having first "revolutionized American music" (U.S. Postal Service, 28–29). Elvis Presley's role in the performance of circum-Atlantic memory is thus well defined: his airbrushed face on a postage stamp, the circulating pantheon of national effigies, silently commemorates the staggering erasures required by the invention of whiteness, while his voice still echoes in the bone.

BETTERTON'S FUNERAL

The first kings must have been dead kings.

- A. M. Hocart

In a somber, even haunting Tatler number (May 4, 1710), Richard Steele recounts his evening walk to the cloisters of Westminster Abbey, there to attend the interment of the remains of Thomas Betterton, the most celebrated actor of that age. As Steele stands in the lengthening shadows of the burial place of English kings, awaiting the corpse of a stage player, he reflects on the kindred significance of two kinds of performance: first, the public rites and obsequies accorded to the venerated dead; second, the expressive power and didactic gravity of the stage. "There is no Human Invention," he concludes, "so aptly calculated for the forming [of] a Free-born people as that of a Theatre" (2:423). In the civic-minded Augustan language of liberal moral instruction, Steele's eulogy sets forth the principal argument that I want to make about the stimulus of restored behavior to the production of cultural memory.

The memory of which I speak accretes in practices and ceremonies, including the great "Human Invention" of the theater as a European high-culture form, particularly as it was constituted in and by the bourgeois public sphere in Britain. From this sphere *The Tatler* and *The Spectator* papers emerged, and to its formation at home and across the seas they contributed a not insignificant share (Habermas; Warner). The modernity of the question is striking. On a scale of organization any larger than that of the village, how is a deep sense of common culture to be instilled? Although there is no reason to dispute here Benedict Anderson's claim that the rise of the novel and the newspaper was conducive to the imagination of secular communities, the theater of Northern Europe has also been nominated for that honor on good evidence (Senelick, *National Theatre*). Beginning in the eighteenth century, a number of visionaries from George Farquhar to Friedrich Schiller turned to the concept of a national stage. Loren Kruger, in *The National Stage: Theatre and Cultural Legitimation in England, France, and America* (1992), has excavated attempts to create what she calls "theatrical nationhood," a project that she finds first articulated in Schiller's "idealist hope of summoning the nation into being by representing it dramatically" (86). More intensely than the solitary experience of readership, the provocative spectacle of the theatrical audience summons the idea of nationhood in the poignancy of its absence. In *Theatre and Disorder in Late Georgian London* (1992), for instance, Marc Baer has documented the role of rioting theater audiences in arguing the "rights" and "freedoms" of the unwritten British constitution, concluding that the London stage provided the key public arena "where a variety of social orders heard and saw national virtues demonstrated, and could therefore learn together how to be English" (193). Without taking exception to either Kruger's mordant genealogy of "founding discourses" (26) or Baer's emphasis on the formative role of late Georgian politics, I am proposing an alternative investigation at an adjacent site, one that permits me to expose the Augustan genealogy of subsequent national and imperial performances. Taking a different angle of approach to the questions raised by Susan Staves in her indispensable *Players' Scepters: Fictions of Authority in the Restoration* (1979), I argue that some Englishmen came to see Betterton, or at least the Betterton created by the hagiographic accounts, as a shadow king, a visible effigy signifying the dual nature of sovereignty, its division between an immortal and an abject body, and the ultimate symbolic diffusion of the former into a body of laws.

To understand how a funeral oration links the public image of Betterton, whose life on the London stage spanned the fifty years from 1659 to 1710, to the historic hopes and fears about the national fate of a "Free-born people" is, however, only part of the question, though a very necessary part. By examining the amplitude of Steele's threnody and the celebrity of the actor whose career it memorializes, I propose to demonstrate how together they also dramatize the power of performance to disclose their unavowed complicity in the catastrophic histories of the circum-Atlantic rim. By 1710 these histories were conjoined by intensified networks of production and consumption, a juncture epitomized by the London chocolate and coffee houses in which the papers of Steele and Addison were read and discussed by patrons who refreshed themselves with stimulating beverages extracted from the labor of West Indian slaves. Sales of slaves were conducted in the coffee and chocolate houses, advertisements for which *The Tatler* carried.

In this light, the practices of memory that I will discuss also entail a rigorous and highly specialized process of forgetting, the general terms of which should now be familiar. The consequences of its success may be inferred not only from numberless omissions but also from the positive assertions of scholars, even those who have recently contributed many welcome renovations to the theatrical history of the period. Steele's dramaturgical vision of English Liberty still lives, for instance, in the framing statement with which Paula R. Backscheider introduces her stimulating *Spectacular Politics: Theatrical Power and Mass Culture in Early Modern England* (1993), when she says, apparently without irony: "At issue for me is how literature is created and then takes on a life and meaning of its own in a free society" (xi). At issue for me is how freedom is created and then takes on a life and meaning of its own as one of the truth effects of English literature. At issue likewise is how the very concept of English Liberty rested on an edifice (and an artifice) of human difference, a difference propagated by representations of human bodies marked by race as either "Free-born" or enslaved. At issue also is how this constructed alterity proved at once so radical and so deeply ambivalent that at crucial symbolic points it subsumed, I believe, the more fundamental (and yet still ambivalent) cultural distinction between the living and the dead.

Competing with, complicating, and complementing the production of human difference in the performance of life and death, freedom and bondage, are sexuality and gender, the imaginative reconsideration of which has transformed the study of Restoration and eighteenth-century theater (Braverman; Brown; Castle; Markley; Straub; Todd). Without denying the principal claims of this important body of work, as most recently consolidated by J. Douglas Canfield and Deborah C. Payne in *Cultural Readings of Restoration and Eighteenth-Century English Theater* (1995), I want to show how differences between sexes and particularly between races are filtered through a prior alterity that death performs by its regulation of memory through the process of surrogation. My account allows for the fact that the players were despised, as the study of the instability of gender roles so amply demonstrates (Straub), but it also shows why they were simultaneously revered. Performances tend to reveal, whether the performers intend to or not, the intricately processual nature of relationships of difference. To use the keyword in Steele's contradictory phrase, performances provide the ways and means whereby a "Free-born people" can be *formed*. They are formed by viewing representations of actions that might or might not at any moment be substituted for their own through the restoration of behavior. Indeed, peoples can be formed in this way by an "Invention" like the theater even as the threat of surrogation raises questions about the fictional status of their identity and their community.

At a moment of intense promulgation of the Anglo-Saxon myth of origin, with its exceptionalist arguments for the racial entitlement of the "Freeborn" to guarantees of constitutionally limited monarchial powers and liberty, Betterton was ending a fifty-year career, which some have called a reign over the "Mimic State" (Gildon, 10) of the London stage. The image of transcendence he projected was the paradoxically fragile one of the surrogated double, and, like the Shilluk or Dinka king in Nilotic Africa, Betterton underwent, even while he still lived, a rite of passage into memory through the classic stages of separation, liminality, and reincorporation. Steele's account elaborates what the symbolic import of the actor's burial in Westminster Abbey suggests: in death, as in life, he performed not only *for* his public but *instead* of it. What follows here will demonstrate how Betterton's contemporaries consolidated this vision by attempting to record the actions of his body in the traces left by his physical movement and vocal intonations. These inscriptions—deriving from and leading back to incorporations—provide an exemplary instance of how celebrity, performing its constitutional office even in death, holds open a space in collective memory while the process of surrogation nominates and eventually crowns successors. The actor Betterton epitomizes the fact that in the magical extensions of imagined community, the moribund but indestructible effigies of the dead, abstracted as the "body politic," continue to haunt the spaces occupied by the living.

Most of the sources on which I base my claims in this chapter have long been known to theater historians, though they have not previously been read as I am reading them here. To the idea of the memorial constitution of the body politic I will return, guided by the local knowledge of George Farquhar's *Discourse on Comedy in Reference to the English Stage* (1702) and especially by the prescient ethnography in Voltaire's *Letters Concerning the English Nation* (1733), which appreciates the cultural significance of the burial of actors in the cathedral of national memory. In recasting the significance of a performer's life and death as a rite of passage, I will also consider a less familiar source, the *Pinacotheca Bettertonaeana*, a sale catalog of Betterton's books issued in August 1710 that inventories the contents of his extensive library at the time of his death. *Pinacotheca* is an ancient word meaning a place of memory, as in a small picture gallery or museum. I am using this *pinacotheca*, much as the original cataloger did, better to remember Betterton, "that Celebrated Comedian, lately Deceas'd" (*PB*, title page). While I recognize that there is no certainty that what the actor had on his bookshelf at the time of his demise will prove what he must have had on his mind while he lived, the example of Julie Stone Peters's reading of Congreve's library shows what can be done with such an elaborate artifact of material culture as a well-inventoried collection (Peters, 63–74). The *Pinacotheca Bettertonaena* contains what I think are some very suggestive correlations between the collection of books Betterton amassed and the central icon he became in the history of Shakespearean acting and hence in English cultural memory. While most of the details of his life, like all but a few of his performances, went unrecorded, the easily documented interests of his quite meticulous collecting have been overlooked. They disclose, I argue, a life lived on the cusp of literature and orature, poised between the arts of public memory and the secret science of forgetting.

I believe that Betterton's funeral, anticipated in the valedictory prologues and epilogues of farewell performances and in the prefatory pages to Nicholas Rowe's landmark edition of Shakespeare's *Works* (1709), constitutes an epitomizing event in the early development of a particular kind of secular devotion. In a culture where memory has become saturated with written communication distributed and recorded by print, canon formation serves the function that "ancestor worship" once did. Like voodoo and hoodoo, the English classics help control the dead to serve the interests of the living. The public performance of canonical works ritualizes these devotions under the guise of the aesthetic, reconfiguring the spirit world into a secular mystery consistent with the physical and mental segregation of the dead. In this reinvention of ritual, performers become the caretakers of memory through many kinds of public action, including the decorous refinement of protocols of grief. A fiction like "Betterton" defines a cultural trend in which the body of an actor serves as a medium—an *effigy*, as I have defined the word—in the secular rituals through which a modernizing society communicates with its past.

"Sticks and Rags": The Celebrity as Effigy

In the nervous, often demented humor of the theatrical greenroom, deaths and other final exits provide much material for levity among actors. Reports delivered backstage from a performance in progress, whether encouraging—"We're knocking 'em dead"— or defeatist—"We're dying out there"—suggest that only one set of participants, cast or audience, can leave the theater alive. Actors know whereof they speak. The passage between life and art, identity and role, enacted by their bodies as a condition of their employment, heightens their liminality in the rituals that mark their passing between life and death. Even in death actors' roles tend to stay with them. They gather in the memory of audiences, like ghosts, as each new interpretation of a role sustains or upsets expectations derived from the previous ones. This is the sense in which audiences may come to regard the performer as an eccentric but meticulous curator of cultural memory, a medium for speaking with the dead. The state of suspense created by these frequent passages and transformations maintains actors in a continuously uncertain position. This instability finds its most characteristic expression in the historic requirement for successful actors to project clearly two qualities above all others: strength and vulnerability (Barr, 298–99). That these predominant qualities contradict one other follows the logic of simultaneous push and pull at the margins of collective identity. In order for performers to enact the strength and stability of the center, they must boldly march to the boundaries to reconnoiter. There they suffer scarifying marks of contamination at the point of contact, and these stigmata render them vulnerable. By means of such risky alarums and excursions at the outer gates, brushes with death and difference, communities imagine themselves into illusory fullness of being by acting out what they think they are not.

It was the much-traveled actor Anthony Aston who recounted the revealing anecdote about Thomas Betterton taking his country tenant, Roger, to Crawley's puppet show at Bartholomew Fair. The bumpkin could not accept that Punch was not alive but "only a Puppet, made up of *Sticks and Rags*," and insisted on drinking his health, much to Betterton's annoyance, particularly after the puppet master had offered the great actor free admission as a professional courtesy. But while attending a production of Otway's *Orphan* at the Theatre Royal that night, Roger inverted his error by remarking of Betterton's performance: "*Its well enought for* Sticks and Rags" (301–2). Roger's misrecognition enacts a general ambivalence. The laughter that Aston's anecdote seeks to tap has its source deep in the surrogated double's uncanny suspension between life and death, strength and vulnerability, body politic and body natural. The figure of this ambiguous effigy, a monstrous amalgam of regal decorum and low fair-booth lumpishness, recurs in Aston's oft-quoted description of Bettertonian deportment:

> Mr. Betterton (although a superlative good Actor) labor'd under ill Figure, being clumsily made, having a great Head, a short thick Neck, stoop'd in the Shoulders, and had fat short Arms, which he rarely lifted higher than his Stomach.—His Left Hand frequently lodg'd in his Breast, between his Coat and his Waist-coat, while, with his Right, he prepared his Speech.—His Actions were few, but just.—He had little Eyes, and a Broad Face, a little Pock-fretten, a corpulent Body, and thick Legs, with large Feet.—He was better to meet, than to follow; for his Aspect was serious, venerable, and majestic; in his latter Time a little paralytic.—His voice was low and grumbling; yet he could Tune it by an artful Climax, which enforc'd universal Attention, even from the Fops and Orange-Girls. (299–300)

As he peers forth imposingly from Alexander Pope's copy of Sir Godfrey Kneller's portrait of around 1695, Betterton's physiognomy, countenance, and posture do little to contradict Aston's description of either their "majestic" or their "corpulent" aspect (figure 3.1). His left hand disappears approximately where Aston said it usually did. His right hand waits nearby. The collaborative stagecraft of painter and theatrical subject, as Richard Wendorf has shown, developed apace in the later eighteenth century, but here Kneller records the postural signature of a most distinctive exercise of memory and the kinesthetic imagination: the "teapot school" of oratorical delivery, which, on ancient authority, discouraged unsupported gestures of the left hand.

Like Aston, George Farquhar also noted Betterton's double identity onstage, his strength and his vulnerability, in the role of Alexander the Great in Nathaniel Lee's *Rival Queens*. Farquhar struggles wittily with the fact that the stage player divides himself in two to represent a hero from beyond the grave:

> We must suppose that we see the very Alexander, the Son of Philip, in all these unhappy Circumstances, else we are not touch'd by the Moral, which represents to us the uneasiness of Humane Life in the greatest State, and the Instability of Fortune in respect of worldly Pomp. Yet the whole Audience at the same time knows that this is Mr. Betterton, who is strutting upon the Stage, and tearing his Lungs for a Livelihood. And that the same Person shou'd be Mr. Betterton, and Alexander the Great, at the same Time, is somewhat like an Impossibility, in my Mind. Yet you must grant this Impossibility in spight of your Teeth, if you han't Power to raise the old Heroe from the Grave to act his own Part. (2:384)

That Betterton's vulnerable body becomes the medium for raising the dead strikes Farquhar, tongue in cheek, as a cruel but inescapable necessity. What necessitates it is the process of surrogation, the enactment of cultural memory by substitution. The royal effigy fabricated by Betterton derived from the memory of earlier actors as well as that of ancient kings: a chronicler of rehearsal practices recalled that during preparations for a revival of *The Rival Queens*, Betterton "was at a loss to recover a particular emphasis of [Charles] Hart, which gave force to some interesting situation of the part"; when a minor actor with a long memory "repeated the line exactly in Hart's key," Betterton rewarded him with hearty thanks and a coin "for so acceptable a service" (Davies, 3:271–72). In terms of the genealogy of a performance, the successor's deference to the earlier interpreter of the role was well considered. Of Hart's Alexander, the long-time prompter John Downes wrote: "he Acting [the role] with such Grandeur and Agreeable Majesty, That one of the Court was pleas'd to Honour him with this Commendation; that *Hart* might Teach any King on Earth how to Comport himself" (41). To act well is to impart the gestures of the dead to the living, to incorporate, through kinesthetic imagination, the deportment of once and future kings.

Indeed, contemporaries believed that Thomas Betterton stood in a direct line of transmission of theatrical tradition going back to William Shakespeare's original stagecraft. John Downes reverently traced this genealogy of performance from the actor Joseph Taylor across the Interregnum through Sir William Davenant, who also did not discourage the notion that he was Shakespeare's illegitimate son: "*Hamlet* being Perform'd by Mr. *Betterton*, Sir William (having seen Mr. *Taylor* of the *Black-Fryars* Company Act, who being Instructed by the Author Mr. *Shakespeare*) taught Mr. *Bet-*

3.1 Thomas Betterton (1635?–1710).
Copy by Alexander Pope (1713) of Sir Godfrey Kneller's portrait (ca. 1695).
Courtesy the earl of Mansfield

terton in every particle of it" (51–52). However dubious the details of Downes's anecdote may have proved (Bentley, 2:597), the kinesthetic nostalgia that it expresses, in which movements and gestures descend like heirlooms through theatrical families, demonstrates the instrumentality of the theater in the fabrication of what Pierre Nora calls "true memory" (15) and Paul Connerton "incorporating practice" (72). The secular sanctity of Shakespearean stage business—arguably the exemplary form of all English incorporating practices—seems to connect also to the legitimating reciprocity between the sovereign state and the "Mimic State" (Gildon, 10). Downes records another genealogy of bits for Betterton's interpretation of the title role in *Henry VIII*: he learned the business from Davenant, who got it from John Lowin, who had been instructed by Shakespeare in propria persona (55–56).

In public memory Betterton's acting became synonymous with kingly dignity. Summary accounts of his career, which ignore the fact that he portrayed at least 183 parts of all kinds (Milhous), emphasize the decorum of his tragic roles and generally slight his many successful comic parts. The actor Colley Cibber, for instance, in his oft-quoted eulogy, memorialized Betterton's action as "a commanding Mien of Majesty" (1:117). Downes remembered the actor most vividly for ennobling particulars such as the two occasions on which he appeared onstage in the borrowed coronation robes of King Charles II (52, 61). Authenticating details of costume and comportment counted for a great deal in the ritualized consecration, inevitably imperfect, of "sticks and rags" as a symbol of sovereign continuity.

What remains physically present to spectators in the theater is the natural body of the performer with its memento mori of pockmarks, strained lungs, and fat. This dichotomy provokes a constant alternation of attention from actor to role, from vulnerable body to enduring memory, in which at any moment one or the other ought to be forgotten but cannot be. This makes the effigy a monstrosity. As a monstrous double, it reconnoiters the boundaries of cultural identity, and its journey to the margins activates the fascination and the loathing that audiences feel for its liminality. In fact, the conditions of doubleness under which living effigies must work, the constantly fluctuating measure of the distance between identity and role, the mental "Impossibility" at which Farquhar jests, resemble nothing so much as the circum-Atlantic phenomenon of racial double consciousness.

Beginning in the eighteenth century, European theorists of the stage developed the idea of double consciousness as a psychological explanation for the paradox of acting. Hence Diderot: "One is oneself by nature; one is another by imitation; the heart you imagine for yourself is not the heart you have" (140). As defined by W. E. B. Du Bois in *The Souls of Black Folk* (1903), double consciousness expresses the bifurcating pressures exerted by racism on descendants of the African diaspora: "It is a peculiar sensation, this double-consciousness, this sense of always looking at one's self through the eyes of others, of measuring one's soul by the tape of a world that looks on in amused contempt and pity. One ever feels his two-ness,—an American, a Negro; two souls, two thoughts, two unreconciled strivings; two warring ideals in one dark body, whose dogged strength alone keeps it from being torn asunder" (8–9).

This is not to equate the condition of stage performers, who make appearances more or less by their own volition, with that of the constituency defined by Du Bois, who did not choose to be defined as "a problem" (7), though a historical understanding of "the antitheatrical prejudice" does illuminate other phobic responses to the performance of difference (Barish). It is rather to suggest that the performative effects of slavery and race hatred that produced such contradictions as double consciousness did not confine themselves to the plantations of the West Indies: it is precisely the ubiquity and importance of blackface roles on the eighteenth-century stage that summon into remembrance the tangled relations that imposed the burden of double consciousness variously on the far-flung subjects of its representations. In this troubled crucible of reciprocal definition, improvised but potent binaries (such as black and white, free and slave) struggled to dominate the terms of representation in the works of public culture, only to find their ontological status subverted there by the obligatory contributions of liminality to the maintenance of memory.

Liminality helps to explain why transvestism, for instance, seems historically constitutive of performance, a prior urgency to which the theater provides an epiphenomenal elaboration or publicity. Marjorie Garber's insightful account in *Vested Interests* (1992) of the funeral of Laurence Olivier ("a transvestite Olivier") as the surrogated burial of Shakespeare in Westminster Abbey ("only this time, much more satisfyingly, *with* a body") focuses on the uses of liminal antitypes in the creation of national memory: "That impossible event in literary history, a state funeral for the poet-playwright who defines Western culture, doing him appropriate homage—an event long-thwarted by the galling absence of certainty about his identity and whereabouts—had now at last taken place" (33). While I warmly embrace this analysis of the meaning of the event, I argue that it was hardly the first of such rituals but rather one repetition among many in a genealogy of performance that dates at least from the passing of theatrical patentee Sir William Davenant, who in 1668 "was Bury'd in *Westminster-Abby*, near Mr. *Chaucer*'s Monument, Our whole Company attending his Funeral" (Downes, 66). Unlike the anxious atmosphere of homophobia and misogyny that produced the transvestite liminality necessary to Olivier's apotheosis as a surrogated double, however, the sacred monsters of earlier times were produced by playing off the circum-Atlantic world's preoccupation with human difference as it was predicated along the frontier of life and death.

Just such a preoccupation, I think, visited Richard Steele at Westminster Abbey in 1710. Pondering the arrival of the torch-lit procession bearing an actor's corpse, he was moved to a gloomy but irresistibly radical reflection on the constructedness of all human difference, even that marked by the pomp of sovereign majesty:

> While I walked in the Cloysters, I thought of [Betterton] with the same Concern as if I waited for the Remains of a Person who had in real Life done all that I had seen him represent. The Gloom of the Place, and faint Lights before the Ceremony appeared, contributed to the melancholy Disposition I was in; and I began to be extremely afflicted. . . . Nay, this Occasion in me, who look upon the Distinctions amongst Men to be meerly Scenical, raised Reflections upon the Emptiness of all Human Perfection and Greatness in general; and I could not but regret, that the Sacred Heads which lie buried in the Neighborhood of this little Portion of Earth in which my poor old Friend is deposited, are returned to Dust as well as he, and that there is no Difference in the Grave between the Imaginary and the Real Monarch. (*Tatler*, 2:424)

As he walks in the cloisters adjoining the very place where English kings go to be crowned and commemorated, Steele's liberal belief that differences among "Men" are "meerly Scenical" fills him with a feeling of emptiness at the negated prospects for "Perfection" and "Greatness." His response dramatizes the extraordinary occasion for his *Tatler* paper: the bones of Thomas Betterton the stage player, son of an "Under-Cook to King *Charles the First*" (Gildon, 5), doyen of a despised profession, are being laid to rest near those of English kings, some of whom, like Richard II and Henry V, remained stageworthy in the scene of collective memory that was the London theater. What are the implications of the fact that Steele and presumably others among his contemporaries were willing to ratify a public ceremony that put at apparent risk the difference between "the Imaginary and the Real Monarch"? The answer lies not only in the way the effigy functions in the theater but also in the way its memory enters into the vortices of behavior that swirl around public nodes in the circum-Atlantic cityscape, continuously reproducing and transforming the performance of daily life in such public places as coffeehouses, marketplaces, places of assignation, and places of burial.

Vortices of Behavior

In Augustan London, as that historic metropolis emerges from the papers of Steele and Addison, the coffee or chocolate house served as an important locus for the judicious discussion and demonstration of propriety of behavior. There the new issues of *The Tatler* and *The Spectator* were read aloud and debated—precisely the kind of secular ritual that animates Hegel's observation that in the Enlightenment morning papers replaced morning prayers. As sites of performance themselves, the coffee and chocolate houses made the theater one of their most urgent topics. If differences between men are "meerly Scenical," good behavior is available to anyone who can measure up to well-informed scrutiny. As the legitimacy of the actor exists in validating gestures of performance, so individual behavior legitimates itself through speech and action on the stages of the public sphere. As performance by definition offers a substitute for a fugitive original, any social performance under this regime entails a certain element of risk (Ketcham; cf. MacAloon, 9).

A demonstration of the high stakes involved in such social dramas as these appears in the expositional confrontation in the first scene of William Congreve's *The Way of the World* (1700), which takes place at the locus of conspicuous consumption of a luxury commodity, "A Chocolate-House." At the play's premiere, the duel for supremacy between Fainall and Mirabell, carried on over chocolate at the gaming table, began with Betterton, adventuresomely miscast as the villain, alluding to interactive protocols of legitimating performance in his opening lines: "I'd no more play with a Man that slighted his ill Fortune, than I'd make Love to a Woman who undervalued the Loss of her Reputation" (*Works*, 3:15). The juxtaposition of terms in Congreve's balanced antitheses—reputation, value, fortune, and play—define the possibilities and limits of self-actualization through the calculated gamble of social performance.

The body politic, as reimagined in *The Tatler* and *The Spectator*, began to be defined by a proliferation of social performances within a meritocracy that steadily expanded in the improvisation and memory of "Free-born people." Hence the increasing importance of the actor as a surrogate for sovereign authority and the socially liminal space of the coffee or chocolate house as a forum for the transmission and refinement of public culture through performance. The London coffeehouse thus functioned in the role of behavioral vortex, a combination of built environment and performative habit that facilitated not simply the reproduction but also, according to circumstance and opportunity, the displacement of cultural transmission.

On the occasion of a benefit performance of *Love for Love* in April 1709, for instance, a year before Betterton's death, Steele sets aside Congreve's comedy to focus the attention of the "Gaming Gentlemen" (who have taken over Will's Coffee House since the death of Dryden) on the powerful accretion of Betterton's cultural authority on the threshold between "the Imaginary and the Real Monarch." As *The Tatler* notes in its inaugural issue:

> However the Company [of Will's] is alter'd, all have shewn a great Respect for Mr. Betterton; and the very Gaming Part of this House have been so much touch'd with a Sence of the Uncertainty of Humane Affairs, (which alter with themselves every Moment) that in this Gentleman, they pitied Mark Anthony of Rome, Hamlett of Denmark, Mithridates of Pontus, Theodosius of Greece, and Henry the Eighth of England. It is well known, he has been in the Condition of each of those illustrious Personages for several Hours together, and behav'd himself in those high Stations, in all the Changes of Scene, with suitable Dignity. (1:19–20)

Steele's humorous treatment of the element of chance in gambling does not submerge the serious point he wants to make about the actor standing in for the king. In an increasingly secular world of self-fashioning individuals and openly competing interests, the idea of community resides in shared conceptions of legitimate performances. These conceptions are not fixed and immutable; they are subject to fluctuations and negotiations, making social transactions conducted under their aegis more like wagers or sales at auction than fixed-price exchanges. In Betterton, by Steele's reckoning, the regulars at Will's seem to have found their touchstone. Through the printed medium of a *Tatler* paper, his public image as kingly effigy reaches beyond the playhouse audience and word of mouth to the extreme range of the circulation of the journal. In Betterton's art, audiences and readers alike saw mirrored and magnified a mastery of the restored behavior that defines cultural legitimacy in the paradox of a doubled body, necessarily vulnerable to the "Uncertainty of Humane Affairs" but nevertheless enduring through "all the Changes of Scene."

Steele's idea that differences among men are "meerly Scenical" expanded when he walked in a city where some of the traditional forms of cultural transmission were being visibly displaced. In that regard, the more specialized and yet more expansive vortex of social performance in circum-Atlantic London is the Royal Exchange as described by Joseph Addison in his oft-quoted *Spectator* number: the convergence of the world's material cultures performed by the metonymic circulation of their commodities for sale. The "High-Change," the time of the most intense activity, struck Mr. Spectator as a ceremonial performance before the eyes of representatives of the great nations of the world. Here, as a "Citizen of the World," he imagined himself in the role of Muscovite, Armenian, Dutchman, Japanese, Indian, Dane, and Jew. The "grand Scene of Business" swirling through the arcades of the Exchange quadrangle sends tears of joy rolling down his cheeks (1:294). Mr. Spectator weeps for the divine beauty of it all, namely the natural distribution of abundance to the distant corners of the world and its providential return through centripetal interdependencies to a central locus of accumulation: "The single Dress of a Woman of Quality is often the Product of an hundred Climates" (1:295).

In the swirling center of the commercial vortex, however, the national effigies remain fixed. Statues representing the monarchs of England since the Norman Conquest, carved by Caius Gabriel Cibber, Colley Cibber's sculptor father, decorated the arcades of the Royal Exchange. The contrast between the memorialized setting and the intercultural performance continuously improvised within it, which Addison calls "an infinite Variety of solid and substantial Entertainments" (1:294), prompted a characteristically reflexive insight by Mr. Spectator, whose ethnographic gaze mediates between dynastic memory and the transformative power of circum-Atlantic vortices of behavior:

> When I have been upon the 'Change, I have often fancied one of our old Kings standing in Person, where he is represented in Effigy, and

> looking down upon the wealthy Concourse of People with which that Place is every Day filled. In this Case, how would he be surprized to hear all the Languages of Europe spoken in this little Spot of his former Dominions, and to see so many private Men, who in his Time would have been the Vassals of some powerful Baron, Negotiating like Princes for greater Sums of Mony than were formerly to be met with in the Royal Treasury! Trade, without enlarging the British Territories, has given us a kind of additional Empire. (1:296)

Like a theater, the Royal Exchange stages a scene of displaced transmission of constitutional authority. Although the "Effigy" here serves as ideal spectator, not actor, its act of spectation is itself a performance: the imagined animation of the effigy by the king's body natural measures for contemporaries the extent of the historic change Addison has calculated between the feudal hierarchy of ancient memory and its modern replacement by an expanded body politic of "so many private Men." The effigy thus summons the dead to enable the living to get a bearing on what they are becoming.

The symbolic reciprocity of theater and marketplace in Anglo-American thought is a topic in itself (Agnew), but I want to contextualize the idea of the behavioral vortex, a "ludic space" at the point of convergence of entertainment and commerce, within a specific genealogy of London performance. Not coincidentally, this genealogy is also an etymology of the word *liberty*. In *The Place of the Stage: License, Play, and Power in Renaissance England* (1988), Steven Mullaney discovers the liminal position of the Elizabethan theater within the ancient "Liberties of London." Enclaves stood outside the old city walls (or as odd pockets within them) on grounds not subject to normal regulation by the authorities. Like Congo Square, they provided a fertile space for the growth of ludic forms literally on the margins of official culture, including carnivals, bear baitings, public executions, taverns, brothels, and theaters that produced the plays of Shakespeare, Jonson, and Marlowe. Mullaney contrasts the official processions and rituals of the "ceremonial city" with the "marginal ritual and spectacle" that flourished "on the *limen* or threshold of the community" (31). These occurred in a place called a "Liberty." *Liberty*, thus understood, "was not a political or juridical concept but a geographical domain, a literal if ambiguous enclave of license and incontinent rule" (57). As London grew outward and incorporated the Liberties within its boundaries, I believe, some of their residual identity as zones of transgression carried over into the combined market and theater district of Drury Lane and Covent Garden (*Sur-*

vey of London). The reiterated complaints about increasingly flagrant prostitution in and around the playhouses of Restoration and Augustan London, which now operated under the authority of royal patents, dramatize the incorporation of the peripheral ludic economy of the Liberties into the centripetal vortices of the modernizing London urbanscape.

The public sale of human flesh—or the display of flesh to promote the sale of other commodities and services—has become so much a part of circum-Atlantic culture that it has rendered itself invisible through its very pervasiveness. Its genealogy crosses at many points the history of the theater and particularly that of the theater district. The perceived overlap of acting and prostitution from the time of the introduction of actresses on the London stage in 1660 offers a case in point, and even a widely admired actor like Betterton could not escape guilt by association: called "brawny *Tom*" by the author of the "Satyr on the Players" (ca. 1684), Betterton stands accused of pimping for the "Drabs" of the playhouse, which the satirist indicts as a "Whore's Rendezvouze" (quoted in *Biographical Dictionary*, hereafter *BD*, 2:84). But the lurid association of theater and the "Vizard-Masks" represents only one of the more sensationally publicized features of the London sex industry. A foreign theatergoer in London in the year 1710, Zacharias von Uffenbach, was shocked by the prevalence of prostitutes and beggars, including "Moors" of both sexes, who freely plied their trade in the pleasure district around the theaters. "The females wear European dress," Uffenbach recounted, "with their black bosoms uncovered, as we often saw them" (88).

In this circum-Atlantic vortex, the flesh of Africans and West Indians was not the only erotic flotsam in the mix (Burford). As the centralizing effects of urbanization drew unskilled labor from the countryside to London, the euphemistic phrase "newly come upon the Town" to describe young girls recruited to prostitute themselves came into general usage. Richard Steele, in the persona of Mr. Spectator, dilates on this phrase by narrating an encounter in the market square nearby both Will's Coffee House and the Theatre Royal, Drury Lane:

> The other Evening passing along near Covent-Garden, I was jogged on the Elbow as I turned into the Piazza, on the right Hand coming out of James-street, by a slim young Girl of about Seventeen, who with a pert Air asked me if I was for a Pint of Wine. . . . We stood under one of the Arches by Twilight; and there I could observe as exact Features as I had ever seen, the most agreeable Shape, the finest Neck and Bosom, in a Word, the whole Person of a Woman exquis-

> itely beautiful. She affected to allure me with a forced Wantonness in her Look and Air; but I saw it checked with Hunger and Cold: Her Eyes were wan and eager, her Dress thin and tawdry, her Mein genteel and childish. This strange Figure gave me much Anguish of Heart, and to avoid being seen with her I went away, but could not forbear giving her a Crown. The poor thing sighed, curtisied, and with a Blessing, expressed with the utmost Vehemence, turned from me. (2:534–35)

This episode constructs an urban scene parallel to both Steele's evening walk in the cloisters of Westminster Abbey and Addison's visit to the Royal Exchange. Through the eyes of Mr. Spectator, the pedestrians behold as spectacle the performance of everyday life in a behavioral vortex, the staging of ceremonial practices within the architectural setting of a place marked by custom for those purposes. In Covent Garden, as at the Royal Exchange, the restoration of certain behaviors designates a "Liberty," the point of intersection of business and pleasure for "many private Men." Here the concept of an effigy may be demonstrated not only in the actions of a particular celebrity or king but in those of a stock character or type. As in the commedia dell'arte, stock characters serve as conduits of memory for social performances, providing a zone of play within which improvisatory variations may be staged. In the scene of assignation in Covent Garden, both Mr. Spectator and the girl "newly come upon the Town" play familiar roles, improvising and negotiating their identities within a scenario provided by the behavioral vortex of the setting itself and their apparently random meeting within it.

The prostitute's body has two aspects: her air of "Wantonness" suggests a standard repertoire of flesh marketing that possesses a kind of immortality in circum-Atlantic performance. The fact that this performance is "checked with Hunger and Cold," however, by a desperate child thinly wrapped against the London January, interpolates a memento mori into the erotic semiosis (Bataille, *Erotism*, 129–39). Although she apparently stops Mr. Spectator cold, the improvisation that the prostitute actually brings off—charity as performance—warms the heart with a gesture of sacrificial expenditure. Such a tribute between negotiating parties Marcel Mauss calls the *prestation*, a "Gift" for which reciprocity is implicitly expected. Reciprocity comes in this instance by way of the girl's vehement performance of gratitude, punctuated with her delectable curtsy. She delivers value for value received, affording Mr. Spectator a joy too exquisite for ejaculation.

The supposed meritocracy and social gambles of the coffeehouse, as well as the transactions performed at the Royal Exchange and in Covent Garden, take on an added layer of meaning when they are juxtaposed to another behavioral vortex only then emerging in London and other circum-Atlantic cities: the cemetery. Like a city wall, death marks a boundary on either side of which subordinate perimeters may be delineated. The "Liberties" of London included a graveyard located outside the city walls, called "No Man's Land," which custom reserved for noncitizens (Mullaney, 39). The designation of a burial ground within the confines of a "ludic space" seems counterintuitive, but such a perception of incongruity stems from a distinctive cultural attitude towards death. Like the proximity of DePauger's *cimetière* to the Place du Cirque (Congo Square) on the outskirts of colonial New Orleans, the location of "No Man's Land" in a "Liberty" of London marks death, like other circum-Atlantic performances, as an exploration of corporate identity at the outer limits of imagined community.

At the same time Sir John Vanbrugh was proposing to end burials in London churches by segregating the dead "in the Skirts of Towne," Addison produced his famous *Spectator* number on funerary monuments in Westminster Abbey (March 30, 1711). Happening on grave diggers at work under the stones of the nave floor, Mr. Spectator noted how every shovelful threw up "the Fragment of a Bone or Skull" from the remains of the "confus'd" multitudes—"Men and Women, Friends and Enemies, Priests and Soldiers, Monks and Prebendaries"—whose bodies "were crumbled amongst one another, and blended together in the same common Mass" (1:110). In the taxonomic priorities of a newly imagined community, this clearly will not do for Mr. Spectator. His meditation on the anonymity of such burials is deflected by his inspiration about the extreme importance of proper inscriptions and memorials to set apart those among the dead who have proven truly worthy of enshrinement in a place of national memory: "As a Foreigner is very apt to conceive an Idea of the Ignorance or Politeness of a Nation from the Turn of their publick Monuments and Inscriptions, they should be submitted to the Perusal of Men of Learning and Genius before they are put in Execution" (1:110). In the renovated commonwealth of memory, "Learning and Genius," not lineage and title, must approve the credentials of embassies from beyond the grave.

Like the statuary at the Royal Exchange, the effigies of the notable dead at Westminster Abbey must perform for the edification of the "Citizens of the World": if this behavioral vortex works as it should, memory and imagination "fill the Mind with a kind of Melancholy, or rather Thoughtfulness, that is not disagreeable" (1:109). Mr. Spectator reorganizes the medieval untidiness of a common grave, where the unsegregated community represents itself anonymously, into a proper pantheon, where "Monuments and Inscriptions" of selected worthies represent the best that the nation has engendered. Death, the supposed leveler of all distinctions, becomes the very agent of their enunciation. The question that must be addressed now is this: on what basis did an actor qualify for early inclusion as an ambassador to posterity?

The Life of Betterton: Talking with the Dead

The familiar sources on Thomas Betterton's life read like eyewitnesses accounts of his mummification, the sacred purification of a secular relic, a venerated effigy fit for a king. In the eighteenth-century critical and biographical commentaries of Charles Gildon, Colley Cibber, John Downes, Richard Steele, and Anthony Aston, the imperishable character of "Betterton" is constructed out of the materials of Thomas Betterton's failing body. Each of the memorialists wrote mainly after the actor's death (Cibber and Aston not until 1740), and in each case (except for Downes) he saw the actor perform only late in his career, when age and failing health limited at least some of his former powers. Although Charles Gildon made Thomas Betterton the subject of what appears to be a booklength theatrical biography, *The Life of Mr. Thomas Betterton, the Late Eminent Tragedian* (1710), putatively the first of that genre in English, the facts about the actor's life contained therein are few, and most of those contested (*BD*, 2:73–96; Lowe; Milhous). A single narrative thread, however, links almost every one of Gildon's biographical assertions with many of the occasional remarks about the actor-manager in other sources: Betterton's status as a living incarnation of Shakespearean tradition, as a worthy representative of the English stage under the Stuart monarchy, and the implicit parallel between the "Mimic State" or the "Government" of the patent theaters and the nation-state itself (Gildon, 5–10).

The measurement of historical time involved in Betterton's career, like that of the Congo slave belonging to "Madam Fitzgerald," belongs to what I have termed epochal memory, a chronotrope that historians might or might not readily periodize but that contemporaries can recognize as having been specially marked by the limits of generational recollection (Postlewait). An exemplary meditation on popular performance as a measure of epochal memory occurs in James Wright's *Historia Histrionica* (1699), the first history as such of the English stage, in which an "Old Cavalier," one of a dwindling tribe, reflects on the actors and playwrights of "the last Age," meaning the end of Charles I's reign and the beginning of Charles II's, and those who can remember them: "We are almost all of us, now, gone and forgotten" (li). Wright's method of weaving together memories of actors and kings to define an "Age" attests to the power of effigies like Betterton to imbue time with narrative, reconstructing a genealogy of performance out of the remains of dead or dying celebrities.

Betterton's powers of endurance, compelled by financial necessity as well as public demand, stood out as remarkable even at a time when actors customarily tried to hold on to their roles as lifelong investments. Steele, in a significant move, exempted Betterton from the ordinary decay of time, even when he was forced to act, toward the end, in a slipper that eased his gout-stricken foot. In the persona of Mr. Greenhat, *The Tatler* noted of the actor's interpretation of Hamlet (which Pepys had first remarked on fifty years before): "Your admir'd Mr. *Betterton* behav'd himself so well, that, tho' now about Seventy, he acted Youth; and by the prevalent Power of proper Manner, Gesture, and Voice, appear'd through the whole *Drama* a young Man of great Expectation, Vivacity, and Enterprize" (1:493). A more skeptical Anthony Aston, in his *Brief Supplement to Colley Cibber*, allowed as how the gouty septuagenarian "appear'd a little too grave for a young Student," particularly in the play scene when he threw himself down at Ophelia's feet. Yet Aston, like Steele, finally had to marvel that even in parts impersonating younger men "no one else could have pleas'd the Town, he was so rooted in their Opinion" (Aston, 300–301). It was that rootedness in public opinion that drew attention from Betterton's physical infirmity to his other body, the one that existed outside itself in the fact of his performance of it. Transcending the body of flesh and blood, this other body consisted of actions, gestures, intonations, vocal colors, mannerisms, expressions, customs, protocols, inherited routines, authenticated traditions—"bits." Like the king's body politic, the actions of this theatrical body could not be invalidated by age or decrepitude.

Despite the paucity of its details regarding the Bettertonian curriculum vitae, Gildon's *Life*, the bulk of which is a pastiche of seventeenth-century rhetorics and potted manuals of decorous gesture (dedicated to Richard Steele withal), *is* a biography in a very special sense—as the memorial inscription of an incorporated effigy. The impression Gildon's account leaves on the reader is of a single public life standing in for an epochal memory (Betterton came in with the Stuart Restoration and exited in their dynastic twilight). This is true for two reasons. First, a narrative that begins with the memory of Charles I and concludes a few pages later by recounting a burial "with great Decency" in Westminster Abbey (Gildon, 5–11) invites comparison, in the Plutarchian tradition of parallel lives, between what Steele called "the Imaginary and the Real Monarch." Reading about Betterton's funeral, few contemporaries could have failed to note that the dismembered body of Charles the Martyr lay in an unmarked grave at Windsor where it had been rudely entombed without services. Alexander Pope, revising his poem *Windsor-Forest* at about this time, rebuked the failure of national memory that such an abomination disclosed and lamented the damage to the body politic that it continued to inflict:

> Make sacred Charles's Tomb for ever known,
> (Obscure the Place, and uninscrib'd the Stone)
> Oh Fact accurst! What Tears has Albion shed,
> Heav'ns! what new Wounds, and how her old have bled?
>
> (*Poems*, 1:180)

Investing the body of the dead king with hallowed powers that act over distances of space and time, Pope trades on the folkloric tradition that regards with special awe and dread a corpse that has been dismembered, disturbed, or improperly laid to rest (R. Richardson, 17). *The Life of Betterton* seeks to link the life of the theater to this national memory by having Betterton preface his remarks on the decay of the art of acting and the decline of stage with a pointedly nostalgic reminiscence: "Plays were acted at Court, in the Time of the Royal Martyr, even on *Sundays*" (18).

Second, Gildon's *Life* constitutes a biography in its entirety because it is also a poetics of orature. In its formidable compendium of elocutionary strategies, whether or not Betterton actually donated his own compilation of notes to the cause, as Gildon claims (17–18), the book tries to write a life not of the actor's career but of his bodily art. It offers an anthology of corporeal actions under the two broad headings of physical gesture and vocal intonation. The *Life* attempts to modernize the *pronuntiatio* and *elocutio* of classical rhetoric, and Gildon advertises them on the title page as the

"ACTION and UTTERANCE of the *Stage*, *Bar*, and *Pulpit*." Referring to Betterton in apocalyptic terms as "the last of our *Tragedians*," Gildon claims that his "Design" is to perpetuate the actor's memory, "conveying his Name with this Discourse at least to a little longer Date, than Nature has given his Body" (1). The biographer then proceeds to provide a copious archive of restored behaviors, physical and vocal, for contemporaries to utilize in the professions and for posterity to ponder as the monumental record of what eloquence meant to their forebears.

Eloquence resides in the credible embodiment of vulnerability and strength, and the mastery of those qualities enhances the longevity of the actor's "Name." Employing a taxonomy of the passions derived from the French painter and theorist Charles Le Brun, Gildon examines the play of strength and vulnerability in the "Passion of Grief." He puts in the mouth of Betterton an analysis of *The Lamentation* by Jordaens of Antwerp (figure 3.2). It delineates the refined states of grief in the various figures of the composition as the body of Christ is taken down from the cross:

> The Passion of Grief is express'd with a wonderful Variety; the Grief of the Virgin Mother is in all the Extremity of Agony, that is consistent with Life, nay indeed that leaves scarce any Signs of remaining Life in her; that of St. Mary Magdelan is an extreme Grief, but mingled with Love and Tenderness, which she always expressed after her Conversion for our blessed Lord; then the Grief of St. John the Evangelist is strong but manly, and mixt with the Tenderness of perfect Friendship; and that of Joseph of Arimathea suitable to his Years and Love for Christ, more solemn, more contracted in himself, and yet forcing an Appearance in his Looks. (36–37)

The distribution of tenderness and manliness, agony and stoicism here described segregates a range of human responses to death and memory into discrete moral spaces. The constituent emotions to the grand Passion of Grief exist only one at a time and one per mourner. A similarly nice delineation characterizes the rationalization of the passions by Le Brun, who separates emotions into irreducible and autonomous categories, like the primary colors or the table of elements.

The culture that produced such a compendium of restored behavior had pointedly distanced its relationship to the dead by regulating the behavior of the bereaved. In contrast to the mortuary rituals observed by Latrobe, here the spirit world exists in an abstract and disembodied relationship to living

3.2 Jacob Jordaens, *The Lamentation*, ca. 1650. Hamburger Kunsthalle. Photo: Elke Walford

memory. On the evidence of Betterton's reading of *The Lamentation*, appropriate memory requires one emotion at a time and that measured by strict standards of decorum in gesture and expression, even as the devastated survivors open their limp, white arms to cradle the mutilated body of their crucified god.

Similar protocols were amply demonstrated when Thomas Betterton talked with the dead, as he was called on to do from time to time in plays that featured ghosts, such as *Richard III* (figure 3.3). Most of the anecdotal lore concerning Betterton's acting centers on his performance in *Hamlet*, that

3.3 *Richard III*. From Nicholas Rowe's *Shakespear* (1709), vol. 4.
Howard-Tilton Memorial Library, Tulane University

play in which death and memory cruelly inflict the uncertainties of proper conduct on the victim of an overwhelming but imperfect grief. Several contemporary sources document the famous response of Betterton's Hamlet to the Ghost. Colley Cibber's oft-cited description, a favorite of theater historians and Shakespeareans, needs to be reexamined in light of its praise for the rational curtailment of the emotion of grief. Cibber reports that Joseph Addison shared his opinion that the excessive vociferation of other actors in the role violated the proper regulation of bereavement and outrage. But "This was the Light into which *Betterton* threw this Scene; which he open'd with a Pause of mute Amazement! then rising slowly to a solemn, trembling Voice, he made the Ghost equally terrible to the Spectator as to himself! and in the descriptive Part of the natural Emotions which the ghastly Vision gave him, the boldness of his Expostulation was still govern'd by Decency, manly, but not braving; his Voice never rising into that seeming Outrage or wild Defiance of what he naturally rever'd" (Cibber, 1:101). If the principles that operate here may be generalized, decency and reverence guide the amazed and the aggrieved to a more stoic relationship with the dead, and to regulate their bereavements they must master their rage (cf. Rosaldo, 1–21). Such considerations obtain, it would seem, even when murdered relations rise from the grave, as if from a primordial past, and demand bloody vengeance from the living.

Embodying Hamlet's response to the second appearance of his father's ghost, Betterton further explored and codified an explicit mode of conduct governing conversations with the dead. By its protocols, the secular reverence appropriate to social memory in the Enlightenment could be extracted from the residual cultural fear and worship of the once omnipresent ancestors. The engraving that accompanies the text of *Hamlet* in Nicholas Rowe's *Shakespear* of 1709 depicts the closet scene with a staginess that many theater historians accept as a plausible representation of Betterton's performance (figure 3.4). The heavily armored Ghost materializes as if through a wall, admonishing Hamlet with his raised scepter. The seated Gertrude, who does not see the Ghost, opens her arms and legs wide in astonishment at her son's sudden and inexplicable start. Hamlet, garter unbraced, opens his arms and his mouth in shock but also in awe. In the technical section of *The Life of Betterton*, Gildon attributes the following remarks on this scene to the actor himself: "In all regular Gestures of the Hands, they ought perfectly to correspond with one another, as in starting in a Maze, on a sudden Fright, as *Hamlet* in the Scene betwixt him and his

3.4 *Hamlet*. Closet scene
from Nicholas Rowe's *Shakespear* (1709), vol. 5.
Howard-Tilton Memorial Library, Tulane University

Mother, on the Appearance of his Father's Ghost—*Save me, and hover o'er me with your Wings, You Heavenly Guards!* This is spoke with Arms and Hands extended, and expressing his Concern, as well as his Eyes, and Whole Face. If an Action comes to be used by only one Hand, that must be by the *Right*, it being indecent to make a Gesture with the *Left* alone" (74). In the first decade of the eighteenth century, the wide dissemination of conduct books, dancing lessons, military manuals, and general advice on deportment of all kinds consolidated the kinesthetic imagination into a repertoire of incorporable memories. The prescriptive nature of the gestures so scrupulously defined here suggests that Gildon's *Life* participates, along with the general proliferation of seventeenth- and eighteenth-century conduct books, in what might be termed the secular rationalization of expressive gesture. The concept of bodily control as a moral imperative moved from the confessional to the salon as a visible index of social acceptability. Indeed, Gildon plagiarizes from at least two Jesuit rhetorics (Roach, 30–31), converting their spiritual exercises into a semiotics of secular affects, now appropriate to divinity principally as it relates rhetorically to the worldly professions of theater and law.

In the Rowe engraving, Hamlet appears in contemporary dress with periwig while the Ghost wears armor of an antiquated look. On the eve of Vanbrugh's proposal for the banishment of burial sites to the "Skirts of Towne" and Addison's reflection on the mediation of memory through national deputies and their cenotaphs, this representation seems to suggest the obtrusiveness of the unfashionable dead. The Ghost has rudely burst in on a modernized domestic space, almost Ibsenesque in its well-furnished boxiness, a boudoir in which familial remembrance (a particular sore point for Hamlet) reposes in trendy three-quarter-length portraits on the wall.

Most pertinent here, however, is the belief that Shakespeare himself had originally played the role of the Ghost, a mix of lore and surmise that had already congealed as "Tradition" when Cibber wrote his *Apology* (1:89). Betterton's colleagues turned this venerable anecdote to flattering effect when they argued that he alone could perform what the dramatic poet had written:

> Had you with-held your Favours on this Night,
> Old SHAKESPEARE'S Ghost had ris'n to do him Right.
> With Indignation had you seen him frown
> Upon a worthless, witless, tasteless Town;

> Griev'd and Repining you had heard him say,
> Why are the *Muses* Labours cast away?
> Why did I only Write what only he could Play?
> (quoted in Gildon, xiii–xiv)

Nicholas Rowe wrote these lines in 1709 on the occasion of a benefit for Betterton, one of several final farewell performances given by the aging star, who had invested his life savings in a West Indian argosy and lost everything when the ship was captured by French privateers (Lowe, 145, 186). In that same year, the publication of Rowe's edition of Shakespeare's *Works*, with its biographical introduction indebted to Betterton for details, created an early milestone in "reinventing Shakespeare"—the inauguration of a scholarly industry in his name (G. Taylor, 52–99). Betterton collaborated with the editor in compiling the materials for "Some Account of the Life, &c., of Mr. William Shakespear" that prefaced the edition (Rowe, 1:xxxiv). Rowe's testimonial allusion to *Hamlet*, with the Ghost rising to reproach inaction and demand justice, substitutes Shakespeare for Old Hamlet and Betterton for his progeny as the only qualified executor of paternal obligation and memory. Rowe's idea that the words the poet wrote can truly live only through the medium of the actor's voice and bodily expression attests to the continuing prestige of orature even (or perhaps especially) in an expanding culture of literacy accelerated by the dissemination of print. Rowe's idea also offers clear testimony in support of the effigy's role as a surrogated double, an efficient way to remember the otherwise obsolescent dead.

The growing embarrassment that the Ghost caused enlightened stagecraft reached its nadir fifty years later at the French premiere of *Hamlet* in Jean-François Ducis's neoclassicized version. Ducis cut the Ghost entirely; instead, he had Hamlet carry around his father's cremated remains in an urn (figure 3.5). Here as elsewhere in the period, decorous behavior contains death's invasion into the space of good sense. Yet it also proposes a new way of talking to the dead: with reverence, with abstraction, and with careful layers of mediation.

Canonical Memory and Theatrical Nationhood

Philosophes like Voltaire wanted to speak *for* the dead but not necessarily *with* them. They needed a medium through which they could negotiate the

3.5 *Hamlet*. Closet scene, Paris premiere, 1769. Hamlet reproaches Gertrude with the urn containing his father's remains. From Jean-François Ducis, *Oeuvres*. Washington University Libraries

reformation of what they regarded as popular superstition into social memory. As Benedict Anderson pithily puts it: "Absurdity of salvation: nothing makes another style of continuity more necessary" (11). A front-running candidate for chief medium of continuity was the canon of classics as enshrined in a national theater. Through the rational magic of theatrical performance, the spirit world metamorphosed into the cultural pantheon of the public sphere, in which the dramatic poets maintained pride of place. This complex of issues—the segregation of the dead, the symbolic diffusion of sovereignty, and the sanctification of a secular canon through the surrogated burial of performers—stands most revealingly defined in the juxtaposition of two sources: George Farquhar's *Discourse Upon Comedy* (1702), which contains an early proposal for an English national theater founded on the secularization of the body politic, and Voltaire's *Letters Concerning the English Nation* (1733), which explains the rationale for theatrical nationhood ethnographically.

Scholars may read in one of the principal documents of Augustan theatrical history and criticism exactly how the mystified doctrine of the king's two bodies was appropriated to suit the national vision of Whig patriots and constitutionalists, avatars of Steele's "Free-born people." Farquhar's *Discourse* calls for new English plays for the specific instruction of "an *English* Audience," an audience that represents a nationality in the modern sense, as an insular ethnicity organized by the historic fiction of race into an imagined community. Deploying the cultural memories revived by the enthusiasts of Anglo-Saxon history and institutions, Farquhar presents the English in exceptionalist terms as "a People not only separated from the rest of the World by Situation, but different also from other Nations as well in the Complexion and Temperament of the Natural Body, as in the Constitution of oure Body Politick" (2:378–79). Imagining the legitimation of the English state by means of a national stage, the Anglo-Irishman Farquhar transforms the ancient duality of the king's two bodies into the conjunction of race (the body natural) and nation (the body politic): the unique "Constitution" of the latter depends upon the particular "Complexion" of the former.

The word *constitution* in this passage ascends through many layers of historical usage. Farquhar's desired union between the natural body of flesh ("Complexion and Temperament") and the body politic leads him to an admission that the very uniqueness of the English "Constitution" stems from its compound nature: "As we are a Mixture of many Nations, so we have the most unaccountable Medley of Humours among us of any People upon Earth" (2:379). This genealogy confesses the disparity and contradiction present within English origins, as does Daniel Defoe's oft-quoted ridicule in *The True-Born English-man*: the contradiction between the supposed purity of Anglo-Saxon roots and the actuality of the composite scum left by the illegitimate union of every invader's garrison and the local camp followers:

> From this Amphibious Ill-born Mob began
> That vain ill-natured thing, an Englishman.
> (Defoe, 11)

But as Anglo-Saxonism flourished, the increasingly dominant narrative of pure autochthony erased the prolific evidence of such promiscuous liaisons.

In the transformation of the dynastic state into the modern nation-state, ethnicity has more than once offered a fable of legitimate origin to authorize subsequent performances. Voltaire's trenchant observations on life in England take a critical but enthusiastic line. Like Malinowski or Lévi-Strauss, twentieth-century anthropologists living among indigenous societies, the philosophe's fieldwork among the English from 1726 to 1729 inspired an extended meditation on the relations of cultural difference. His observations made the strange practices of the natives more familiar to Frenchmen and, at the same time, the familiar practices of the French more strange to themselves. His ethnographic project, which concludes in high Gallic fashion that the British Isles have thirty religions but only one sauce, comes to a crucial episode in letter 23, "On the Regard that Ought to be Shown to Men of Letters," in which Voltaire discusses the burial of the actress Anne Oldfield in Westminster Abbey. Remarking on the secular monument to Isaac Newton in that sanctified place, Voltaire observes: "What raises the Admiration of the Spectator is not the Mausoleums of the *English* Kings, but the Monuments which the Gratitude of the Nation has erected, to perpetuate the Memory of those illustrious Men who contributed to its Glory" (*English Letters*, 166). Here civic worship bleeds national glory out of the bodies of kings and infuses it into the memory of celebrity subjects—"illustrious Men."

Still more remarkable to the French ethnographic eye, however, was the monument that the English erected to the memory of an actress. This choice of effigy struck the philosophe as singular, and well it might, for his hosts could not have been dedicating thereby a monument to the conventional female virtues—certainly not to chastity. In the version of letter 23 that he wrote directly to the French actress Clairon, Voltaire pointedly draws the contrast between the reverence of the English as they buried *their* beloved starlet in the national cathedral and the insults his countrymen heaped on the wretched corpse of Oldfield's French counterpart, Adrienne Lecouvreur: "It is true that beautiful Oldfield, England's leading actress, enjoys a handsome mausoleum in the Church of Westminster like the country's kings and heroes and even the great Newton. It is also true that Mademoiselle Lecouvreur, the leading actress of France in her time, was brought to the corner of the then unpaved Rue de Bourgogne in a cab, that she was buried there by a street porter and has no mausoleum." This leads Voltaire to the climax of his argument for that ethnic peculiarity of the English, their tendency to bestow honors where they are properly deserved: "The English have established an annual holiday in honor of the famous actor and poet Shakespeare. We still do not have a holiday for Molière" (*Selected Letters*, 257). Voltaire refers to David Garrick's Stratford Jubilee, a rain-soaked fiasco, but that same actor had also arranged for several pieces of funerary sculpture to memorialize Shakespeare, who was in fact already marbelized in national memory by the statue carved by Peter Scheemakers for Westminster Abbey (Dobson, 137–46).

In this chain of surrogations, the rites and monuments raised to stage players stand in for the memory of the dramatic poets, who in turn represent the sanctity of secular memory, which in its way defines the legitimating authority of the culture at large. Theatrical interments in eighteenth-century England, I believe, functioned as a prototype for tombs dedicated to the Unknown Soldier, those cenotaphs of the nominated double of which Benedict Anderson says, "no more arresting emblems of the modern culture of nationalism exist" (9). They constituted a place or a site of memory (in Nora's sense) where the symbolic burial of one surrogated body in a special place with special obsequies authorized the general disposal of others in newly rationalized and segregated spaces of death. They eternalized an effigy dedicated to those who would otherwise remain anonymous to one another in the fictive kinship of race and nation.

The singular body politic of the "Free-born" therefore requires unique surrogacy in the rites of selective memory. In letter 8, Voltaire takes up further evidence of English exceptionalism. As he wondered at the burial of Oldfield in Westminster Abbey, so he pondered with admiration another exotic national virtue—Liberty. "The *English*," Voltaire concludes, "are the only people on earth who have been able to prescribe limits to the power of

Kings by resisting them" (*English Letters*, 41). As the concept of a "Liberty" transformed itself from a ludic space on the fringes of English society into a recognized practice of privileged self-invention, death and surrogation enabled the reaffirmation of the "*socially* peripheral [as] *symbolically* central" (Stallybrass and White, 5). The connection Voltaire implies between the English constitution and the peculiar local custom of burying celebrated (and even notorious) performers with dignity in hallowed ground is not arbitrary. The autonomy of the sovereign subject, in such a momentous scheme of resistance, must be perpetually performed and so, perforce, must the purity of its origins be continuously reinvented.

The *Pinacotheca Bettertonaeana*: Bibliography of Origin

Betterton's funeral did not end the public rites initiated by his physical disintegration and death. Four months later, in the closing act of disposing of his pitiful estate, Jacob Hooke auctioned off the actor's books. The sale catalog inventories the contents of the impressive library—books, prints, drawings, and paintings—once belonging to "that Celebrated Comedian, lately Deceas'd," who had already spoken with ghosts. In the anthropology of death, the act of distributing the possessions of the dead may function to implement reincorporation, a movement out of liminality and into the final phase of the rite of passage. As the auctioneer emptied out the contents of Betterton's Covent Garden lodgings, a larger and more diffuse space of memory filled up with totemic markers.

The *Pinacotheca Bettertonaeana*, the grand title of Hooke's auction catalog, puts the actor's cultural capital on the line by preparing the community for the test of an auction. It makes the powerful point that these were not just books, but Thomas Betterton's books. Hooke clearly thought that fact raised their value, but he could not be certain how much. An auction, unlike the fixed-price or private treaty exchange, ascertains value publicly in cases where it may be in question. It does so by bringing together for the occasion an "auction community" (C. Smith, 80–81). As was customary, Jacob Hooke prepared the market for his auction of Betterton's books by offering them for public viewing for three days before the sale and by placing copies of the catalog "at the following Coffee-houses, *viz. St James*, near St. *James*'s Palace; Mr. *Ellars* at *Westminster-hall* Gate; the *Grecian* at the Temple Back-Gate; Mr. *Nixon*'s in *Fleetstreet*; Mr. *Squire*'s in *Fuller Rents*, in *Hol-*

bourn; St. *Paul's* near the West-end of St. *Paul's* Cathedral; *Will's* in *Cornhil*, near the Royal Exchange, and at the place of Sale [Betterton's former lodgings]" (*PB*, title page). The physical locations dot the map of London; the social location is, I think, more singular—Steele's imagined community of the "Free-born."

The sale catalog of approximately 560 books reveals certain distinctive strengths of Betterton's collection. There are, of course, many plays, including Rowe's new edition of Shakespeare, but not nearly as many as might have been predicted. The actor more or less systematically acquired the complete nondramatic works of canonical English authors, including Chaucer, Spenser, Milton, and Dryden (*PB*, 1–3). He kept up with the burgeoning publications of philosophy and natural history, his collection including two editions of Hobbes, several of Locke, Boyle's *Experiments*, and Robert Hooke's eye-popping *Micrographia* (*PB*, 2–3). Somewhat more predictably, but still revealingly, he owned rhetorics and books on gesture (*PB*, 4–5), including John Bulwer's classic *Chirologia; or, The Natural Language of the Hand* (1644), and conduct manuals such as Richard Brathwait's *The English Gentleman* (1630) and *The English Gentlewoman* (1631). Betterton maintained standard sets of geographies and travel books, especially rich in circum-Atlantic materials, including Hakluyt's *Voyages* (*PB*, 3), Thomas Gage's *Survey of the West Indies* (*PB*, 8), Ogilby's *History of Africa, Illustrated with Notes, and Adorn'd with Sculptures* (*PB*, 2), and a more surprisingly specialized publication designed for Native America, Eliot's Algonquian-English Bible (*PB*, 6).

The largest single category, however, containing approximately 145 titles, including most of the expensive folios, is European history, especially English history. Here Betterton's collection approached comprehensiveness. It included separate lives by diverse authors of Henry V, Henry VII, Henry VIII, Edward I, Edward II, Edward III, Edward IV, Edward VI, Richard II, Richard III, Elizabeth I, James I, Charles I, and Queen Anne. It likewise included historical surveys and reference books such as Sir Bulstrode Whitlock's *Memorials of English Affairs, from Brute to the End of James the Ist's Reign* (1709), Sammes's *Britannia; or, The Antiquities of Ancient Britain* (1676), Sir Richard Baker's *Chronicle of the Kings of England* (1696), Samuel Daniel's *History of Great Britain* (1626), and many more (*PB*, 1, 4, 5).

Most emphatically, however, Thomas Betterton's library of English history contained all the principal works published in the 1600s concerning one of the great historical projects of the century: the search for the racial origins of the British people. The results of this effort devolved so massively into the imperialist ideologies of the eighteenth and nineteenth centuries that scholars too often lose sight of the fact that its essential terms emerged from much earlier debates about the founding of Britain. If no other reference had survived, the controversy could be reconstructed almost in its entirety by using the *Pinacotheca Bettertonaeana* as a bibliography.

Some of the Anglo-Saxon myth's key early texts included William Camden's monumental *Britannia; or, A Chorographical Description of Great Britain* (1586), which burst the bubble of the Trojan diaspora (vi); John Speed's *History of Great Britaine* (1632) and John Toland's *Anglia Libera; or, Limitation and Success of the Crown of England* (1701), both of which claimed an exceptionalist heritage of liberty in the Saxon origins of the English constitution; and above all Richard Verstegen's revisionist and protoracist *Restitution of Decayed Intelligence in Antiquities Concerning the Most Noble and Renowned English Nation* (1605), of which Hugh MacDougall, in *Racial Myth in English History*, judiciously concludes: "It represents the first comprehensive presentation in English of a theory of national origin based on a belief in the racial superiority of the German people, a theme repeated a thousand times in succeeding centuries" (49). In 1710 each of these titles was put up for auction as having belonged to Thomas Betterton (*PB*, 1, 4, 6, 10).

Born with the family name Rowlands, the author of *Restitution of Decayed Intelligence* changed his moniker to claim the Saxon kin he revered. Like Farquhar, Verstegen believes in Anglo-Saxon exceptionalism. Unlike Farquhar, he insists that this exceptional status derived from ethnic purity: as a Germanic people, he claims, the English descended from a racial stock of unconquered and unmixed blood. They occupy a completely different branch of the world's family tree than the descendants of Ham, for instance, who "did plant themselves in divers places of Africa" (96). In characterizing their ethnic identity, Verstegen finds them equally fit to govern themselves peacefully and to conquer and rule their inferiors: "They were a people very active and industrious, utterly detesting idleness and sloth; still seeking war to enlarge the bounds of their own territories: fierce against their enemies, but conversing together among themselves in great love and friendliness" (44). Indeed, their ancient virtues of industry and fair play at home plus armed expansionism abroad resemble those often ascribed by Richard Steele's contemporaries to themselves a hundred years after Verstegen wrote and by the Anglo-Americans who took over the Louisiana Territory a hundred years after that.

In a fascinating digression explaining away any possible impurities in English origin, Verstegen argues that the invading Danes and Normans were really Germans as well (146). Moreover, the racial and linguistic unity of the Teutonic peoples derives from the geohistorical fact that Britain was once a peninsula of Europe. Verstegen cites fossil evidence, "the bones of fishes" unearthed in the Kentish countryside, to prove that what was once dry land had become ocean and vice versa (83). This claim (which happens to be true, though not in the time frame Verstegen imagined) is most significant. If Britain was not an island, then Verstegen can contest the diasporic narrative of Britain's founding by amphibious invasion, the culmination of the Mediterranean and circum-Atlantic voyage of the Trojan Brute (73–74). He can also supplant it with a countermyth of an eternally inviolate Germanic homeland fortified by absolute ethnic homogeneity, bellicosity, and xenophobia: "That they have been the only, and ever possessors of their Country [and] they have ever kept themselves unmixed with foreign people, and their language without mixing it with any foreign tongue" (35). He thus creates out of natural history and linguistic memory an imaginary locus in which purity of origin establishes world-historical entitlement. He exemplifies the tendency of the historic search for Anglo-Saxon origins to erase evidence of diaspora and mixture wherever possible in order to promote myths of monocultural autochthony. Preaching the restoration of memory, he practices the science of forgetting. If there has ever existed anything like a transhistorical ethnicity, the strange fluctuation in Verstegen's argument between elasticity and rigidity illustrates the perverse and apparently timeless genius of Anglo-Saxonism to perpetuate itself by simultaneously expanding its boundaries in the name of freedom and disavowing its consequent affiliations in the name of race.

White Skin, Black Masks

Improvised secular rituals coalesce as memory in the process of forgetting that creates circum-Atlantic identities. The ghosts of the sacrificed still haunt these historic spaces. Effigies accumulate and then fade into history or oblivion, only to be replaced by others. So it is with Thomas Betterton's Othello, which, for Richard Steele, represented the actor's definitive performance. As Steele waited in the cloisters of Westminster Abbey, he reviewed his memories of the paragon of English orature. Of the nearly two hundred roles that Betterton had played, Steele chose one by which to memorialize the actor's contribution to the "Human Invention" that was vital to "the forming [of] a Free-born people":

> I have hardly a Notion that any Performer of Antiquity could surpass the Action of Mr. Betterton on any of the Occasions in which he has appeared on our Stage. The wonderful Agony which he appeared in, when he examined the Circumstances of the Handkerchief in Othello; the Mixture of Love that intruded upon his Mind upon the innocent Answers Desdemona makes, betrayed in his Gesture such a Variety and Vicissitude of Passions, as would admonish a Man to be afraid of his own Heart, and perfectly convince him, that it is to stab it, to admit that worst of Daggers, Jealousy. Whoever reads in his Closet this admirable Scene, will find that he cannot, except he has as warm an Imagination as Shakespeare himself, find any but dry, incoherent, and broken Sentences: but a Reader that has seen Betterton act it, observes there could not be a Word added; that longer Speech had been unnatural, nay impossible, in Othello's Circumstances. The charming Passage in the same Tragedy, where he tells the Manner of winning the Affection of his Mistress, was urged with so moving and graceful an Energy, that while I walked in the Cloysters, I thought of him with the same Concern as if I waited for the Remains of a Person who had in real Life done all that I had seen him represent.
> (*Tatler*, 2:423–24)

Betterton, stately vessel of Anglo orature, thus transmits Shakespeare to a new order of generations by fleshing him out, but he does so wearing blackface.

The illustration of *Othello* in Nicholas Rowe's 1709 edition of Shakespeare suggests the effect of the stage business in which a blacked face regards and blacked hands caress (and later suffocate) a pallid Desdemona (figure 3.6). Theater historians debate the degree to which this image depicts an actual staging, Betterton's or otherwise, but the exploitation of the actress's seminudity seems plausible enough to some (Howe). Although the early history of burnt cork is beyond my scope here, blackface did remain powerful enough as a stage effect that Charles Lamb used the "revolting" theatrical appearance of "a *coal black Moor*" offering "wedded caresses" to this "Venetian Lady, of highest distinction" as unanswerable

3.6 *Othello*. From Nicholas Rowe's *Shakespear* (1709), vol. 5.
Howard-Tilton Memorial Library, Tulane University

evidence that Shakespeare's plays should be read but not staged. Lamb's first premise *is* unanswerable: "What we see upon the stage is body and bodily action" (Lamb, 1:108).

It was that very corporeality that Steele emphasized in commending Betterton's ability to flesh out with action and expression the "dry, incoherent, and broken Sentences" of *Othello* (3.4), but the scene most frequently illustrated was that of the murder of Desdemona. The image of Othello standing over her pathetic corpse offers more than a cautionary tale, though it offers that too. In 1711 two cases were reported from Suriname in which black slaves impregnated white women of the planter class, the penalty for which was flogging and branding for the woman and death for the slave (Mintz and Price, 29). The scenic economy of Rowe's *Othello* engraving makes an instructive comparison to the closet scene from *Hamlet* (cf. figures 3.4 and 3.6). In each case a domestic interior dominated by a bed is entered violently by a figure in martial trappings: Othello wears a British officer's coat and waistcoat while his three-cornered hat rests on the nightstand; he brandishes a pillow in place of the Ghost's baton. The uniform underscores the official status of the effigy created by the manipulation of identity and role. Here the doubleness of the actor's art, a black mask covering his white face, a European general's uniform covering his history as a slave, poignantly reverses the polarities of Du Bois's double consciousness: "two souls, two thoughts, two unreconciled strivings; two warring ideals in one dark body" (9). In a world predicated on African slavery, the actor in blackface stands astride the threshold of social death.

As death and its rituals offer occasions to mark and question the boundaries of circum-Atlantic identities, so miscegenation and its representation enact the fears of some that the artifice of those boundaries will collapse. That is, no doubt, why death so frequently seals off such liaisons with sacrificial violence. But death and miscegenation also enact a deeper terror that lurks at the heart of surrogation as a cultural process: the fear of being replaced, a fear that plays itself out in tropes of monstrosity and especially cannibalism. In his *Tatler* eulogy, Steele remarks on Betterton's "moving and graceful Energy" in the "charming Passage" wherein Othello recounts his courtship of Desdemona. So vivid is Steele's memory of this scene that he reports his inability to separate the stage business from the actor's "real Life" actions offstage. It is important that the scene about which Steele professes his inability to draw the line between life and art is also the scene in which the title character narrates his seduction of an important white man's daughter (*Othello* 1.3.128–46). That Othello has been "taken" in battle and "sold to slavery" reminds Desdemona and the spectator of the fierce customs once pertaining to prisoners of war, which honored the imbrication of slavery and death: to spare the life of a captive was to own that life; to yield to captivity was to give up one's life to the captor.

At the time Richard Steele saw Betterton's performance, however, Othello's narrative turn of escape and "redemption" from slavery chafed against a reality in which African slavery was increasingly rationalized not under the rubric of the fortunes of war but as a perpetual and naturally inherited condition, in contrast to bonded servitude, into which whites might fall temporarily. What remained from the romance of chivalric captivity was the correspondence of slavery and living death. As the *History of Virginia* (1705) explains: "Their servants they distinguished by the Names of Slaves for Life, and Servants for a time. . . . Slaves are the Negroes, and their Posterity, following the Condition of the Mother" (Beverley, 271). In nature "whiteness" nowhere exists; it must be produced by artful contrasts, by legerdemain, by stage tricks, or by laws. For a limited number of members of select groups participating in the benefits of the circum-Atlantic economy, freedom came to be understood as a right bestowed by "white" birth, inalienable from life itself. As for the others whose freedom was obtainable only beyond the grave, the fatality of Anglo-American law was nearly absolute: those living free could treat them as if they were the living dead.

In *Slavery and Social Death* (1982), Orlando Patterson sets forth the comparison between the "natal alienation" inherent in slavery and a state of living death (7). The horror of such a condition finds itself weirdly reflected in proliferating customs that treated the dead as if they belonged to a race apart. That is why to a culture predicated on the segregation of the dead, ghosts, even when they are mediated by living effigies, are so deeply threatening. As audiences project an array of their anxieties about surrogation onto the body of the performer, in his or her voice they may hear what they themselves dare not name. It is no wonder that the effigy becomes a sacred monster and that Thomas Betterton shared in the opprobrium as well as the adulation. In the "Satyr on the Players" (ca. 1684), the satirist aggregates in Betterton's physique and voice the preoccupations with human difference that Restoration theatrical performance titillated but could not exhaust. In this vicious review of Betterton's Othello, issues of social class within English conventions of place holding and degree find their monstrous double physically embodied by race and rendered grotesquely visible in Betterton's surrogated physique. Locating him among the shops and bagnios of Covent Garden, where the sight of "Moors" of both sexes prostituting themselves shocked Uffenbach in 1710, the "Satyr" burns the actor's body in effigy:

> For who can hold to see the Foppish Town
> Admire so sad a Wretch as Betterton?
> Is't for his Legs, his Shoulders, or his Face;
> His formal Stiffness, or his awkward Grace:
> A Shop for him had been the fittest place;
> But Brawny Tom the Playhouse needs must chuse
> The Villain's Refuge, and Whore's Rendezvouze.
> When being Chief, each playing Drab to swive,
> He takes it as his chief Prerogative.
> Methinks I see him mounted, hear him Roar,
> And foaming Cry Odsblood, you little Whore,
> Zounds, how I ____! I ____ like any Moor.
>
> (quoted in *BD*, 2:84)

The trope of sexual excess, a frequent charge brought against players (Straub), here plays itself out against an actor who, functioning as the sacred medium through which the "Free-born People" could speak with their canonical dead, blacked himself up. In *Black Skin, White Masks* (1952), Frantz Fanon never lets the reader lose sight of the salient principle that in many dominant representations of miscegenation "one is no longer aware of the Negro but only of a penis; the Negro is eclipsed. He is turned into a penis. He *is* a penis" (170). This terrible instrument, in combination with aroused female fertility, threatens to produce a superabundance of "monsters," mulattoes who eat ideologies of origin raw. So at the limits of transgressive performance, the effigy burns, and by its flickering light the villagers try to see if the center has held.

Steele was not the only Englishman to remark on the impact of Betterton's staging of Desdemona's seduction in its current circum-Atlantic context. In 1710 the earl of Shaftesbury expressed his fear that "a thousand Desdemonas" had become so obsessed with romantic stories of Africans in travel literature that they would abandon their menfolk to "follow the fortunes of a hero of the black tribe" (quoted in Cowhig, 13). And if the sentiments of one contemporary correspondent are to be credited, responsiveness to the tragedy of the Moor of Venice became a kind of litmus test of frigidity, which in the sexology of the time was the key to fertility. As Sir

John Percival wrote to Elizabeth Southwell in 1709: "I declare that they who cannot be moved at Othello's story so artfully worked by Shakespeare and played by Betterton, are capable of marrying again before their husbands are cold, of trampling on a lover when dying at their feet, and are fit to converse with tigers only" (quoted in *BD*, 2:90–91). The power of this performance to galvanize memory stems from the depth of its penetration into the anxieties of the public that brought it forth, so much so that the only way to ensure their full (though temporary) relief was to see the blackened body of the actor, standard bearer of their collective affinities, safely buried under the hallowed entablature of their deepest tomb.

Of all the fictions that summon a people together into a community, the concept of *nation* is the most labile. This is so conspicuously true of Great Britain that its constitution has not been written down—hence the added importance of orature in its ceremonial transmission of memory. In the kingly roles that Betterton played, animating in speech and gesture a number of the personages from the chronicles he collected, the actor as effigy sustained the living memory of a past that allowed his contemporaries to imagine a number of possible futures. By 1710, as theories of diasporic origin receded and those founded on autochthony advanced, these futures could repose themselves on the increasingly well-upholstered myth of the Anglo-Saxons' special place in Providence. One of the titles in Betterton's library, a conduct book by Richard Brathwait descended from Castiglione's *The Perfect Courtier* in the genealogy of social performance but pointedly entitled *The English Gentleman*, imagines a vast array of behaviors regulated within a particular framework of historical knowledge (*PB*, 4). Read in connection with the racist Saxonism of Verstegen's *Restitution of Decayed Intelligence* (*PB*, 6), *The English Gentleman* offers a practical guide to the performance of origins in the guise of self-fashioning.

For the English gentleman, the framework of historical memory ought to include "how his Countrey was first planted; how by degrees it became peopled; how to civilitie reduced; how by wholesome Lawes restrained; and how by the providence of the *Almighty*, in so calme and peaceable manner established" (Brathwait, *Gentleman*, 218). In his account of the powers of improvisation imputed to Iago in *Othello*, Stephen Greenblatt, citing Castiglione, maintains that the "spur-of-the-moment quality of improvisation is not as critical here as the opportunistic grasp of that which seems fixed and established" (227). The historical order of succession available in Betterton's library, fixed and established in the English gentleman's hindsight, became visible to the theatergoing public (and the coffeehouse self-fashioners) through Betterton's acting of English pageantry—Henry IV, Henry V, Richard III, and Henry VIII (Gildon, 174–76)—and English decorum: the "Action and Utterance of the Stage, Bar and Pulpit" (Gildon, title page). In the precise regulation of public deportment, an actor like Betterton could make these national virtues seem spontaneously visible and accessible: in the proper containment of grief, for instance, in the demonstration of the destructiveness of the passions, or in the solemn but hallow gravity with which the spirits of ancestors are now to be addressed. Betterton's eloquence impressed contemporaries not only as exemplary but as exemplary in its Englishness. His later career was conceived as a struggle waged by orature for the control of living memory within theatrical nationhood. For Charles Gildon in *The Life of Mr. Thomas Betterton*, the counterpoise to French dance and Italian opera was English acting: comparing Betterton to Roscius, who represented "*Roman* Virtue" before it "was lost with their Liberty" (14), Gildon maintained that the English actor stood as proof against such national moral decay: "Let the Excellence of the *Roman* be never so great, that of the *Briton* was the greatest we had" (2). From Betterton's "Action," Steele confessed, not from foreign song and dance, he "had received more strong Impressions of what is great and noble in Human Nature, than from the Arguments of the most solid Philosophers, or the Descriptions of the most charming Poets I had ever read" (*Tatler*, 2:422).

Spoken or written, this memory was canonical. Alexander Pope, who arranged for Betterton's translations from Chaucer to be published to benefit the destitute Widow Betterton (*Correspondence*, 1:142), proposed this epitaph from Cicero, "which will serve him well in his Moral as Theatrical capacity," to adorn the actor's grave: "The sweetest part of a life well-lived is the remembrance" (*Correspondence*, 1:88; translated by Lucy Appert). In the Victorian consolidation of theatrical history, such a residual memory of Betterton did indeed endure. In 1862, for instance, an article by John Doran in *The Cornhill Magazine* entitled "Frozen-Out Actors" enthused over the English Roscius as the key link in a chain that joined the past, spanning the gulf of the Interregnum, to the present. In this genealogy of performance, Shakespeare's sibling lives just long enough to bless the succession of an Everlasting Club of Thespians: "[Betterton's] acting was witnessed by more than one old contemporary of Shakespeare,—the poet's younger brother being among them,—he surviving till shortly after the accession of Charles the Second; and a few of Betterton's younger fellow-actors lived to speak of his great glory to old stagers who were loquacious in the early days of elderly men yet paying scot and lot among us" (177). Doran's invocation of the permanence of royal effigies, linking the sovereign succession of the body politic to the continuity of the English stage, is likewise explicit: "The humble lad, born in Tothill Street, before monarchy and the stage went down, had a royal funeral in Westminster Abbey, after dying in harness almost in sight of the lamps. He deserved no less, for he was the king of an art which had well-nigh perished in Commonwealth times, and he was a monarch who probably has never since had, altogether, his equal" (177).

But theater historians learn to take the bitter with the sweet. Like Alexander Pope, himself doubly excluded by reason of his Catholicism and his physical deformity (Deutsch), Betterton performed his role of national effigy as a variety of freak. In his *Historical Memorials of Westminster Abbey* (1886), Arthur P. Stanley uneasily records what he clearly regards as the peculiar period in the eighteenth century when actors and actresses—Anne Oldfield, Anne Bracegirdle, Spranger Barry, Samuel Foote—were buried there, and he notes with a certain relief that the last interment of a player's corpse was that of John Henderson in 1785, though later monuments were raised to the memory of Sarah Siddons and John Phillip Kemble (287–88). A century after Steele's *Tatler* eulogy, Charles Lamb had only withering sarcasm to offer over David Garrick's effigy, which was then gathering dust, an excrescence in Poet's Corner, a monument to mortuary architecture's usefulness in segregating the dead (1:97). Betterton's grave had no stone, and certainly no statue memorialized his artistry. Yet by the flickering light of the torches at his interment, Steele thought he saw a Shakespearean hero rise up in the actor's shroud, animated by a corpse that could still not only speak and gesture but also impersonate the quick and the dead.

Of all the hallucinations on which Steele and Addison report after walking in the city, then, Betterton's funeral may have been the most ethnographically surreal, certainly a strong rival in that regard to Mr. Spectator's account of the parade of Mohawk "Kings" that had taken place earlier that same week, during the actor's final illness. The blurring of boundaries between "the Imaginary and the Real Monarch" occupies both *The Tatler* and *The Spectator*: Betterton's burial inspires Steele's meditation on the interchangeability of actors and kings among a "Free-born people" (*Tatler*, 2:423); Addison refers to the Iroquois diminutively as "this little Fraternity of Kings" who nevertheless have the ear of the "Queen of the Country" (*Spectator*, 1:212–13). Voltaire admired the Englishness of "Liberty," which he defined as the singular accomplishment of limiting royal powers, while Steele employed the trope of death as the great leveler, a truly constitutional limit on sovereignty. Within these diffusively egalitarian sentiments, however, there operates another, far more precise grid of cultural meaning, one more inclined to categories of radical inequality: living or dead, white or black, "Free-born" or not.

The uncanniness of Steele's description of Betterton's Othello derives in part from its experimentation with the dissolution of the distinction between life and art on the liminal cusp of life and death: he remembered Betterton as having done what Othello did, "winning the Affection of his Mistress" with talk of slaves and cannibals, "in real Life." The threatening possibilities of that reality, which cannot be entirely repressed, are best contained by forgetting, which is the function of figures like Betterton or Elvis. Amid the necessarily imperfect erasures of circum-Atlantic memory, such effigies reaffirm the identity of the "Free-born" by sacrificing their whiteness as they take the place of kings.

FEATHERED PEOPLES

Epic loves a parade.

- DAVID QUINT

ON THE DAY OF BETTERTON'S FUNERAL, A REMARKABLE EMBASSY CONCLUDED ITS mission in England, and on the next day, May 3, 1710, it departed for America. Its members had arrived at court for an audience with Queen Anne in mid-April. She royally entertained them for the next two weeks, during which they became the talk of the town, as enthusiastic crowds turned out to follow their progress through the streets of London. Accompanied by colonial sponsors and translators, this embassy consisted of four Indian "Kings," as their English hosts called them—actually three Mohawks and an Algonquian Mahican. As documented by Richmond P. Bond in his excellent *Queen Anne's American Kings* (1952), the English recorded three names for each Indian: his Iroquoian or Algonquian name, phonetically rendered, his Christian name, and his invented title. Most prominent among the Mohawks was Theyanoquin, known to the colonials as Hendrick, who accepted the title while in England of "Emperour of the Six Nations." Next there were Sagayeanquaphrahton, or Brant, who was introduced as "King of the Maquas," and Ohneeyeathtonnoprow, or John, "King of the Generethgarich." Then there was the Mahican Elowohkaom, or Nicholas, who passed as "King of the River Nation" (Bond, 1–16). Like the effigy-kings of the theater, these royal guests reigned transiently in the negotiated territory between truth and fiction, but their liminal position did not make the interests they represented any less consequential.

Ethnohistorians have shown how Native American languages record the symbolic inventiveness of the material relationships between Iroquoia and northern Europe at this historic juncture: the traditional Mohawk word for the Dutch, *Kristoni*, "metalworkers," complemented their term describing Europeans in general, *Asseroni*, or "ax makers" (Richter, 75). These words, duly noting the most prodigious aptitude belonging to the cultures thus delimited, were opposed to the name by which the Mohawks knew themselves—*onckwe*, "human beings" or "the Real People" (Richter, 184). The Real People linked themselves to the ax makers by a valuable trade alliance known as the Covenant Chain. The concept of the Covenant Chain derived from a word with the Iroquoian root, *teHonane:-tosho:t*, meaning "to link arms in a chain of friendship." Linking arms represented a traditional gesture characteristic of the ritualized dramas of Forest Diplomacy, the formal negotiations whereby the Covenant Chain was kept "polished" (Jennings, *Iroquois Diplomacy*, 116). Fundamental to the conduct of Forest Diplomacy and the maintenance of the Covenant Chain was the periodic convocation of Condolence Councils, ancient rites of collective memory wherein the dead were mourned, new chiefs, or sachems, installed, and kinship ties celebrated. Since the European designation "King" had no equivalent meaning in matrilineal Iroquoia, the visiting Forest Diplomats might more properly have been addressed as sachems, but their actual titles, like their portfolios, were obscured by the subtle stagecraft of intersocietal diplomacy during "Queen Anne's War," as the War of the Spanish Succession was known in Anglo-America.

A crisis of royal succession is necessarily a crisis of cultural surrogation, but when the vacant Spanish throne passed into the hands of the French Bourbons, the ensuing struggle engulfed the ax makers in eleven years of war, arguably the first world war. The outcome entailed many consequences for the circum-Atlantic world of the eighteenth century and beyond, one of which was the French attempt to consolidate their interior position in North America along the water routes from Canada to Louisiana, and another of which was the greater influence of Anglophile "Praying Mohawks" like Hendrick over the conduct of Iroquois Forest Diplomacy. Along with their colonial sponsors from New York, whose interest in the lucrative fur trade they shared, and with the support of Great Britain's emerging Tory leaders, who favored a peripheral Atlantic strategy as an alternative to direct confrontation with France on the European continent, the Native American ambassadors urged on Queen Anne an undertaking of considerable scope and daring—the joint Anglo-Iroquois invasion of Canada. In their speech to the queen, which was printed and circulated, they argued that the "Reduction of *Canada* is of such Weight, that after the effecting thereof, We should have *Free Hunting* and great Trade with Our *Great Queen*'s Children" (quoted in Bond, 94n).

In this chapter, I propose to foreground not the fateful geopolitical contest between these nations and peoples—imagined communities in their modern, bellicose infancy—but rather some of the symbolic representations of that contest as staged through intercultural performances. Along with the public spectacles of various kinds occasioned by the Iroquois embassy to London, including revivals of Sir William Davenant's operatic version of Shakespeare's *Macbeth* (1664), at which the American Kings were spectators, as well as John Dryden's *The Indian Emperour; or, The Conquest of Mexico by the Spaniards* (1665) and Thomas Southerne's dramatic adaptation of Aphra Behn's *Oroonoko; or, The Royal Slave* (1694), both of which played during their embassy, I will treat Alexander Pope's celebration of the Treaties of Utrecht in *Windsor-Forest*. This ode, which proclaimed global emancipation even as Great Britain cornered the West Indian slave trade, features Native Americans as partners and beneficiaries in its expansive vision of a Pax Britannica. Though troubled by images of intractable violence, *Windsor-Forest* projects the effects of transoceanic alliances like the Covenant Chain as ushering in an era of unimaginable superabundance.

I intend to look at these London performances and Pope's poem in comparison with another Atlantic celebration of the Great Peace: the Iroquois Condolence Council, that festive and sometimes elegiac but far from disinterested act of mediation between the past and the future, between memory and renegotiated identity, and between a procession of dead ancestors and the arrival of "painted Chiefs," who act the roles of precursors of a renewed "Race of Kings" (Pope, *Poems*, 1:192). The Condolence Councils, which remain in memory to this day as performances in New York State and Canada and as historic texts in transcriptions made by literate scribes, are outstanding examples of orature. *Windsor-Forest*, which has recently been shown to inscribe the ancient dance meters of festival panegyric and the Pindaric ode (Quintero), must also be understood as belonging to this genre, which I am interpreting as the collaboration of oral and literate techniques in the service of collective memory. Yet any performance of memory also enacts forgetting. Like Richard Steele's account of Thomas Betterton's funeral, I argue, these works by Shakespeare, Davenant, Dryden, Behn, and Southerne, dominant contributors to the London theatrical repertoire at this historic moment, and by Pope, then emerging as England's dominant poet, were pressed into the service of a particular project: the memorial condensation of race and nation in the interstices of circum-Atlantic amnesia.

Through the spectacular manipulation of restored behaviors, these works perform variations on a persistent Atlantic occasion particularly subject to forgetting: encounters between and among white, red, and black peoples. Representations of these encounters show how Europeans, Native Americans, and Africans, real or imagined, acting in one another's presence, real or imagined, repeated their special rites of surrogation. Through these rites, they performed not only their identity but also their threatened continuity. In representations of such triangular encounters, at least one of the parties seems fated to disappear from the selective memory of another. Such disappearances are necessary to ensure the untroubled performance of a dominant trope: that of genealogical succession, imagined as a stately procession, as an everlasting club whose members succeed one another as if on parade. In a world continuously reinvented by intercultural propinquity, however—and that is precisely what the circum-Atlantic world was and is—the order of any procession may be threatened with interruption or usurpation. Underlying the intense images of violence—in *Windsor-Forest*, the blood of hunted birds and men; in *Macbeth*, the blood of kings; in *The Indian Emperour* and *Oroonoko*, the blood of millions—there is the pressure exerted by the implicit menace of this usurpation. The fear that blood will be mixed, a fear that intensifies the ritual expectation that blood must be shed, haunts these representations like a vengeful ghost: the specter of future generations threatening to be born.

The cultural materials under consideration here, especially the English ones, tend to support the psychoanalytic truism that for most people anxiety is the longing for what they fear. Examining closely the highlights of the public performances given in London over a period of several weeks, I will examine three special signifiers of this anxiety—women, children, and feathers—that emerge, in turn, from representations of a remarkably turbulent contradiction: the fear of superabundance. This superabundance, whether apparent or real, persists in circum-Atlantic memory. It serves as a historic provocation for what Georges Bataille calls "profitless expenditure" or what I call the performance of waste. Its ritual enactments involve the conspicuous consumption of nonutilitarian objects and forms of all kinds, including theatrical productions and other incarnations of excess. On the dangerous cusp of violence and the aesthetic, the performance of waste deflects the anxieties produced by a sense of having too much of everything—including material goods and human beings—onto specially nominated surrogates—effigies, as I have defined them in the preceding chapters. In the following section, before turning specifically to the Condolence Councils and then to the performances occasioned by the Mohawk embassy of 1710, I will set forth the specific terms that identify them both as circum-Atlantic events.

The Accursed Share:
Abundance, Reproduction, and Sacrifice

Building on Marcel Mauss's *The Gift*, Georges Bataille develops a theory of what he calls "General Economy" in the first volume of *The Accursed Share* (1967). He extends the argument from the "archaic societies" examined by Mauss to include the technocultures of modernity. Rejecting models founded on scarcity and utility, Bataille examines diverse but mutually illuminating Atlantic phenomena of abundance and profitless expenditure, ranging from human sacrifice among the Aztecs to the Marshall Plan. In the natural history of the world, according to the premise of the "General Economy," the "dominant event is the development of luxury, the production of increasingly burdensome forms of life" (33). Human cultures somehow must cope with the profuse excesses produced by nature and reproduced by their own increasingly fecund manipulations of it. Their strategies for coping with this superabundance include such forms as potlatch, feasting, ritualized warfare, and sacrifice—performing the waste of excess objects, produce, and human life. As the vivid introductory example of a particular operation of the "General Economy," Bataille offers a section entitled "Sacrifices and Wars of the Aztecs," in which he concludes that the "passion that made the blood stream from the pyramids generally led the Aztec world to make unproductive use of a substantial portion of the resources it commanded" (63). For Bataille's argument, as for so many other dramatizations of the terrors of excess, indelible images of Mesoamerica provide the touchstone.

From the arrival of Cortés in Mexico, exposure to the New World's vast cultures of profitless expenditure shocked and fascinated Europeans, who found in such performances of waste an echo of and an affront to their own. For its part in circum-Atlantic memory, Mesoamerica has maintained certain syncretic traditions, such as carnival in Zinacantan, which represents the conquest itself as sacrifice, with a "Montezuma-impersonator" who doubles in the role of St. Sebastian, dying with a hail of arrows in his heart, dismembered at precisely that moment at which he is most adored (Bricker, 138–47). Bataille locates the focal point of such ambivalence in the sacrificial victim, the "accursed share": "The victim is a surplus taken from the mass of *useful* wealth. And he can only be withdrawn from it in order to be consumed profitlessly, and therefore utterly destroyed. Once chosen, he is the *accursed share*, destined for violent consumption. But the curse tears him away from the *order of things*; it gives him a recognizable figure, which now radiates intimacy, anguish, the profundity of living beings" (59).

The truth belonging to this provocative description of the effigy appears in performances where it metastasizes into a fetish, which Karl Marx in *Capital* defines as the vesture of material objects in an aura of mystery. Under such a spell, the relations between human beings assume "the fantastic form of a relation between things" (165; cf. Taussig). The idea of a "General Economy" founded on the violent consumption of flesh—and its exchange through warfare or sale at auction, as in the slave trade—sets up a dynamic play of meaning between *fetish* and *effigy*. The received African meaning of *fetish* pulls against the sense of doubleness and surrogation in *effigy* by investing the fetish object itself with original motive powers. Pulling back hard in the opposite direction is the general cosmology of the spirit world, a system of forces in which the charm of the fetish functioned and on which its value depended. In this sense, the fetish does not conceal the labor of its production, as Marx said, but renders its value visible and manifest in the work of cultural magic through and on it.

What stands out in Bataille's theoretical model of a "General Economy" is the way in which the specific economy of material abundance is symbolically superimposed on that of human reproduction. This superimposition particularly obtains in the circum-Atlantic world, where entire populations existed as actual or potential commodities and where the triangular trade in human flesh, manufactured goods, and raw materials rapidly produced a superabundance unprecedented in both extent and maldistribution. The enduring effects of this superimposition still operate in the fiercely laminating adhesion of bodies and objects, in which the exchange of human flesh signifies the prolific availability of all commodities. Bataille's critique demystifies this process not at the point of exchange but at the point, unaccounted for by conventional economists, of profitless expenditure: "Sacrifice restores to the sacred world that which servile use has degraded, rendered profane" (55). His insight illuminates the aestheticized depiction of a variety of scenes, including those where ritualized violence expends a human surplus or those where women play prominent roles as consumers of luxury goods, including exotic pets, chocolate, and Negroes. These representations themselves, in the form of paintings, sculptures, plays, and operas, became more widely available as objects of lavish expenditure as circum-Atlantic economies selectively expanded the wealth and leisure necessary to their cultivation. In the resulting semiotics of superabundance and sacrifice, as I have suggested, the heaviest burden of signification was born by the frailest of their accoutrements: women, as both consumers and the consumed; children, as both the auguries of surrogation and its realization in the fullness of time; and feathers, as both exotic tokens of otherness and the polychromatic markers of its alarming copiousness and profusion.

This particular concatenation of fetishes appears uncannily in the image of the actress Anne Bracegirdle playing the fabulously overdressed role of an "Indian Queen." A mezzotint engraving (figure 4.1) depicts either the title role in a revival of Dryden and Howard's heroic drama with music by Purcell (Ganz, 30; see Pinnock) or possibly Semernia, who offers herself up as the interracial sex interest in Aphra Behn's *The Widow Ranter; or, The History of Bacon in Virginia* (1689). Like Behn's novella *Oroonoko; or, The Royal Slave* (1688), *The Widow Ranter* dramatizes a failed rebellion in an American plantation. It is tempting to suppose that the mezzotint shows Semernia's grand entrance at the top of act 4, where she ceremoniously approaches the sacred altar at which the Indians offer sacrifices to the god Quiocto. Feather-crowned train and parasol bearers, seminude children with decidedly African features, attend the even more opulently befeathered Indian Queen. In these attendants the blood of Indians and Africans seems already to have mixed. As threatening as interracial sex between Africans and Europeans may have been, fecund liaisons between African slaves and Native Americans posed a different kind of menace to whiteness. The multiplication of Maroon communities (the social and military alliances of Indians and escaped slaves that flourished in parts of South America, the Caribbean, and Louisiana) offered more than practical resistance to Euro-

4.1 Anne Bracegirdle as an Indian queen. Engraved by R. B. Parkes after the picture by J. Smith and W. Vincent. Howard-Tilton Memorial Library, Tulane University

colonial interests. They also provided a subversive alternative to the self-proclaimed ascendancy of white people as sole proprietors of circum-Atlantic contact and exchange. The miscegenistic lushness of this particular staging raises the level of ritual expectancy in anticipation of the predictably catastrophic consequences of erotic encounters among red, black, and white peoples.

In each of the works considered here, such threatening varieties of human abundance compel expenditures of blood, for which the carnage in

Behn's *Widow Ranter* sets the general scene. Although, in fact, Semernia is not herself officially sacrificed to the local deity, neither is she destined to survive the sanguinary fifth-act rites of English tragicomedy: disguised as an Indian warrior, she perishes by accident at the hands of her white lover, the defeated rebel Nathaniel Bacon, who kills himself in remorse. Performed in the same year that the expensive young women at Josias Priest's school sang and danced in *Dido and Aeneas*, the stage deaths of the English hero and Indian queen in *The Widow Ranter* thus point a Virgilian moral on the entanglement of origin, eros, and fate: theirs is another profitless expenditure of surrogated royalty on the altar of race. Standing in as intercultural double for the Indian King, Bacon presides over the propitiative rites: "I have too long survived my queen and glory," he concludes, "those two bright stars that influenced my life are set to all eternity" (321). Profitless as this expenditure may be, it is nevertheless precisely motivated as a stringent method of contraception in the service of race and nation. The prenuptial sacrifice contributes to the fiction of the originary whiteness of the Virginians and thus to the "safer repose" of the Anglo-Americans' "country" (324).

The theatrical fate of Semernia and her unborn progeny illustrates a more general point: the representation of women and children in the production of theatrical nationhood, including its regional and local ethnic affiliates, derives at least in part from their role as caretakers of memory. As Laura Brown argues in *Ends of Empire: Women and Ideology in Early Eighteenth-Century English Literature* (1993), there occurred a "Feminization of Ideology" in the Augustan period, a feminization made manifest in literature but enunciated even more emphatically by means of performance. For Brown, the nexus of the problem exists in "the interaction of the woman and the slave, as figures of commodification" (20). The effigy-producing magic of performance creates out of the materials of this interaction one of the most memorable of fetish objects: the "Gift" offered between men as a sacrificial expenditure under the sway of abundance and in the implicit expectation of reciprocity (Hyde, 93–108; Rubin). The presentation and adornment of women, as one of the most efficacious of aesthetic productions, makes conspicuously public this performance of waste.

Africans often appear in representation as infantilized, feminized objects of domestic luxury and consumption. Here, like women, their labor is effaced even as their value as possessions is performed. The portrait of Louise de Kéroualle, duchess of Portsmouth, by Philippe Mignard (1682), for instance, suggests the conventions whereby the European incorporation of Africa and Africans may be at once acknowledged as conspicuous consumption and disavowed as the vital business of the nation (figure 4.2). Involuntary servitude is domesticated, privatized, trivialized. The African serving girl, collared with pearls and positioned in the composition where the spaniel would otherwise be, lovingly presents her ladyship with sprigs of red coral and a conch shell filled with even larger pearls. Mignard's composition brings together the images opulently suggestive of total *prestation* (Mauss) and unproductive expenditure (Bataille) that send a youthful shiver of ritual expectancy through the hoary voice of Father Thames, speaking the climactic peroration of Pope's *Windsor-Forest*:

> For me the Balm shall bleed, and Amber flow,
> The Coral redden, and the Ruby glow,
> The Pearly Shell its lucid Globe infold,
> And *Phoebus* warm the ripening Ore to Gold.
> (1:190)

The sacred conveyance of this ornamental excess, however, like Pope's Belinda in *The Rape of the Lock* (L. Brown, *Ends of Empire*, 113–18), is the body of the woman whose captive flesh the slave both doubles and adorns.

Mignard's duchess recalls Addison's "beautiful Romantick Animal," in whose idolatrous worship "the Sea shall be searched for Shells, and the Rocks for Gems; and every Part of Nature furnish out its Share towards the Embellishment of a Creature that is the most consummate Work of it" (*Tatler*, 2:195). She likewise gives proof of Mr. Spectator's dazzled observation, as he stood under the gaze of the kingly effigies at the Royal Exchange, of the multinational derivation of a single English lady's gown and accessories: "The Muff and the Fan come together from the different Ends of Earth. The Scarf is sent from the Torrid Zone, and the Tippet from beneath the Pole. The Brocade Petticoat rises out of the Mines of *Peru*, and the Diamond Necklace out of the Bowels of *Indostan*" (*Spectator*, 1:295). She might even evoke the scene in *The Female Tatler*, no. 67, for December 7 to 9, 1709, in which Arabella and Emilia watch Lady Praise-All peruse the wares of an "India House," clearing the shelves of this "nick-nackatory" (135).

Placed between the richly brocaded and slightly parted thighs of Mignard's duchess, the cornucopia of pearls opens up like the lips of a lush pudendum. The background in turn opens up on the seascape beyond, the

4.2 Louise de Kéroualle, duchess of Portsmouth.
Portrait by Philippe Mignard, 1682.
National Portrait Gallery

wealth-engendering colonial islands invisible over the horizon, beckoning unseen on the shimmering perimeter where horizon becomes mirage. In this sumptuous, seductive, and deeply disturbing paean to imperial commodification, the slave child seems to exist to reproduce blackness for and somehow also to produce the whiteness of the white woman, an effect eerily evoked two hundred years later (on another social plane) by the West Indian negress presenting flowers to the linen-skinned prostitute in Edouard Manet's notorious portrait *Olympia* (see figure 5.12). But children, like death, have many uses. The presence of the slave girl, performing her role of sacrificial expenditure in a composition that quotes Raphaelesque templates of Madonna and Child, dramatizes human reproduction amid an iconology of material superabundance.

Like the opulent scenery of portraiture, the details of physical staging highlighted the sacrificial economy of abundance in Restoration heroic plays. Even in a theater where costume tended to be generalized, the original staging of Dryden and Robert Howard's *The Indian Queen* (1664), the play for which Dryden provided a sequel in *The Indian Emperour*, evidently made use of certain authenticating details to underscore the cultural difference of the Americans: in a word, feathers. According to the introductory matter of *Oroonoko*, Aphra Behn returned from a journey to South America bearing native specimens suitable to a cabinet of curiosities, including snakeskins, rare flies, baskets, aprons, weapons, and, above all, "Feathers, which they order into all Shapes, make themselves little short Habits of 'em, and glorious Wreaths for their Heads, Necks, Arms and Legs, whose Tinctures are unconceivable. I had a Set of these presented to me, and I gave 'em to the King's Theatre, and it was the Dress of the *Indian Queen*, infinitely admired by Persons of Quality, and was unimitable" (2). This ethnographic account complements the image of Anne Bracegirdle festooned as an Indian queen, perhaps the one in Behn's own play, but in the semiotics of heroic stagecraft generally, feathers undertook a key role: "The ordinary method of making an Heroe," Addison complains, "is to clap a huge Plume of Feathers upon his Head." The same conventionality applied to ghosts in bloody garments—"A Spectre has very often saved a Play"—and physical violence—"that dreadful butchering of one another which is so very frequent upon the *English* stage" (*Spectator*, 1:178, 186–87). In the "General Economy" of the heroic play, then, the performance of waste, enacted amid the haunted vestiges of the European spirit world, occurred on the level of material extravagance in adornment, especially feathered plumes, as well as in blood. As a material object, the feather marks an act of violence: what it cost to produce was the original wearer's life, and what it served to dramatize was the predication of overarching symbolic systems on the material basis of waste.

What these representations accomplished, in my view, was the accommodation of exotic accounts of Atlantic superabundance and sacrifice into the normalizing regimes of whiteness. Cognizant of ritual practices, like the taking of captives in the Aztec Flower Wars (the object of which was not to achieve victory per se but to obtain victims for sacrifice), Europeans depicted Native Americans as cruel prodigals. As such, they performed as dual substitutes, doubling as sacred priests and sacred offerings, their bodies methodically clothed and unclothed. No wonder that from Montaigne to Artaud, Native American and especially Mesoamerican customs and practices have played the roles of ethnographic provocation and hyperbolic mirror. The ambivalence of Europeans toward profitless expenditure, an economy of excess at once so alien and so familiar, haunts the debate that Tzvetan Todorov, in *The Conquest of America: The Question of the Other* (1984), traces throughout the documents of the conquest: the Spaniards' more or less absolute choice between identity and equality, on one hand, and difference and inequality, on the other (146–67). Although the North American Indians lacked the vastly opulent material culture that overawed the conquistadors even as they put it to the torch, both Aztec and Iroquois rituals also entrusted societal renewal to the performance of waste (Clendinnen, 87–88). They did so believing in the efficacy of a particular rite of symbolic kinship: different bloods could be mixed but only after a certain portion of them—the accursed share—had been spilled.

Condolence Councils and the Great Peace

Paramount among the performances that defined the historic moment of the Mohawk embassy in April 1710—the subsequently erased rubric under which all the English examples might be subscribed—is a Native American form of intersocietal communication known as the Condolence Council. This ritualized drama of treaty negotiation and cultural renewal came into play diplomatically among those peoples whose destinies remained interdependent as allies and rivals in North America. The key to this balance of interests was Forest Diplomacy, of which the Condolence Council was a principal medium. In Amerindian tradition, the Condolence Councils reaffirmed the compact of the Great Peace instituted by Deganawidah and Hiawatha before the arrival of Europeans (Dennis). Initially, the councils regulated relations among the five nations of the Iroquois Confederacy—Mohawks, Oneidas, Onondagas, Cayugas, and Senecas—also known as the Great League of Peace and Power. Later, as flexible yet evocatively structured rites of intercultural communication, they particularly flourished in New France and New York as the centrally located Iroquois dealt with the rival ax makers. During the closing years of the seventeenth century, the English, inept at first, grew more confident at performing their part in this sophisticated interplay of protocol, negotiation, and expression of mutual interests.

The success of the Condolence Councils forms a most necessary feature of the background of the London performances of the Mohawks, for reasons that anthropologist William N. Fenton explains when he uses theater as a metaphor to describe the Native American tradition:

> Underlying protocol of treaties and the drama of forest diplomacy was an Indian ceremony for renewing their political forms and restoring society known as the Condolence Council. This developed into a drama in which the actors were Indian sachems and colonial governors. With different casts and slight changes in the script it ran for more than a century, principally at Albany. . . . There were French actors when the play was staged in Montreal. But in its purest form it was celebrated at the great drama festivals held each fall at Onondaga where it was said the ceremony originated with the founding of the [Iroquois Confederacy] before the Dutch came to America. Deganawidah was the playwright and Hiawatha its leading actor. (18)

Through singing, dancing, and heightened speech, the line of chiefs descended from Deganawidah, the fatherless boy who brought peace to the Iroquois, was evoked. Deganawidah defeated witchcraft and founded the Great Law. Deganawidah taught the ceremonies of lasting peace, of which the Condolence Council, wherein the parties became of "One Mind" by solacing past griefs and exchanging presents, was the most efficacious. Presents typically took the form of "wampum," exquisite strings of glass or shell beads that served at once as gifts and as mnemonic records of the councils. Predicated on the "requickening ceremonies," which existed to mourn the dead and to install their successors, the Condolence Councils represent more than an occasion for the performative affirmation of reciprocal obligation. With their recitation of the notable dead, they also offer a most powerful instance of a performance of origin, located through a genealogy of linked surrogations that functioned as cultural definition in the face of the other.

In the cycle of death and surrogation, intense contradictions emerge that cannot go unaddressed. Through requickening ceremonies, the Iroquois mourned losses to the community by assigning the name and social role of the deceased to a younger kinsman or, alternatively, to a captive taken from another tribe. Among the Iroquois, women typically made these life-and-death decisions. As the caretakers of memory, they were not only the bearers but also the makers of meaning within strict protocols. Under the supreme direction of the matriarchs, the Iroquois assimilated captives in one of two ways. If the bereaved women especially approved of the captive, he or she would be assigned the name and place in society of the deceased, decked out in the tribal vestments, and welcomed forever after as kin. If the bereaved women questioned the auspiciousness of such an appointment for any reason—surviving observers found the criteria for this decision deeply mysterious—the captive was given his or her adoptive name, decked out in the tribal vestments, and then, at the festively appointed time, ritually murdered, typically by slow fire, cooked, and feasted on by his or her new kin (Richter, 35–36). Either way, the surrogated double was taken in by the Real People as one of their own.

Suffice it to say that the problem of surrogation is handled differently at different times by different peoples. After early attempts to exterminate the indigenous population proved unduly burdensome, the French adopted a system of officially encouraged miscegenation in Canada, some features of which carried over into the customs of Louisiana. They called this assimilationist policy "One Blood" (Johnson, "Colonial New Orleans," 23). The English and Anglo-Americans, by contrast, maintained a policy of segregation (Nash). Sublimated in countless dramas and narratives that fantasize interracial liaisons, such associations tend to culminate in one form of non-consummation or another, often that of violent death.

The visit of the sachems to London, for instance, occasioned the production of a ballad, called *The Four Indian Kings*, that fancifully recounts the love affair between one of the Mohawks and an English noblewoman. Although this ditty remained one of the most frequently reprinted ballads of the eighteenth century (Bond, 70), its immense popularity was eclipsed by the many versions of Richard Steele's poignant tale of Inkle and Yarico (Hulme, 225–63). Writing in the eleventh number of *The Spectator* (March 13, 1711), one year after the visit of the Kings, Steele elaborated the story, which he first read in Richard Ligon's *True and Exact History of the Island of Barbadoes* (1657), of the English merchant Thomas Inkle and the Carib maiden Yarico (*PB*, 2): Yarico rescues Inkle from the massacre of his landing party; they then spend an idyllic time together as castaway lovers. On their return to "*English* Territories," however, he repays her devotion by selling her into slavery, and her heartrending plea that he spare her because she is pregnant with their child only serves to drive up her price (1:50–51). The banality of this tale is in no way alleviated by the urgency of Yarico's condition. Time and time again, even on the level of fantasy, the sobering fact that exotic mates make even more exotic offspring reminds Englishmen to snap out of it.

Although Indians had been brought to England and treated as curiosities, dead or alive, since the reign of Henry VIII, the visit of the Four Kings represents an occasion of a far different order at a unique historical moment. The twentieth-century reader should keep in mind that their embassy predated most of the genocidal ruin of North America and that the situation of the English, thinly settled close to the Atlantic seaboard in 1710, was not yet such that they could expect to dictate terms to the Iroquois Confederacy, the influence of which extended across the Great Lakes to the Mississippi Valley. As casualties mounted in the European land war against more populous France, and as the expansion of the British military through intensified recruitment provoked national anxiety over the expensive threat posed by a standing army, Tory opposition to the Whig faction supporting the duke of Marlborough's brilliant but Pyrrhic campaign in Flanders gained ground (Trevelyan). Tories like Pope could point to a war weariness that had become a general malaise by 1710. In *The Life of Betterton*, Gildon attributes to the actor an opinion that the recent decline of the arts and sciences stemmed from "the Sowerness of our Temper under the Pressures of so long and heavy a War" (12). In *The Tatler* Steele employs the same dyspeptic term to describe the way in which the regulars at Will's Coffee House received the news of Marlborough's great but costly victory over the French at Malplaquet: "I came hither this Evening, and expected nothing else but mutual Congratulations in the Company on the late Victory; but found our Room . . . full of sowr Animals" (1:447–48). As an alternative to the increasing butcher's bill in Flanders, a peripheral strategy of naval blockade and smaller-scale amphibious actions at distant but vital points overseas emerged from Tory councils of war, particularly at the urging of Colonel Francis Nicholson, one of the Anglo-colonial sponsors of the visit of the Kings. What the Americans brought with them from Tiononderoge was a plan, based on their experience of maintaining a far-flung trading empire amid more populous rivals arrayed along water routes, that fit the concept of a peripheral strategy very conveniently: a strike not at the heavily defended borders of metropolitan France but at its more vulnerable outpost in Montreal.

In the realm of the representation of violence as the performance of waste, larger geopolitical interests may be condensed into the tangible form of proxies and surrogates. In its characteristic metaphor of the hunt, Pope's *Windsor-Forest* compares peripheral overseas military expeditions to the surprise capture of an unsuspecting partridge in the stealthy hunter's snare:

> When *Albion* sends her eager Sons to War,
> Some thoughtless Town, with Ease and Plenty blest,
> Near, and more near, the closing Lines invest;
> Sudden they seize th'amaz'd, defenceless Prize,
> And high in Air *Britannia*'s Standard flies.
>
> (1:161)

This passage better describes the amphibious descent of Iroquois raiding parties on Huron villages (or the British coup of capturing Gibraltar in 1704) than it does the increasingly ponderous and complicated set-piece battles on the European continent. The largest battles of the seventeenth century engaged 30,000 to 40,000 soldiers, but at Malplaquet in 1709 Marlborough commanded 110,000 allied troops, opposed by 90,000 French (Van Creveld). At that time, the entire Iroquois population did not exceed 20,000 (Jennings, *Iroquois Diplomacy*, xiii), but it dominated the waterborne fur trade from the Mississippi to the Hudson nonetheless. The interdependence of rivers and oceans in a strategy of naval domination of trade routes whereby a relatively small population can exert disproportionate influence on a large system fairly characterizes the elegiac geography of empire in Pope's *Windsor-Forest*:

> Let *India* boast her Plants, nor envy we
> The weeping Amber or the balmy Tree,
> While by our Oaks the precious Loads are born,
> And Realms commanded which those Trees adorn.
>
> (1:151)

Historically, oceans have served to separate nations and peoples. To the power possessed of naval and maritime supremacy, however, the very cause in which the trees that Pope calls "our Oaks" have been sacrificed, oceans serve rather more to join than to sunder.

Although the Tory-backed offensive against Canada in 1711 ultimately succeeded in conquering only Nova Scotia (Acadia) for queen and country, British collaboration with those Pope called the "Feather'd People" (1:191) had a number of indirect consequences for the conduct of the war in its final stages and for imperial strategy in the longer term. In *The Influence of Sea Power Upon History* (1890), Alfred Thayer Mahan accounts for the results in carefully chosen words that could also describe the strategy of the Iroquois, if, as in *Windsor-Forest*'s preoccupation with rivers, interior water routes may stand for sea lanes:

> The noiseless, steady, exhausting pressure with which sea power acts, cutting off the resources of the enemy while maintaining its own, supporting war in scenes where it does not appear itself, or appears only in the background, and striking open blows at rare intervals, though lost to most, is emphasized to the careful reader by the events of [the War of the Spanish Succession] and of the half-century that followed. The overwhelming sea power of England was the determining factor in European history during the period mentioned, maintaining war abroad while keeping its own people in prosperity at home, and building up the great empire which is now seen; but from its very greatness its action, by escaping opposition, escapes attention. (209)

In this light, as French-allied Huron survivors or the Louisiana-bound expatriates of the Acadian—"Cajun"—diaspora might have viewed it, the historic record suggests the timeliness of the London visit of the Kings. Poised at the balance point of circum-Atlantic relations in 1710, as the Anglophiles gained ascendancy over the Francophiles among the Iroquois, their embassy dramatized the powerful consequences attending on success or failure in Forest Diplomacy.

The key to success was the Condolence Council. That sequence of ritual events was arranged according to the dramaturgy of cultural renewal: a procession, which included calling out the roll of the founders; the welcome at the fire by the woods; the wiping away of blood and tears; the roll call and eulogy to the ancestral dead; the farewell chant to the Dead Chief; the recitation of laws; the exchange of condolences and wampum strings; the showing of the face of the new chief; the charge to the new chief and to the public; and the feast and celebration dance (Fenton, 18–19). As the council increasingly lent itself to intercultural negotiation between hosts and guests, the importance of the exchange of gifts, including wampum, grew, transferring the prominence devoted to the rite of succession to the enactment of renewed relations between the negotiating parties. Items in the negotiation were reinforced by means of wampum, beads arranged in strings or belts that served a mnemonic purpose as well as one of mutual empowerment through gift exchange. The kinesthetic performance of handling wampum was of the utmost importance: the belt was passed, like a proposition, between the parties, and the quality of their gestures in taking up or setting down the wampum signified their intentions (M. Foster).

That the French policy of One Blood had support from at least some on the Native American side is demonstrated by the first recorded description of a Condolence Council, "The Mohawk Treaty with New France at Three Rivers, 1645" (reprinted in Jennings, *Iroquois Diplomacy*, 127–53), a meticulous Jesuit record of the performance of the Council that includes admiring descriptions of the pantomimed action and eloquent singing of the chief Mohawk negotiator, Kiotseaeton. According to this record, the participants in the council celebrated intersocietal fraternity through gestures of consanguinity and abundance. Costumed to portray the spirit of sacrificial expenditure, Kiotseaeton appeared at the council swathed in wampum from head to foot: "He was almost completely covered with Porcelain beads" (137). His performance showed that the wampum signified the physical as well as the spiritual unity of One Mind, as the Iroquois understood it, or One Blood, as the French put it. As a demonstration of the faculty of kinesthetic imagination to minimize the language barrier, the Mohawk's performance was virtuosic. On the formal presentation of the tenth wampum belt (or "collar"), for instance, "[Kiotseaeton] took hold of a Frenchman, placed his arm within his, and with his other arm he clasped that of an Alguonquin. Having thus joined himself to them, 'Here,' he said, 'is the knot that binds us inseparably; nothing can part us.' This collar was extraordinarily beautiful. 'Even if the lightning were to fall upon us, it could not separate us; for, if it cuts off the arm that holds you to us, we will at once seize each other by the other arm.' And thereupon he turned around, and caught the Frenchman and the Alguonquin by their two other arms,—holding them so closely that he seemed unwilling to leave them" (141).

The gesture of linking arms represents the kinesthetic foundation of what was to become the concept of the Covenant Chain. When the council was renewed several months later, the eighth beaded protocol made explicit what Kiotseaeton's pantomime had suggested: "This is to assure the French that, if they wish to marry in this country, they will find wives here, since we are their friends and allies" (147). By 1677, however, when the Mohawks celebrated a great council with the English at Albany, the Covenant Chain linked North America to Great Britain, which had no concept comparable to the French doctrine of One Blood but accepted in theory the proposition that two peoples might be joined at a safe distance by a symbolic chain of reciprocal trade and mutual defense.

In a bisocietal relationship between a predominantly oral culture and a literate one, written texts—such as treaties or works of literature—may serve as powerful instruments of forgetting. Performance, however, works on behalf of living memory by bringing the parties together as often as necessary. The common goal of the Condolence Councils was the maintenance of the Covenant Chain. In its service, they had to be regularly repeated up and down the line in a cycle of renegotiations—"polishing the Chain." The idea of continuous reiteration (and possible revision) of multiparty obligations ultimately provoked the willful misunderstanding on the part of Anglo-Americans that gave to English the term "Indian giver," but at the height of the success of the Covenant Chain, the more astute among the Europeans well understood the principle that operated behind oral tradition and the Great Law (Lafitau): among performance cultures the law functioned, as Bernard J. Hibbitts explains, "not as rules or agreements but as processes constituting rule or agreement . . . not [as] an object, but a routine of words and gestures" (959). The records of the councils disclose recurring annoyance on the part of the Indians at the distracting effect of "pen and ink work" during the negotiations, as colonial secretaries scribbled away, futilely trying to put down on paper understandings that could exist only in the meeting of eyes and hands and voices.

One reason why "epic loves a parade," as David Quint wittily puts it in *Epic and Empire: Politics and Generic Form from Virgil to Milton* (1993), is that processions resemble genealogies or other lists of successive eminences (31). They favor the processes of memory without writing (Vansina, 34–56). Thus roll calls of the dead oriented the participants in Condolence Councils to what they were about to become by recounting who they had been. In such performances, the prestige of origin asserts itself forcefully, and the recitation of the Deganawidah epic provided a means of remembering the laws and protocols of the Great Peace through a recitation of the names and deeds of the successive "Founders" (Fenton, 14–15). The movement of the Condolence Council from grief and loss to harmony and festivity, as Fenton observes (19), illustrates Alfred R. Radcliffe-Brown's paradigm of ritual transformation from dysphoria to euphoria. While this form dominated the political dialogue at one end of the Covenant Chain, the people at the other end turned to the works of their poets, and to one in particular.

Windsor Forest Diplomacy

Alexander Pope began *Windsor-Forest* in 1704 as a pastoral reminiscence of his boyhood in Binfield (near Windsor), and he published it in 1713, revised and expanded, as an encomium to the Tory Peace of Utrecht (Mack, 199–207). This treaty marked not only the end of a war but also the end of the unrivaled preeminence of the Mediterranean in the geopolitics and poetics of Eurocentric imagination. *Windsor-Forest* proclaims the maritime leadership of the newly established United Kingdom in the new world order. By the protocols of this order, nations invent themselves through and among imperial rivals, allies, and subject peoples. For this and other reasons, I regard *Windsor-Forest* as a quintessential circum-Atlantic text. In it the poet reinvents Windsor as a national cemetery, a suburb of the dead. Such a claim reflects my understanding of what Pope insinuates and elides as well as what he explicitly contends, for *Windsor-Forest* belongs in the genre of poetry of allusion more fittingly than it does in the poetry of statement (Brower). Its contradictions mirror those of a world in which the best chance for the survival of tradition was through improvisation. Its supple couplets are thick with memories, ancient and modern, which are then displaced by surrogations—a new Augustan age stands in for the old, the Spanish imperial tradition gives way to Northern European ambitions, Plantagenet catastrophe yields to Stuart reparation, while "Fair *Liberty*, *Britannia*'s Goddess" raises her head again "and leads the Golden Years" (1:159).

Pope predicates these surrogations on the simultaneous presence of the living and the dead: Windsor, like Westminster Abbey, serves as a burial place for English kings, and Queen Anne goes to hunt there, near the bones of her predecessors, including those in the unmarked tomb of Charles I. Consciously reviving Virgilian topoi of nostalgia (Morris, 103–30), Pope constructs Windsor Forest as a "place of memory" in Pierre Nora's sense—a shrine-studded site at which classical allusion dignifies the transformation of dynastic memory into modern national and imperial priorities (Carretta; Clements). The pervasiveness of the hunting imagery in *Windsor-Forest* underlines the theme of sacrificial violence that returns to the poet like the repressed. This reading takes into account Earl R. Wasserman's acute appreciation of the politics of *Windsor-Forest* in *The Subtler Language* (1959) and Laura Brown's critique in *Alexander Pope* (1985). For Brown, the poem's "elaborate attempts to rationalize imperial violence in the name of peace result in a circular and obsessive return to the theme of violence even in its most pastoral scenes" (40). Taking up the related theme of the law as performed memory, Pope reviews the devastating consequences of the invasive Norman legal concept of a "Forest" as the exclusive preserve of the king outside of common law, an issue still vexing to eighteenth-century theorists of inalienable property rights, including the right of property in the flesh of other human beings (Michals). On the subject of slavery, *Windsor-Forest*'s premature proclamation of emancipation enacts a strange substitution in the triangular relationship of red, black, and white peoples: the visibility of freed Native Americans obscures the existence of enslaved Africans. Finally, in its juxtaposition of history and natural history, the placement of the succession of kings and empires beside the encounter of cultures and races, *Windsor-Forest* raises the unanswered question by which circum-Atlantic communities, past and present, are haunted: by whom shall they (or we) be replaced?

As a work of literature—that is, as a printed repository of restored behavior—*Windsor-Forest* contains the traces of several genres of performance, including its largely neglected formal indebtedness to the choric meters of the ancient festival panegyric (Quintero, 44–56). Performative traces also reside in the poem's inscription of incorporated practices: its highly kinesthetic imagery of acts of extreme violence, the performance of waste, juxtaposed to conciliatory gestures of condolence, the performance of negotiated plenty. Like the contemporary *Rape of the Lock*, *Windsor-Forest* is a poem animated not only by rhetorical figures but also by gestures. Pope's cadenced evocation of the festival chorus, with its dancelike shifts of direction and mood—strophe, antistrophe, epode—accounts, I believe, for the distinctive but mysterious movements of the poem.

The ode begins by calling on the "Forests" of Windsor and the shades of the monarchs and muses who wander there to "Invite" the poet's song (1:148). Pope makes it clear, in the richly allusive language of his distinctive topophilia ("Consult the Genius of the Place in all," he later advised Lord

Burlington [*Poems*, 3.2:138]), that Windsor Forest will both represent an actual geographical locus, with fields and trees known to the poet since boyhood, and serve as a protean signifier of England, English history, and British global entitlement in world-historical terms: "Not proud *Olympus* yields a nobler sight" (1:151). Windsor Forest presents a landscape reminiscent of "Groves of Eden" (1:148), redolent with origins, visited by classical deities—Pan, Flora, Pomona, Ceres, Diana—yet hallowed by the graves of English kings, its variety of historical associations permeated by an underlying foundationary order, a *concordia discors*, "where, tho' all things differ, all agree" (1:150). Out of the memories of Windsor Forest, personal and patriotic, the poet constructs a topographical *lieu de mémoire* to celebrate a national vision of global peace and plenitude following war and sacrifice:

> Rich Industry sits smiling in the Plains,
> And Peace and Plenty tell, a *STUART* reigns.
> (1:152)

Pope effects the poetical union of local cultural traditions, assumed to have roots as deep as time, with the victory consummated by Tory strategy and negotiation in the final years of a global war: the waters of Father Thames, flowing past Windsor, empty ultimately into all the oceans of the world, and on those same waters the sturdy oaks of Windsor Forest sail as the hulls of English warships and merchantmen.

The imagery of the circum-Atlantic circulation of the waters of the Thames, bringing back with compound interest what they have carried away, returns toward the end of *Windsor-Forest*, where Pope devotes his penultimate verses to a climactic, prophetic vision:

> The time shall come, when free as Seas or Wind
> Unbounded *Thames* shall flow for all Mankind,
> Whole Nations enter with each swelling Tyde,
> And Seas but join the Regions they divide;
> Earths distant Ends our Glory shall behold,
> And the new World launch forth to seek the Old.
> Then Ships of uncouth Form shall stem the Tyde,
> And Feather'd People crowd my wealthy Side,
> And naked Youths and painted Chiefs admire
> Our Speech, our Colour, and our Strange Attire!
> Oh stretch thy Reign, fair *Peace*! from Shore to Shore,
> Till Conquest cease, and Slav'ry be no more:

Till the freed *Indians* in their native Groves
Reap their own Fruits, and woo their Sable Loves,
Peru once more a Race of Kings behold,
And other *Mexico's* be roof'd with Gold.

(1:190–92)

Scholars generally agree that the "Feather'd People" and "painted Chiefs" in this passage refer to the Indian Kings (1:191–92 n), the continuing excitement over whose visit coincided with Pope's ongoing revisions of the poem and whose embassy supported by its very presence the Tory policies that led the way to Utrecht. The court diarist Narcissus Luttrell recorded the special visit of the Indian Kings at Windsor on their way home (6:577).

What has been largely overlooked in the above passage is the defamiliarizing impact of Pope's Citizen-of-the-World reversal of the terms of the encounter: he transforms the "Ships of uncouth Form" into Native American ethnological wonder at the bizarre forms of "Our Speech, our Colour, and our Strange Attire!" He reverses the direction of voyages of encounter. Like Horace Walpole's later prognostication of a time when New World "Augustan" empires would rise to replace the Old—"a Virgil in Mexico, and a Newton at Peru" (24:62)—Pope predicts successor realms to the tyrannical rule of Spain: new gilding for the domes of Mexico and a new "Race of Kings" for Peru. This powerful trope recurs in the circum-Atlantic literature and orature of imperial surrogation, whereby the past and present must be reinvented to serve the needs of a hallucinatory future.

Windsor-Forest, then, like the Iroquois Condolence Council, uses the devices of epic memory to elaborate the occasion of its celebration, especially the "roll call" of oral recitation. As the poem reviews dark memories—Norman tyranny, the Wars of Roses, the martyrdom of Charles I—and epic highlights—Edward III claiming the throne of France, Queen Anne rebuilding the churches and palaces of London—it inscribes as literature a festive pattern of orature: the dancelike movement from dysphoria to euphoria. As in the Condolence Council, there is early in the poem much "wiping away of blood and tears" and mourning the ancestral dead. The tyranny and violence of Norman kings, cited in a sixty-line passage about "savage laws," "savage beasts," and the chaos of human predation ("A mighty Hunter, and his Prey was Man"), serve as a pointed contrast to Stuart beneficence (1:152–59). They also give warning that Peace and Plenty may not be taken for granted: "The levell'd Towns with Weeds lie cover'd o'er" (1:156). This imagery of violent devastation returns to the poem in a later passage on the burial of English kings. Edward IV and Henry VI, "th' Oppressor and th' Opprest" (1:179), fateful antagonists in the Wars of Roses, mingle their remains in Windsor now, their juxtaposed graves a monument to a dearly purchased peace. Near the Yorkist and Lancastrian graves, the resting place of Charles I dramatizes the dangerous fragility of that peace: his execution, Pope avows, set in train the Great Plague, the Fire of London, and the continuing threat of bloody civil war—as tangible a menace in 1713 as at any previous date in English history, the throne occupied by an aging, childless queen, the last of her line. Peace and plenty come not unbidden but need tending to—"polishing the Chain" through wise policy at home and abroad.

As in the Native American imagery of the Condolence Councils, where "Free Hunting and great Trade" will ensue from careful maintenance of the protocols of the Great Peace, *Windsor-Forest* extols the recuperation of violence in the "Sylvan" arts of the Pax Britannica after Utrecht:

> The shady Empire shall retain no Trace
> Of War or Blood, but in the Sylvan Chace,
> The Trumpets sleep, while chearful Horns are blown,
> And Arms employ'd on Birds and Beasts alone.
> (1:186–87)

The contrasted choric movements of Pope's poem, its strophic assertion of peace and plenty opposed by an antistrophic reply of displaced violence, in which "gasping Furies thirst for Blood in vain" (1:193), converge in the synthesizing epode of the hunt, where nature's abundance offers up a copious portion of itself as sacrifice.

Pope was not alone at this time in proposing blood sport as the moral substitute for war between factions, nations, or races (1:139). Through its subtle poetry of allusion, however, *Windsor-Forest* links this sacrifice to the violence done when women become the prey of men. Eros, like Diana, deflects dangerous urges to make war onto alternate objects of desire. Pope's Ovidian recounting of the rape of the huntress Lodona by Pan locates this predation at the originary site of the poem's aqueous meanderings, the tributary waters of the Thames in the river Loddon. The bitter tears of the violated girl flow copiously ever after. They gurgle into the "great Father of the *British* Floods" and thence empty into the seas and oceans of the world (1:169 ff). The overlay of pastoral sentiments on the bodies of surrogated victims, however, cannot completely exile "Terror" and "mad Ambition," as Pope's peroration nervously hopes, "from Earth to deepest Hell" (1:192–93). "Unbounded *Thames*" fails to conceal its nourishing source in Lodona's tears. More urgently, Pan, who raped her, is a liminal creature of mixed ancestry, which identity defers the specter of miscegenation to the originary source, threatening *panic* (Bernal). Captive of its own allusive meanings, then, *Windsor-Forest* is a poem of circum-Atlantic memory for what it tries and fails to forget.

The pastoral trope of "freed *Indians* in their native Groves" (1:192), which envisions global emancipation, seemingly erases the facts of the Atlantic system: triumphantly proclaiming the end of slavery, *Windsor-Forest* omits mention of the Asiento clause of the Treaties of Utrecht, which granted Great Britain a thirty-year monopoly on the slave trade to the Spanish West Indies. Moreover, the South Sea Company numbered among its investors Alexander Pope (1:192n). What appears to be a complete erasure of the violence done to Africans, however, is in reality a palimpsest. Like the river Thames, which traces its mysterious hydrological source to the rape of Lodona by Pan, the poem locates its erasures of violence in racial surrogation. When he imagines the Edenic paradise of peace and plenty that will follow the reconstruction of a devastated Mesoamerica under the Pax Britannica, Pope makes what his eighteenth-century verbal critics censured as an error in diction, a slip wholly uncharacteristic of the poet: liberated by Britain from the tyranny of Spain, Pope writes, the Americans will be free to "woo their Sable Loves" (1:192). To the adjective *sable*, meaning a "Colour between Black and Brown," Joseph Warton objected, saying "they are not negroes" (quoted in 1:192n). Like Pope's *Rape of the Lock*, which refers to "*Africk*'s Sable Sons" (*Poems*, 2:171), *Windsor-Forest* is in fact notably meticulous in its description of colors. Pope's use of the word *sable* accurately reflects the ambiguous categories of race among West Indian populations. Like the uncertain derivation of the chaconne that Purcell's Dido sang or the polymorphous family tree of the Afroasiatic Pan, the genealogy of the "Race of Kings" in *Windsor-Forest* belongs not to autochthony but to diaspora. Hence its very multiplicity and profusion—the plenitude of the *concordia discors*—justify Pope's projection of a dynamic "new World" that will now "launch forth to seek the Old" (1:191).

The Empire of the Sun

On March 13, 1710, while the Iroquois Kings were at sea en route from Boston to London, the Queen's Theatre revived John Dryden's *The Indian Emperour; or, The Conquest of Mexico by the Spaniards* (1665). Betterton took the title role as the sacrificial Montezuma (*London Stage*, hereafter *LS*, 204, 215). As a perennially popular sequel to Dryden and Sir Robert Howard's *Indian Queen* (1664), the play treats, in Dryden's own words, a "story [that] is, perhaps the greatest, which was ever represented in a Poem of this nature; (the action of it including the Discovery and Conquest of the New World)" (*Works*, 9:25). *The Indian Emperour* remained in the English repertoire for seventy years, one of the most successful representatives of a genre known as the Restoration heroic play, the inspiration for which Dryden ascribed to the opening lines of Ariosto's *Orlando Furioso* and Davenant's earlier experiments, which included *The Cruelty of the Spaniards in Peru* of 1658 ("Commentary," *Works*, 9:298).

In *The Indian Emperour*, Dryden varies history to suit his dramaturgical needs, principally by attaching a villainous and greedy Pizarro to the expedition of the noble and heroic Cortez. That is one of several interesting bifurcations in the play, including a scene (2.2) in which the ghost of the Indian Queen rises from the underworld in a stage machine, very likely costumed in the feathered headdress from Suriname that Aphra Behn described (Dryden, prologue, 9:29). The ghost of the Indian Queen, bloody dagger still in her breast, appears in order to haunt Montezuma, the lover for whom she killed herself. This Didoesque situation is doubled in the next scene when Cydaria, Montezuma's daughter, who has fallen in love with Cortez, wants to revive his dead lover, whom she physically resembles but of whom she is insanely jealous, so that she may kill her or, failing that, "kill my self for but resembling" her (9:57). Aside from the oft-parodied exaggeration of confused motives in Dryden's heroic plays, his dramaturgy of reprised characters deepens the scheme of surrogation on which he constructed this drama of superabundance, miscegenation, and sacrifice.

Abundance looms threateningly from the outset. While Spain appears in this characteristically English representation as senile, its empire ripe for superannuation, Dryden's curtain-raising version of the New World burgeons with youthful energy, fecundity, and plenitude. On their arrival, Dryden's conquistadors admire the native topography with eyes that marvel in discovery and with language that speaks in reproductive imagery of infancy and new birth:

CORTEZ: On what new happy Climate are we thrown,
So long kept secret, and so lately known;
As if our old world modestly withdrew,
And here, in private, had brought forth a new!

The earl of Rochester made sport of Dryden's inelegant simile of midwifery, but it was apt enough in capturing the superimposition of material abundance on maternity:

VASQUEZ: Methinks we walk in dreams on fairy Land,
Where golden Ore lies mixt with common sand;
Each downfal of a flood the Mountains pour,
From their rich bowels rolls a silver shower. (9:30–31)

Montezuma makes an extravagant gift of Mexican gold to the Spaniards, offering them all they can find, "Save what for sacred uses is design'd" (9:42). This gesture of gift giving links plenitude to the sacred in a way that the ethnographically alert would have been wise to hear as ominous.

Dryden's understanding of the meaning of Aztec ritual drama and its vast scope draws on Montaigne as well as on Spanish sources ("Commentary," 9:308 ff). As Adam Versényi demonstrates in *Theatre in Latin America: Religion, Politics, and Culture from Cortés to the 1980s* (1993), drawing on Diana Taylor's *Theatre of Crisis: Drama and Politics in Latin America* (1991), the communication between the Spanish conquistadors and the Mesoamericans relied on reciprocal stagings and theatrical devices: "representational actors, spectators, a defined stage, and a thematic content carried to conclusion, dialog, music, and dance" (10). In particular, the staging of the rituals of human sacrifice, variously reported during and after the conquest, made a deep impression on Europeans, who noted the spectacular theatrical conventions (Clendinnen, 87–110). Dryden made use of reports of these rituals not only for local color in the background of his play but for the spine of its action, which dramatizes the sacrificial performance of waste in the midst of incalculable abundance.

"The victim," to reiterate Bataille's fundamental insight into the relationship between abundance and sacrifice, "is a surplus taken from the mass of *useful* wealth" (59). Of the performance traditions along the Atlantic rim, Aztec rituals most clearly exemplify the process that *The Accursed Share* describes. Though repelled by the bloody carnage, the Europeans, who were themselves engaging in a genocidal rampage at the time, could not but identify themselves with the perpetrators (Las Casas). The conquest itself has frequently been interpreted as a drama in which Cortés played the part of the vengeful god prophesied by Aztec augury and Montezuma that of his sacrificial victim; in fact, *The Indian Emperour* inverts the roles of the antagonists in a way that replays such a sanguinary scene. First, establishing the importance of the mass offering of captive blood to the Sun, Dryden has the Indian High Priest report:

> The Incense is upon the Altar plac'd,
> The bloody Sacrifice already past.
> Five hundred Captives saw the rising Sun,
> Who lost their light ere half his race was run.
> (9:32)

But shortly thereafter Montezuma addresses Cortez as a god and offers to make further sacrifices to *him* (9:40). The Aztec people worshipped their emperor as a semidivine being, among them but not fully of them, and they addressed him by a most terrifying title: "our lord, our executioner, and our enemy" (Clendinnen, 80). Montezuma's abdication of this role, which Dryden carefully dramatizes, foreshadows rapidly unfolding surrogations.

Chief among these dramatically ironic developments is the forging of the crucial anti-Montezuma alliance between the Spanish and the Native American people that Dryden knew as "Taxallans." Rival nation to the Aztecs in the ritualized "Flower Wars," Tlaxcala was militarily indispensable to the conquest of Mexico, "providing Cortés with his only secure because unambivalent allies" (Clendinnen, 33). Dryden knew better than to accept the remarkably persistent myth that a few hundred determined Spaniards defeated the Aztecs by overawing them with horses and weaponry (Prescott) or semiotics (Todorov). The playwright puts in the mouth of Pizarro the realpolitik of conquering the empire of the sun: "Our men, though Valiant, we should find too few, / But *Indians* joyn the *Indians* to subdue" (9:31). Tlaxcala shared interests and therefore enemies with Spain, as later, at the time of the revival of *The Indian Emperour* in 1710 and thereafter until the American Revolution, the Mohawks shared them with Britain.

Heroic drama also loves a parade. In a play animated by bold, formal gestures, Dryden capitalizes on the pompous cadences of his heroic couplets to underscore the ritualized actions of the Americans, who on their first entrance, staged as a procession with "Train," are instructed by the stage directions to "place themselves" ceremoniously before their High Priest commences the dialogue with a solemn prayer (9:32). Invoking the kinesthetic imagination in this manner initiates the double action of defamiliarization: on one hand, the stylization of movement highlights the strangeness of the Aztecs; on the other, their nobility and decorum link them to the Herculean heroes, Euro-exotics like Cortez or Almanzor, from whom extravagantly honorable conduct was de rigueur in any heroic play (Waith).

Like the Spanish accounts on which it is based, *The Indian Emperour* draws on the horrors of human sacrifice to establish not only the uncanny otherness of the Indians but also their uncanny familiarity. In Aztec culture, warfare itself was a highly ritualized affair aimed at acquiring those prisoners whose sacrifice provided an appropriately lavish gift of human blood to Huitzilopochtli, the god of war and of the sun, and Quetzalcoatl, "The Feathered Serpent God" (Keegan, 106–15). The sacrifices followed a period during which the captive victims enjoyed the opulent pleasures of special adornments, food, music, and concubines. Like the Iroquois, the Aztecs addressed their doomed victims "with kinship terms" and even mourned their deaths. In *The Conquest of America*, Todorov draws attention to the duality of the victim: taken from among outsiders but assimilated by the period of preparation, the surrogate becomes familiar enough to stand in for his hosts but at the same time remains sufficiently strange to stand apart from them (144). Most significantly for a theory of surrogation and performance, the Aztecs identified victims with the gods to whom they were to be sacrificed, and after their hearts had been cut out and their blood caught in drinking bowls, their skin was artfully flayed from their bodies in one piece to be adorned and worn as costumes (figure 4.3). Such a second skin identified the wearer with the god through the memory of the victim (Clendinnen, 96). In *Violence and the Sacred*, René Girard locates the need for the sacrifice of the "monstrous double" in the social investment in stability, a homeopathic diffusion of uncontrolled destruction by ritualized acts of violence (269–73). Girard's insight illuminates the relationship of expenditure, surrogation, and continuity. The monstrous double offers itself up as an effigy, the immolated provider of the new skin in which the god—and perforce the community summoned into being by its memory—may continue to return. In the symbolic utterances of profitless expenditure, as the wearing of the flayed skins of sacrificial victims demonstrates, carnage and costume converge in the "requickening" performance of waste.

The Indian Emperour credits these expenditures to the Aztecs through the evocation of offstage rites and the bloody apparition of the sacrificed queen. They return, however, in the form of Spanish atrocities, the ones actually brought onstage, much to Addison's discomfort (*Spectator*, 1:186–87). Dryden, through his dramatization of the cruelty of Pizarro, places the onus of sacrificial expenditure back on the conquistadors. He

libro. 2. de las cerimonjas.

quitoznequj, amo mictlan iauh: yoan ipampa inquitzoncuja, quj mopialtiaia ynitzon: iehica caic oqujmomaceuj, in mavizcotl, in xuchitl ynietl, intilmatli: ynic amo çan nenpoliuiz itiiacauh io: iuhqujnma ic contlcioaujli aia malli. Auh intlamanj vm pa muchichioa inteuanma, te nochtitla, iztac totolihujtl, ynic mopotonja, injuh omoteneuh ipan quaujtleoa. Auh in vncan momanaia tototecti, tecpantimanj vipantimanj ticapan, anoço caca pan: ipampa caticatl antoca in vn can momanaia. Auh incana alte petl ipan, cacatl motzetzeloa, yni pan qujnoalmana, qujnoalquetza, qujnoalteittitia: tlaixco qujnoalma na inxipeme, ynonmaqujaia tlaca coatl. Auh ynaqujque, mihi vintia, iautlauelilo que, mixtlapa loanj, acan ixmauhque, iollotla paltique, iollochicaoaque, quipopo anj ynjntiiacauhio, moqujchnenc quj, qujmonpepeoaltia, qujmontlac hecalhuja, oiaiaopeoa, qujnmoia iaopeoaltia. Auh inic vel qujntla uelcujtiaia, ynic vel qujmolima ia, ynic vel intlauel, inqualan qujcuja, qujmonxiccuja, qujmo xiccuj, qujmonxiccotona: ic nj man in xipeme tlapaynaltiaia ymjcampa intepuztco icatiuh ce

4.3 *Above*: Aztec ritual flaying. *Below*: wearing the second skin.
Bernardino de Sahagún, Florentine Codex, book 2.
Archivo General de la Nación, México

introduces a scene of torture in which the villain and a "Christian Priest" stretch Montezuma and an Aztec priest on the rack to make them divulge the location of their stores of gold. Since the emperor has set no limit on the gold that the Spanish may acquire, this expenditure seems pointedly profitless. As Montezuma's "Veins break" and "Sinews crack" (9:98), he engages the Christian priest in a debate about the theological meaning of divine kingship and the sacrificial body: "When Monarchs suffer, gods themselves bear part" (9:99). The real drama of the scene, however, exists in the foreknowledge that Montezuma's crucifixion and flaying constitute the ritual whereby destiny prepares him to be replaced:

> Old Prophecies foretel our fall at hand,
> When bearded men in floating Castles Land.
> (9:36)

Before the play ends, Pizarro will remove the royal victim's skin, metaphorically speaking, but Cortez will wear it.

The ominous forecast of surrogation in *The Indian Emperour* plays off the tragicomedy's erotic subplots of promiscuous miscegenation. The stage directions for act 4, scene 3, call for a "pleasant Grotto" provided with a "Fountain spouting," around which are discovered "*Spaniards* lying carelessly un-arm'd, and by them many *Indian* Women" (9:83). The scene provides an occasion for a lyric interlude of songs and a racy dance number, "a Saraband with Castanieta's" (9:84). The miscegenistic program of the Spaniards culminates at the highest level, when Cortez himself, caught between the jealous love of two Indian women, Almeria and the princess Cydaria, pairs up with the latter. The former, now redundant, performs the self-sacrificing courtesy of stabbing herself to death. Even in a tragicomedy, where reprieves are more generously available, miscegenation represents an excess that must induce an expenditure of blood. As was the case in Aphra Behn's *Widow Ranter* and *Oroonoko* and, in a slightly different way, in Pope's *Windsor-Forest*, the anxiety about surrogation in *The Indian Emperour* looks not to the past but to the future. It entertains the threat posed to the purity of origins by the new order of generations.

It seems odd to conceive of Dryden's play as containing material suitable for children to act, but notables of the period did exactly that. In 1731 William Hogarth made a visual record of the prison scene of *The Indian Emperour* (4.4), the scene that follows the miscegenistic orgy, as it was acted in a private theatrical by children in the household of John Conduitt, mas-

4.4 Robert Dodd, after William Hogarth, *The Indian Emperour; or, The Conquest of Mexico*, 1731. Act 4, scene 4.
Northwestern University Library

ter of the mint (figure 4.4). Shown in the audience are members of the royal family, who shortly thereafter ordered a repetition of the production at St. James's Palace (Paulson, 2:1–4). Hogarth's conversation piece records the incisiveness of performance in crystallizing the effects that remain invisible or diffuse to the reader. Cortez, who has been captured by the Aztecs at this point, is in chains. Accompanied by a waiting woman, Cydaria has just entered to find her lover kissing Almeria's hand. She seethes with jealous passion and tearful reproach. The strength of her emotion is suggested by the two handkerchiefs depicted in the scene, one held in her left hand, another, the spare, clutched in the hands of her attendant.

Why children? Hogarth's details, as they so often do in his depiction of theatrical subjects, document an intricate genealogy of performance. In *Hogarth's Blacks: Images of Blacks in Eighteenth Century English Art* (1987), David Dabydeen argues for the complicated effects of doubling and inversion of dark skins and white in Hogarth's representation of excess. The occasion of the Conduitt production does dramatize its conspicuous consumption and leisure. The luxury of the furnishings and appointments, including the quite professional job of scene painting on the wings and backcloth, enhances the opulence of the scene. Theophilus Cibber of Drury Lane was engaged to coach the children, all of whom were about ten years old (Paulson, 2:1). Like the adornment of women, such an expenditure signifies the elevation of aesthetic forms into a realm marked as existing above and beyond utility. In the limits of a domestic space, the amateur theatrical production enunciates a high bourgeois reply to the court spectacles of Europe, which allegorized dynastic legitimacy and world-historical entitlements in canvas and gilt. A distant mirror of the sacrifice-saturated culture it reconstructs and appropriates, the parlor *Indian Emperour* is a secular offertory, a play about golden empires of the sun, staged at the behest of the master of the mint.

Amid the erotic cross-purposes and genocidal preparations, order rules. The children act formally, imitating the large gestures, stern expressions, and heroic poses illustrated by the acting manuals of the period. Like dance notation, these rhetorics served a role as kinesthetic recipe books, disseminating readily restorable behaviors to a wider public. In the Lilliputian *Indian Emperour*, the children's formal gestures seem to enact a struggle to govern adult passions that surely cannot be contained within their diminutive bodies. There is thus a surplus of passion in the scene that cannot be accounted for, not in the sense of being lost, but in the sense of being conspicuously wasted. Flooding the stage with tears and copiously adorned with plumes, the female Indians vie for the attentions of the miniature conquistador. The genealogy of their performance, as Dryden explained, descends from no less august an origin than "the Discovery and Conquest of the New World." But its fundamental signification, played out on the bodies of the children, is to represent the succession of empires and the mixing of races as coefficient threats in a reproductive economy of excess.

Oroonoko and the Empire of the World

On April 21, 1710, three days prior to the Mohawk *Macbeth*, the Theatre Royal, Drury Lane, revived Thomas Southerne's *Oroonoko; or, The Royal Slave* (1694). The management did not advertise the production as one staged "for the Entertainment of the Indian Kings" (*LS*, 219), but for reasons that will become clear, Southerne's adaptation of Aphra Behn's novella powerfully summarizes many of the issues raised by the circum-Atlantic encounters that the Iroquois embassy both symbolized and embodied. *Oroonoko* enjoyed what John Downes liked to call "the life of a Stock-Play" (100), with revivals throughout the eighteenth century, during which it provided ammunition for both sides of the slavery debate. The frequency of its revival in the period from 1700 to 1728, for instance, made it third in popularity among all the tragic dramas in the repertoire, surpassed only by *Hamlet* and *Macbeth* (G. W. Stone, 198).

Like ritual observances among the Aztecs or requickening ceremonies among the Iroquois, the English theater helped British subjects to imagine a community for themselves by making a secular spectacle out of the deeply mysterious play of ethnic identity and difference. Like the scribal transcriptions of the Condolence Councils or the meticulous ethnographic record of Aztec ritual compiled by the Franciscan Bernadino de Sahagún, surviving playscripts from the London stage supply the historian of performance with a detailed record. It is admittedly only a partial record, and few would deny that it is a deeply problematic one, but it contains nonetheless a transcription of most of the words spoken and a few of the gestures delivered on significant public occasions. Related documents sometimes disclose the affects of the performers and the response of the audience. Reading these records today therefore ought to be like eavesdropping at a popular rite of intense but often opaque cultural significance, something on the order of gaining possession of a blow-by-blow account of the Balinese cockfight attended by Clifford Geertz. Historians ought to attend to the "deep play" in the stock plays. What the stock playscripts—*The Indian Emperour* and *Macbeth* as well as *Oroonoko*—disclose at the historic juncture of April 1710, for example, is a preoccupation with the sacrificial expenditure of surrogated doubles.

In his dedicatory epistle to *Oroonoko*, Southerne wonders that a dramatist of Behn's "command of the stage" would "bury her favorite hero in a novel," and he quotes secondhand an opinion to the effect that she often told the story out loud more "feelingly" than she wrote it down (Southerne, 4). Self-serving apologia for the stage aside, Southerne rightly discerns that the story contains material that can emerge fully only by means of performance. Narrated from the point of view of a putative eyewitness, Behn's novella tells the story of an African prince, who, "betray'd into Slavery" and brought in captivity to Suriname, leads a failed revolt against the English authorities (*Oroonoko*, 33). Behn predicates the narrative on the heroic romance between Oroonoko and Imoinda, "the beautiful Black *Venus* to our young *Mars*" (9), the woman he finally kills rather than let her give birth to a child destined for slavery.

The circum-Atlantic background for *Oroonoko* has long been available to literary historians (Sypher), but its implications have recently undergone reexamination and critique (Azim; Ferguson). Charlotte Sussman, in "The Other Problem with Women: Reproduction and Slave Culture in Aphra Behn's *Oroonoko*" (1993), has shown how the conflicting ideologies of population growth in the West Indies—whether to contain or encourage reproduction among the slaves—shaped Behn's narrative at key moments, providing "a crucial point of intersection between the historical context of the slave trade and an ahistorical heroic romance" (215). Laura Brown has demonstrated how Aphra Behn's characterization of Oroonoko encapsulates the historic contradictions of slavery in a narrative that links the fate of the martyred African prince to that of Charles I. Behn thereby incorporates, Brown argues, a scheme of "radical contemporaneity," which, in the terms defined by Johannes Fabian in *Time and the Other*, subverts the chronopolitics of difference by placing Europeans, Africans, and Native Americans in the same framework of epochal memory. Brown also shows how Behn juxtaposes "the figure of the woman, ideological implement of a colonialist culture, with the figure of the slave, economic implement of the same system" (*Ends of Empire*, 62). What I propose to add is a disclosure of how these distinctively circum-Atlantic relationships—reproduction and abundance, surrogation and memory, miscegenation and violence—emerge out of the performance of Behn's narrative through the staging of Southerne's dramatic adaptation.

Southerne makes three additions of great importance to the materials provided by Behn's novella. First, he adds a comic subplot involving the attempts of the Widow Lackit and the sisters Charlotte and Lucy Welldon to find husbands in colonial Suriname. Second, he has Oroonoko succeed in the assassination of the corrupt governor, who lusts after Imoinda, before killing himself. Third, and most significant, he changes Imoinda's color from black to white. The overall effect of these revisions is to make the issue of surrogation the focal point by adding miscegenation to Behn's tragic plot of doomed lovers and to intensify its threat by interpolating scenes of husband hunting among a dwindling field of white men. Southerne emphasizes the slim pickings among the male gentry through the comical interjections of Daniel, the Widow Lackit's idiot son. When the public distribution of slaves by lots leaves the widow without a male African, she complains: "Here have I six slaves in my lot and not a man among 'em, all women and children; what can I do with 'em, Captain?" (Southerne, 23). Teasing her for not being content with her lot, the captain suggests that she "try" Oroonoko: "Have you a mind to try what a man he is? You'll find him no more than a common man at your business" (24). The widow responds violently to this insult, but like Etherege's Loveit or Congreve's Lady Wishfort, her enraged denials cannot convincingly overcome the inertial semiotic forces exerted by her name: no citation of Fanon is required to establish what the "it" is that she "lacks."

Southerne several times reiterates the comparison between the sexual barter of marriage and the institution of slavery. When Charlotte Welldon, disguised as a man, tries to arrange for her sister Lucy's marriage, she has to insist on removing the transaction from the market square: "This is your market for slaves; my sister is a free woman and must not be disposed of in public" (27). What happens in private does little to distinguish the flesh of the "free woman" from that of the enslaved. The Welldon scenes thus prepare dramatically for the introduction of Imoinda, the white slave, into a scene that radically condenses the circum-Atlantic crucible of sex and race into an imagined community of the dispossessed. Imoinda's appearance inspires a rape attempt by the English governor, which is shortly followed by an Indian attack: "Indians or English!" she dithers, in the ambivalent manner of a New England captivity narrative, "Whoever has me, I am still a slave" (54).

In one sense, Southerne's blanching of Imoinda merely continues a pronounced tendency on the part of the Africans in this story to turn white, a metamorphosis that is stunningly accomplished by Oroonoko's homily on slaves, including himself, as private property under English law, which he believes at this point must be respected. Exculpating his masters, the Royal Slave opines:

> If we are slaves, they did not make us slaves,
> But bought us in an honest way of trade . . .
> They paid our price for us and we are now
> Their property, a part of their estate,
> To manage as they please.
>
> (64)

The relentless assimilation of African identity into European ideology is forecast by Behn's overdetermined characterization of Oroonoko. Not only was he schooled by a French tutor in the courtly manners of Europe, but his sensitive royal blood shudders at the tale of the barbaric execution of King Charles I of England. Commensurate with his sovereign demeanor, he accepts the local pseudonym of "Caesar." Behn takes care to assure the reader that Caesar's physiognomy matches his sensibility: "His Nose was rising and *Roman*, instead of *African* and flat. His Mouth the finest shaped that could be seen; far from those great turn'd Lips, which are so natural to the rest of the Negroes." Although his regal qualities, physical and mental, rival or excell those of the most "civiliz'd" of princes (Behn, *Oroonoko*, 8), Behn's narrator adds a frequently overlooked but very significant amendment to her description of his physique:

> I had forgot to tell you, that those who are nobly born of that Country, are so delicately cut and raised all over the Fore-part of the Trunk of their Bodies, that it looks as if it were japan'd, the Works being raised like high Point round the edges of the Flowers. Some are only carved with a little Flower, or Bird, at the sides of the Temples, as was *Caesar*; and those who are so carved over the Body, resemble our antient *Picts* that are figur'd in the Chronicles, but these Carvings are more delicate. (Behn, *Oroonoko*, 45)

Behn's ethnographic use of the African practice of scarification marks Oroonoko's body in several ways. First, it adds to the fact of his color, which was "perfect Ebony, or polished Jett" (Behn, *Oroonoko*, 8), an ineffaceable insignia of origin, like the brand name on a grand piano. Second, like feathers and other less permanent adornments, the ornamental scars serve as a physical incorporation of excess expenditure, a luxurious emblem of distinction, which suggests to Behn's narrator japanning, a style of raised marquetry on expensive, imported furniture. Third, the narrator's evocation of the scarified Picts, though qualified, works against the radical contemporaneity of Oroonoko's characterization by linking the customs of his people to those of the most notoriously savage inhabitants of prehistoric and Roman Britain. Southerne said of Behn's decision not to risk Oroonoko on the stage, "She thought either no actor could represent him, or she could not bear him represented" (4). Given the contradictions of her requirements for this prodigious effigy, her surrogated double of Charles I—African yet European, scarified yet smooth as classical "Statuary" (Behn, *Oroonoko*, 8), slave yet royal sovereign—her reluctance to sacrifice him to the representational machinery of the stage is understandable.

Where angels feared to tread, Southerne rushed in Jack Verbruggen. Interpreted carefully, casting choices sometimes offer a revealing glimpse behind the scenes into the orature of stage production. The assignment of roles can mediate decisively between inscription and expression, and playwrights at this time enjoyed varying degrees of influence over the process (Holland). Anticipating the desires of the theatergoing public, Southerne's choice for the title role was a significant exercise of his authorial function. One of the young actors who remained behind after Betterton and other veterans left the Drury Lane company in 1695, John Verbruggen emerged as a leading man in Betterton's absence, a succession that made comparisons to the departed star inevitable (Cibber, 1:108, 157). On the advice of the duke of Devonshire, the dedicatee of the printed version of *Oroonoko*, Southerne asked that Verbruggen, despite his relative inexperience, create this most difficult of roles, which might otherwise have been designated for a more senior actor (Southerne, 4).

Out of Verbruggen's success as Oroonoko, Anthony Aston constructed for him the reputation by which theater historians have for the most part uncritically remembered his acting: an "unpolish'd Hero" in whose spontaneous performances "Nature" predominated over "Art." Aston continues: "You may best conceive his manly, wild Starts, by these Words in *Oroonoko,—Ha! thou hast rous'd the Lyon [in] his Den; he stalks abroad, and the wild Forest trembles at his Roar*:—Which was spoke, like a Lyon, by *Oroonoko*, and *Jack Verbruggen*; for Nature was so predominant, that his second Thoughts never alter'd his prime Performance" (311). Aston's description exemplifies the utility of the kinesthetic imagination in creating the fiction of race. His collapsing of the African character into the public identity of an English actor (and of both into the king of beasts), aside from its conventionally racist formulation of the instinctive behavior of the noble savage, elides blackface and whiteface roles. Aston was not alone in this elision, which evokes the characteristic duality of strength and vulnerability in a theatrical effigy. When Verbruggen was compelled to humiliate himself by making an obsequious public apology before one of Charles II's bastards, whom he had called, not implausibly, the son of a whore, he did so from the stage, dressed and blacked up for the part of Oroonoko (Davies, 3:447).

Vulnerability succeeds. Aston recorded the poignant affect of Verbruggen's reading of the line in which Oroonoko first contemplates murdering Imoinda to save her and their unborn child from a fate worse than death: "He was most indulgently soft, when he says to *Imoinda,—I cannot, as I wou'd bestow thee; and, as I ought, I dare not*" (312). According to all the printed versions of the play (Southerne, 117), the words Oroonoko speaks here are in fact "dispose of thee," not "bestow thee," as Aston recalled. The doomed hero is responding to Imoinda's pathetic query, "Which way would you dispose of me?" (116). Aston's emendation, however, is not so wide of the mark. Its subtle slippage shows what a close reading of the transcripts of play texts in performance can reveal: both *bestow* and *dispose* fit within the context of sacrificial expenditure, in that the former suggests gift giving, the latter a final settlement. Once Imoinda has introduced the word *disposed* into their West Indian *liebestod*, Oroonoko seizes upon it:

> Yet this I know of fate, this is most certain:
> I cannot as I would dispose of thee;
> And as I ought I dare not. O Imoinda!
>
> (117)

To dispose of something generally means to liquidate a surplus, as in the concept of disposable income. As the Royal Slave puts it, "My heart runs over" (117). Southerne carefully prepares for this moment, raising the tensions of ritual expectancy, by earlier expositional speeches in which Imoinda begs to be killed in order to terminate her pregnancy, a "fountain" of "flowing miseries" that "swells so fast to overwhelm us all" (65). Oroonoko's reply takes up her theme of disposing of a sacred but expendable excess, the accursed share:

> Shall the dear babe, the eldest of my hopes,
> Whom I begot a prince be born a slave?
> The treasure of this temple was designed
> T'enrich a kingdom's fortune. Shall it here
> Be seized upon by vile unhallowed hands
> To be employed in uses most profane?
>
> (66)

Bataille's account of the Aztec victim made holy by being torn from the mundane world and expended illuminates this distinctively circum-Atlantic moment on the London stage. The child is a "treasure" saved by sacrifice from "unhallowed hands" and "profane" uses. Its fate is sealed by a crisis of violence and legitimacy: "like a naked new-born babe, / Striding the blast, or heaven's cherubim" (*Macbeth* 1.7.21–22). Like Macbeth, whose character in Davenant's version was served up to the Iroquois Kings later that same week, Oroonoko worries the issue of dynastic succession. From their different vantage points, both tragic heroes ponder the paradox of surrogation: to be replaced by others is a threat, but it is also a need.

In their climactic stichomythic exchanges, Oroonoko and Imoinda prepare for the consummation of their sacrifice by offering themselves to the sun, the "great god / That rises on the world" (118). Oroonoko's prolonged hesitation, which Verbruggen made "indulgently soft," is illustrated in the 1735 edition of the play, which shows a blacked-up hero turning away from his pale but most willing victim, whose pregnancy seems to be represented by the generous drape of her gown (figure 4.5). Here the circum-Atlantic emphasis of Southerne's transformation of Behn's "Black *Venus*" into a sentimental white heroine declares itself in a remarkable speech that imputes totalizing desire to miscegenation:

> O! That we could incorporate, be one,
> One body, as we have been long one mind.
> That blended so, we might together mix,
> And losing thus our beings to the world,
> Be only found to one another's joys.
>
> (120)

This is precisely the conclusion that cannot be allowed, however recurrently it may have been imagined. In a scene of violence filled with verbal and visual echoes of *Othello*, Oroonoko *disposes* of Imoinda, their unborn child, the villainous governor, and finally himself. In the ironic contradictions of interracial desire and hatred, it is the English governor who has previously spoken the epitaph of his rival Oroonoko, whose courage "In a more noble cause would well deserve / The empire of the world" (91). It is fully representative of such symbolic condensations of the circum-Atlantic performance of waste that Oroonoko's "more noble cause" has included the violent extirpation of the local Carib Indians on the governor's behalf (2.3). In both Behn's *Oroonoko* and *The Widow Ranter*, the potential liaison of African and Native American peoples operates as an invisible or only partially visible threat to Eurocolonial domination. This liaison appears in representation only to disappear, as it does in Southerne's *Oroonoko*, so that the hero has a nonwhite adversary to rout. It also fades from Alexander Pope's memory of the Treaties of Utrecht. But Oroonoko's plan to establish a Maroon community on the edges of colonial Suriname, in which the rebellious slaves will "live Free" in their "native innocence" (Southerne, 71),

4.5 Frontispiece to *Oroonoko*, by Thomas Southerne, 1735 edition.
Northwestern University Library

evokes the alliances between African and Native American cultures that flourished at various points around the Caribbean, from Suriname to Louisiana. It also provides a powerful reminder of the fact that the conquest of a new "empire of the world," as Britain was then imagining, like the conquest of the empire of the sun, as Spain and Tlaxcala had once accomplished, required, above all other necessities, strategic alliances with the locals.

The Mohawk *Macbeth*

The way in which Queen Anne and her ministers received the four American Kings shows British willingness to adopt the protocols of Forest Diplomacy, which they had learned from a new generation of skilled translators, colonials who had lived among the Iroquois and who understood their language and culture. In that regard, it is important to keep in mind two things. First, every detail of the Mohawks' visit, which included appearances at court, at Woolwich Arsenal for a military review, at the Society for the Propagation of the Gospel in Foreign Parts, at a cockfight, at an Italian opera, and at the Board of Trade, constituted an item on a diplomatic agenda. Second, the scope of the public visibility and success of their embassy was unprecedented, though the Kings were not alone among recent visitors in attending the London theater to see and be seen. In 1702 *The Emperour of the Moon* played "for the entertainment of an African Prince, Nephew to the King of Banjay." In 1703 it was repeated for "the entertainment of His Excellency Hodgha Bowhoon, Envoy to Her Majesty from the Great King of Persia." In 1708 *Othello* played "for the entertainment of the Ambassador of the Emperour of Morocco" (*LS*, 29, 34, 178). No other visitation, however, seems to have created the sensation that the Four Kings' did, and in no other negotiation was the theatrical offering so pointedly chosen to dramatize the significance of the event, though one would certainly like to know more about the Moroccan ambassador's impressions of Betterton's *Othello*. As befits a predominantly oral culture, the Iroquois embassy was greeted in London by performances in which the celebrants acted out in song and dance the ancestral history of the negotiating parties. The Iroquois knew, and the sophisticated Anglo-colonial negotiators accepted, that performance can articulate what otherwise may not be properly communicated. One of the formulaic moments of Iroquois treaty protocol was the lead-in phrase, "Let me drive it into your mind with a song," followed by a musical number (Fenton, 29). The orature of the London theater in 1710 could powerfully emulate this feature of Forest Diplomacy.

Davenant's musical *Macbeth* resonated with a sense of its own allegorical role in living memory. As a suspenseful roll call of Stuart genealogy, which, "being drest in all it's Finery, as new Cloath's, new Scenes, Machines, as flyings for the Witches; with all the Singing and Dancing in it" (Downes, 71), Davenant's adaptation evoked at its premiere the usurpation and murder of Charles I and the recent restoration of his progeny (Spencer, 2–3). The extravaganza was again revived with new music and new scenes following the Act of Union between England and Scotland in 1707 (*LS*, 159). It then served as a timely celebration of continuity and change between the reigns of James I, the first of the Stuart monarchs, and Anne, the last of them, on the occasion of the landmark political event of her reign: the establishment of the United Kingdom. As if to illustrate Robert Weimann's argument that Shakespearean drama has no fixed meanings but many uses (65–81), Davenant's operatic *Macbeth* was revived again at the Queen's Theatre, Haymarket, on April 24, 1710, expressly "For the Entertainment of the Four *INDIAN KINGS* lately arriv'd" (*LS*, 220).

This performance provided a climactic scene of public welcome for the embassy, second only to their appearance at court. Arriving to attend the spectacle, the Kings had already become a spectacle themselves. They were escorted to *Macbeth* by a "Mob" of Tory sympathizers who saw in them a vindication of their religious values—the Kings, as Praying Mohawks, fell under the aegis the High Church Society for the Propagation of the Gospel in Foreign Parts—and grand strategy—the Anglo-Mohawk alliance offered an alternative to the long casualty lists at Malplaquet. What E. P. Thompson has called the "moral economy" of the English crowd operated here in the wake of the "Sacheverell Riots" of March 1–2, 1710. This insurrection took place when a "popular Tory mob" (Holmes), demonstrating on behalf of a High Church clergyman and against the Whig government's conduct of war and its policy of religious tolerance, ritually desecrated and demolished the largest dissenting chapels in London. In a year of political turmoil, the novelty of the Mohawk-Mahican brotherhood left other imitative affiliations swirling in its wake as it passed through the turbulent crowds. Of the progress of the four Indian Kings through the London streets, Mr. Spectator reports that it was followed everywhere by "the Rabble" (1:211). The "Mob," according to an account in John Genest's history of the stage, took a vociferous, proprietary interest in "the Swarthy Monarchs" (2:451). Two years later, after the sweeping Tory victory in the parliamentary elections of November 1710 and the preliminary implementation of the allied invasion of Canada, letters to *The Spectator* would complain of gangs of young toughs calling themselves "Mohocks" terrorizing the streets of London under the leadership of an "Emperour" (3:187–88). Jonathan Swift was sure that they were Whiggish thugs, and John Gay wrote a play about them, which remained unproduced, perhaps because the subject was politically unpalatable for the patent theaters (Winton, 11–25). The actual existence of the "Mohock Club" is uncertain, but the very fact of its discursive life as a imaginary instrument of violence and political reprisal demonstrates that the Iroquois alliance had a symbolic impact that reached beyond diplomatic circles into the popular imagination of the "Free-born." The boundaries of national consciousness are invented to include and exclude, as any boundaries must, but they are also subject to complex negotiation and adjustment in the presence of others: they advance to meet external and alien cultures on the cusp of empire, and they contract to define internal affiliations of party, religion, and class.

The "Rabble" had a great deal to say about the staging of the Kings' visit to the theater. Built in 1705 by the architect Sir John Vanbrugh, who would shortly propose segregated Cities of the Dead to replace interments in London churches, the Queen's Theatre, Haymarket, was in itself a behavioral vortex. Like the appointments of the other London theaters, but even more so, the architectural design of the Queen's Theatre, home of the Italian opera in London, accommodated and implicitly reinforced the social demarcation of the audience. Before the production of *Macbeth* could begin, Robert Wilks, the actor-manager, had to mollify a curious crowd in the cheap gallery seats. They wanted a better view of the Iroquois, who, through no fault of their own, upstaged the English actors. Genest's history of the stage offers what it takes to be an eyewitness account:

> The curtain was drawn, but in vain did the players attempt to perform—the Mob, who had possession of the upper gallery, declared that they came to see the Kings, "and since we have paid our money, the Kings we will have"—whereupon Wilks came forth, and assured them the Kings were in the front box—to this the Mob replied, they could not see them, and desired they might by placed in a more conspicuous point of view—"otherwise there shall be no play"—Wilks assured them he had nothing so much at heart as their happiness, and

> accordingly got four chairs, and placed the Kings on the stage, to the no small satisfaction of the Mob. (Genest 2:451)

The Kings were initially honored with a desirable front box, though not the royal box. It was then common practice, however, to have dignitaries and would-be dignitaries seated onstage during the performance: it was an honor to be invited but an extra expense for the social climber who wanted to be seen in the act of seeing a play. Like royalty, the stage spectators acted the roles of an ideal or surrogate audience. The public wanted to enjoy their enjoyment, seeking in their responses a reaffirmation or perhaps a correction of their own. This is what the "Mob" demanded, and this is what the "Kings" graciously provided.

There is persuasive evidence that the Kings outfitted themselves especially for the occasion to establish in the public eye their native authenticity, their legitimacy as sovereign representatives, through symbolism the English public could understand. They performed their roles quite theatrically—literally so in that they borrowed their outfits from the playhouse wardrobe—yet they also performed, it would seem, within the formal traditions of diplomatic condolence in the North American manner. As John Oldmixon recounts in *The British Empire in America* (1741): "On the Arrival of these Kings, the Queen was advised to make the most of shewing them; and the Dressers at the Play-house were consulted about the clothing of these Monarchs, and it was determined that part of their Dress should be a Royal Mantle. The Court was then in Mourning, and they were clothed with black Breeches, Waistcoat, Stockings, and Shoes, after the *English* Fashion, and a Scarlet in grain Cloth Mantle, edg'd with Gold, overall. They had Audience of the Queen with more than ordinary Solemnity" (1:247). Queen Anne and her court were still mourning the death of the royal consort, Prince George of Denmark. Narcissus Luttrell reports how the grief-stricken queen buried George with obsequies modeled on those accorded Charles II: his interment, like Betterton's also, was at night by torchlight in Westminster Abbey (6:366–67).

Experts in the condolence of loss on the occasion of intersocietal negotiation, the Iroquoian ambassadors seem to have played their parts in the drama consummately. The results of their raid on the collection of stock costumes are reproduced on the playbill for Powell's puppet theater (figure 4.6). The Kings (labeled A, B, C, and D on the playbill) were incorporated into the puppet theater's rendition of the duke of Marlborough's most recent victory over the French. That the Indians were in fact mere puppets

4.6 The four Indian Kings. Handbill for Powell's Puppets (detail), dated May 1, 1710.
Northwestern University Library

in eyes of some of the English cannot be doubted, but their representation here as generic royals, somewhat reminiscent of the adoring Magi—with multiracial features, pasteboard scimitars, and school-play crowns—might also indicate their self-promoting integration within a symbolic economy of intercultural effigies that accommodated their adoptive titles. Amid the strange eclecticism of the other costumes and properties, the feathers placed beside the Kings' ears stand out as a distinctively Mohawk adornment, a piece of Americana cast up in London out of the turbulence of the circum-Atlantic vortex. What Oldmixon describes as the "more than ordinary Solemnity" of their audience with the British empress, then, could refer equally well to English court protocols or the venerable customs instigated by Deganawidah at the time of the Great Peace. Most likely it refers to both, reciprocally intertwined, as in the exchange of gifts.

An epilogue written for the occasion of the Kings' visit to the Queen's Theatre, spoken by William Bowen, whose benefit night this was, thanks them for swelling the audience to a house-filling crowd "that even Avarice might please." In expressing Bowen's gratitude, the epilogue marks the auspicious nature of the occasion in relation to the purpose of the embassy:

> May Fortune in Return, your Labours Crown,
> With Honour, Safety, Riches, and Renown.
> And that Success attend you Arms in Fight,
> Which he has by your Means obtain'd this Night.
> (Danchin, 471)

The epilogue also plays host by introducing the Kings to the segregated classes of English men and women in attendance, who were seated by category in socially marked sections of the playhouse: the ladies, occupying the circle of boxes, shine like "Stars," which would not have come out that night without the lure of the "Planets," meaning the Kings; the "*Beaux*," or fashionable young men about town, who will be induced to stay seated in the side boxes only by the novelty value of their Iroquoian majesties; finally, "the Citizens and their Wives," the former bringing along the latter for fear of "Cuckholdom at Home" (Danchin, 471). Unanticipated, or at least unremarked, is the "Mob" in the cheaper gallery seats. Observant visitors from America, whose matrilineal kinship networks produced three cooperating, nonstratified clans—the Bears, the Wolves, and the Turtles—could learn a great deal about their hosts from the ambiguously enforced but publicly reiterated hierarchy—the pit, the box, and the gallery—of the English playhouse. The Queen's Theatre had the Royal Arms emblazoned on the proscenium, under which the crowd insisted the Indians be seated while they heard their praises sung as proxy Kings fighting Queen Anne's war.

The theme of the epilogue spoken by Bowen anticipates the lines of Pope's *Windsor-Forest* that projected the rebuilt Whitehall Palace as a future global imperial seat: "There Kings shall sue, and suppliant States be seen" (1:188). Pope echoes the Prophet Isaiah (60:3): "And the Gentiles shall come to thy light, and kings to the brightness of thy rising" (1:188n). The extended allusion of the epilogue to *Macbeth* was likewise biblical, and, appropriately enough, it cited the first book of Kings:

> As *Sheba*'s Queen with Adoration came,
> To pay Her Homage to a greater Name,
> And struck with Wonder at the Monarch's Sight,
> Thought the whole Globe, of Earth that Prince's Right.
> Since Fame had fall'n much short in it's Report,

Of so renown'd a King, and so enrich'd a Court.
So now Great *Anna*'s most Auspicious Reign,
Not only makes one Soveraign cross the Main;
One Prince from Lands remote a Visit pay,
And come, and see, and wonder, and obey:
But wing'd by Her Example urges Four,
To seek Protection on *Britannia*'s Shore.
O Princes who have with Amazement seen
So Good, so Gracious and so Great a QUEEN;
Who from Her Royal Mouth have heard your Doom,
Secur'd against the Threats of *France* and *Rome*;
A while some Moments on our Scenes bestow,
Scenes that their being to Her Favours owe.
(Danchin, 470–71)

The epilogue thus reverses the roles of the biblical text (1 Kings 10:1–13), in which the queen of Sheba brings an embassy to the court of the kings of Israel and departs in awe at its greatness and Solomon's wisdom.

In both the biblical and the modern visit, however, gift exchange facilitated the negotiations. Responding to his royal guest's gift of a camel train of spices, gold, and precious stones, "king Solomon gave unto the queen of Sheba all her desire, whatsoever she asked" (1 Kings 10:13). As Marcel Mauss points out in his classic essay, and as the Queen's Theatre epilogue pointedly demonstrates through its choice of biblical text, "the Gift" is never disinterested. It is a performance of generosity that affirms reciprocal obligation by initiating a "system of *total prestations*" that binds the parties together contractually:

> In the systems of the past we do not find simple exchange of goods, wealth and produce through markets established among individuals. For it is groups, and not individuals, which carry on exchange, make contracts, and are bound by obligations; the persons represented in the contracts are moral persons—clans, tribes, and families; the groups, or the chiefs as intermediaries for the groups, confront and oppose each other. Further what they exchange is not exclusively goods and wealth, real and personal property, and things of economic value. They exchange rather courtesies, entertainments, ritual, military assistance, women, children, dances, and feasts; and fairs in which the market is but one part of a wide and enduring contract. (3)

Here Mauss describes a pointed cultural performance, cognate with and sometimes expressed through potlatch, in which the parties attempt to outdo one another in sacrificial expenditure. Like the queen of Sheba during her visit to Solomon, the Mohawks came to Queen Anne bearing gifts: wampum belts, porcupine-quill headbands, and a "purification stick," probably a mnemonic "cane" on which the succession of the Founders was carved. In return the Kings departed carrying Queen Anne's bounty of bolts of cloth, mirrors, brass kettles, scissors, razors, a "magic lanthorn," swords, pistols, muskets, four hundred pounds of gunpowder, and an agreement in principle to invade Canada (Bond, 12–13). The performance of "polishing the Chain," however, required more than the presentation of valuable items; it also required the exchange of what Mauss calls "courtesies, entertainments, ritual . . . dances." When the Kings appeared at court, the most dramatic moment of their "Speech to Her Majesty" came with the ritual presentation of "*BELTS* of *WAMPUM*" to record and solemnify the council (Bond, 94). By means of such restored behaviors, which gave form to events at which a certain amount of improvisation was necessarily required, the interdependent dramas of surrogation and sacrificial expenditure could be staged. Their staging featured the performance of memory, turning on the vacancies created by death, sometimes violent death, condoled by the rejuvenating imperative of legitimate succession.

Within the "system of *total prestations*," *Macbeth* was an apposite choice. Congreve's comedy *The Old Batchelor* had been advertised for the entertainment of the Kings on April 24, and Richmond P. Bond speculates that Betterton's final illness prompted the substitution of *Macbeth*, in which Wilks had taken over the title role (3). Bond's explanation certainly fits the facts of the occasion—Betterton died four days later—but it underestimates the sophistication of intersocietal calculation invested in the success of a performance such as a Condolence Council. In the promulgation of canonical memory, as Betterton's career as an effigy attests, Shakespeare numbered first in veneration among the spirits who spoke to the living from the tribal pantheon of the English dead. It would be unpromising to try to reconstruct the Kings' possible responses to an English comedy of manners by extrapolating from what is known about eighteenth-century Native American humor, but there is no reason to suppose that they would find Congreve any more accessible than American audiences generally do today. Shakespeare, however, casts a wider net, and it is far less difficult to grasp the symbolic and narrative immediacy for the Iroquois of the events depicted in *Macbeth*. These events represent the successful invasion of a northern wilderness country by heroic yet benevolent English forces in alliance with progressive local tribes. They culminate with the usurpation of the tyrant Macbeth and the proclamation of peace founded on dynastic legitimacy and the rule of law.

The scenes of the Davenant version unfold in what must have seemed a pointed similarity to an Iroquois Condolence Council, enacting a movement, as in Pope's *Windsor-Forest*, from dysphoria to euphoria. "Royall Master Duncan," the dead chief, like Charles I, is mourned. There is a preoccupation with the wiping away of blood and tears. The new chief, Malcolm, like Charles II, returns from exile to his rightful throne and is given his charge, to reign with "One Mind," by Macduff, "showing the face of the new Chief":

> So may kind Fortune Crown your Raign with Peace
> As it has Crown'd your Armies with Success.
> (Davenant, 60)

Finally, Fleance, the fatherless child and Stuart progenitor, like Deganawidah, defeating witchcraft and factionalism, returns to join the final scene of general rejoicing and peace. Shakespeare did not provide a final entrance for Fleance, son of Banquo and the ancestral link to the Stuart clan, but evidently Davenant, like Pope, could not pass up such an opportunity to reiterate the meaning of this dynastic triumph over the forces of darkness.

Like *Dido and Aeneas* in its seriocomic depiction of evil, *Macbeth* draws on supernatural phenomena, an animistic magic that the flight through the air of the Three Witches (played by cross-dressed men in a flying machine) emphasized visually in Davenant's adaptation. Here the spirit world infiltrated the magic of the modern state. The English themselves did not have settled views on such matters—Queen Anne still cured "The King's Evil" with the laying-on of hands, and the last public witch burning in England was in 1712, and in 1722 in Scotland. With regard to Anglo-Mohawk intercultural understanding, death and the hereafter, as they so often do, provided an occasion for the clarification of identity and difference. Enlightened Joseph Addison offered a skeptical but sympathetic introduction to relevant Iroquoian beliefs in the second of two *Spectator* numbers he devoted to the visit of the Kings:

> The *Americans* believe that all Creatures have Souls, not only Men and Women, but Brutes, Vegetables, nay even the most inanimate things,

> as Stocks and Stones. They believe the same of all the Works of Art, as of Knives, Boats, Looking-glasses; and that as any of these things perish, their Souls go into another World, which is inhabited by the Ghosts of Men and Women. For this Reason they always place by the Corpse of their dead Friend a Bow and Arrows, that he may make use of the Souls of them in the other World, as he did of their wooden Bodies in this. How absurd soever such an Opinion as this may appear, our *European* Philosophers have maintain'd several Notions altogether as improbable. (1:236–37)

The fair degree of sensitivity in this comparative ethnography mirrors the earlier *Spectator* number in which Addison presents what Mr. Spectator describes as a report on the Iroquois Kings' response to the wonders of English culture. That essay is an early instance of the Citizen-of-the-World device, which Pope briefly adopts in *Windsor-Forest*, in which the innocent observations of alien visitors defamiliarize the values of their hosts. In Mr. Spectator's version of their touristic impressions of London, the Indians wonder at the inexplicable blood feud between two ravening monsters, one called "Whig" and the other "Tory." They remark on the vast emptiness of St. Paul's Cathedral, which they assume to have been painstakingly carved out of a single block of white stone and from which they conclude that religion, once very important to the English, has now been forsaken by most of them. They become fascinated by sedan chairs, men's wigs—"Instead of those beautiful Feathers with which we adorn our Heads"—and women's cosmetic patches, which they identify as symptoms of a most mysterious disease—"when they disappear in one Part of the Face, they are very apt to break out in another" (1:211–15). In comparison to such bizarre practices, the Shakespeare-Davenant *Macbeth* demonstrates the feasibility of cross-cultural communication on the basis of mutually intelligible beliefs about the afterlife. The play's strange images of death dramatize the active presence of a spirit world, interpenetrating and acting on the physical one, creating a dual community out of the ghostly correspondence between the living and the dead.

Nicholas Rowe's 1709 edition of Shakespeare illustrates the cauldron scene of *Macbeth*, in the midst of which, on one side or another, the Iroquois would have been seated (figure 4.7). The costume is "modern dress," contemporary to the eighteenth-century audience (not to the hoary events of the play), further pointing the currency of the action. Malcolm and the English captains, for example, wore the scarlet coats and ivory waistcoats of

British line officers, laying siege to the forested castle of Dunsinane (Montreal?) and leading the confederated Anglo-native armies to decisive victory. The three conjuring witches show Macbeth the line of kings—a "roll call of the Founders"—leading to the Stuarts. Consistent with Davenant's stage direction "A Shadow of eight Kings, and Banquo's Ghost after them pass by" (43), the last king holds a mirror to reflect the dynastic future. Macbeth poses the burning question of surrogation as he sees the lineage of the Stuart clan materialize before his eyes, its legitimacy reflected in the order of its identical succession, its destiny maddeningly written in Banquo's smile:

> Thy Crown offends my sight. A second too like the first.
> A third resembles him: a fourth too like the former:
> Ye filthy Hags will they succeed
> Each other still till Dooms-day?
> Another yet? a seventh? I'll see no more:
> And yet the eighth appears;
> Ha! the bloudy Banquo smiles upon me,
> And by his smiling on me, seems to say
> That they are all Successors of his Race.
>
> (Davenant, 43–44)

Semiopera also loves a parade. The grotto scene from Rowe's *Shakespear* here depicted must be reconstructed with the four Indian Kings as represented by Powell's puppets—A, B, C, and D—seated onstage (cf. figures 4.6 and 4.7): they were playing a part in the scene, mirroring the procession of British kings and thus offering to the public eye a symbolic reiteration, an intercultural doubling, of the legitimacy and the inevitability of the "empire of the world" as reflected in the cultural mirror of its allied peoples.

In one sense, the future implied by these intersecting parades of effigies is that of a world linked through surrogations and proxy kingships—a Covenant Chain. In another sense, however, the juxtaposition of royal genealogies recalls a more dysphoric maxim: uneasy lies the head that wears a crown. Macbeth's fears about Banquo's usurpation by means of progeny—"That they are all Successors of his Race"—articulates the contradiction of aspiration and anxiety that often tortured even the festive occasions of circum-Atlantic contact. Based on its recurrence in Iroquois requickening ceremonies, as well as in *Windsor-Forest*, *The Indian Emperour*, *Oroonoko*, the Mohawk *Macbeth*, and many other events and represen-

4.7 *Macbeth*. From Nicholas Rowe's *Shakespear* (1709), vol. 5.
Howard-Tilton Memorial Library, Tulane University

tations, historians must reckon with the consequences of the threat posed by this contradiction. Whenever the sweet desire to assimilate or to be assimilated curdles into the fear of being replaced, the moment is propitious for the performance of waste.

Epode: Albion's Golden Days

For all the vivid color of Alexander Pope's circum-Atlantic scene painting, there is, as has been noted, a powerfully suppressed presence revealed by the ecstatic phrase in *Windsor-Forest*, "Slav'ry be no more." Also noted are the ways in which Pope's amnesia is structural, a pattern of erasure that links many representations across the Atlantic interculture. Feathers and children recur as signs of this absence, the deferred memory of the American holocaust. Depicting the luxuries of an elaborately staged domestic scene, Justus Engelhardt Kühn's *Portrait of Henry Darnall III as a Child*, painted in Annapolis, Maryland, in 1710, embodies the pervasiveness of the central fact of African slavery in the circum-Atlantic world, here represented by the silver-collared boyservant who faithfully retrieves his young master's yellow-feathered kill (figure 4.8). In the formality of their play, these children of different worlds within the same world juxtapose past and future as well as black and white. Native Americans do not populate the scene except through the metonym of the bow and perhaps that of the dead bird. Conversely, Africans have only a ghostly place in Pope's vision of the Pax Britannica, mocking his abolitionist prediction, yet pressing in on the meaning of the poem through the very fact of their unexplained disappearance.

In New York City in 1712, a combined force of African and Native American insurrectionaries (the dreaded red-black ligature of *marronnage*) burned down a warehouse and killed ten "Christians" before the combined Manhattan and Westchester militias restored order. The rebels had bound themselves to secrecy with a blood oath and had covered their bodies with a magical ointment, prescribed by an African shaman, that they thought would render them invulnerable. Most committed suicide rather than surrender, but the remainder were captured and sentenced to die by various methods—one was to be "burned with a slow fire that he may continue in torment for eight or ten hours and continue burning in the said fire until he be dead and consumed to ashes." On June 23, 1712, as *Windsor-Forest* was beginning to take its final poetical form, Governor Robert Hunter wrote to the Lords of Trade in London and described the executions of twenty-one

4.8 Justus Engelhardt Kühn, *Portrait of Henry Darnall III as a Child*, Annapolis, Maryland, 1710.
Maryland Historical Society, Baltimore

rebels: "Some were burnt, others hanged, one broken on the wheel, and one hung alive in chains in the town, so that there has been the most exemplary punishment inflicted that could be possibly thought of" (quoted in Hofstadter and Wallace, 187–89). Although Governor Hunter justified this spectacle of the scaffold on grounds of utility, the imagination that his administration devoted to the particulars brings it under the aegis of the performance of waste.

Performing the ineffaceable memories within circum-Atlantic amnesia, the violence of *Windsor-Forest* erupts in the vivid imagery of predation as a kind of sacrifice. Pope finds these bloody rites enacted on the lives of birds, which cannot but evoke the "Feather'd People" who populate the expansion of Windsor Forest, as the waters of Thames circulate through the circum-Atlantic vastness:

> See! from the Brake the whirring Pheasant springs,
> And mounts exulting on triumphant Wings;
> Short is his Joy! he feels the fiery Wound,
> Flutters in Blood, and panting beats the Ground.
> Ah! what avail his glossie, varying Dyes,
> His Purple Crest, and Scarlet-circled Eyes,
> The vivid Green his shinning Plumes unfold;
> His painted Wings, and Breast that flames with Gold?
> (*Poems*, 1:161)

Like the game bird in Kühn's portrait of Henry Darnall, Pope's sacrificial pheasant signifies that at least one party to the triangular relations of African, Native American, and European peoples becomes marked as excess and violently disappears.

Such representations had to struggle to erase the fact that in the circum-Atlantic world, diaspora was a material fact, autocthony a fiction of origin. Sir William Young describes how the "Black Charaibs" of St. Vincent's, whose society began by chance with the wreck of a slave ship from the Bite of Benin in 1675, had organized a fully assimilated Maroon community by "about the year 1710":

> The savage, with the name and title, thinks he inherits the qualities, the rights, and the property, of those whom he may pretend to supersede: hence he assimilates himself by name and manners, as it were to make out his identity, and confirm the succession. Thus these Negroes not only assumed the national appellation of Charaibs, but

4.9 "Savages of Several Nations," by Alexandre de Batz, New Orleans, 1735. *From left*: "Chef," "Sauvagesse esclave," "Dansseur," "Illinois," "Sauvagesse," "Negre," "Atakapas." From the Smithsonian Miscellaneous Collection, vol. 80, no. 5, 1928.

Courtesy The Historic New Orleans Collection, Museum/Research Center, acc. no. 1974.25.10.98

> individually their Indian names; and they adopted many of their customs: they flattened the forehead of their infant children in the Indian manner: they buried their dead in the attitude of sitting, and according to Indian rites: and killing the men they took in war, they carried off and cohabited with the women. (8)

By the terms of Young's account, allowing for the condescension and unconscious projection of its racism, the black Caribs of St. Vincent's demonstrate the leading practices of intercultural surrogation through performance: they adopt and presumably adapt the restored behaviors of the red Caribs, displacing their transmission of burial rites, bodily adornment, and even naming. Assisted by miscegenation, voluntary or otherwise, two or many peoples mingle to become something new, but rarely without cost, and never without ambivalence (figure 4.9).

Turtle Island

Perhaps, as Kwame Anthony Appiah claims, "only something as particular as a single life" can capture the multiplicity of surrogated identities as they are (or were) continuously reinvented on the Atlantic rim (191). In the decisive years from 1680 to 1755, one of the four Kings, the Praying Mohawk Theyanoquin, or Hendrick, lived such an exemplary life. Also known as Teoniahigarawe, Tiyanoga, Tee Yee Ho Ga Row, Deyohninhohhakarawenh, White Head, King Hendrick, Hendrick Peters, and Emperour of the Six Nations, Theyanoquin was born Mahican but was "adopted" by the Mohawks (Jennings, *Iroquois Diplomacy*, 253). A pious Anglican, Theyanoquin served ably as a leader in the long struggle against France, of which the London embassy of 1710 was but one episode. Like the African "savage" in Young's account of the black Caribs of St. Vincent's, Hendrick "assimilate[d] himself by name and manners, as it were to make out his identity, and confirm the succession." His place onstage in the line of Kings at the Mohawk *Macbeth* proved to be prophetic. In the loyal service of king and country, Theyanoquin was killed in action at the outset of the Seven Years' War, during which the hinge of fate forever closed the door on the French empire in North America: Canada was surrendered to Great Britain; Louisiana was secretly ceded to Spain, and when Napoleon reacquired it in 1803, he quickly sold it to the United States. The anglophone ascendancy in North America did enable, as Theyanoquin and his colleagues had predicted, "great Trade with Our *Great Queen*'s Children," but it also brought forth much else that could not have been predicted or even imagined.

"I went out into this no-man's land," said Sam Phillips, Elvis Presley's first agent, when he booked the singer on the Louisiana Hayride in 1954, "and I knocked the shit out of the color line." For Phillips, reminiscing about the year in which the United States Supreme Court handed down its decision in *Brown v. Board of Education of Topeka* and the Louisiana legislature responded by proclaiming "Massive Resistance" (Rogers, 35–37), Elvis's blackness "was almost subversive, sneaking around through the music" (quoted in Guralnick, 134). For others, it was more palpable, closer perhaps to the appropriating spirit of Young's Caribbean "savage," who "thinks he inherits the qualities, the rights, and the property, of those whom he may pretend to supersede." In the consciousness of American identity, this surrogation remains exemplary, as evidenced by the way in which the United States Postal Service puffed the Elvis Presley commemorative: "The influence of the rock 'n' roll revolution is now felt throughout American culture in movies, fashion, and politics" (U.S. Postal Service, 31). In this sense, something more than the particularity of a single life must somehow take precedence in the performance of memory.

The way in which the United States Postal Service uses the word *culture* here can perhaps best be illustrated anecdotally. Traveling with my ten-year-old daughter on the way home from a family wedding in 1977, I happened to change planes in Memphis on the day of Elvis Presley's funeral. After the interment at Graceland, crowds of grieving fans were, like the two of us, hurrying through the airport on their way to their various destinations across the country. My daughter carried her cousin's bridal bouquet, which she, thinking herself very lucky, had caught, but somehow word circulated that the flowers had come from Elvis's grave. For a tense moment, several mourners stood across our path, sending mixed signals of reverence and resentment. Before I could think to say "Relatives of the Bride," my ten-year-old, sensing the moment, invented a tradition. She offered each of the people standing in our way a sprig of flowers from her souvenir bouquet. The recipients seemed to accept this wordless gesture as a gift, a sacrificial expenditure, a Maussian *prestation*. In fact, it was. This episode demonstrates the fantastic speed at which a secular ritual—even one improvised at an airport concourse, one of Rosaldo's "busy intersections"—can create something like the basis for a community among strangers who have nothing more meaningful in common than the fact that they have come together within a powerful effigy's ambit. Sharing what they took to be the enactment of a collective loss, they could better imagine a common purpose. So the celebrants of the impromptu condolence ceremony gave way, letting us pass, as we resumed our journey across "Turtle Island," which is what the Iroquois called America before the ax makers came.

ONE BLOOD

Will the court hold that a single drop of African blood is sufficient to color a whole ocean of Caucasian whiteness?

– ALBION W. TOURGÉE

"HERE WE ARE," SAYS THE RAISONNEUR IN DION BOUCICAULT'S *THE OCTOROON; or, Life in Louisiana* (1859), alerting the audience that he is about to locate the scene of the action. His announcement is at once precise and mysterious: "We are on the selvage of civilization." In the mouth of Salem Scudder, a homespun character in the Anglo-American tradition of Yankee Jonathan, the word *selvage* does a lot of work in Boucicault's play. It literally means the edge of a fabric, woven thickly so that it will not unravel. It more figuratively suggests a margin, a boundary, or a perimeter that by opposition defines the center—in short, a frontier. *The Octoroon*, a popular melodrama of miscegenation and intercultural displacement, is constructed on a number of frontiers, real and imagined, between "white" and "black," "civilization" and "savagery," "justice" and "revenge."

In one sense, Scudder's sibilant "selvage of civilization" presents a puzzling contradiction to the subtitle of the play, *Life in Louisiana*. Terrebonne Plantation, the locale of the action, sits just downriver from New Orleans, which by 1859 had become America's fourth largest city and one of its busiest ports, a circum-Caribbean cosmopolis with old family fortunes and colonial architecture already in various stages of decay (more like Venice, say, than Dodge City), through which the commerce of the nation's regions and world's nations passed. In another sense, however, Scudder's phrase is apposite: when he thinks of life in Louisiana as living on the edge of the world—between cultures, between languages, and between races—he defines another kind of frontier, or complex of frontiers, in which human difference, like a selvage, forms the seams at which separate worlds meet.

The Octoroon, along with the "Life in Louisiana" that it purports to depict, provides the touchstone for this chapter, in which I propose to examine several genres of performance as memorials to the circulation of cultures, material and symbolic, in the circum-Atlantic vortex. The record of the earlier life of this circulatory system, New Orleans, which announces itself as the "City that Care [Time] Forgot," has become today a "place of memory" in Pierre Nora's sense. As a favorite tourist destination, it performs as a simulacrum of itself, apparently frozen in time, but in fact busily devoted to the ever-changing task of recreating the illusion that it is frozen in time. Nora writes: "For if we accept that the most fundamental purpose of the *lieu de mémoire* is to stop time, to block the work of forgetting, to establish a state of things, to immortalize death, to materialize the immaterial—just as if gold were the only memory of money—all this in order to capture a maximum of meaning with the fewest signs, it is also clear that *lieux de mémoire* only exist because of their capacity for metamorphosis, an endless recycling of their meaning and an unpredictable proliferation of their ramifications" (19). New Orleans is the only inhabited city that exists simultaneously as a national historical park. Unlike Colonial Williamsburg or Disney World, each of which it resembles in certain respects, the Crescent City's picturesque inhabitants do not change clothes and go home at the end of their working day to what they erroneously have come to regard as the real world (Baudrillard).

The mythic original that the present city of New Orleans represents appears as an environmental setting, a *milieu de mémoire*, for Boucicault's *Octoroon*. How is it that a humble melodrama can condense meanings of such geohistorical scope? Two axes, one running north and south, the other east and west, intersect in Boucicault's play, as they once did in Louisiana: the former axis conjoins the river systems of the Mississippi basin with the Caribbean; the latter follows the path of national expansion conceived by Anglo-Americans as preordained. Though Horace Greeley's famous admonishment to the young man was not addressed to the Five Civilized Tribes—Choctaws, Chickasaws, Cherokees, Creeks, and Seminoles—it did define movement along the east-west axis in the imperative, as the

Indian Removal Act of 1830 did by mapping out the Trail of Tears. Similarly obligatory movement along the north-south axis is remembered colloquially in the ominous phrase, "sold down the river." Set at the point where these two axes crossed, *The Octoroon* stages a narrative of encounter, a dramatization of Anglo-American contact with the creolized interculture of the Latin Caribbean. It enacts the story of the radical reduction of one kind of frontier—that of multiple identities, which are primarily a matter of culture—into another kind of frontier—that of the catastrophic antinomies of manifest destiny, which are primarily a matter of "blood."

Against the generic lineage of *The Octoroon*, however, which descends from the so-called mortgage melodrama, a specialized performance of Euro-bourgeois anxieties concerning entitlement and dispossession (Brustein, 168–69), I also propose to juxtapose two other exemplary performance genealogies. The first involves the Mardi Gras parades of New Orleans's "Black Indians," the African-American "tribes" or "gangs" who masquerade as Native Americans during carnival and share some of their traditions with such diverse sources as Afro-Caribbean festivals and nineteenth-century Wild West shows. The second takes up select occasions featuring the performance of race in daily life in Louisiana, culminating in the staging of *Plessy v. Ferguson*, the visionary but disastrous New Orleans civil rights case that was adjudicated by the Supreme Court of the United States in 1896. The principal effect of *Plessy* was to establish "separate but equal" not just in the Louisiana Separate Car law, which had been disobeyed by the appellant, but as the law of the land.

The performance of race—as an alternative to an ontological commitment to its reality—counted for a great deal in a society that began under the displaced influence of the French colonial doctrine of One Blood but then experienced a century-long transformation by means of more or less obligatory surrogations. The essays in Arnold Hirsch and Joseph Logsdon's *Creole New Orleans: Race and Americanization* (1992) meticulously document previous instances of what these spectacles continue to perform: as Latin laws and customs were hollowed out, remodeled, and reinhabited after the Anglo-American occupation, a new social order was improvised. I want to examine the contingent and opportunistic performance of those improvisations, which include antebellum slave auctions, sex circuses in the legalized brothels of Storyville, and finally the apocalyptic Anglification of the old *Code noir* in *Plessy v. Ferguson*.

Common to these restorations and reinventions of behavior—the commodity at auction, the victim of sacrificial expenditure, and the transgressor before the law—is the liminal figure of the octoroon. Such ubiquity was neither accidental nor the consequence of pervasive numbers. Defined as a person of one-eighth African ancestry, an octoroon was legally black but in most cases passed for white. In fiction and in drama, as well as now and then in the practice of everyday life, the so-called "tragic mulatto" became an effigy whose fate, prepared in the crucible of gender and sexuality as well as race, condensed hatred and desire in the same imaginary liquid—mixed blood. In this strange world, where bipolar laws and customs attempted to sort out kaleidoscopic tints and hues, mulattoes of any kind might be expected to induce crises of surrogation, but even more so when the marks of mixture were ambiguous or invisible.

In their representations of Native Americans and African Americans, I will argue, as well as in their depiction of the forms of violence that I have termed the performance of waste, certain condensational events—performances of *The Octoroon*, New Orleans slave auctions, Mardi Gras Indian parades, Wild West Shows, and the staging of the Plessy case—thematize the "law" of manifest destiny and the doctrine of monoculturalism that it inscribes. But they also propose, each in its own way, the historic opportunity to accept or reject an alternative to the bloody frontier of conquest and forced assimilation: the paradigm of creolized interculture on the Caribbean model—a plural frontier of multiple encounters, another version of "Life in Louisiana."

Circum-Atlantic America

My argument unfolds in a context shaped by the current revision of the field of American studies, a reconfiguration heralded by Karen Halttunen's *Confidence Men and Painted Women: A Study of Middle-Class Culture in America, 1830–1870* (1982) and Lawrence Levine's *Highbrow/Lowbrow: The Emergence of Cultural Hierarchy in America* (1988) and now hastened by the publication of works such as Eric J. Sundquist's *To Wake the Nations: Race in the Making of American Literature* (1993), Jay Fliegelman's *Declaring Independence: Jefferson, Natural Language, and the Culture of Performance* (1993), and Eric Lott's *Love and Theft: Blackface Minstrelsy and the American Working Class* (1993). Haltunnen and Levine found in performance the occasion of the exquisite production of hierarchies of exclusion. Heeding the prophetic voice of W. E. B. Du Bois, Sundquist defines Pan-African cultural forms as central to an understanding of American law, politics, religion, folklore, and music, as well as literature. Both Fliegelman and Lott grant orature pride of place as testimony to the fact that difference is one thing that most Americans have in common. To the discussions enabled by their research into the complex reciprocities of culture and national identity, I would add an observation on the timeliness of the reexamination also currently under way of the questions raised by the fact of global English.

It should come as no surprise at this stage of the argument that I see the study of circum-Atlantic literatures and oratures in English (as well as in other languages) as more promising and more urgent than the study of canons organized around the existence of national borders. No taxonomy is innocent, of course, but the deeply ingrained division within English studies between American literature, on the one hand, and English or British literature, on the other, has foreclosed the exploration of certain historic relationships in a particularly invidious way. Thinking in terms of regional and hemispheric intercultures, of which the circum-Atlantic world is but one, will, for instance, allow canons and curricula to accommodate more readily the extraordinary florescence of contemporary drama, poetry, and prose fiction from Africa and the Caribbean. By accommodation I do not mean simply the opening up of an isolated specialty within the "coverage model" of English or any other literature (Graff) but rather the reorganization of ways of thinking about how cultural productions at every level and from many locales dynamically interact.

The Octoroon, for example, was written after a brief period of residence in New Orleans by an Anglo-Irishman of French ancestry who learned his trade as melodramatist in Paris. He wrote *The Octoroon* for a New York premiere in 1859 and rewrote it for a London opening in 1861. Although the play is one of the most frequently anthologized in collections representing drama in the United States, Boucicault's status as an American dramatist has, understandably, been the subject of prolonged but largely inconclusive debate (Kosok). No doubt there is still much to be learned by reading *The Octoroon* in connection with, say, Royall Tyler's *The Contrast* (1787), with its treatment of the frivolous Anglophile, Billy Dimple, and his down-to-earth foil, the original Yankee Jonathan. There is more to be learned now, however, by reading *The Octoroon* in connection with, say, Thomas Southerne's *Oroonoko*, the work of another Anglo-Irish playwright, or *An Echo in the Bone*, by Jamaican Dennis Scott. All three plays dramatize a narrative of diaspora and enslavement in the plantation economy at different times and from different vantage points along the Atlantic rim. Like *The Octoroon*, *Oroonoko* is a drama of encounter among white, black, and red peoples, and, also like both *The Octoroon* and *An Echo in the Bone*, it turns on the forbidden—and violently punished—desire between lovers characterized as belonging to different races.

Even the best histories of American melodrama (Grimsted; McConachie; Mason) generally omit mention of the fact that plays like *Oroonoko* remained in the English-speaking repertoire well into the nineteenth century. But that play's triangular entanglement of races, its improbable but providential rescues, its noble savages and sentimental heroines, its deployment of the sexual aggression of a white villain against the doomed miscegenistic couple, in short, its obsession with identity and difference could play effectively to the audiences that also applauded *The Octoroon*. Such scenes could still play, perhaps above all, because those audiences were composed of patchwork collections of diverse circum-Atlantic identities and interests thrown together "on the selvage of civilization."

In this light, the ritual performances embedded within *Oroonoko*, *The Octoroon*, and *An Echo in the Bone*—human sacrifice, rites of passage, and the return of the dead on Nine Night—can be reinterpreted in relationship to a variety of nontheatrical performances from Condolence Councils to jazz funerals. They existed and continue to exist to make something like common sense out of the challenge posed by the gabble of different tongues to the echo of dimly remembered voices. They broadly conform to the practices that I have delineated as pertaining particularly to the formation of circum-Atlantic identities under the pressure of contact and exchange: death and burials, violence and sacrifices, laws and (dis)obedience, commodification and auctions, origins and segregation. These are the structural mainstays of performances that define America as an ever-shifting ensemble of appropriated traditions. They must be sought both inside and outside the venues that so presumptuously refer to themselves as legitimate theater, organized religion, and the dominant culture. They also must be sought both inside and outside reductive binaries such as black and white or minority and majority, which suggest that human skin and social position exist as reciprocally fixed polarities rather than as a color wheel that turns over through time, the changing hues or tints of which bear no fixed or essential relationship to cultural affiliation and social position. Even from a perspective standing at Plymouth Colony and looking west (Schlesinger), the truth of this vision of America could be perceived by those with sufficient acuity.

And from a perspective standing in New Orleans along America's Third Coast, such a vision is impossible not to see, however often (and however violently) it has been disavowed.

Walking in the city makes this truth visible. In a letter to Albion W. Tourgée, the attorney who prepared the principal briefs for the Plessy case, civil rights pioneer Louis Martinet described the historic effects of One Blood, which included the large-scale assimilation of the Native American population into the African-American, as well as the African into the European and vice versa. As he surveyed the streets of New Orleans in 1891, Martinet pointed out the absurdity of juridical assignments of racial identity in such a place: "There are the strangest white people you ever saw here. Walking up & down our principal thoroughfare—Canal Street—you would [be] surprised to have persons pointed out to you, some as white & others as colored, and if you were not informed you would be sure to pick out the white for colored & the colored for white" (quoted in Olsen, 56–57). Among those who would most certainly have been "picked out" for white was Homer Adolph Plessy, the creole octoroon whose arrest for riding in the "Whites Only" passenger car of an East Louisiana Rail Road train set the eponymous legal case in motion. The logically desperate situation of those who argued for the binary "separation of the races" in the face of its unassailable risibility is best summarized by some touristic verses, penned around 1829 by Colonel James R. Creecy:

> Have you ever been in New Orleans? If not you'd better go,
> It's a nation of a queer place; day and night a show!
> Frenchmen, Spaniards, West Indians, Creoles, Mustees,
> Yankees, Kentuckians, Tennesseeans, lawyers and trustees,
> Clergymen, priests, friars, nuns, women of all stains;
> Negroes in purple and fine linen, and slaves in rags and chains.
> Ships, arks, steamboats, robbers, pirates, alligators,
> Assassins, gamblers, drunkards, and cotton speculators;
> Sailors, soldiers, pretty girls, and ugly fortune-tellers;
> Pimps, imps, shrimps, and all sorts of dirty fellows;
> White men with black wives, *et vice-versa* too.
> A progeny of all colors—an infernal motley crew!
>
> (quoted in Latrobe, 172)

A sense of burdensome superabundance, so characteristic of Anglo-American responses to the teeming human and material panoply of the circum-

Atlantic cityscape, weighs heavily on these already limping verses. There are too many incommensurate objects, species, mixtures, and colors, the propinquity of which the entrepot of New Orleans makes continuously visible.

Anxiety over a perceived surplus of difference, of course, is not new to American studies, nor is it, more surprisingly, entirely a thing of the past. "My definition of race," writes Eric Sundquist, "is deliberately limited to the relationship between black and white cultures." With only a barely perceptible blink of his scholarly eye, Sundquist drops "the very different set of questions raised by American Indian literature and oral tradition" from further consideration in his study of race in American literary history (8). The pioneers in the academic study of American theater and drama who were exploring a new disciplinary frontier forty years ago arrived at a similar impasse. It seemed to them as if cultures and races could best be imagined one, or at the most two, at a time. In the first sentence of his important and influential survey, *Theatre U.S.A, 1668 to 1957* (1959), one of those texts that define the boundaries in which subsequent research agendas would be imagined, Barnard Hewitt moved decisively to end a controversy that had arisen about the scope of the field: "Theatre or the stuff of theatre existed in the ceremonies and dances of the American Indians when the first settlers arrived in what is now the United States, but our theatre owed nothing in its beginnings to native sources" (1). Hewitt was rejecting the vigorous case, jointly put forward by A. M. Drummond and Richard Moody in 1953, that American Indian peace treaties, performed with songs, dances, and speeches by tribal members of the great Iroquois Confederacy—the Condolence Councils—should be canonized as the first American dramas. Their premise was that Amerindian rituals, like the Greek "songs and dances on the threshing floor," constituted foundational texts in the field of American theater research.

Although scholars in the new field of theater history, emerging from what they saw as their Babylonian captivity in departments of English, agreed that the study of performance is indispensable to the proper understanding of dramatic literature, Drummond and Moody went further. They wanted to extend the scope of the field of American theater and drama to include all varieties of what they termed "theatre-in-life" events. This was a remarkable move, enlarging the canon of legitimate objects of study: "Some of these 'theatre-in-life' events we participate in playfully: charades, initiations, parades, costume dances, foot-ball celebrations, snake dances, and the like. Others we act in more solemnly and oftentimes unwillingly: burials, marriages, commencements, church services, courtroom trials, and such. In all of them we easily recognize the theatrical, show-like qualities. . . . The Indian Treaties were 'theatre-in-life' dramas of the highest order" (15).

In rhetoric aimed at legitimating the study of performance, Drummond and Moody would have opened up the field of Anglo-American drama to the study of other American cultures and ethnic traditions, embracing orature as well as literature in the evaluation of cultural forms of "the highest order." Their concept of "theatre-in-life," later called "invisible theatre" (MacNamara), decenters the role of high-cultural forms of theater—those primarily reflecting the interests of the dominant, anglophone middle and upper classes—and implicitly supports (by promoting bisocietal treaty negotiations as drama) Mikhail Bakhtin's insight that "the most intense and productive life of culture takes place on the boundaries" (*Speech Genres*, 2).

At an early moment of disciplinary self-definition, other scholars rejected Drummond and Moody's proposed canon as too inclusive, arguing instead for a thoroughgoing, stringently focused exploration of what Barnard Hewitt called "our theatre." The clearest articulation of the reasons for concentrating research efforts on a more limited sphere appears in Walter Meserve's pointedly subtitled history, *An Emerging Entertainment: The Drama of the American People to 1828* (1977). Contrasting Amerindian performance culture to Anglo-Puritan antitheatricality, Meserve allows that "one people in America who did not object to theatre but incorporated it into their daily ritual were the American Indians." Their performances, however, "though clearly dramatic in a general sense," nevertheless lacked "the artistry and imagination imposed by a dramatist." Hence they "do not belong in the history of American drama" (5–6).

The numerous representations of Native Americans brought on stage through the imagination and artistry of white dramatists, however, play a paradoxically central role in the formation of a self-consciously national drama: "For many writers interested in establishing a sense of nationalism in literature," Meserve writes, "the American Indians seemed ideal characters" (246). In this schema, Native Americans can enter into the history of "the Drama of the American people" only as they are represented by white authors and actors. In such roles—cast as effigies—they become integral to the self-invention of "the American People" only through literary "artistry and imagination." Even in a field supposedly predisposed to value performance, then, literature prevails over orature. Without aesthetics, there is no real drama, just as without writing, there is no real history.

From the point of view of narrative typology, Walter Meserve's account of Native Americans—first invoked, then erased, then reinvented as aesthetic objects or "ideal characters" by Euro-Americans seeking native spiritual authenticity without having to deal with living autochthons—participates in a larger project: the legitimation of manifest destiny, in which the inevitability of Anglocentric displacement of indigenous peoples and rival colonial interests takes on the golden penumbra of a creation myth (Slotkin). The immense economic and social energy released by westward migration generated a voracious appetite for legitimating images and representations from which the expanding frontier and "America" emerged as coextensive imaginative spaces (Truettner, 149–89). What Francis Jennings has called "the cant of conquest" develops two main themes in depicting the Indian (*The Invasion of America*), both of which help to erase memories such as the mutual regard attained under the Covenant Chain. The first, which stresses the unremitting and vindictive barbarism of the "savages," suited the ideological needs of the Calvinist New Englanders especially, though it did not end with the bloody Indian wars of the seventeenth century. The second, which develops the notion of a transcendently wise and just Indian, living in innocent harmony with nature but doomed by the advance of civilization, predicates doctrines of tribal purity and authenticity that have yet to run their course in American belief and law (Pagden). The two sides of Anglo-American imagery, the wanton savage and the noble savage, might be seen to reflect, in an eerily doubled projection, the duality of American justice—the retributive violence of the law of the frontier, which is to say vigilantism, and the grandly sweeping constitutional appeal, over the heads of all previously existing civilizations, to the Enlightenment's "Laws of Nature," of which manifest destiny, which is to say cultural vigilantism, was one.

In this narrative, the function of the surrogated aboriginal is to disappear, and historians of American drama have recounted in detail the contributions of nineteenth-century popular entertainment to the wistful celebration of the vanishing Indian (Jones; Wilmeth). Both the novel and the stage play exploited the sentimental fascination of "the last of" stories: *Last of the Mohicans*; *Logan, The Last of the Race of Shikellemus*; and the celebrated melodrama *Metamora; or, The Last of the Wampanoags* (1829), by John Augustus Stone, whose work had a second life in the popular parody by John Brougham, *Met-a-mora; or, The Last of the Pollywogs* (1847). In the original, which premiered concurrently with the debates leading to the passage of Indian Removal Act of 1830 (which relocated the Five Civilized Tribes from the southeastern United States to Oklahoma), a scenery-chewing Edwin Forrest played the title character (Grose). Stone meant to give Metamora equal measures of savagery and nobility, and Forrest died grandly and very extensively before a tableau of burning wigwams with the words, "We are destroyed—not vanquished; we are no more, yet we are forever" (38). In the deflationary burlesque version, the chorus of stage Indians, the Pollywogs, massacred by an army of popgun-firing whites, sings, "We're all dying." Theirs was something of a specialty act within the aesthetic priorities of Anglo-American representation, taking their place in a genealogy of Indian death scenes: puritan John Eliot's *Dying Speeches of Several Indians* (1685) seems to have founded a popular American genre that continues today at every performance of Tom Jones and Harvey Schmidt's *The Fantasticks* (1960), in which the Old Actor recites Shakespeare and the Indian dies, obediently beginning his final agonies whenever he hears the command, "Mortimer, die for the man" (51).

Not to belabor the elements of national wish fulfillment in these genocidal fantasies, I want simply to point out that the issue of race in America is hard to reimagine without considering Native Americans. The stark polarity of the frontier trope of center versus margin traps the imagination of historians as well as dramatists in a monotonously self-replicating closure, a monologic foregone conclusion in which only the victor remains to mourn his vanquished victim. The violence of this narration reinscribes the violence of laws such as those mandating Indian removal: the Native American disappears, at the stroke of the white man's pen, and only the aesthetic Indian remains behind, in memory, in representation, in effigy, and (very often) in fact.

I believe that an alternative historical model of intercultural encounter, one based on performance, will suggest an alternative historical narrative of American literature and culture, one more resistant to the polarizing reductions of manifest destiny and less susceptible to the temptations of amnesia. Such a model would emphasize the truly astonishing multiplicity of cultural encounters in circum-Atlantic America, the adaptive creativity produced by the interactions of many peoples. Such a model would require a performance genealogy in which the borderlands, the perimeters of reciprocity, become the center, so to speak, of multilateral self-definition.

When Native Americans, for instance, speak of their cultures, they tend to do so with a recognition of their vast diversities of language, custom, and experience. Amerindian encounter narratives (recounting interactions with other tribal groups as well as with whites and blacks) are apt to contest the monolithic story told in Anglo-American fiction, historical or otherwise. David Whitehorse, for example, an authority on the contemporary pan-Indian powwow, explains the performance genealogy of the Trail of Tears, showing how one of the consequences of Indian removal was a productive cross-fertilization between extremely remote cultures: "Eastern ceremonial expressions such as the Busk, the Green Corn Dance and the Stomp Dance were retained by the Five Civilized Tribes. With the removal of these tribes to Indian Territory (present-day Oklahoma) in the 1830's, they carried their ceremonies from an agrarian based society to a marginal Southern Plains environment. Within the span of two generations, the dances and ceremonies of preexisting Southern Plains tribes had been interspersed with those of the Five Civilized Tribes through the process of cultural diffusion. In this manner, the southern variant of the inter-tribal pow-pow had its genesis" (5).

Whitehorse, whose lineage is Sioux, Comanche, and Irish, reminds scholars not only that Indians live in different yet dynamically interactive cultures but also that they are capable of a far wider range of human behavior than retreating, dying, and vanishing. The Indians he describes innovate, improvise, and adapt. One major influence on intertribal powwows, Whitehorse explains, was the popular Anglo-American Wild West show, which provided disparate Indian traditions with "commonly understood frameworks within which to conduct the affair" (12; see Laubin and Laubin, 81, 455). The powwow, which follows no written text, illustrates some of the dynamic opportunities of a truly interactive dramatic performance, one that Drummond and Moody would call a "theatre-in-life" event.

Whitehorse also articulates by vivid example a theory of contemporary cultural politics, a new epistemology of difference, which disrupts received conceptions of circum-Atlantic identities. His account shows how intertribal powwows embody the kind of permeable, negotiable, and fluctuating boundaries described in contemporary social environments by postmodern ethnography (Clifford; Conquergood; Rosaldo). But postmodernity, whatever its uses, promises nothing like utopia, as postmodern ethnographers are the first to admit. Perhaps the most troubling and informative essay on this subject is James Clifford's probing examination of identity in Mashpee, an account of the legal struggles of a New England community to establish its people as members of an authentic Native American tribe (277–346).

Their purpose was to reclaim Wampanoag ancestral lands from Massachusetts real-estate developers. They claimed in effect that, contrary to Stone's melodrama and Forrest's famous death scene, Metamora was not the "Last of the Wampanoags." The vexed question before the court was: What constitutes an authentic tribal culture in the eyes of the law? The verdict was that a mere oral tradition, handed down since the seventeenth century through generations of forced and voluntary assimilations, massacres, intermarriages, and acculturations, was insufficient proof, in the absence of proper written documentation, of the existence of an "organic" or historically continuous "whole" tribal culture. With the typically solemnified violence of American law, the federal court reenacted an apparently inexhaustible scenario of erasure, staging the melodrama of the vanishing Indian against a poignant backdrop, not of burning wigwams, but of rising condos.

The marginal condition of life between powerful categories, the condition that postmodern ethnographers find so rich in cultural expressiveness, renders the people actually trying to live within it extremely vulnerable to the punitive consequences of their undecidability. Whether they choose not to take the path of "straight-line assimilation," a decision that ultimately leads perhaps to "symbolic ethnicity" at most (Gans), or are forbidden this path by some uncorrectable accident of their births, they live, for better or worse, in a double culture, invested in two worlds (at least) yet faced with powerful laws and customs favoring unitary identities (Du Bois). One reason for this phenomenon in American society, I believe, is a historic juridical tendency, epitomized by the majority opinion in *Plessy v. Ferguson*, first to collapse culture into categories of race and then to try to enforce those categories as absolutes, as if they were set down in black or white. Such racialist thinking surfaces in the very conception of a tribe or a people necessarily existing as an "organic whole."

Challenging the view of human culture as organic in any biological sense, Clifford speaks for a quite different conception of American legitimacy when he writes, "Groups negotiating their identity in contexts of domination and exchange, persist, patch themselves together in ways different from a living organism. A community, unlike a body, can lose a central 'organ' and not die. All the critical elements of identity are in specific conditions replaceable: language, land, blood, leadership, religion. Recognized, viable tribes exist in which any one or even most of these elements are missing, replaced, or largely transformed" (338). Such an entity is less like a plant and more like a quilt, pieced together over time by many hands out of odds and ends, the borders doubled over as selvage, multiple edges of contact among the particolored patches. As an alternative to the mirage of monocultural continuity or to its related hallucination, the binary of two impermeable races opposed, Clifford explores the possibility, suggested by the history of the Caribbean basin, of "organic culture reconceived as inventive process or creolized 'interculture' " (15). Responsive to such consequential world-historical events as the African diaspora and the geopolitics of rival Eurocolonial systems, this view has many promising implications for the study of genealogies of performance, exemplified in my account by that of the Mardi Gras Indians of New Orleans.

The last decade has seen a great florescence of this extraordinary tradition. As the Big Chiefs and other Indian masqueraders have challenged each other as to who is the most "pretty," their consummate mastery of a total art form of costume, music, dance, heightened speech, and dramaturgy has transformed the streets of the city during the extended Mardi Gras season. Chiefs such as Allison "Tootie" Montana of the Yellow Pochahontas, Bo Dollis of the Wild Magnolias, Larry Bannock of the Golden Star Hunters, Victor Harris of the Spirit of Fi-Yi-Yi, and others too numerous to mention have become world-historical messengers. The message they share has roots as deep as memory, but it must reinvent itself anew every year in hosannas of feathers, beadwork, gesture, and song. In Japan such messengers would be revered as Living National Treasures. In New Orleans they are still harassed by the police for parading without permits.

Life on the (Caribbean) Frontier

There is no agreed-on explanation for the origins of present-day Mardi Gras Indians in New Orleans, and it would be surprising if one were ever established. As the beneficiary of slave importation under the French, Spanish, and American regimes, Louisiana, in the words of one historian of life on its sugar plantations, "shared the socio-economic experience of the larger circum-Caribbean culture" (Fiehrer, 4). Recent scholarship has explored the cosurvival and coadaptation of West African festival performance genres in the Jamaican "John Canoe" (Junkanoo) Christmas celebrations, the Amerindian Masquerade of St. Kitts-Nevis and Bermuda, the Trinidad carnival, the Cuban *comparsas*, and New Orleans Mardi Gras Indians (Hill, *Trinidad Carnival*; Nunley and Bettelheim).

The musical structure of the Indians' call-and-response songs, with counterrhythms supplied by a percussive Second Line, certainly suggests West African derivations (Sands). An ethnomusicological account of the tribes as they were in the early 1970s dates the first activity to the "early nineteenth century" and connects the gangs' structure to traditional African mutual assistance societies, which developed in nineteenth-century New Orleans as social aid and pleasure clubs (Draper). The standard sociology of African-American New Orleans relates the Indians to "neighborhood groupings within the Negro population," which remain "a salient feature of its social life." The city of New Orleans is divided into "Uptown" and "Downtown," the latter referring to the older, historically creole French Quarter and environs, the former to the more Anglo-Americanized sections; the Indians were likewise divided into Uptown and Downtown "gangs" (Rohrer and Edmondson, 38–39). After the release of Maurice Martinez and James Hinton's documentary film, *The Black Indians of New Orleans* (1977), a controversy developed over Martinez's acceptance of the Indians' own accounts of their authentic Amerindian origins dating to colonial times (De Caro). Yet just such a claim of genuine ethnicity, including family ties, is a recurring theme in the oral histories. Big Chief Allison "Tootie" Montana of the Yellow Pocahontas, for instance, affirming his family history of "Indian blood," says of his cousins, "Man, they just look like an Indian" (quoted in Berry, Foose, and Jones, 210–11).

In America, blood is the talisman of authentic identity, but the history of the Mardi Gras Indians frustrates unitary explanations. New Orleans photographer Michael P. Smith, an acute and knowledgeable observer of cultural traditions of the African-American community, has suggested some connections between the Mardi Gras Indians and the special reverence for the Sauk Indian chief, Blackhawk, a feature of worship in local spiritual churches (*Spirit World*, 43, 66). Both Samuel Kinser, in his study of Gulf Coast carnival, and Smith, in his recent *Mardi Gras Indians* (1994), point to the 1880s as the most likely decade for the formation of the Mardi Gras Indian practices that continue today, and Smith has developed some suggestive evidence that the visit of Buffalo Bill's Wild West in 1884–85, along with later visits by other shows, including the Creole Wild West Show and the African Wild West Show, influenced the Mardi Gras Indians (97–105). More than a few Mardi Gras Indians find the suggestion that Buffalo Bill's Wild West influenced their traditions deeply offensive, but fortunately there is no shortage of alternative genealogies. Smith elaborates what he sees as a number of linkages between present-day Indian gangs and the renegade bands of Afro-Amerindian Maroons who tormented the colonial authorities in Louisiana (*Mardi Gras Indians*, 21–25), as they did the overseer in *The Octoroon* (Boucicault, 8), the English governor of Suriname (Southerne, 92), and his counterpart in Jamaica (D. Scott, 102–6). Reid Mitchell, in his recent *All on a Mardi Gras Day: Episodes in the History of New Orleans Carnival* (1995), sums up (and gives up) by citing Hobsbawm and Ranger's *Invention of Tradition* (1983): "With the Mardi Gras Indians, the working class black people of New Orleans too 'invented a tradition' " (115).

Such diverse claims for the origin of Mardi Gras Indians provide a crux for the construction of collective memory out of genealogies of performance. The tangle of creation narratives—the romantic reaching back to extracolonial encounters between black and red men and women, the Afro-Caribbean ties to Trinidad, Cuba, and Haiti, the links to West African dance and musical forms, the social hypothesis stressing fraternal African-American bonds in the face of oppression, the presence of a strong spirit-world subculture, and the catalyst of the Wild West Show—does not exhaust the possibilities. I believe that each story contributes its own grain of truth—the trace of a once powerful surrogation. Taken together, the stories exemplify Clifford's reformulation of a contemporary cultural politics of authenticity: "If authenticity is relational, there can be no essence except as a political, cultural invention, a local tactic." This line of thinking leads him finally to his summary of Mashpee Indian identity: "Groups negotiating their identity in contexts of domination and exchange . . . patch themselves together" (15, 338).

By reinvoking the metaphor of patchwork amid exchange, I do not mean to imply that there is anything haphazard about Mardi Gras Indian performance. On the contrary, the extraordinary artistry and craftsmanship of the costumes, which may take a year to build, taken together with the many-layered protocols of Sunday rehearsals, parade-day tactics and strategy, and music-dance-drama performance, make the honor of "masking Indian" a New Orleanian way of life (figure 5.1). The victories earned in intertribal competition, their exact meanings, and their deep significance, like the solidarity won by thousands of hours gossiping at the sewing table, cannot be shared with outsiders. The tribes, brilliant apparitions on Mardi Gras, St. Joseph's Day, and Super Sunday keep the secrets of their undecidability. "Nobody ain't never gonna find the code," as Larry Bannock, Big Chief of

5.1 Larry Bannock, Big Chief of the Golden Star Hunters, 1984.
Photo: Michael P. Smith

the Golden Star Hunters, put it: "The map has to be in your heart" (Bannock, personal interview).

The map certainly must be in the heart of the Big Chief because the parade routes followed by the gangs are unannounced, except to the tribal inner circle, led by the First Spy Boy, who serves as scout. The Flag Boy relays signals between the Spy Boy and the Big Chief. Each office is multiplied, so that there are Second and Third Chief, Second and Third Spy Boy, and so on. There is also a Wildman or Medicine Man, distinguished by the cow or buffalo horns on his headdress, who dances from side to side across the line of march, both inciting and holding back the crowd. Queens sometimes accompany the Chiefs. The formation takes up several blocks, and the costumed Indians are supported by the Second Line of supporters and respondents. (There is also, according to Michael Smith, now a "Third Line," which is how the revelers sardonically refer to the band of ethnographers, ethnomusicologists, and English professors taking pictures, making recordings, and compiling notes [Smith, "Hidden Carnival," 7].) The Spy Boy, who must be the most savvy Indian next to the Big Chief, looks out for the other tribes in the vicinity, but the Big Chief decides whether to accept or to avoid a confrontation.

Violence punctuated the earlier history of Mardi Gras Indians. Its present role is unclear. Contemporary Big Chiefs point out that the object of the confrontations now is to show excellence in costume and performance style, to make the enemy Chief "bow" by superior display. Some also admit to carrying weapons and stashing them with their Second Liners. This carries on a tradition. The great jazz musician Ferdinand "Jelly Roll" Morton (ca. 1885–1941) contributed his memories of growing up in New Orleans to the Library of Congress archive of oral histories. Mr. Jelly Roll, who was a Spy Boy around the turn of the century, recalls that the tribes "wanted to act exactly as the Indians in days long by. . . . To dance and sing and go like regular Indians." They would "form a ring, in a circle, dancer in the center, sending his head way back," while the tribe members made "a kind of rhythm with their heels." There were friendly and unfriendly tribes, and when "they'd meet a real enemy, . . . their main object was to make the enemy bow." If the enemy did not bow, there could be real trouble. "Some even carried pistols," Morton recalls; "The next day there would be someone in the morgue" (*Jelly Roll Morton*).

What did it mean for Jelly Roll Morton and the tribal members for whom he scouted to "act exactly as the Indians in days long by"? Granting the undecidability of pure origins and "organic" cultural "wholes," what connections recur and thus point toward a genealogy of performance? The earliest detailed description of a gang of Indians is Henry Rightor's note in his history of New Orleans, published in 1900, actually a promotional effort for New Orleans tourism. Rightor noticed something that I have not seen commented on elsewhere but that I think is highly significant. Though the phrase "masking Indian" is used to describe the Mardi Gras performances and the way of life that supports them, Mardi Gras Indians don't always or even often wear masks. Every body part of an Indian Big Chief may be covered with sequins or rhinestone beads and ostrich plumes, completely altering his silhouette and hiding every inch of his skin, but, as Rightor notes, the Indian's face, then as now, usually remains exposed, except perhaps for war paint:

> The favorite disguise with the negroes is that of the Indian warrior, doubtless from the facility with which it lends itself to a complete transformation of the personality without use of the encumbering and embarrassing mask; and in war paint and feathers, bearing the tomahawk and bow, they may be seen on Mardi Gras running along the streets in bands of from six to twenty and upwards, whooping, leaping, brandishing their weapons, and, anon, stopping in the middle of a street to go through the movements of a mimic war-dance, chanting the while in rhythmic cadence and outlandish jargon of no sensible import to any save themselves. (631)

The secrets and occult powers of their "jargon" served as another kind of mask, disguising their meanings from uninitiated observers and adding to their mystery, but the absence of facial masks suggests several other possibilities. First, masking was illegal in the city of New Orleans, and although the law may have ignored the violations of the white krewes, there is no reason to suppose it would have overlooked a black Indian who crossed the line. Second, Rightor's impression that the Indian's personality was completely transformed (a problematic observation about someone Rightor could not have known) evinces another meaning of disguise in cultural politics. What the masquerade transformed was the stereotypical "[Negro] personality." It accomplished a carnivalesque inversion of the ordinary experience of working-class blacks in post-Reconstruction Louisiana, in which the laboring body was exposed while the facial expression remained masked. That today's Mardi Gras Indians expose their faces should be understood, I believe, not merely as a literal unmasking but as self-fashioning revelation. "Every Indian," Larry Bannock says, "parades in his own way" (Bannock, videotaped interview). At the same time, the way in which every Indian parades does not, precisely speaking, belong to him alone, no matter how virtuosic the productions of his musical and kinesthetic imagination might be. He performs the gestures and actions, he sews the feathered and beaded costumes, and he sings the songs, all of which constitute living artifacts, spirit-world messages passed on through the medium of his performance. Occupying and transforming the streets in the "back of town," an Indian in his new suit on Mardi Gras morning is ambulant architecture, a living *milieu de mémoire*.

The Performance of Waste

Like powwows and Mardi Gras Indian parades, the so-called legitimate theater enacts what the community imagines to be most important to its survival: the connections between its collective memory and its possible fates. Audiences at the premiere of *The Octoroon* did not need a weatherman to tell them which way the wind was blowing (Erdman). The play opened at the Winter Garden Theatre in New York City on December 6, 1859, four days after the execution of John Brown. Dion Boucicault, who spent the season of 1854–55 in New Orleans as manager of the Gaiety Theatre, seized his opportunity to dramatize the emergency of race in a key locale of circum-Atlantic memory in North America. His melodrama retails the plot of Captain Mayne Reid's romance *The Quadroon; or, A Lover's Adventures in Louisiana* (1856), which was itself only one of dozens of novels, biographies, and other representations dealing with "tragic" octoroon or quadroon heroines, beginning in 1836 with Hildreth's *The Slave* (Zanger). In both Boucicault's play and Reid's novel, a rare beauty of delicate manners and mixed race, legally exposed by the foreclosure of a mismanaged plantation, finds herself auctioned off as a slave to the highest bidder, who turns out to be the moustache-twirling villain. Reid's hero rescues the quadroon and then marries her. Boucicault reversed the outcome for the New York version of play: the octoroon (Zoe) takes poison moments before the letter of credit saving the plantation arrives.

Violence in *The Octoroon* includes, but is not limited to, the villain (Jacob M'Closky) torching and sinking the steamboat *Magnolia* on the Mississippi River, murdering the slave boy, Paul, with a tomahawk, and in turn meeting his own fate at the hands of the vengeful Choctaw Indian, Wahnotee, the slave boy's faithful companion. Ostensibly, these atrocities stem from M'Closky's attempts to seize Terrebonne Plantation and its human property, namely Zoe. On a deeper level, they stem from a more violent fear. The multiplied instances of interracial and intersocietal contact in Boucicault's scenario add to the threatened displacements of the stock plot of the mortgage melodrama. They intensify anxieties born of the Louisiana "frontier," a historic zone of circum-Atlantic encounter, for which the play soothingly—in careful increments of blood—substitutes binary oppositions based on variations of the theme of manifest destiny.

Boucicault plays on the manifold possibilities of frontier life, beginning with a Cooperian image of three men—one white, one red, one black—going off together into the woods to hunt. The hero (George) sets the scene in act 1: "Aunt, I will take my rifle down to the Atchafalaya. Paul has promised me a bear and a deer or two. I see my little Nimrod yonder, with his Indian companion. Excuse me, ladies" (8). Such a piece of staging evokes Leslie Fiedler's well-known formulation of "the relationship between sentimental life in America and the archetypal image, found in our favorite books, in which a white and a colored male flee from civilization into each other's arms" (Fiedler, xii). This describes the mythic embrace of Natty Bumppo and Chingachgook, Ishmael and Queequeg, Huck and Jim, but it also echoes the sacrificial offering of the hunt, performed as an act of bloody surrogation amid the violent couplings and unnerving palimpsests of Pope's *Windsor-Forest*:

> Proud *Nimrod* first the bloody Chace began,
> A mighty Hunter, and his Prey was Man.
> (*Poems*, 1:155)

Alexander Pope and Dion Boucicault would be thought an odd couple indeed on any syllabus, but they participate in the symbolic representation and memorialization of a hemispheric interculture "built up," as Paul Gilroy puts it in broad terms, "across the imperial networks which once played host to the triangular trade of sugar, slaves and capital" (*Union Jack*, 157). Apart from the menacing biblical allusions—Nimrod stalks his prey in Genesis—the variety of skin colors alone would suggest that among Boucicault's dramatis personae somebody must be superabundant.

In *The Octoroon*, the homosocial idyll of the hunt places a white man in a triangular relationship with an African American and a Native American.

When another plantation owner complains that the Choctaw Wahnotee should "return to his nation out West" (i.e., postremoval Indian territory) and M'Closky accuses him of thieving and drinking, Zoe defends him: "Wahnotee is a gentle, honest creature, and remains here because he loves that boy with the tenderness of a woman. When Paul was taken down with the swamp fever the Indian sat outside the hut, and neither ate, slept, or spoke for five days, till the child could recognize and call him to his bedside. He who can love so well is honest—don't speak ill of poor Wahnotee" (8). Here the historic juncture of Africans and Amerindians, the key cultural linkage in the performance genealogy of the Mardi Gras Indians, emerges in a representation destined for consumption by whites as the deep, innocent, and essentialized love among the children of Nature. The Indian doubles the white man, standing in for him in the role of frontier companion and lover. Today's Mardi Gras Indians also tend to sentimentalize the African-Amerindian encounter; as Chief Larry Bannock explains: "They were the first people to accept us as human" (Bannock, videotaped interview). But Bannock's memory of the contact is positioned in historical memory (albeit the imprecise reminiscence of oral tradition) rather than in Fiedler's Nature, the mythic, timeless, and homosocial realm of the North American wilderness.

As his foreshadowing exposition suggests, Boucicault also gives Wahnotee a dark purpose in the essentializing symbolic action of *The Octoroon*. He is the agent of violent revenge against the villainies of Jacob M'Closky and, by extension, against all the vicious features of white culture that M'Closky, the grasping, bullwhip-wielding Connecticut Yankee, could possibly represent. The crucial scene in the play for my purposes is the kangaroo court set up on the Mississippi wharf in act 4. Here Salem Scudder, the sympathetic Yankee Jonathan, presides over the trial, first of Wahnotee, who is falsely suspected of Paul's murder (since his tomahawk was used in the deed), and then of M'Closky, who is soon enough found out as the culprit. Scudder first argues against the summary stringing up of Wahnotee: "This lynch law is a wild and lawless proceeding. Here's a pictur' for a civilized community to afford: yonder, a poor ignorant savage, and round him a circle of hearts, white with revenge and hate, thirsting for his blood: you call yourself judges—you ain't—you're a jury of executioners. It is such scenes as these that bring disgrace upon our Western life" (32). Scudder convicts the jury, which is "white with revenge," of acting like a bunch of savage Indians. He appeals to the famed due process of American law. Yet a few lines later, when the villain M'Closky stands in the improvised docket, Scudder completely reverses himself and the play's presentation of the essence of American justice:

> Fellow-citizens, you are convened and assembled here under a higher power than the law. What's the law? When the ship's abroad on the ocean, when the army is before the enemy, where in thunder's the law? It is in the hearts of brave men, who can tell right from wrong, and from whom justice can't be bought. So it is here, in the wilds of the West, where our hatred of crime is measured by the speed of our executions—where necessity is law! I say, then, air you honest men? air you true? Put your hands on your naked breasts, and let every man as don't feel an American heart there, bustin' with freedom, truth, and right, let that man step out—that's the oath I put to ye—and then say, Darn ye, go it! (33)

It seems that the Yankee Jonathan speaks with forked tongue. He now appeals beyond the law to a higher power that acts in the hearts of free men and exists outside and above due process—an American tree bearing some mighty strange fruit. He speaks as if he were in some wilderness outpost, the "selvage of civilization," instead of in a long-established colony with laws in three languages and plenty of lawyers already (G. Richardson). In fact, the frontier on which he stands is that of cultural difference and simmering racial hatreds, one that Boucicault's dramaturgy—and not only Boucicault's dramaturgy—wants to confuse with the Wild West.

As the net of vengeance closes, drawn ever more tightly with increasingly ferocious invocations of Judge Lynch, the stage directions read: "Wahnotee rises and looks at M'Closky—he is in his war paint and fully armed" (33). Boucicault's faulty pronoun reference underscores the weird substitution of the red man for the white: the gentle child of Nature has been transformed into the terrifying agent of vigilante justice. Through the course of the remaining scenes of the play, Wahnotee silently pursues an increasingly hysterical Jacob M'Closky, who, at one point in the chase, mistakes the Indian swimming after him for an alligator, a kind of Louisiana bayou anticipation of Captain Hook and the crocodile (34). In the final tableau of the play, while George holds the lifeless body of Zoe downstage, the stage direction gives an explicit cue to focus the ending of *The Octoroon* on the theme of bloody vengeance: "Darken front of house and stage. Light fires.—Draw flats and discover Paul's grave.—M'Closky dead on it.—Wahnotee standing triumphantly over him" (40). Here, amid the pious terrors of

American justice, Boucicault pulls off a very complicated piece of racial surrogation and inversion: a white man is lynched by an Indian for the murder of a Negro. Scudder unscrambles the code of this anagram when he refuses to intervene to save M'Closky from being "butchered by the red-skin" and explains to the condemned man the true nature of the crime for which he must die. Scudder also confirms that while the frontier in Louisiana is more intercultural than geographical, the natural law of manifest destiny must nevertheless remain in force: "Here we are on the selvage of civilization. It ain't our side, I believe rightly; but Nature has said that where the white man sets his foot, the red man and the black man shall up sticks and stand around. But what do we pay for that possession? In cash? No—in kind—that is, in protection, forbearance, gentleness, in all them goods that show the critters the difference between Christian and savage. Now, what have you done to show them the distinction? for, darn me, if I can find out" (37).

Scudder's sentimental apostrophe of the white man's rule of law, sanctioned by Nature, evokes the qualities that Wahnotee has shown in loving Paul, the womanly and maternal virtues of "protection, forbearance, gentleness." That the Indian ends the play standing over the dismembered body of the victim of his merciless revenge completes Boucicault's inverted presentation of the dual symbolism—and the dual reality—of American justice as the performance of waste.

Ghost Dance: Buffalo Bill and the Voodoo Queens

Henry Rightor's description of a Mardi Gras Indian humbug of around 1900—"a mimic war-dance, chanting the while in rhythmic cadence and outlandish jargon" (631)—makes a revealing comparison to one published in the *Daily Picayune* sixteen years earlier, which refers to "an onslaught of a whole band of whooping red-devils." Like Rightor's account, it stresses costume, speech, and dance: "The Indians wore their semi-civilized garb, were gorgeous in their native warpaint and spoke their own guttural language . . . and they went through the weird dances of their race." The reporter, however, was recounting the street parade and premiere of Buffalo Bill's Wild West, December 22–23, 1884 (*Daily Picayune*, December 24, 1884).

Before it departed New Orleans on April 11, 1885, Buffalo Bill's Wild West performed daily for mixed crowds, including a "Grand Performance" on Mardi Gras day (*Daily Picayune*, February 17, 1885). Bad weather and a transportation strike frustrated William F. Cody's design to make a killing off the crowds at the World's Industrial and Cotton Exhibition, which had opened that rainy winter (Deahl). Nevertheless, the show came to town with two hundred cowboys, Indians, and Mexicans to enact its simulacrum of manifest destiny: the Pony Express and the Deadwood Coach getting through, the buffalo hunt, the duel with Yellowhand, the Indians' scalp and war dances, the nostalgic adieu to a proud and vanishing race (Blackstone). Annie Oakley joined the company for the first time in New Orleans, and a big attraction was added when Chief Gall, the Sioux sachem, strategist of the victory at the Little Big Horn, arrived for a special guest appearance, including "pow-wows, dances, and a feast" (*Daily Picayune*, January 3, 1885).

At fifty cents, the admission price (plus carfare or a long walk) was pretty steep in an economy where the newspaper editorialized about overpayment—"Demoralized Negro Labor"—when wages for field hands hit one dollar a day (*Daily Picayune*, February 16, 1885). The company, however, offered itself free of charge when it paraded on December 22 through the streets of the city, especially the Uptown areas (*Daily Picayune*, December 22, 1884). It is important to imagine the spectacle of costumed and armed Plains warriors, some of them recent victors over Custer, striding proudly through the streets of New Orleans on the days before Christmas 1884. Uncontained within the arena of the Wild West Show, which depicted the white man's view of the Indians' subjection as well as their nobility, they would have made a greater impression, I think, on those who saw them move through the neighborhoods, speaking "their own guttural language" and performing "the weird dances of their race" than they would have in the arena, though that spectacle was by all accounts quite impressive in its own way.

The parades of the Wild West Show, inviting the public "To see Scenes that have Cost Thousands their Lives to View" (advertisement, *Daily Picayune*, December 22, 1884; figure 5.2), manifested a double nature, their identity falling somewhere between a folklore procession, with its gala emphasis on crafts and special skills, and a military parade, with its emphasis on the display of national power and national will. Anthropologist James Fernandez explains this distinction: "A folklore procession is, by definition, a show of local culture and a manifestation of local identity, just as a military parade is a parade of national culture and national identity. . . . The military parade is a parade of the 'instruments of violence' of which the nation-state enjoys the role of possession and legitimate use, just as a

EDUCATIVE --- INSTRUCTIVE --- ENTERTAINING.

J. M. BURKE...GENERAL MANAGER

"It is grandly realistic and historically reminiscent."—Gen. W. T. Sherman.
"After a century's reign, the circus is dethroned."—Dan Rice.
"The sports of ancient Rome's arena excelled."—Brick Pomeroy.

GRAND

Opening Day, Tuesday, Dec. 23,

—AT—

OAKLAND PARK,

Reconstructed and Improved. New Amphitheatre, Seating 15,000.

THE CENTURY NOVELTY! TOO LARGE FOR A CANVAS!

THE GRANDEST EXHIBITION ON EARTH.

"W. F. CODY—BUFFALO BILL—the Sphinx of the Prairie—is a man with a history, a record and a name, won by merit, sustained with honor and borne without reproach.—Earl Dunraven, in London Telegraph.

The most celebrated of all Scouts, Guides and Indian Fighters known in American history. Marvelous Equestrian Marksman.

Capt. A. H. BOGARDUS, Champion Wing Shot of the World.

EUGENE BOGARDUS, America's Coming Champion.

Major FRANK NORTH, White Chief of the Pawnees.

Two Hundred Indians, Scouts, Mexicans, Cowboys.

"Our President and Cabinets, our Generals, our Public and our Press accord it patronage and praise."—Washington Republican.

A VISIT WEST IN THREE HOURS,

To see Scenes that have Cost Thousands their Lives to View.

EXHIBITIONS AFTERNOONS ONLY, AT 1 P. M. GATES OPEN 12 M. (Sundays included) DAILY. EXHIBITION RAIN OR SHINE.

Admission 50 Cents; Children 25 Cents. Easy to get there in 18 minutes. Beautiful Groves, Interesting Surroundings, Enjoyable Drives. PICTURESQUE WESTERN CAMP. Canal street city horse and steam cars to gate. Carriages admitted free. STREET

5.2 Buffalo Bill's Wild West: America's National Entertainment. Advertisement in the New Orleans *Daily Picayune*, December 22, 1884.
Howard-Tilton Memorial Library, Tulane University

folklore parade is a parade of the instruments of conviviality" (280). Encompassing these contrasting modes of performance, the Plains warriors performed complex and contradictory roles of enemies and American heroes, of local specimens and national symbols.

With or without their permission, Indians participate in the often violent struggle over what and who is or is not American. In the symbolic economy of Wild West violence especially, American Indians are richly polysemic, and Cody exploited every nuance. Indians could signify reckless defiance in face of oppression and tyranny. Through the repetition of the word *wild* in several of their tribal names, the Mardi Gras Indians seem to invoke this association, just as the Anglo-Americans did a century before at the Boston Tea Party. Creole Wild West was the first Indian gang name to be recorded, and it dates from the 1880s (Kinser, 162–63). Disenfranchised of a continent, American Indians could also signify holders of legitimate entitlement to either repatriation or revenge. From the time of Plymouth, the Indian appeared in the bad conscience of white mythology as a symbol of savage retribution, the dark agent of God's wrath. Those a generation away from slavery, exiles from a home they would never know, could identify with Native Americans, bitter exiles in their own land. The slave-holding propensities of the Five Civilized Tribes (so-called by whites in part *because* they held slaves) emphasize the double, inverted nature of the Indian as a symbol for African Americans: the nonwhite sign of both power and disinheritance. The theme of frontier space—and its control by nomads—illuminates, I think, the importance of the border skirmishes and alarums enacted by Mardi Gras Indians. On Mardi Gras day Indian gangs claim the space through which they move, like a passing renegade band, and the broad arm's-length gestures they make show off more than just their costumes. They occupy the constantly shifting borderlands, protected on their flanks by scouts (Spy Boys) as they migrate from block to block, from bar to bar. They perform a rite of territory repossessed to assert not sole ownership, perhaps, but certainly collective entitlement to fair use. It would be narrowly ethnocentric but not wildly misleading to describe them as performers in a mortgage melodrama on a world-historical scale, an unsettling vision, when one thinks of it this way, for the incumbent title holders.

Double identities, however, usually have more than two sides. The particularly masculine emphasis of the gangs, their fraternal organization, and their patriarchal dedication to the Big Chief, as well as their death-before-retreat bellicosity, recall the post–Civil War rhetoric of resurgent black manhood. African-American newspapers of the period often referred to the bravery of the black regiments on behalf of the Union cause, a rhetoric that intensified with the collapse of Reconstruction in the 1870s and 1880s, as Louisiana and the nation lurched backward into Jim Crow (Blassingame, 181). In the "old days," at the edge of living memory for today's maskers, Mardi Gras Indian processions ended on "the battlefield" or at the "Bucket o' Blood," a place where challenges could be answered and scores settled (Mitchell, 121). The polarity machine of the Wild West "Exhibition"—Cody never allowed it to be called a "Show"—was sanctified as a historical simulation of catastrophic expenditure. Steeped in the violence of gunfire, it certainly enacted the theme of machismo in the face of race war. Buffalo Bill also dramatized the despoliation of the West, the wanton slaughter of the buffalo, in a way that exemplifies my definition of violence as the performance of waste.

That is one reason why the shift by Mardi Gras Indians from confrontation based on nerve and spears and guns to competition based on patience and sequins and hems is so very interesting. It is no accident that competitive stitchery, beadwork, and opulent adornment have edged out violence in the confrontation between rival gangs. At carnival everyone wants to be seen in acts of conspicuous consumption and expenditure. For the urban underclasses in the United States at the end of the twentieth century, violence is one of the few forms of excess expenditure available in the absence of money. People spend their own and one another's blood. For this kind of investment, however, Mardi Gras Indian suits offer themselves as a substitute. In the year of exhaustive labor that it takes to make them, their designers "sweat blood" (Bannock, personal interview). The same gorgeous costume must be worn no more than once. The certainty that it must be sacrificed—ritually dismembered at the end of the Mardi Gras season—adds poignancy to its beauty and credibility to its role as a surrogate for the body of its creator.

The suits should not be thought of as artifacts but as performances in themselves. They seem to want to move out of the closed arena of curatorial manifest destiny and into the streets. That is their eloquence. Like other Afrocentric ritual and festival arts, Mardi Gras Indian parades unfold dynamically in time—simultaneously as memory and improvisation. In setting aside the necessary conjunction of ritual and cultural stability in African performance, Margaret Thompson Drewal contends "that rapid social change stimulates a traditionalizing process in which rituals and ritual symbols proliferate, constructing their pasts at the same time that they construct themselves" ("Ritual Performance," 25). So it is for the Indians. As Fu-Kiau Bunsekei, founder of the Kongo Academy in Bas-Zaire, said of African processional and masking festivals: "People are allowed to say not only what they voice in ordinary life but what is going on within their minds, their inner grief, their inner resentments. . . . Parades alter truth" (quoted in Nunley and Bettelheim, 23). In New Orleans the truth that Mardi Gras Indian parades seem to alter, by reenacting African-American memory through the surrogation of Native American identities, is the infinitude of Anglo-American entitlement.

At least a partial answer to the question about what Mr. Jelly Roll meant by "actual Indians in days long by" may now be formulated, particularly by attending to his mysterious hint of nostalgia for something irretrievably lost. I believe that one deep purpose of the gangs, their secret preparations, and their spectacular but nomadic performances is publicly to imagine a space, a continent, from which the white man and his culture have vanished or retreated to the peripheries. The tribes on this fictive continent are richly differentiated, Uptown and Downtown, friendly and unfriendly, but they all communicate through expressive performance across the shifting borders of their imagined community, the living and the dead. In other words, I believe that performance in New Orleans permits, through the disguise of "masking Indian," the imaginative re-creation and repossession of Africa (figure 5.3).

In his account of the sacred vision of Wovoka, the Paiute messiah of the Ghost Dance religion, the Cheyenne known as Porcupine calls Wovoka "Christ." The promise of the Ghost Dance religion was that if the Indians could keep dancing in the right spirit, their dead would return to life, and their world would be replenished and restored to them. White folks, an excrescent superabundance in America, would disappear. Porcupine continues: "When we were assembled, he began to sing, and he commenced to tremble all over, violently for awhile, and then sat down. We danced all that night, the Christ lying down beside us apparently dead" (795). As the Ghost Dance religion swept across the Great Plains in 1890, the authorities panicked, too fearful even to accept Buffalo Bill Cody's attempt to mediate with Sitting Bull, who was killed while resisting arrest (D. Brown, 436). Banned for the next thirty years, Ghost Dancing had struck a particular nerve, demonstrating the power of the kinesthetic imagination over the aspirations a people and the fears of their adversaries.

5.3 Yellow Jackets on Mardi Gras morning in New Orleans:
Chief Sterling Desmond and his queen.
Photo: Ed Newman, New Orleans, 1995

The Ghost Dance, like Mardi Gras Indian observances, was a rite of memory with spirit-world claims on the return of the ancestral dead. Porcupine saw this resurrection in terms of Christ, in something like the way that voodoo in New Orleans adopted Christian terms alongside the Afro-Caribbean. In neither case did syncretism necessarily deflect the practice of the arts of resistant memory (J. Scott). Revived (or at least more intensely publicized) in the 1880s, voodoo in nineteenth-century New Orleans is popularly associated with the successful practices of two Voodoo Queens, a mother and daughter, both bearing the name Marie Laveau. Operating through the intervention of spirits, or *loas*, the Voodoo Queens, caretakers of memory, resisted the segregation of the dead. The ethos of spirit-world possession pointedly focuses attention on the autonomy and ownership of living bodies, an attention most unwelcome to slaveholders in antebellum times as well as to their heirs in the era of Jim Crow. White or black,

Louisiana Creoles live closer to the dead than do most Anglo-Americans: the tombs of the ancestors are visited and tended on All Saints' Day, for instance. Increasingly, however, the line between the living and the dead in New Orleans worked as a symbolic reiteration of the color line, particularly with the increasing popularity in the 1870s and 1880s of expanding "Whites Only" cemeteries, segregated Cities of the Dead.

There is anecdotal support for the trend toward a more radical segregation of the dead in a remarkable account printed in the *New Orleans Bulletin* for May 29, 1875: "Buried alive. Sickening tale of our hospital dead: A man in the charity wagon revives. He attempts to get out of his coffin. The driver smothers him." It seems that the driver of the hearse, one Jim Connors, could not accept the fact that a nineteen-year-old smallpox victim, a black man named George Banks, had been pronounced dead prematurely. "You —," shouted Connors, hitting Banks over the head with a brick and then suffocating him with the couch seat of the hearse, "I have a doctor's certificate that you are dead, and I'm going to bury you" (quoted in Saxon, Dreyer, and Tallant, 342–43). As a tribute to the power of the written word in a literate society, the story is hard to excel, but not all societies maintain such a punctilious segregation of the dead from the living or black from white.

Mardi Gras Indian beadwork repays close study. Three panels adorn the suit of a child masker (figure 5.4). On the headress there is a death's head. The panel at the boy's waist shows Mohawk warriors dancing in victorious celebration around the fire in which a paleface is being sacrificed. The panel over the young Indian's heart depicts a circum-Atlantic Ghost Dance: two masked African shamans tenderly raise a Native American from the dead. Here the spirit-world faiths of African and Native American memory define an imagined community that opens the frontier between the living and the dead as it acknowledges the violence of the border between white and not-white.

A body possessed of its social memory—call it a "spirit"—is a body in some sense possessed of itself. It is even possessed of itself as property, to put it in the mystified but ennobling legal jargon whereby Anglo-Americans claimed certain inalienable rights. This amends somewhat the idea that the Mardi Gras Indians, or the Plains Indians, danced for the repossession of territory, though that is true; they also danced to possess themselves again in the spirit of their ancestors, to possess again their memories, to possess again their communities. They danced to resist their reduction to the status

5.4 Young Mardi Gras Indian Warrior, 1990.
Photo: Michael P. Smith

of commodities. In other words, they danced—and they still dance—to possess again a heritage that some people would rather see buried alive.

Slave Spectacles and Tragic Octoroons

One particularly informative guide to the operation of a behavioral vortex is the institutional convergence of business and pleasure. The staged exhibition of bodies for the purpose of selling them is an obvious enough marketing strategy that marks those bodies publicly as not possessed of themselves as property. Nineteenth-century historians of slavery traced the performance genealogy of the slave market to the ancient world, in which they professed to find detailed precedents for contemporary practice. Thus W. O. Blake's *History of Slavery* (1857) describes Athens: "On this occasion [market day] the slaves were stationed in a circle in the marketplace, and the one whose turn it was to be sold, mounted a table, where he exhibited himself and was knocked down to the best bidder. The sales seem to have been conducted precisely like those of the present day in Richmond, Charleston, New Orleans, and other cities of the South" (29). That the Greek and Roman exhibitions included nudity or seminudity likewise lent a legitimating dignity or, at least, time-honored pragmatism (in the eyes of the buyers) to the custom of exposing and examining all the surfaces of the slave's body: "They were placed on a raised stone, or table, so that everyone might see and handle them, even if they did not wish to purchase them. Purchasers took care to have them stripped, for slave dealers had recourse to as many tricks to conceal defects, as a horse-jockey of modern times" (50). The less obvious but more enduring strategy was to use the traffic in bodies to promote the sale of other commodities as well. This technique gave slave spectacles utility as drawing cards even for the customers who "did not wish to purchase" slaves, but who might be induced to spend their money in any number of other ways, their mimetic desire released by the eye-filling scenes of the public flesh market.

In antebellum New Orleans particularly, slave auctions proved a popular and highly theatrical spectacle. The most popular of them took place in a magnificent theaterlike rotunda, designed and built for this purpose, in the St. Louis Hotel. The management provided music from a stage band. Of the entertainment value of the slave auctions of the mid-1850s, the local press remarked: "Amusements seldom prove attractive here unless music is brought to the aid of other inducements to spend money" (*Daily Picayune*,

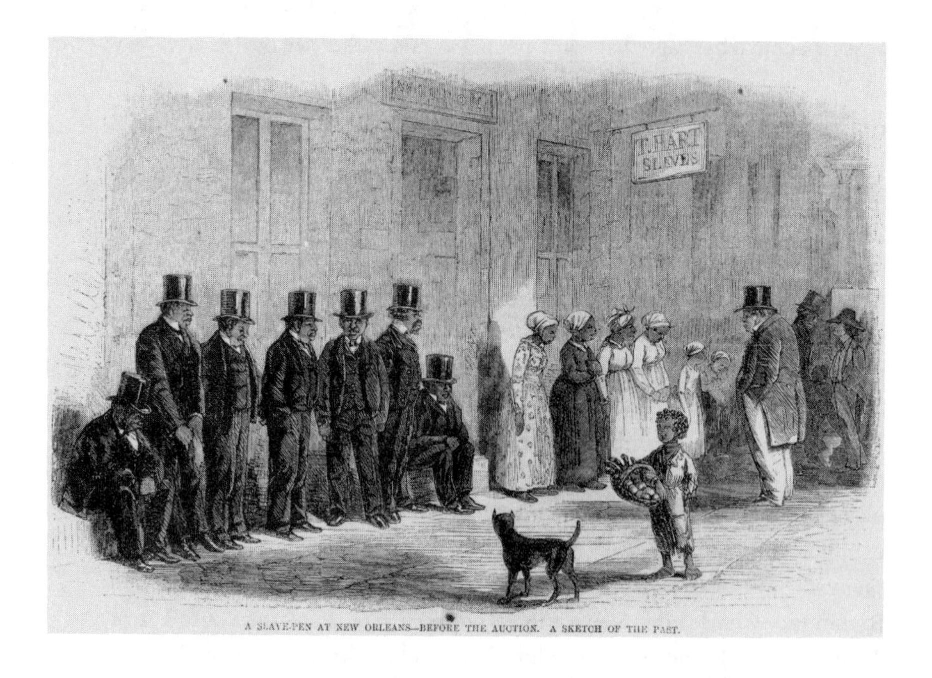

A SLAVE-PEN AT NEW ORLEANS—BEFORE THE AUCTION. A SKETCH OF THE PAST.

5.5 Exchange Alley. *Harper's Weekly*, January 21, 1863.
Courtesy The Historic New Orleans Collection, Museum/Research Center, acc. no. 1958.43.24

March 26, 1853). The brokers also provided special theatrical costumes: formal wear for the male slaves and brightly colored dresses for the women. These are shown in an illustration from *Harper's Weekly* in which the preauction display of merchandise takes place on the street in "Exchange Alley," part of the St. Louis Hotel complex (figure 5.5). Captioned "A Slave-Pen at New Orleans—Before the Auction. A Sketch of the Past," the text and image, "by a foreign artist," offer a retrospective view of slave marketing before the outbreak of the Civil War: "The men and women are well clothed, in their Sunday best—the men in blue cloth of good quality, with beaver hats; and the women in calico dresses, of more or less brilliancy, with silk bandana handkerchiefs bound round their heads. Placed in a row in a quiet thoroughfare, where, without interrupting the traffic, they may command a good chance of transient custom, they stand through a great part of the day, subject to the inspection of the purchasing or non-purchasing passing crowd. They look heavy, perhaps a little sad, but not altogether unhappy" (*Harper's*

Weekly, January 21, 1863). The shock of such a revived memory, a picturesque scene that someone stumbled on casually while walking through the city, is increased by the recognition of the very normality of the slave trade in the performance of daily life in New Orleans. The restored behavior of the marketplace created by its synergy a behavioral vortex in which human relationships could be drained of sympathetic imagination and shaped to the purposes of consumption and exchange. Under such conditions, the most intolerable of injustices may be made to seem natural and commonplace, and the most demented of spectacles normal. But normality does not happen by accident. It thrives on exposure (and construction) through extraordinary performances. Why else dress up slaves in top hat and tails?

Antebellum New Orleans, which had the earliest American suburb to be linked to the urban hub by public transport, was in some respects a prototypical circum-Atlantic city. In this urban plan, the Exchange complex, surpassed in scale only by the St. Louis Cathedral in Jackson Square, comprised not only a commercial center but a ludic space, a stage of cultural self-invention through restored behavior. Its promoters, ridiculing the old marketplaces of the French and Spanish colonial period (in which, under the Spanish liberalization of the old *Code noir*, slaves could earn the price of their freedom), touted the Exchange as the Louisianian staging point of a new circum-Atlantic empire: "We can't say how it is elsewhere, but here, the going-going-gone of the auctioneers, and the clinching 'bang' of their hammers, follow the rounds of our city and keep company with the streets, as the roll of the British drum is poetically said to follow the sun, and keep company with the hours around the world" (*Daily Picayune*, February 20, 1853). In this estimation, slave spectacles expand the centripetal pull of the behavioral vortex to the suburban perimeters of the metropolis and beyond.

The eye of the vortex, however, was the rotunda of the St. Louis Hotel. The building was designed in 1838, by the French architect J. B. Pouilly, as the anchor of one end of Exchange Alley. Pouilly conceived the alley as a mall-like promenade cutting through the French Quarter to link the rotunda to Canal Street, a major thoroughfare of commerce and the symbolic dividing line between the Latin and Anglo-American zones of the city. The concept closely resembles a contemporary suburban shopping mall with anchor department stores at each end of a promenade of smaller specialty shops. Pouilly's protomall featured male-oriented ateliers such as tobacconists, gunsmiths, and fencing masters, mixed in with slave brokers, lining each side and leading to the imposing urban landmark of the St. Louis Hotel itself.

The hotel was a kind of homosocial pleasure dome with overlapping commercial and leisure attractions. The informative *Historical Sketch Book and Guide to New Orleans* recalled: "This exchange not only contained the finest bar-room in the city, but the principal auction mart, where slaves, stocks, real estate, and all other kinds of property were sold from noon to 3:00 P.M., the auctioneers crying their wares in a multitude of languages, the English, the French, and the Spanish predominating. The entire upper portion of the building was devoted exclusively to gambling and billiard rooms. . . . Adjoining the exchange [was] a cockpit" (77). The auction itself began with a "promenade," a kind of production number in which the chorus of commodities paraded to the auction block, led by a high-strutting master of ceremonies. According to an account in the Louisiana WPA oral history project: "Some of the traders kept a big, good-natured buck to lead the parade (of slaves to be sold) and uniforms for both men and women, so that the high hats, the riot of white, pink, red and blue would attract the attention of prospective buyers" (quoted in Saxon, Dreyer, and Tallant, 226).

The fancy costumes came off as the merchandise was stripped to permit close examination. In her narrative, former slave Lu Perkins recalls having been stripped at her own sale, noting that there was a practical motive for the exhibition of her upper body: "I 'members when they put me on the auction block. They pulled my dress down over my back to my waist, to show I ain't gashed and slashed up. That's to show you ain't a mean nigger" (quoted in Mellon, 292). Slaves on the block were sometimes expected to dance in order to show at once their liveliness and their docility. They also had a motive, it was supposed, to increase their sale price: the more valuable the slave, the less willingness on the part of the master to inflict harm. In his slave narrative, James Martin recalls: "Then, [the auctioneer] makes 'em hop, he makes 'em trot, he makes 'em jump. 'How much,' he yells, 'for this buck? A thousand? Eleven hundred? Twelve hundred dollars?' " (quoted in Mellon, 291).

Here resides a plausible, if as yet relatively unexplored, genealogy of performance. With music, dance, and seminudity, the slave auction, as a performance genre, might be said to have anticipated the development of American musical comedy. It certainly had important linkages to the black-faced minstrel show, which enacted the effacement of the cultural traditions of those whose very flesh signified its availability for display and consumption. But they were not the only descendants of slave auction performance art.

In terms of drawing power, the "fancy-girl" auctions, the sale of quadroons (one-quarter African-descended females) and octoroons, proved an exceptionally popular New Orleans specialty (Genovese, 416–17), performed in an atmosphere charged not only with white privilege but with male privilege. As anxious buyers bid up the price many times that of a good field hand, the sale of relatively well-educated and relatively white women into sexual bondage raised the erotic stakes higher in a public, democratic spectacle that rivals all but the most private of pornographic exhibitions in aristocratic Europe (Senelick, "Erotic Bondage").

The compelling, even hypnotic fascination inspired by slave spectacles resides, I believe, in their violent, triangular conjunction of money, property, and flesh. In the rotunda of the St. Louis Hotel, as it was represented by an engraving in 1854, three kinds of property go under the gavel at once: pictures on the left, real estate on the right, and slaves in the middle (figure 5.6). In the dramatic lighting provided by the bull's-eye window in the classical, pantheonlike dome, the centrality of naked flesh signifies the abundant availability of all commodities: *everything* can be put up for sale, and everything can be examined and handled even by those who are just looking. In the staging of New Orleans slave auctions, there is a fiercely laminating adhesion of bodies and objects, the individual desire for pleasure and the collective desire to compete for possession. As competitions between men, the auctions seethe with the potential for homosocial violence. As theatrical spectacle, they materialize the most intense of symbolic transactions in circum-Atlantic culture: money transforms flesh into property; property transforms flesh into money; flesh transforms money into property. As circum-Atlantic performances, they epitomize the dependence of commodification on auctions, organizing an auction community around the event itself and serially reorganizing that community and intensifying or transforming its consciousness of value with each new performance. As Charles W. Smith explains in *Auctions: The Social Construction of Value* (1989): "Where most forms of economic life occur within established communities and in terms of accepted values, auctions require that such communities and values be continually reproduced" (14). It could also be said that auctions require such communities and values to be continually *performed*. What an auction organizes is close to sacred ritual in circum-Atlantic terms because it disposes of luxury fetishes in the form of excess expenditure: bread is not often auctioned off, but

5.6 W. H. Brooke, "Sale of Estates,
Pictures and Slaves in the Rotunda, New Orleans," 1854.
Courtesy The Historic New Orleans Collection, Museum/Research Center,
acc. no. 1953.149

(where value is shifting, labile, unfixed) slaves, paintings, plantations, and fancy girls are.

Into this highly charged scene, the entrance of the tragic octoroon or quadroon, sometimes advertised as a "Yellow Girl," introduced the effigy's uncanny doubleness. Abolitionist tracts appropriated such spectacles to heighten the pathos of the flesh market, while not coincidentally trading on its erotic titillation. In this genre must be numbered John Theophilus Kramer's *Slave Auction* (1859), an eyewitness account of the New Orleans slave market designed for readers in the North: "There stands a girl upon the platform to be sold to the highest bidder; perhaps to a cruel, low and dissolute fellow, who, for a day or two since, won a few thousand dollars by playing his tricks at the faro table. She is nearly white; she is not yellow, as they call her. She has a fair waist, her hair is black and silky, and falling down in ringlets upon her full shoulders. Her eyes are large, soft, and languishing" (26). Her flesh disguises the invisible truth of her blood. She could pass, but the law and the act of sale label her, stripping her of her whiteness. In the politics of performance, she is "marked" (Phelan). The performance of a "fancy-girl" auction and its representation in nineteenth-century art and literature definitively illustrate the function of an effigy in the process of symbolic substitution—of a white-appearing body for a black one, of gender difference for racial difference, and of one commodity for another. They exemplify the role of surrogation in both the transmission and the displaced transmission of cultural forms and attitudes.

Dion Boucicault's own residence in New Orleans, at the height of the spectacular slave auctions of the mid-1850s, offers an example of how the performances of everyday life may be reconstructed for the stage. He made his New Orleans debut on January 23, 1855, though his plays had long been popular in the Crescent City before his arrival in person. Looking for a likely venue to establish a permanent company, Boucicault secured local backing and assumed the role of actor-manager-playwright of the Gaiety Theatre, which opened on December 1, 1855 (Durham, 502). The big success of the season was the acting of Boucicault's wife, Agnes Robertson. She excelled in roles, often written for her by her husband, in which she could take on several different identities. In *The Chameleon*, her Gaiety debut, she played the part of an actress who impersonates three different characters to win the heart of her skeptical father-in-law to be. She followed up this role with two other star vehicles, *The Cat Changed into a Woman* and *Violet; or, The Life of an Actress* (*Daily Picayune*, December 28, 1855, and January 14, 1856). Robertson's ability to suggest liminality and the consequent instability but great attractiveness of her image made her acting style particularly amenable to surrogation—the metamorphosis of one symbolic identity into another, an exchange of bodies and souls.

New Orleans high society welcomed Boucicault and Robertson hospitably, a generosity that became the source of great local bitterness after the premiere of the play that purported to show contemporary "Life in Louisiana." Boucicault could not but observe the weird demimonde of *plaçage*, the creole custom of arranging extramarital liaisons with educated *mulatas*: some New Orleans theaters set aside one performance a week for gentlemen and their quadroon mistresses; at these miscegenist fetes, the managements desegregated the seating and disinvited white women (Kendall, *New Orleans Theater*, 38–39).

After a brief return appearance in 1857, Boucicault left New Orleans for brighter prospects in New York and London. One of the brightest of these was the chance to craft another role for Agnes Robertson—Zoe—in which she could excel in her specialty of multiple identity, a poised walk along the borders of difference, before the clarifying moments of the final tableau, when she is purified by death: "O! George, you may, without a blush, confess your love for the Octoroon!" (40). The *Daily Picayune*, drawing on accounts of the production in the abolitionist papers in the North, responded with a savagely vituperative review, headed "The Last of Mr. Boucicault," especially noting Robertson's willowy rendering of the title role as "a delicately colored young female, enwrapped in white muslin, sentiment, and poetry" (*Daily Picayune*, December 24, 1859). Two years later, as the Civil War raged in the States, Boucicault took his play to London, where it initially failed because the audience rejected the unhappy ending: London theatergoers could not accept Agnes Robertson's death in any role. Boucicault cobbled together a new version, "composed by the Public," as he put it, "and edited by the Author," in which the octoroon revives (Degen). One of the most widely reproduced illustrations of a scene from that copious archive of sensation that Michael Booth calls "Victorian spectacular theatre" appeared in the *Illustrated London News* (figure 5.7), but more than a simple spectacle, the image is a *realization* in the deep sense that Martin Meisel has imparted to that word. The scene depicts a climactic moment from act 3 of *The Octoroon* in which Zoe, amid the financial collapse of Terrebonne Plantation, stands on a table in the mansion she once graced. This action represents onstage the restored behavior of the slave auctions of the New Orleans Exchange, the transformation of cash into flesh and of flesh into property.

What happens to Zoe happens in a room filled with men, both spectators and combatants, who have assembled for the purpose of selling "Estates, Pictures, and Slaves." Boucicault's placement of the public auction in a private parlor (though no doubt motivated in part by scenic economy) brings the scene of slavery home to the domestic sphere, a setting that middle-class audiences outside the South could also recognize. Many authors appropriated the ever-useful mortgage melodrama master plot (Chekhov warmed it over in *The Cherry Orchard*) as a surefire appeal to bourgeois anxieties of displacement. But the variant involving the tragic octoroon substituted expendable female bodies for the foreclosed properties of the melodramatic master narrative. Slavery, including the genteel servitude of the fancy girl, is social death: Zoe is property, but she is dispossessed of any property in herself.

5.7 Dion Boucicault, *The Octoroon*, Adelphi Theatre, London.
Illustrated London News, November 30, 1861.
Howard-Tilton Memorial Library, Tulane University

What Boucicault engineers in the build-up to the auction scene is a symbolic and material linkage between the representation of race and the representation of gender. Both become commodities, but it is the scarcely visible presence of black blood that provides the signifier of commodification. When George ardently proposes marriage, Zoe takes her somewhat obtuse lover on a frank fact-finding tour of her body, including her extraordinary blood count:

ZOE: And what shall I say? I—my mother was—no, no—not her! Why should I refer the blame to her? George, do you see that hand you hold? look at these fingers; do you see the nails are a bluish tinge?

GEORGE: Yes, near the quick there is a faint blue mark.

ZOE: Look in my eyes; is not the same color in the white?

GEORGE: It is their beauty.

ZOE: Could you see the roots of my hair you would see the same dark, fatal mark. Do you know what that is?

GEORGE: No.

ZOE: That is the ineffaceable curse of Cain. Of the blood that feeds my heart, one drop in eight is black—bright red as the rest may be, that one drop poisons all the flood; those seven bright drops give me love like yours—hope like yours—ambition like yours—life hung with passions like dew-drops in the morning flowers; but the one black drop gives me despair, for I'm an unclean thing—forbidden by the laws—I'm an Octoroon! (16–17)

Zoe's blood is exposed and marked as if it has already been shed. The body of the white-appearing octoroon (played by the fascinatingly liminal Agnes Robertson) offers itself as the crucible in which a strange alchemy of cultural surrogation takes place. In the defining event of commercial exchange, from flesh to property, the object of desire mutates and transforms itself, from African to woman: its nearly invisible but fatal blackness makes it available; its whiteness somehow makes it clean.

Such a slave spectacle is, I think, as American as baseball. Boucicault drew on a large and growing repository of images and descriptions of this pathetic and erotic scene. The hostile review of the New York *Octoroon* in the New Orleans *Daily Picayune* referred to "a delicately colored young female, enwrapped in white muslin." In the competing images of the slave auction scene circulated in high-culture venues through easel paintings and sculptures of the period, the delicately colored young female was more often unwrapped than enwrapped (Honour). The image of Robertson's Zoe fully clothed on the auction block must be viewed in the context of antebellum slave sales and their representation in several popular circum-Atlantic media (McElroy). In that context, Zoe would have had to strip, and she would have been stripped by association in the minds of the viewers as she stepped up on the tabletop (T. Davis).

Such a strong cultural signification marks American sculptor John Bell's masterpiece *The Octoroon*, which was exhibited at the Royal Academy in 1868 (figure 5.8). The octoroon's smooth skin glows childlike and white, Bell's marble medium helping here to reinforce his message. That message seems to be that slavery is more tragic and exciting when it is suffered by innocent white women. The octoroon repines unresistingly in the almost ornamental chains of her bondage. Like Rapunzel, she sweetly, and very

5.8 John Bell, *The Octoroon*, 1868.
Courtesy the Blackburn Museum and Art Gallery, Lancashire, England

carefully, lets down her hair. In the social semiotics of Victorian nudity, the absence of pubic hair, such as in those smoothly modeled plaster casts of classical statues that ruined John Ruskin's wedding night, signified purity. This signifier of innocence promised a body as yet untouched—acquiescent, passive, virginal, ownable—the body of a slave, the body of a child.

"The Quadroon Girl," by Henry Wadsworth Longfellow, retails many of the same images but with the added narrative complication that the unnamed girl is being sold off in the front parlor by her bankrupt planter father. Three of Longfellow's twelve stanzas allow the reader to catch his drift:

Her eyes were large, and full of light,
Her arms and neck were bare;
No garment she wore save a kirtle bright,
And her own long, raven hair.

And on her lips there played a smile
As holy, meek, and faint,
As lights in some cathedral aisle
The features of a saint.

"The soil is barren,—the farm is old,"
The thoughtful planter said;
Then looked upon the Slaver's gold,
And then upon the maid.

(28)

The liminal status of the Quadroon Girl opens up a space for erotic play even in the most earnest of abolitionist tracts, the kind of play facilitated by the duality of the subject—white and black, child and woman, angel and wench. It was through this kind of weirdly bifurcated imagery that the circum-Atlantic world viewed slavery and race in America.

To the public nudity by association in the auction scene of *The Octoroon*, Boucicault adds another erotic twist. This one amplifies the racial and gendered doubling of the octoroon by playing her off sexually against a "white" woman. Zoe stands at the apex of a compositional triangle (see figure 5.7). She is anchored on one side by the scene of gladiatorial male violence (between M'Closky, the villain, and George, her boyfriend, backed up by Salem Scudder, the amiably murderous Yankee Jonathan). On the other

5.9 St. George Hare, *The Victory of Faith*, 1891.
Reproduced by permission of the National Gallery of Victoria, Melbourne

side she is anchored by the neighboring plantation belle Dora Sunnyside's heaving bosom. All those along the base of the triangle, including Dora, bid on Zoe. Dora's bid intensifies the erotic effects of the scene by linking the two women sexually. Dora's participation in the male-centered activity of bidding on property at an auction makes hers a kind of breeches role, recalling that the comparable scene in the source novel, Reid's *Quadroon*, has the Dora character cross-dress so that she can enter the rotunda at the St. Louis Hotel to procure the slave girl (Reid, 308–9). The implicitly lesbian coupling of two women, one fair, the other dark, proliferates in the Victorian erotica of the circum-Atlantic exchange. For instance, in a painting entitled *The Victory of Faith*, the Royal Academician St. George Hare exploits this erotic theme in the guise of a religious painting (figure 5.9). The otherwise puzzling title is explained by the narrative program, which invites the beholder to believe that these nudes represent two Christian virgins in ancient Rome sleeping innocently together in the holding pen of the Colosseum on the last night before their fatal rendezvous with the lions. The presence of the (unchained) black girl, on which the grasp of the white girl's hand insists, insinuates what the unrepresentability of pubic hair cannot: the pressure of sexual desire from within even the whitest body. The sexualized virgin martyr rises transcendent from the flesh of her black double. These two bodies might miraculously appear from the blood of one octoroon.

The Victory of Faith epitomizes the interracial and sexual doubling whereby the "tragic" sale of white women displaces the representation of black slave sales, in which the generic prototypes of white culture's musical comedy predominates. The scene from Boucicault's *Octoroon* is so rich because it shows in action this process of surrogation (of white for black) and transformation (from buffo comedy to noble tragedy). Obscured in the corner of the room (see figure 5.7, stage right, background) stand the other slaves who have been on the block earlier in the scene: Lot "No. 1" is Solon; Lot "No. 2, the yellow girl Grace, with two children—Saul, aged four, Victoria, five (*They get on the table*)." These slaves happily celebrate their good fortune when they are sold as a family, then Ole Pete, the Uncle Tom character, stands on the block as Lot "No. 3" and dances cheerfully to show how spry he is and to raise his bid accordingly (27–28). But all this is preparatory to the sale of Zoe: when she stands on the table, the tone of the scene shifts from minstrelsy to melodrama, the tragic heroine literally taking the stage, pushing the comic supernumeraries off to the right. Even from a slave sale, black people are excluded.

To accomplish such a coup de théâtre, Boucicault must purify Zoe of her own traces of African blood. He does this by having her die by her own hand and then—miraculously—turn white. As Zoe expires, Dora reverently reports: "Her eyes have changed color." Ole Pete explains, "Dat's what her soul's gwine do. It's going up dar, whar dere's no line atween folks" (39). Out of the ruptured chrysalis of the octoroon's body floats a miraculous American angel. Her ritualized death and transfiguration suggest that God, like Monsieur Colbert, ultimately favors the policy of One Blood.

Storyville

In terms of the genealogy of performance, New Orleans slave spectacles themselves undergo a process not of complete cessation but of transformation and displacement. Slavery was quite explicitly and officially sexualized—and thereby at least symbolically recuperated—in the development of legally sanctioned prostitution during the 1890s. Unique in the history of American tenderloin or red-light districts, the area that came to be known as Storyville was established by city ordinance, and it was included as an important hub in the new streetcar system. Its architecturally elaborate houses, built from the ground up to serve their designated purpose and marked by prominent rooflines featuring Victorian cupolas, made Storyville an important urban and even civic landmark and nodal point.

In the displacement of New Orleanian vortices of behavior, Storyville succeeds Exchange Alley and the St. Louis Hotel, turning the principal ludic space on its axis and moving it a few blocks over, reconstituting the homosocial pleasure dome in the post-Reconstruction era. Storyville was separated from the site of Congo Square, then renamed Beauregard Park, by the old cemetery: like London's Covent Garden, the modern commercial city grew up around the old liminal zones, including the fringe marketplace, creating a specialized behavioral vortex in which the supply of human flesh could meet the ever more specialized demand.

The most prominent cupola on the Storyville skyline belonged to Miss Lulu White's Mahogany Hall, a brothel specializing in mixed-race women and heavily advertised as "The Octoroon Club." The whorehouses published directories or catalogs (called "Blue Books") which advertised specialized sexual services in highly coded language. In their self-representation, if that is what it is, the women stress their skills as performers and their racial categories:

> The beautiful Estelle Russell, now a member of high standing in Miss White's famous Octoroon Club, a few years ago one of the leading stars in Sam T. Jack's Creole Show . . .
>
> Emma Sears . . . the colored Carmencita . . . as a tambourine dancer she has no superior and very few equals. Tall, graceful, winning. (Blue Book, HJA)

In the normalizing courtesies of business cards and consumer guides, the flesh market is once again subsumed into the legitimate economy of the city: at its peak, Storyville employed over a thousand people; it promoted tourism and well-controlled shore leaves for the U.S. Navy; it became, like family dinner at Antoine's, a local tradition for some, a place for fathers to initiate their sons into a privileged knowledge of the world and of their own proper place in it as men.

5.10 Jelly Roll Morton plays the piano
at Hilma Burt's Mirror Ballroom, Storyville, ca. 1904.
Courtesy the William Ransom Hogan Jazz Archive, Tulane University

Some Storyville brothels offered special performances, called "Circuses," three nights per week. The musical accompaniment to such entertainments employed a number of musicians important in the early history of jazz (Lulu White's Mahogany Hall furniture is still in use in the reading room of the Hogan Jazz Archives at Tulane University). In one photograph, the girls gather around the piano, which is played by none other than Jelly Roll Morton (figure 5.10). According to Mr. Jelly Roll's own oral history, the staging here is more demure than usual, for normally the whores danced naked. The madam put up a screen between the piano and the stage, but Mr. Jelly Roll cut a hole in it so that he could see the Circus. The word he used to describe what he saw was "cruel": "I worked for all the houses, even Emma Johnson's Circus House, where the guests got everything from soup to nuts. They did a lot of uncultured things then that probably couldn't be mentioned, and the irony part of it, they always picked the youngest and most beautiful girls to do them right before the eyes of everybody" (Lomax, 127). New Orleans brothel performances have roots deep in representations and behaviors spawned in the slave culture of the antebellum period—and in the reconstructed memories and restored behaviors consciously evoking that period. Storyville establishments featured auctions in which young girls and even children, advertised as "Virgins," were put up on front-parlor tables and gaveled down to the top bidder.

Ernest J. Bellocq photographed a number of the women in Storyville, and his fragile, haunting images suggest the performative character of the self-representation of the sex workers. Bellocq's portrait of a reclining, nude young girl (the scene restaged with Brooke Shields by Louis Malle in the film *Pretty Baby*) evokes the imagery of vulnerability and availability that also characterized depictions of the tragic octoroon (figure 5.11). Mr. Spectator encountered an earlier edition of her specialized type, "newly come upon the Town," plying her trade in Covent Garden. She is the recumbent version of John Bell's statue (cf. figure 5.8), except that wherever the black or mulatto woman is absent, as she apparently is from this photograph, pubic hair tends to appear. The pose in Bellocq's photo quotes another strong tradition of erotic representation in European painting, the reclining nude Venus and her clothed handmaiden, so there is an empty space in Bellocq's composition that connoisseurs could reasonably be expected to fill in. The image of the black woman in the upper right of Edouard Manet's notorious painting of a sixteen-year-old white prostitute, *Olympia*, insists on constructing the linkages between the diverse flesh markets throughout the circum-Atlantic world (figure 5.12). But as much as the image insists, its beholders erased it. The West Indian woman (identified by her headdress) became all but invisible to subsequent commentators—except to those who praised Manet for his formal compositional effects of light and shade—evidence of the success of surrogation as cultural displacement (Boime, 2–4; Clayson, 6, 16).

In the Storyville sex circuses, other popular specialities included dark and fair lesbian acts and even displays of bestiality (figure 5.13). New Orleans historian Al Rose has interviewed a number of those prostitutes who lived into the 1950s and 1960s. Their histories read something like slave narratives, especially when their sexual initiation included being auctioned off like the antebellum "fancy girls." One of Rose's informants speaks

5.11 Storyville prostitute.
Photo: Ernest Bellocq. Courtesy the Howard-Tilton Memorial Library, Tulane University

unsentimentally and explicitly about her sale on the block at Emma Johnson's Circus in about 1915 or 1916, when she was about twelve years old:

> I was in the circus two or three nights a week. There was another kid my age . . . Liz. . . . We used to work together. By this time we were getting a little figure and looked pretty good . . . and neither one of us was afraid to do them things the johns liked, so we'd get a hundred a night to be in the circus. My mother was in the circus, too. She's the one who used to fuck the pony. Emma kept a stable in the yard and a colored man, Wash, used to take care of the two ponies and the horse. In the daytime me and Liz rode the ponies around the yard. . . . Ain't that something? . . . So, Emma . . . made a speech about me and Liz and how everybody in the District knew we was virgins, even though we did all these other things and that if the price was right, tonight

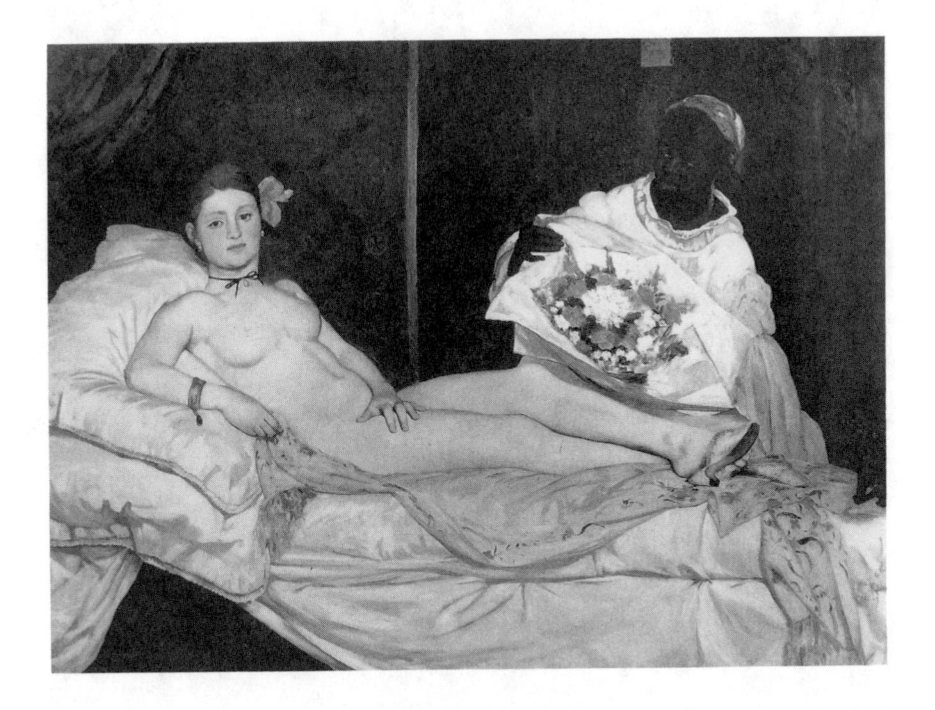

5.12 Edouard Manet, *Olympia*, 1863.
Courtesy the Musée d'Orsay, Paris

> was the night and she'd have an auction. Some snotty kid bid a dollar and Emma had one of the floor men slug him and throw him out in the street. One man bid the both of us in, honest to God, for seven hundred and seventy-five dollars each! A lot of johns bid, and he wasn't gonna be satisfied with just one. He bought us both. Well, we went upstairs with him. He wanted us both together, and you know how it is, we thought he ought to be entitled to somethin' for all that money, so we came on with everything we could think of, includin' the dyke act. . . . We did a dance we had worked out where we jerked ourselves and each other off. (quoted in Rose, 149–50)

Theater historians, alert to the particulars of stage business, will appreciate the detail in which this virtuosic performance is recorded. It actually took two nights, in deference to the premature exhaustion of the patron. The "dyke act," a pornographic mainstay, signals the availability of the girls, their readiness for defloration, while reiterating their status *intacta*, their

GOOD GOD!

The Crimes of Sodom and Gomorrah Discounted.

5.13 Cover story on Storyville in *The Mascot*, October 21, 1893.
Howard-Tilton Memorial Library, Tulane University

sapphic innocence of prior penises. With their purchase comes a fantasy of their possession, an echo of the absolute ownership once possible under the Old Regime:

> The Slaver led her from the door,
> He led her by the hand,
> To be his slave and paramour
> In a strange and distant land.
> (Longfellow, 28)

In New Orleans the transmission of black slavery was displaced to the white variety in more direct and literal ways than in other places. As the Jim Crow laws developed, the liaisons permitted in Storyville became more rigorously segregated. Just before the district closed down in 1917, African-descended women were forbidden to work in white-only brothels. To this day, however, the urban behavioral vortex is still propelled by energies unleashed by slavery, white and black. The question is not whether slavery still exists but whether people still treat each other as if it did. Reconstituted on Bourbon Street, New Orleans's more recent ludic space, Storyville lives symbolically in such pseudofleshpots and jazz joints as Lulu White's Mahogany Hall and Storyville Lounge—Girls, Girls, Girls. These alternate with strip clubs and T-shirt emporia to resituate the homosocial pleasure zone as a synecdoche for the entire city of New Orleans (Wade). This Afro-Caribbean capital, which has now somehow constructed itself as the nation's libido (i.e., "The Big Easy"), publishes some of the most bizarre promotional literature in the history of American boosterism: "A corpulent hostess, patted and powdered and daubed with rouge, New Orleans reclines along the banks of the wide river, straining her corsets of convention and drawing her admirers to her with a languid gesture. A feminine city—not in the girlish sense, but like an aging coquette, a little too perfumed, a bit jaded—New Orleans fascinates the senses without taxing the mind" (Kolb, xi). In such a formulation, the city of New Orleans itself becomes the ludic space, the behavioral vortex, for the rest of the nation.

If that is really so, then my theory of displaced transmission would predict that the homosocial pleasure dome must have reconstituted itself in some significant and prominent way in a vortex-inducing landmark or node. Following out the logic of my line of speculation on the genealogy of antebellum performance, I believe that it has. Roughly equidistant by only a few city blocks from the sites of both the St. Louis Exchange and Storyville, the Louisiana Superdome consummates the performance genealogy of the North American traffic in money and flesh. The dome is built over the site once occupied by the "Bucket o' Blood," the place where Mardi Gras Indians met to settle old scores. It is now the cyclonic center of a complex of mall-like avenues of shops and department stores, and at times of peak use it becomes a prime procurer of trade for prostitutes during such events as tractor pulls, trade shows, and the 1988 Republican National Convention. It is also the most prominent stage for North America's most popular national spectacle, NFL Football. Such spectacles—the commodification of flesh in an economy of ever more highly specialized greed—display immensely valuable black bodies sweating for white people who still unblinkingly call themselves owners. This is not to negate the very different degrees of agency involved in the sale of flesh then and now, but it is to link them in a genealogy of surrogations, a line of descent from the past into the future.

In the postmodern circum-Atlantic world of late capitalism, what Paul Gilroy calls "the sound system culture" both symbolizes and embodies the syncretism whereby African, North American, Caribbean, and European forms circulate together in a plagiarized interculture. Sound system culture "redefines the meaning of performance by separating the input of the artist who originally made the recording from the equally important work of those who adapt and rework it so that it directly expresses the moment in which it is being consumed" (*Union Jack*, 165). The image of Boucicault's tragic octoroon, borne up "Like a Virgin" to displace the experience of African-Americans with the image of a White Goddess, has yet to exhaust its powers of recirculation. Madonna's sixty-million-dollar contract with Time-Warner is worth pondering in the context of auctions, recycled commodities, and displaced spectacles. Flesh sells; it sells itself, and, more important, it sells everything else. As effigy du jour of the 1980s, Madonna rode the crest of a dark wave of subordinated African-American performers and performances. She was their surrogate (hooks, 157–63). Around that substitution, Madonna fashioned the complex web of intercultural and subcultural appropriations—gay, queer, Catholic, and working-class rituals—that defined her as a "Material Girl." Through flirtations with blackness, though not with blackness alone, she produced herself as the multipurpose effigy of the decade. As in the case of Zoe in *The Octoroon*, the invisible presence of blackness marks her flesh as a commodity even as her whiteness changes its value. "Blackness" and "whiteness" have extraordinary meaning to a performer in this system of ornate fetishizations. Now more than ever, the proximity of human flesh to virtually all material objects offered for sale drives an economy of catastrophic expenditure. By its terms, race constitutes a form of property—something a performer can own, sell, or exchange. "Indeed," asked Albion W. Tourgée in his preliminary brief for *Plessy v. Ferguson*, written in 1895, "is it not the most valuable sort of property, being the master-key that unlocks the golden door of opportunity?" (quoted in Olsen, 83).

Homer Plessy and Whiteface Minstrelsy

The categories defined by "whiteness" and "nonwhiteness" are at once the most powerful and the most fragile creations of circum-Atlantic performance. The strangeness of a society produced by insisting on the visibility of these fictions of identity is poignantly evoked by Patricia J. Williams in *The Alchemy of Race and Rights: Diary of a Law Professor* (1991). Not coincidentally, her memory of her own debut into the obligatory performance of race, her entrance into the cruel lights of its scopic regime, was jogged while walking through the city on a visit to New Orleans in 1989: "I recall the first time I shifted vision internally and beheld myself with my mind's eye. Unlike the intimacy of my mother's voice, the eye belonged to someone I did not know. The eye beheld that I was 'not white'; this awareness did not make me wonder about the source of the eye's vision—I was too caught up in horrible fascination of the news it brought: I learned, through it, to hate the black mirror image that confronted me in every store window; in public places and in the eyes of others, I was revealed." What catches her eye—or what catches her in its eye—is the restored behavior of the old slave dances of Congo Square, now revived specifically to meet the tourist gaze: "In New Orleans, I notice, it is only the black residents who dance in the street; it is only white tourists who can bear to stand and watch. If whites do dance it is in imitation of blacks-who-are-watched. If whites dance it is a separate form of entertainment, like the limbo. It is a seen dance, rather than a felt or a transporting dance" (213). In Williams's account, as in the elaborate stagecraft of the Plessy case, the play of visible and invisible properties turned into actions brings into question—even as it reflects the real human costs of—the fantastic category of "not white" (figure 5.14)

The complaint signed by Detective Chris C. Cain charges one Homer Adolph Plessy with offenses against "the peace and dignity of the State" of

5.14 One Blood: Alfred R. Waud,
life sketches of New Orleanians, *Every Saturday*, 1871.
Louisiana Collection, Howard-Tilton Memorial Library, Tulane University

Louisiana. It alleges that on June 7, 1892, Plessy, "being a passenger of the colored race on a train of the East Louisiana Rail Road," a line "wholly operated within the said state, unlawfully did insist upon going into and remaining in a compartment . . . assigned to passengers of the white race." He did so even though he had available to him on the same train "equal but separate accommodations . . . for persons of the white and colored races" (*The State vs. Homer Adolph Plessy*, ARC). Plessy stood accused of violating section 2 of act 111 of the state of Louisiana, enacted in 1890. He spent the night in jail and was released the next day on a $500 bond. Plessy did not deny the charges: he and his colleagues of the American Citizens Equal Rights Association and its successor organization, the Citizens Committee, had scripted every move beforehand, including the revelation, elusive to the eye, that Homer Plessy was not white. As an octoroon, Plessy held a particular place in creole society, a place descended from the position of Free Persons of Color under the *Code noir*, many of whom could and did pass for white. They played a unique role in Louisiana and American history: some of their number, slave owners themselves, enlisted to fight for the Confederacy; many others disappeared entirely into whiteness, particularly during the growing polarization of the races under intensified Anglo-American vigilance in the 1850s. The Citizens Committee of Plessy's generation inherited the historic consequences of the doctrine of One Blood: the color line in Louisiana was a frontier but not in any practical sense a border. Their narrow goal, ambitious enough in itself, was to challenge the constitutionality of the discriminatory public accommodations act of 1890, one of many passed during the era. Their broader—some have said utopian—goal was to challenge the legality of the concept of race itself.

To the lay reader of the decision written for the majority by Justice Henry Billings Brown and the justly famous dissent by John Marshall Harlan, the most striking thing about *Plessy v. Ferguson* is what the court does *not* deal with. In the assignment of errors of January 5, 1893, and in subsequent briefs, Plessy's attorneys, citing the "due process" clause of the Fourteenth Amendment, argued the unconstitutionality of a law that failed to define (because it could not define) what it meant when it said "white" and "colored" races. Tourgée's brief asks: "Is not the question of race, scientifically considered, very often impossible of determination? Is not the question of race, legally considered, one impossible to be determined, in the absence of statutory definition?" (quoted in Olsen, 81). On one hand, having failed to define what it meant, because it could not define what *race* meant, the law in effect deputized the railroad conductors of Louisiana to make their own personal judgments, while punching tickets, about what the legislators might possibly have been thinking when they said "white" and "colored" races. On the other hand, Tourgée's brief continues, if whiteness can somehow be proven to exist, then on a railroad conductor's say-so the court in effect deprived Homer Plessy of his claim to its benefits. In other words, the court denied him his property in himself—the quiet enjoyment of his "seven-eighths Caucasian blood"—without due process of law (quoted in Olsen, 99). This deprivation, argued Tourgée, also therefore violated the Thirteenth Amendment, which prohibits slavery in the United States, because slavery, by definition, denies the enslaved their right to property in themselves. The majority opinion of the Supreme Court, however, swept aside all these arguments. Although the legal issues involved received tortured scrutiny (Lofgren, 174–95), all the majority felt compelled to do was to reiterate the assertion, unsupported by the facts of the case, that there is a clear distinction between "white and colored races—a distinction which is founded in the color of the two races, and which must always exist as long as white men are distinguished from the other race by color" (*Plessy v. Ferguson*, 163 U.S. 537).

But Homer Plessy was *not* to be distinguished from the other race by color. In order to provoke Detective Cain, the octoroon had to perform his "blood," first its predominant whiteness, by entering the "Whites Only" car unquestioned, then its invisible colored remainder, by getting himself ejected and arrested (Robinson). This is what I want to call whiteface minstrelsy, which trades on stereotypical behaviors—such as white folks' sometimes comically obsessive habits of claiming for themselves ever more fanciful forms of property, ingenious entitlements under the law, and exclusivity in the use of public spaces and facilities. Not the least farcical of these music-hall turns in *Plessy* was the "Mammie Exemption" of the Louisiana Separate Car Law: nurses attending children were permitted in segregated black or white cars, which in practice could mean only one thing, since not many white nurses attended black children at that time (Olsen, 75). Whiteface minstrelsy also pokes fun at the foibles of white amnesiacs: the gumshoe Cain forgetting to keep his eyes peeled for octoroons; absent-minded Chief Justice Brown forgetting that their "color" is invisible; the tap-dancing chorus line of the majority of the Supreme Court of the United States, with only Justice Harlan out of step, forgetting that justice is blind.

The long run of "separate but equal" (emphasis on separate) in popular custom, even after its supposed repudiation by law in 1954, remains visible to those walking in any city, especially along the perimeters of those neighborhoods evacuated by white flight or patrolled by white fear. Surveying the sharply drawn boundaries of the contemporary urbanscape—not all pervasive, of course, but pervasive enough—makes Tourgée's reductio ad absurdum in his *Plessy* brief of 1895 seem prophetic: "Why not require all colored people to walk on one side of the street and the whites on the other?" (quoted in Olsen, 98). In the practice of laws and (dis)obedience, the staging of Homer Plessy's transgression provided a fateful occasion to join a bitter struggle over the behavioral vortices of the American public sphere, including accommodations, facilities, schools, places for work, places for play, final resting places, and places of memory.

Chief among those who should have been able to explain the historical depth of this struggle to his colleagues at the time of the *Plessy* decision was the new associate justice appointed to the Supreme Court by President Grover Cleveland in 1894, Louisianian and New Orleanian Edward Douglas White. White would, in the fullness of time, become chief justice. The young lawyer White, however, had been steeped in the unique traditions of his home state, which included the living vestiges of the doctrine of One Blood and its ritualized Anglo-American nemesis, the race-conscious festivities of upper-class Mardi Gras. White is known to have been a member of the most exclusive of the anglified everlasting clubs of New Orleans, the Pickwick Club and its masked double, the Mistick Krewe of Comus, cofounded in 1857. The ironies of White's career mark the version of local memory and circum-Atlantic performance that I will seek to elucidate next by examining the interdependent traditions of carnival and the law in the "City that Care Forgot."

CARNIVAL AND THE LAW

Stateways cannot change folkways.

– William Graham Sumner

On June 15, 1993, the Advisory Committee on Human Relations, which reports to the New Orleans City Council, held a hearing on the disposition of the Liberty Place Monument, a cenotaph erected to honor a handful of fallen defenders of white supremacy during Reconstruction in Louisiana. The hearing was open to the public. In the spirit of Mr. Spectator, though not pretending to his fine impartiality, I included it on my walk through the city. Like Joseph Addison's look into the catacombs of Westminster Abbey, however, the event proved to be a case study in the uncanny. It featured a performance of origin, played out in an agonistic struggle over a specific "place of memory," one formally dedicated to the segregation of the living as well as the dead. The businesslike cadence of the proceedings sounded to my ears like a shovel in a shallow grave, methodically turning over the ashes and fragments, troubling the spirits in their fitful sleep.

The hearing was chaired by Rabbi Edward P. Cohn. Among the prominent witnesses who testified, some very eloquently, pro and con, former Louisiana State Representative, Klansman, and Hitler enthusiast David Duke made the most unforgettable presentation. Duke, who has denied the Holocaust, began by lecturing Rabbi Cohn on the importance of preserving "our memories." As he warmed to his theme of Liberty, linking it to "our heritage" as enshrined in the Liberty Place Monument, he insinuated in every way he could the essential liaison of liberty with "Anglo-Saxon" whiteness. He did not use Steele's phrase, "Free-born People," but it resonated nonetheless in the few silences that punctuated his testimony. In fact, the setting of the Liberty Place Monument hearing provided the kind of stage of misremembrance on which whiteness is traditionally performed. Duke wears his everywhere like a mask: the skin, scraped shiny by his cosmetic surgeon, brilliantly reflects the glare of the television lights. Standing a few feet away, he seems more fragile in person than his telegenic image suggests, and certainly more weird: the newly concise nose, as pink as his tongue, is sculpted as if from the same mold as Michael Jackson's.

Duke and his associates, the Friends of the Liberty Monument, were opposed by a number of civil rights leaders, academic experts, and ordinary citizens, who, defending their own stake in civic memory, denounced the monument as a racist provocation. The contending parties were debating more than the fate of a twenty-foot-high granite obelisk, itself carved and burnished white in the imposingly funereal tradition of circum-Atlantic amnesia. Embossed with the word *Liberty*, the plinth was originally intended to mark the final resting place of a local white supremacist named Fred Nash Ogden. It eventually came to memorialize more generally those who died under his command on the occasion that assured his place in Louisiana history.

On September 14, 1874, at the head of a paramilitary organization called the Crescent City White League, Ogden and several other former Confederate officers directed the armed overthrow of Louisiana Governor William Pitt Kellogg and his racially integrated administration. The authors of the blueprint for this coup d'état, the *Platform of the Crescent City White League*, including Ogden, proclaimed in advance the victory of what its signatories called "that just and legitimate superiority in the administration of our State affairs to which we are entitled by superior responsibility, superior numbers, and superior intelligence." Although Governor Kellogg survived to be reinstated by federal troops several days later, Reconstruction in Louisiana was soon effectively aborted, and the era of Southern Redemption begun (J. Taylor, 253–313).

Phrased in the past tense, the factual account disguises a continuous reenactment of a deep cultural performance that many New Orleanians call the present (Landry, *Battle of Liberty Place*). As historian Lawrence Powell explains: "Where other Southern towns and cities could celebrate Confederate battlefield valor, upper-class whites in New Orleans found it deeply satisfying to concoct a history in which their brave young men actually won the peace—and this on the ground where early in the Civil War the city fathers had been forced to surrender. The Fourteenth of September was their tradition, and they were proud of it. Fathers passed it down to children through dramatic retellings of those heroic days" (42). Over the years, this oral tradition has been reiterated by official acts. In 1932 the city added an inscription at the base of the monument to specify the importance of the coup in bringing about the end of Reconstruction in Louisiana, which termination, as the words carved in the granite base of the plinth put it, "recognized White Supremacy and gave us [back] our State." In 1981 Dutch Morial—the city's first "black" mayor, actually a Creole of color in the tradition of Homer Plessy—failed in his efforts to remove the monument: the city council, then dominated by traditionalists, enacted a preventive ordinance to preserve it. By the end of the 1980s, however, supporters of the monument no longer held a majority on the city council. In connection with street improvements in 1989, the monument was removed and placed in storage, where it remained until a lawsuit by "historic preservationists" forced the city council reluctantly to reerect it (Eggler, B-1). In 1993, contemplating its removal for the second time on the grounds that it represented a "nuisance" and honored those who had shot dead a number of city and state policemen, the council asked its Advisory Committee on Human Relations to render an opinion on the nature of the memories evoked by the monument. It charged the committee to take into account the implications of those memories for the city's "great cosmopolitan population consisting of large numbers of people of every race, color, creed, religion, age, physical condition, national origin, and ancestry" ("Scope of the HRC Hearings"). Such a performance is, for reasons that I hope have become obvious by now, not only a local event but a circum-Atlantic crux.

In this final chapter, I want to review a particular history of the present. This history must include an estimation of the local consequences of the Liberty Place Monument controversy in the context of two interlocking systems of collective memory through performance: carnival and the law. Although the precise intersection of these distinctive mnemonic traditions is unique to New Orleans, their genealogies descend from the reinvention of circum-Atlantic practices—origins and segregation, laws and (dis)obedience. The litigation concerning the Liberty Place Monument erupted simultaneously with the legislative attempt by the New Orleans City Council to integrate the old-line Mardi Gras krewes, first tentatively in 1988 and then more adamantly in 1991–92. That timing was far from coincidental (Vennman, "New Orleans 1993 Carnival"). Both the Mardi Gras and the Liberty Monument controversies intertwine around one of the key questions in *Plessy v. Ferguson* and subsequent civil rights cases based on the principle of fair and equal access to accommodations: the legal control of public spaces despite the persistent folkways of racial prejudice. At issue is the power to maintain—or to reconstruct—the urban vortices of behavior along the Atlantic rim.

Once and Future Kings

A headline in the New Orleans *Times-Picayune* for September 22, 1992, culminated a remarkable year in the history of Mardi Gras in New Orleans: "Rex Broadens Membership in Carnival Revolution." Two subheads followed. The first justified the word *revolution*: "120-Year-Old Color Barrier Falls." The second tried to take it back: "Tradition Reigns Amid Change." These contradictory assertions record the effects of the explosive Mardi Gras Ordinance passed by the city council in December 1991 that proscribed discrimination on the basis of race, sex, religious affiliation, or sexual orientation in organizations previously considered private (and thus constitutionally protected) that now could be shown to have social functions extending beyond any reasonable definition of privacy. Mardi Gras parades use public streets, for instance, and the social activities at so-called private clubs may mask occasions on which business in the public interest is frequently discussed. Rather than obey such a law, the krewes of Comus, Momus, and Proteus have packed up their baubles and papier-mâché, ending a century and a half of Mardi Gras tradition. They also opened up their parade dates for newer, upwardly mobile krewes, some of which have already integrated. The banner headlines came out when Rex, in the name of its motto (Pro Bono Publico), integrated its membership—to the dismay of many who believe that carnival tradition ought to supersede the law. As a concession to that tradition, discrimination on the basis of sex was dropped from the prohibitions of the ordinance.

Like New Orleans itself, carnival and the law in Louisiana share an origin, at once documentable and deeply mythologized, in Latin traditions, namely the pre-Lenten revelries of Mardi Gras and the French and Spanish civil codes. But these intertwined historic roots have grown far denser than that, entangling Anglo-American and prolific African traditions and customs through centuries of struggle. In an ethnically complex and divided city, carnival and the law still provide antagonistic sites for the playing-out of the cultural politics of social identity and difference. Both carnival and the law have operated as agents of cultural transmission, especially in conserving the exclusionary hierarchies of the social elite, yet both have also served as instruments of contestation and change: in the struggle for dominance between creole and Anglo-American interests in the mid-nineteenth century, for instance; in the agony of Reconstruction and resegregation in the late nineteenth and twentieth centuries; and, most recently, in the furor over the ordinance, a law that in actuality represents only one link in a chain of attempts to bring carnival under the regulating thumb of legislation.

At first glance, pairing the terms *carnival* and *law* may seem contradictory, a perverse shackling of opposites. Carnival, an occasion for festive transgression, limited only by human imagination or stamina (whichever exhausts itself first), apparently flourishes beyond the law, above the law, and even against the law. In the Bakhtinian construction of the European carnivalesque, seasonal revelry and masquerade offer release from the oppression of official culture, a suspension of its laws, an exhilarating inversion of its authority, a momentary state of topsy-turvydom, in which the common people become powerful and the powerful people become ridiculous. To the august majesty of the law, the carnivalesque says, "Bottoms up!" (Bakhtin, *Rabelais*). The laws and customs relating to carnival in New Orleans, however, have necessarily taken different forms from the ones developed by more homogenous societies, even those European traditions afflicted by deep religious hatreds and class resentments (Le Roy Ladurie, *Carnival in Romans*). Under a violently self-terrorized slave culture and then under its only partially reconstructed successor regimes, Louisiana law has created a number of contradictory regulations concerning carnival.

On the one hand, the law has deliberately created in its interstices a space for easily overlooked transgression, which heightens the fleeting pleasures of apparent escape from its reach, if only because enforcement, in the absence of a wronged and privileged constituency, is unrewarding. Performers and performances have often traded on the fruits of this variety of guilty pleasure. In Louisiana, however, overlooked transgression seems to have offered a release of pent-up furies, a publicly enacted dream of escape from race hatred's waking nightmares. That is one reason why theorists of carnivalesque inversion debate to what degree, if any, ludic transgression

6.1 Rex Parade, 1901.
"King," "Contentment," "Riches." *Human Passions and Characteristics.*
Louisiana Collection, Howard-Tilton Memorial Library, Tulane University

contributes even momentarily to the subversion of the dominant orders and the majesty of their laws (Falassi; Kinser; Stallybrass and White). This skepticism seems all the more persuasive (to put the case in its most defeatist terms) in situations where groups of differently empowered people have tolerated living together side by side for centuries without the hope of justice among them.

On the other hand, Louisiana law relating to Mardi Gras tends eventually to annex the ludic space at its margins simply by legalizing the offenses it declines to prosecute. Carnival becomes law. This is a historical process: in earlier times, especially under slavery, many carnivalesque practices were unpunished illegalities; today, they have entered into law. In the absence of a law that makes one race the property of another, there seems to be greater need for a more elaborated regulation of carnival activity to sustain at least the symbolic supremacy of the favored group. This process, whereby once transgressive activities become dignified, sanctioned, and even legally protected practices, seems to reflect the anomalous origins of New Orleans street parades as upper-class performances by a closely knit local aristocracy, in contrast to the predominantly vernacular culture of other popular American parading traditions like those of Philadelphia (S. Davis; Ryan, "American Parade"). Amid the experience of total civic participation in a collective cultural performance (figure 6.1), carnival tradition asserts and enforces historic claims of entitlement, priority, and exclusivity. As I propose to demonstrate, these claims date especially from the post–Civil War period of Reconstruction and Southern Redemption, though their history reaches back to colonial times. Nurtured in the fierce legalities and illegalities of racial politics, they remain festering there, rendered intensely visible at Mardi Gras but present on a year-round basis. At carnival time, race serves as a master trope for a broad spectrum of exclusionary designs and practices: classism, anti-Semitism, sexism. Even now, standing in the public gaze of other kinds and other classes of people at the end of the twentieth century, the ultraelite will not, and perhaps cannot, renovate the stage on which its dignity, usurped from the Creoles in the 1850s, fought for outside the law and "won" in the 1870s, and gradually consolidated within the law ever since, is still seasonally performed. Even in the meticulously exclusive privacy of its own social gatherings, which is all that remains after the cancellation of the parades, the members of these everlasting clubs seem to insist on acting out the self-reassuring spectacle of their historic privilege beyond the uttermost limit of superannuation.

The subject matter of the traditional festivities—the transformation of a bourgeois elite into a mystified pseudoroyalty through the iconographic manipulation of costumes, tableaux, and floats—reiterates hierarchies even as it boasts, more or less accurately, of involving the whole city (and its hordes of cash-bearing guests) in a communal rite of fleshly participation. For New Orleanians steeped in the tradition of Mardi Gras, everything depends on where one participates, with whom, and at which occasions, public and private, and thus on the minutely detailed laws, written and unwritten, of inclusion and exclusion by which one is socially located and judged. The established pecking order of the old-line krewes, for instance, with the Mistick Krewe of Comus (founded in 1857) at the apex, enforces social discipline on the families of the elite, including those accepted under the seemingly more democratic aegis of the Rex, that annually selected monarch who ascends to the honor of "King of Carnival" (see figures 1.2 and 1.4).

What kind of carnival is this? Not an occasion for seeking release from a way of life, it would seem, but an institution dedicated to its perpetuation. After summarizing the supposed violence and vulgarity of New Orleans street carnivals of the 1850s ("the disgraceful actions of ruffians") before the advent of the Anglo-American krewes, the commemorative pamphlet issued by the Mistick Krewe of Comus on the occasion of its centennial constructs the history of New Orleans carnival in Pavlovian rather than Bakhtinian terms. Remarking on the good behavior of the crowds that Comus is assumed to have elicited, it observes: "Undoubtedly, this is due to the fact that the people of the city, naturally orderly, are 'conditioned' to restrain themselves to innocent fun. Also the Carnival is conducted by the leading citizens and representative people of the City. Comus has done more than its share to bring about this sense of dignity and orderliness which characterizes the Mardi Gras celebration in New Orleans" (*One Hundred Years of Comus*, 5–6). Anyone who has experienced the excesses of Mardi Gras in the streets of the French Quarter might wonder at this description, but it actually asserts the prior claim of traditions that serve a more explicit social function than the generalized license of pre-Lenten crapulence and its expiation.

The power of such traditions may be seen in the images of the minikrewes organized a generation ago for the enculturation of children, whose experience presumably "conditioned" them from an early age to read correctly the relationship between the symbolic gestures of carnival and their future social positions (figure 6.2). Perry Young, historian of the Mistick Krewe of Comus, once explained the salient peculiarity of the local culture's historic rites of kinship—the intervention of its patriarchy into a sphere that most high societies delegate to women: "The carnival—this fashionable end of it—is the social system of New Orleans. Its season is the social season, no matter how sociable the others. And the social system of New Orleans is run by men. Women have their place, dowagers their say, but when there's justice to be done, carnival defies the female fiats. It is generous and adamant, and male. . . . The most-beloved man in town may have a wife that simply could not dance, friends that would not fit. It is the Membership Committee that preserves the inner social equilibrium" (*Carnival*, 64). By regulating krewe memberships and ball invitations through discreet and rigorous blackballing, fathers and brothers have renewed the homosocial compact annually, exerting themselves to keep the dance floor safe from threats of misalliance. In a society of complex genealogies and mixed ances-

6.2 Children's Carnival Club of New Orleans, 1938.
Courtesy The Historic New Orleans Collection, Museum/Research Center, acc. no. 1979.325.7532

tral blood, debutante balls are apparently too important to be left to women, in something like the way that war, as Clemenceau said, is too important to be left to generals. That the uninvitable are themselves still Mardi Gras participants (by virtue of their performance on the streets, cast as social inferiors) is made excruciatingly plain in Young's celebration of the proper role for "Negroes and *Gens de Couleur*" in carnival (figure 6.3), which is to reenact festively their assigned place of menial servitude in Young's racist version of real life:

> In the white parades no element is more essential, or more sincerely part and parcel, than the thousand or fifteen hundred black torchbearers and muleherds, white-shrouded, cowled, that dance before the cars, between them, alongside, toiling, but dancing. They think that they belong, and they earn the affiliation. A dollar apiece they get, or a dollar and a half, the way is long, the asphalt hard, the blazing torches hot and heavy—but they dance. Not for the dollar and a

6.3 Joseph Pennell, *In Carnival Time—New Orleans*, 1884.
Courtesy The Historic New Orleans Collection, Museum/Research Center,
acc. no. 1974.25.19.389

> half—they do it for being part of the parade—a part that can't be done without—a part that cook and chambermaid, scrub-woman and black mammy, admire as much as madame on the Avenue admires the masks that might be son and heir, lord and master, or fine and chosen true-love. (Carnival, 63)

The responses from big houses seem to enact the present and imagine the future as the seamless restoration of antebellum behaviors.

Prominent though they may be in the consciousness of carnival in New Orleans, the old-line krewes actually represent a small fraction of the overall scene. For days leading up to Fat Tuesday, the streets of New Orleans and its suburbs fill with revelers drawn from every segment of the community. As of 1995, there are over forty other parading krewes, including the newer, larger superkrewes of Bacchus and Endymion and all-female krewes such as Venus and Iris (Hardy). The newer krewes ape the pseudoclassical names, the parading practices, and some of the traditional icons of older groups. Although outsiders may be forgiven for failing to mark distinctions based on outward spectacle, insiders master the coded relationships between exclusivity and cultural capital: "It is understood," remarked Young with a wink, knowing that a word to the wise is sufficient, "that a king of Hermes was a Jew" (*Carnival*, 73). Anticipating objection to the exclusion of Jews from other clubs, the official historian of Comus offers this consolation: "Of carnival business the Jews get their full share—they control Canal street, where carnival merchandise is bought" (*Carnival*, 73). "Bless the Jews," he concludes, in his version of expansive fellow feeling, "we couldn't be gentiles without them" (*Carnival*, 74).

The krewe-centered images of hierarchies and polarities tend to be recycled by the promiscuous maskers in the streets (figure 6.4). Here, freestyle masquerading yields up fantastic substitutions of social identities, crossing and recrossing differences of race, class, gender, and sexuality. Gay krewes and maskers in the French Quarter have developed elaborated traditions of drag performance, which reflect back, with irony and romance, on the parades and tableau balls of the traditional krewes. Then there is Zulu, shadowing and sometimes interrupting not only the route of the Rex parade but also the festively absolutist claims of its monarch (see figures 1.3 and 1.5). Along the back streets and under the highway overpasses, Mardi Gras Indian tribes seek each other out for humbugs, their movements and music an expression of their powerful countermemories. No one can experience this cornucopia comprehensively during one season or several. New

6.4 Maid and Lady. Promiscuous maskers, Mardi Gras, 1934.
Courtesy The Historic New Orleans Collection, Museum/Research Center, acc. no. 1979.325.3870

Orleans on Mardi Gras day is a whirling maelstrom of intercultural surrogations, condensed in space and time, each an eddy in the larger circum-Atlantic vortex.

Any understanding of these complex genealogies of performance must somehow take into account the contradictory claims they inspire about festivity and tradition. On the one hand, Henry Rightor, writing in 1900, thought that carnival in New Orleans would be utterly ruined by innovation of any kind: "There are enemies of this Carnival; not those chill-hearted, shrivel-skins who frown on it as a device of the devil; not the clergy, nor any overt opposition. It is the innovators who are to be feared, they do not understand the carnival spirit, and seek to have it new" (629). On the other hand, Fu-Kiau Bunsekei, of the Kongo Academy in Bas-Zaire, believes that festivals are themselves instruments of critique, redress, and transformation: "Festivals are a way of bringing about change. People are allowed to say not only what they voice in ordinary life but what is going on within their minds, their inner grief, their inner resentments. They carry peace. They carry violence. The masks and the songs can teach or curse, saying in their forms matters to which authorities must respond or change. Parades alter truth. Parades see true meaning" (quoted in Nunley and Bettelheim, 23). Rightor sees seasonal festivals as symbolic of a world that ought to be kept as it is. Bunsekei views them as a way of imagining the world as what it ought to become. These contrasting opinions about carnival parallel contrasting interpretations of the law: as a precedent-bound bulwark of continuity or as an agent of expansive change. These contradictions also characterize a culture that invents and keeps two kinds of time: one constructed as the slow, peristaltic rhythms of social custom and cultural transmission over what historians of the French *annales* school call the *longue durée* (Braudel), which New Orleanians like to call "timelessness"; the other conceived as the history of events, as eruptions of sociopolitical topicality, the key word of which is "timeliness." During the Mardi Gras season of 1991–92, these positions collided head-on in the council chambers and in the streets, but they were spun out of the same centrifugal distribution and centripetal reconstitution of laws and customs.

The French *Code noir*, by limiting Afrocentric public culture in the form of slave assembly, provided the first of many precedents for the regulation of carnival activities under Louisiana law (*CN* 1724, article 13). Subsequent legislation, spurred by the bloody slave revolution in St. Domingue, refined the law further, as in the 1807 amendments to the anglicized "Black Code" of

1806: "Every person is prohibited from permitting in his or her negro quarter, any other assemblies but those of his or her own slaves, and from allowing his or her said slaves the liberty to dance during the night" (Lislet, 120). Here the official culture, wrapping itself in the majesty of its laws, asserts its interest in regulating carnivalesque leisure activities, even if those activities occur on private property and involve celebrants who are themselves defined as private property ("real estate" under the Black Codes). The official existence of the Black Codes made festivity something for slaves to get away with, a transgressive and even subversive act, the origins and meanings of which, for safety's sake, were best effaced or at least disguised.

The enactment of rigorous laws, however, and the rigorous enforcement of those laws are two different things; at least they were under the notoriously lax French and Spanish regimes. Evidence from the entire colonial period shows an increasingly prominent performance culture, organized particularly around the festivities of the pre-Lenten period, in which slaves, free men and women of color, and creole high society participated. The emergence of costume balls and masquerades, open-air gatherings on the levee, and eventually the famous bamboulas in Congo Square show not only a pattern of transgression indulged but also one of transgression carefully channeled into regulated conduits of time and space. These included toleration of certain condensational events, like slave dances, within approved vortices of behavior, like Congo Square. The law thus created on its margins a space for play, a liminal zone in which dances, masquerades, and processions could act out that which was otherwise unspeakable.

Carnival and the law conspire together to craft a contingent margin of behavior that remains easily within the laws' reach, if need be, but hovers provisionally outside their grasp. Slaveholders liked to think or at least to pretend to think that carnival provided them with a holiday from the rigors of enforcing their own laws, and the Mardi Gras spirit even allowed the slaves to mimic, and no doubt parody, in the sophisticated West African way, the forms and customs of their masters, while at the same time secretly re-creating their own. In such communication across races and cultures, there resides a kernel of understanding that could grow into mutual appreciation; but in the very same caricatures, there also fester the bitter seeds of mutual hatred.

In fact, violence in Louisiana flourished in such surfeit that only a small portion could be surrogated as play. The best-organized slave revolt in North American history, the Louisiana uprising of 1811, took place during carnival season, when a force of over five hundred hundred freedom fighters marched on New Orleans under Haitian officers, with flags unfurled and drums beating. When local militia put down the revolt, the captured rebels were savagely executed and their severed heads displayed on pikes at intervals on the Mississippi levee (Hofstadter and Wallace, 190). In his abolitionist novel *Blake; or, The Huts of America* (1859–61), Martin Delany evokes the memory of these events. Plying the imaginative spaces between fact and fiction, Delany shows how the threat of a slave revolt flickers amid the "games, shows, exhibitions, theatrical performances, festivals, masquerade balls, and numerous entertainments and gatherings" on the eve of Mardi Gras in New Orleans: "It was on this account that the Negroes had been allowed such unlimited privileges this evening. Nor were they remiss to the utmost extent of its advantages" (98–99). Yet, despite Delany's wishful thinking, many accounts confirm that planters said they found the sights and sounds of celebrating Negroes irresistibly reassuring. For instance, in the New Orleans *Daily Picayune*, on the eve of the Civil War, a few days after the execution of John Brown, and on the same page as the review of Boucicault's *Octoroon*, an editorial entitled "Contentment of the Blacks" soothed its readers with contrasting images of the horrors of the working poor in the North and the idyllic conditions enjoyed by slaves in the South, as evidenced by the very performances and festivities legally forbidden by the Black Codes: "Day and night, the sounds of merriment ring forth from plantation negro quarters and the merry dance never ceases" (December 24, 1859). This is the scene that Perry Young thought he saw reenacted by the Mardi Gras flambeaux.

With the Louisiana Purchase and thereafter, the Anglo-Americans sought to dismantle the three-caste system—the living memorial to One Blood—in favor of a strict black-white dichotomy, imposing broad segregationist restrictions beyond the provisions of the original *Code noir*. In 1806, for instance, the revised Black Code stipulated for the first time the same penalty—death—for "any slave, free negro, mulatto, Indian or mustee" who committed arson, poison, vandalism, or "rape upon the body of any white woman or girl" (Lislet, 115). Not surprisingly, the revised Black Codes attempted to channel the remnants—and reinventions—of African public culture into acceptable, even desirable directions, further mixing it with traditions and values drawn from European sources. In the revisions to the Black Code of 1855, slaves were still forbidden assembly (under penalty of ten to twenty-five lashes), but exceptions were made explicitly for church, funerals, and a strictly controlled public recreation: "They may assemble on the commons for the purpose of dancing, or playing ball, or cricket, permission to that effect being first obtained from the mayor, but such permission to that effect shall be granted by the mayor for no other day than Sunday, and shall expire at sunset." In other provisions, slaves were prohibited from attending masked balls where free persons of color were admitted or to "quarrel, yell, or sing obscene songs, or in anywise disturb the public peace" (Leovy, 258–59). These laws seek to open a narrow, carefully regulated space for collective expression, a space that Frederick Douglass and others denounced as a sinister illusion in which insurrectionary emotions could be released through a safety valve of revelry, dance, and play (Genovese, 577). This genealogy of slave performance interprets sanctioned assemblies such as the bamboulas in Congo Square as surrogates for rebellion, as symbolic substitutions of uninhibited physical performance for unconstrained physical violence, as trade-offs of carnival for carnage.

The measure on Sunday recreations, which governed the mixed assemblies at Congo Square, was passed to regulate a practice that had clearly been tolerated for some time, and in that respect it fairly characterizes the general development of Louisiana law governing festive activities. The open question was for whom and under what circumstances the law could be suspended; or, differently put, in whose interests would it be more definitively rewritten? In the years between the Louisiana Purchase and the Civil War, the Anglo-Americans appointed themselves. In the "Offenses and Nuisances" section of the *Laws and General Ordinances* of 1857, for instance, the first year in which the upper-class, Anglo-American Mistick Krewe of Comus officially paraded on Mardi Gras in masquerade costumes, the city of New Orleans re-reiterated an ordinance that made it unlawful "to abuse, provoke, or disturb any person; to make charivari, or to appear masked or disguised in the streets or in any public place." Another, related ordinance stated: "No person on Mardi Gras, or at any other time, shall throw flour or any other substance on any person passing along the streets or any public place" (Leovy, 173).

The contradiction between these laws in plain English and the emerging practice of Anglo-American krewe parades, in which masked revelers throw objects from floats, is revelatory. Irish, Italians, and other working-class ethnics made charivari and rough music, throwing flour, fecal matter, and even quicklime on passersby during Mardi Gras. The Mistick Krewe of Comus, however, masqueraded by night, and its exotic floats carried the masked and

6.5 Mistick Krewe of Comus parade, "Dreams of Homer," passing before city hall, 1872. *Frank Leslie's Illustrated Newspaper*, March 9, 1872. Courtesy The Historic New Orleans Collection, Museum/Research Center, acc. no. 1974.25.19.366

hooded Anglos through public streets cleared for their passage, protected from the mixed and swirling crowds, in flagrant, public violation of the city ordinances (figure 6.5). The ad hoc vortices of Latin street festival, in which chance encounters among maskers put ordinary social and racial distinctions at risk, parted before the regulated entry of "royalty." Rather than opening the streets for willy-nilly mischief, krewe parades occupy them in a style evoking the civic entries of Renaissance princes, a grandeur supported by themes drawn from literary classics. A local reporter's description captures the already imposing pretensions of an early Comus parade, which drafted marching bands, police escorts, and equestrian pomp into the well-disciplined service of the carnivalesque: "After the usual vanguard of mounted police and torch-bearers, and a military band, appeared the jovial God upon a noble steed, which seemed conscious both of the honor conferred upon him, and of the brilliant trappings with which he was decorated. *Comus*, sitting with an easy grace, smiled recognition of the enthusiastic greeting which met him at every step" (*Weekly Budget*, March 6, 1878). Today's Mardi Gras parade goers will note that basic elements of contemporary parades, including the self-important tone of noblesse oblige, had already become commonplace in the early years of Anglo-American carnival. The early membership of Comus was coextensive with that of the exclusive Pickwick Club, truly an everlasting club on the Anglophile model, with memberships handed down like family heirlooms.

Bourgeois carnival cleanses as it dignifies. The krewes appropriated the insulting act of throwing offensive materials on passersby, a time-honored carnival prank, and transformed it into the condescending but apparently good-hearted act of throwing cheap baubles to the acquiescent crowd, whose members continually plead, "Throw me something, Mister." As New Orleans's hidden carnival substituted revelry for revolution, white carnival substituted trashy "throws" for real garbage: each gesture substitutes an act of festive performance for one of symbolic or actual violence. Every year the floats lumber through cheering crowds, copiously ejaculating beads, cups, and "doubloons," special coins cast with the name of the krewe and the year. Grown men plead for these trifles. Young women flirt with the masked riders, and now some expose their breasts, bartering for the prized tokens. The ritualized adornment of "Bead Whores" is a stunning condensation of the circum-Atlantic tradition discussed in earlier chapters: the creation of an auction community motivated by the transformation of gifts into commodities (Gregory; Hyde; Mauss).

Occasionally, the atavistic violence of earlier Mardi Gras throws breaks forth, as it did in 1992, when a krewe member emptied a bucket of urine on the crowd, an insult that may well have passed unrecorded had not the victims included a captain and a lieutenant of the New Orleans Police Department (*Times-Picayune*, February 26, 1992). Current municipal ordinances elaborate on permissible and impermissible throws. Recently, as a civic rebuke to the countercultural Krewe of Trojan, condoms and "any other sexually oriented device" joined "insects, marine life, rodents, and any other animal (dead or alive)" on the ever-expanding condemned list as "not within the boundaries of good taste and decency," though women's panties, a popular traditional throw, remain legit (*Times-Picayune*, October 4, 1991). Away from the popular euphoria, the ambitious tableau balls continue in private, unchanged in basic pomp and circumstance since the mid-nineteenth century. In terms of Bataille's "General Economy," Mardi Gras in New Orleans is "sacrificial expenditure." In terms of circum-Atlantic memory, it is a spectacular performance of waste, draped in a mantle of privileged disobedience. Like an unwritten constitution, one portion of that privilege—Anglo-Saxon whiteness—is itself a mythic memory performed in specific secular rituals.

The Demon Actors in Milton's *Paradise Lost*

The stirring rhetoric of Anglo-Saxonism resounds in a privately printed history of the Mistick Krewe of Comus, compiled to celebrate its centenary year of 1957: "The people of New Orleans are under three influences—the French, the Spanish, and the Anglo-Saxon. The Spanish influence is especially shown in the early architecture of the city, the French influence by the manner and customs of the people, the Anglo-Saxon by aggressiveness in developing the commercial and business growth of the city" (Herndon, 6). The strong claim of superior aggression and superior industry sets apart the category labeled Anglo-Saxon, concealing its ragtag origins among assorted freebooters, the teeming refuse of several distant shores, a number of whom came to Louisiana via Mobile, Alabama.

Tracing the names and addresses of twenty-seven of the original Comus members of 1857—both homes and offices—discloses that they were representative of an assortment of American opportunists drawn to New Orleans between the Louisiana Purchase and the Civil War to seek their fortunes. A memorandum from the daughter of the first president of the Pickwick Club records the addresses as well as the professions of the founders—steamboat agents, accountants, lawyers, produce wholesalers, and a "cotton pickery"—in all, eighteen merchants, four professionals, three bankers, and two unknowns (Werlein Memorandum). Most have distinctly English-sounding names (there are an Addison, a Pope, and a Newton among the founders), but others, like William J. Behan, who joined after the Civil War, are Irish or Scots. Early on, this was a very fluid kind of association—mostly young men, mostly wholesalers, who met regularly Uptown at John Pope's drugstore on the corner of Jackson and Prytania streets—as yet neither a class nor a caste but rather an imagined kinship network founded on mutual appreciation for each other's industry, invention, and powers of organization. The founding president's daughter sets the scene:

> New Orleans in 1857 was but a comparatively small place spread over a very considerable area and divided into a number of small districts, each of the latter being either under separate administrations or were recently become a part of the City. It was not an unusual thing then,

> as it is now in small cities, for the better element of young business and professional men to gather of an evening at the leading drug store and to sit or stand around, smoke a cigar and pass a few words with one another before returning to their work or going elsewhere. . . . At that time this neighborhood was the centre of the then new residential district; there resided the well-to-do American (as opposed to the French) residents of the City. . . . [At John Pope's drugstore] the early affairs of the Mystic Krewe of Comus were doubtless frequently discussed; and it was here that the inception of the Pickwick Club was made. (Werlein Memorandum, 2–3)

Reinventing creole carnival prior to and immediately following the Civil War was an improvisation by English-speaking Protestants on themes borrowed from Latin Catholic tradition. On one level, the story is mostly of local interest: socially ambitious Anglo-Americans, hanging out together at the neighborhood drugstore, decided to consolidate their toehold on the world by building a clubhouse and conspicuously overspending on party hats and papier-mâché. On a deeper level, the story is more generally a circum-Atlantic one—into the cavities of memory and identity hollowed out by the human floods of manifest destiny, new interests inserted themselves, generating a hybrid performance of social self-sameness. Anglo-American carnival was a displaced transmission of a surrogated memory—something new, admittedly, but hardly original.

One strong proof of this assertion resides, I believe, in the privileged role of English literature in the krewes' early attempts to accumulate cultural capital to complement their material success. Here, canonical memory serves in its political capacity as social self-assertion. Milton, Spenser, and Dickens, for instance, were invoked early on to assert English preeminence and energy in the face of francophone hauteur and reputed creole sloth. The name *Comus* derives from the stately masque of the same name by John Milton. The first procession and tableau ball of the Mistick Krewe of Comus in 1857 impersonated "The Demon Actors in Milton's Paradise Lost." The great Protestant epic provided ample opportunity for costume and characterization—damned characters from the realm of eternal death, of course, but still at heart English: a classical hell, Tartarus, with harpies, furies, and gorgons; the expulsion, with Satan, Beelzebub, and Moloch; the conference of Satan and Beelzebub, with a chorus of the seven deadly sins (Young, *Mistick Krewe*, 61). Another early Comus parade took up Edmund Spenser's *Faerie Queene* and, according to J. Curtis Waldo, in his *History of the Carni-*

val in New Orleans (1882), "illustrated in appropriate groupings the principal episode of that delicate and fanciful creation, which, in the centuries that have elapsed since its birth, has lost no beauty or splendor by comparison" (12). Without completely ruling out the possibility that Spenser's epic romance spoke urgently to the hearts of New Orleans dry-goods merchants, the more likely explanation is that they were claiming kin, performing their intelligence with learned citations.

In the absence of direct ancestors of sufficient prestige, the general concept of collective memory organized by race has served to establish a sense of heritage, however fabricated and illusory. Like Betterton in his library, the Mardi Gras performers enveloped themselves in the spirits of English dead. Like Betterton also, they brought the dead back to life by embodying characters from the fictive ancestral canon. Like voodoo in New Orleans, these rites had both a public and a hidden character. The satanic face of the "Demon Actors" could disappear behind the festive mask of harmless fun. The "Pickwick Club," of course, quoted Charles Dickens, suggesting its generous openness to the good-hearted members of a motley krewe. The by-laws of the club explain that it was formed by Comus members "to give continuity to comradeship born under the mask" and to "conceal the secrets of their other identity" (*The Pickwick Club*, 3).

Secrecy reigned over the krewe protocols, a mystification of their improvised rituals of self-replication. One informative document is a privately printed, first-person account by William J. Behan, wholesaler and sugar factor, later mayor of the city of New Orleans, of his 1871 initiation into Comus, whose membership was and is secret, and into the Pickwick Club. Behan recalls:

> At that time, when a duly elected member was presented to the Pickwick Club, he was met by the Sergeant-at-Arms, booted and spurred, and equipped with the largest and fiercest-looking saber which could be found. The position of Sergeant-at-Arms was filled by the most robust member of the Krewe, and one whom nature had endowed with the most sonorous basso-profundo voice to be heard on the operatic stage. He was an awe-inspiring figure, and the spirit of the newcomer quailed within him, as he was led blindfolded, into the darkened and mysterious chamber where the ceremony of initiation was to take place. The room was draped with sable curtains, and ornamented (if such a word can apply) with owls, death's heads, cross-bones and similar blood-curdling devices. Behind the curtains, the merry Krewe

> of Comus was concealed, but never was this re-assuring fact suspected until having administered the oath to the aspirant, the President asked in a loud and solemn voice: "Are you willing that this stranger be admitted," and then a mighty and unanimous roar burst forth from behind the curtains: "We are," and the curtains were drawn back, disclosing the merrymakers. Now, the room was flooded with light, solemnity yielded to hilarity, and the evening waxed merrier and merrier, for the "Big Mug" had been discovered, filled with the wine of the gods, for Comus and his Krewe. (2)

It is perhaps challenging to keep in mind that the performers in this social drama are not boys, in possession of a tree house, but grown men—social, commercial, and civic leaders of a city that was then reconstituting itself as an Anglo-American version of a Latin-Caribbean capital. By Behan's account, the Comus initiation follows the classic pattern of rites of passage—separation, liminality, and reincorporation—and his hearty effort to take whole affair lightly conceals neither the serious purposes of homosocial affiliation that the rite reaffirms nor the oligarchic entitlements afforded by membership in the community that it secretly and selectively perpetuates.

The Pickwick Club and the Krewe of Comus exerted social discipline over the families of the New Orleans elite by minutely regulating both club membership and the annual invitations to the coming-out balls of the Mardi Gras social season. In the useful *Hand-Book of Carnival* furnished by J. Curtis Waldo in 1873, the Mistick Krewe of Comus's secret rites of social selection are explained in relationship to its public parades at Mardi Gras:

> Not only have the gorgeous and fantastic processions been the occasion of an out-door demonstration on the part of almost the entire population, but the tableaux and ball which terminate the evening's festivities have ever been a subject of the deepest anxiety with a certain class of our population. The beautiful and costly cards of invitation and the mysterious manner of their distribution, combine with the social position of those selected, to invest this part of the entertainment with a still deeper interest. It has grown to be a recognized evidence of caste to be the recipient of one of these mysterious biddings, and here is sole clue we have to the character of the organization. (6–7)

Waldo's choice of the word *ever* to describe a practice that had been instituted fourteen years earlier (and had been interrupted by the Civil War) shows that by 1873 the social position of Comus members and their families had already coagulated into timelessness. To paraphrase the language of Kafka's useful parable, the intruding leopards had established themselves in the memory of some as eternal consumers at the ritual chalices of Mardi Gras.

Darwin's Ghost: Justice White and White Justice

The masked struggle between timelessness and topicality in white carnival takes on a particularly sinister meaning during Reconstruction, 1865–1877. These years were also (not coincidentally) the formative period for the iconographic and thematic material of the old-line floats and ballroom tableaux that exist today. All claims for the transcendence of New Orleans Mardi Gras tradition—its supposedly disinterested existence outside the contingencies of law, politics, and time in "the city that care forgot"—must be weighed against the events of September 14, 1874, and the evidence of krewe participation in the coup. A boast, attributed to a Comus captain by the official historian of the Mistick Krewe, proudly implicates the membership of the men's clubs and secret carnival societies: "It is safe to say that every member . . . capable of bearing arms, participated" (Young, *Carnival*, 34). The centennial pamphlet of the Mistick Krewe lists the coup of 1874 as a historical highlight: "Many Comus maskers took part in the battle" (*One Hundred Years of Comus*, 23). The official historian of the Boston Club, center of the krewe activities of the Rex organization, claims that the plot against the Kellogg government was hatched at the club and quotes approvingly a memoir written in 1899 that states: "The Boston Club party grew into public utterance as an expression standing for the supremacy of the white man and the perpetuation of the white man's institutions" (Landry, *Boston Club*, 115–16). These are boasts, made after the fact, but further research supports their veracity: by comparing the muster rolls of the White League's military formations with the names of known krewe members (whose secret affiliations krewe membership records disclose), one may substantiate with details the general picture of overlapping constituencies.

This research documents (with names) what many native New Orleanians generally know as a commonplace: that the officer corps of the White League (and a not insignificant number of its rank and file) formed an interlocking directorship with the secret membership of the exclusive Mardi Gras krewes and men's clubs, especially Comus-Pickwick. Like the Ku Klux Klan elsewhere in the South, the carnival krewes took advantage of their "comradeship under the mask" to assert the entitlements of their group, most obviously against blacks, but eventually against others with whom they made temporary alliances of convenience: the Crescent City White League had a separate regiment into which Italians were segregated, for instance, and another for the Irish. Unlike the Klan, the krewes have ever since maintained a strict standard of exclusion by caste. Checking the partial roster of White Leaguers in Augusto Miceli's *The Pickwick Club of New Orleans*, a retrospective membership record privately printed in 1964, with *The Roll of Honor: Roster of the Citizen Soldiery Who Saved Louisiana*, complied in 1877 by carnival historian J. Curtis Waldo, confirms a list of 115 names of Comus-Pickwickians who took up arms to fight the Battle of Liberty Place in 1874.

First on Waldo's *Roll of Honor* is Major General Fred Nash Ogden, hemp merchant and member of the Pickwick Club (Miceli, appendix J). Ogden was a Confederate veteran, cited for valor at Vicksburg, and the coauthor of the *Platform of the Crescent City White League*, which justified violent rebellion against the state of Louisiana on the grounds that "the negro has proved himself as destitute of common gratitude as of common sense." The Liberty Place Monument was originally conceived as Ogden's tomb. Next on the list of heroes is Brigadier General William J. Behan, future mayor of the Crescent City, also a wounded veteran of Gettysburg, whose brother was killed at Antietam on his eighteenth birthday and whose Van Gennepian rite of passage into Comus and the Pickwick Club has already been cited.

Most ominously, however, in terms of the history of American race relations in the twentieth century, was the armed service of a young lawyer in Company E of the Second Regiment, "Louisiana's Own" (Waldo, *Roll of Honor*, 24): Edward Douglas White. White, later justice and ultimately chief justice of the Supreme Court of the United States, joined the majority opinion in *Plessy v. Ferguson*. Justice White was also a member of the Pickwick Club and perforce the Mistick Krewe of Comus (Miceli, appendix J).

To historians of cultural performance, the most fascinating phenomenon to emerge from this juncture of coup and carnival is the way in which Comus rehearsed the former by improvising the latter. At Mardi Gras in 1873, eighteen months prior to the Battle of Liberty Place, the theme for the Krewe of Comus parade and ball was "The Missing Links to Darwin's *Origin of Species*." It presented animal-like caricatures of hated public figures from Reconstruction, such as Ulysses S. Grant as a verminous potato bug or the "radical" Republican J. R. Pitkin as "The Cunning Fox [carrying a car-

6.6 Mistick Krewe of Comus parade,
"The Missing Links to Darwin's *Origin of Species*," 1873. *Left*, Charles Darwin, "The Sapient Ass"; *right*, "The Gorilla," or "The Missing Link."
Carnival Collection, Howard-Tilton Memorial Library, Tulane University

petbag] which joins the Coon." This taxonomy, arranged by phyla in a parodic version of "survival of the fittest," culminated in the mock crowning of "The Gorilla," a caricature of the Negro lieutenant governor of Louisiana, strumming a banjo with hairy paws, as the "Missing Link of Darwin's Eden" (figure 6.6). In the tradition of carnivalesque inversion, the lowest changed places with the highest, but this topsy-turvydom mocked the regime that supposedly had created in the first place its own Lords of Misrule by placing black people in positions of power over whites. The White League's *Platform* denounced Reconstruction as "the most absurd inversion of the relations of race," and its members volunteered to set the state of Louisiana right side up again by turning it upside down.

6.7 Rex parade, "Voyages of Discovery," 1992. Darwin and the Gorilla.
Photo: Barbara Vennman

The sense of doubleness provoked by this inversion, however, played itself out in the form of a weird kind of identification through disguise. White carnival during Reconstruction took on the mask of blackness to protest what it saw as the injustice of its postwar abjection and exclusion from power. The Krewe of Momus, for instance, representing a mounted battalion of Moors in blackface, performed such a drama of protest in their street parade for Mardi Gras of 1873: "Trooping down the streets of an American City, between rows of stately modern edifices, came the dusky battalions of the race who could not be conquered, and who fought with blind savagery for things they only prized because the hated Christians desired it. Their swarthy faces and barbaric splendour of their trappings recalled the vanished centuries" (Waldo, *Hand-Book*, 60). In the collective memory of both blacks and whites under slavery, the historic license of carnival had provided a locus in which rebellions in the name of liberty could at least be imagined, if not implemented. The restoration of behavior that such an adventure inspires reappears through the doublings and inversions of white carnival: the face of the "fittest" behind the black mask of the gorilla representing Darwin's missing link certainly belonged to a member of the Mistick Krewe of Comus, perhaps to Brigadier General Behan himself, who was known to have taken a masked role in the parade (Miceli, appendix H).

In that light, the floats and tableaux from the 1870s make for some very instructive comparisons to those of 1992: their shared urgency resides in a kind of two-faced panic—queasy resignation punctuated by eruptions of outrage—that local government and its laws are passing from the control of white people; moreover, in each case, carnival emerges as the site where images of violent ridicule may stand in for violent actions (figure 6.7). Then as now the imagery oscillates between timelessness, the supposedly innocent realm of fantasy and fairy story, and timeliness, direct interventions in local and national politics, including the denigration of African-Americans and their claims for equal protection under the law.

The apostrophe of Darwin, uniting reactionary loathing of modern science with murderous opposition to the Fourteenth and Fifteenth Amendments, culminates in the mock crowning of "The Gorilla," who, holding his banjo in one hand, with the other pushes open the gate of "Darwin's Eden," which the Comus designer depicted as an old Louisiana plantation house. Evocative of the terrors of black usurpation of white privilege and derisive about the evolutionary rise of subspecies, the final tableau at the Comus ball

6.8 Mistick Krewe of Comus tableau, "The Missing Links to Darwin's *Origin of Species*," Varieties Theatre, 1873. *Harper's Weekly*, March 29, 1873. Courtesy The Historic New Orleans Collection, Museum/Research Center, acc. no. 1953.69

of 1873 arranged the phyla of the natural world on a staircase in ironic order of the fittest (figure 6.8). A correspondent from *Harper's Weekly* found this spectacle, a twisted form of carnivalesque inversion, "irresistibly laughable":

> When the curtain rose on the second tableau the Gorilla had just been crowned, and was seated on his throne under a dais, with Queen Chacona [the Baboon] on his right, and Orang, the Premier, on his left. On either side of the broad ascent to the throne the animal and vegetable world were crowding toward the royal presence, each in the order of his rank, the "Toilers of the Sea," kneeling, in loyal awe upon the pavement below. In the midst of the stair were three musicians—the Grasshopper with fiddle and bow, the Locust with his rattle, and the Beetle with his hammer. A pedestal on either hand bore the statuesque forms of the Baboon and the Marikina.
> *(Harper's Weekly*, March 29, 1873)

Its designers meant this tableau to be read as a double inversion: Comus, god of mirth, reigns in perfectly proportioned serenity at the bottom of the hierarchy of grotesques; thus the Bakhtinian displacement of official culture by the grotesque realism of the carnivalesque body turns bottoms up. The tableau offers a symbolic preenactment of the coup d'état in which members of the Mistick Krewe of Comus (among others), attacking "the most absurd inversion of the relations of race," violently displaced the reconstructing "monkeys" at the top. Comus celebrated the final collapse of Reconstruction in 1877 with a triumphant float parade entitled "The Aryan Race" (Young, *Mistick Krewe*, 222).

In these improvisatory rituals staged by men, women played a symbolically central role. In *Women in Public: Between Banners and Ballots, 1825–1880* (1990), Mary P. Ryan decants the literature of the White League to show how the "ladies assumed the role of the endangered to plead for a return to the regulation of race relations in public space" (93; see also Bryan; O'Brien). The control of race relations in public spaces is exactly to the point—concerning laws and (dis)obedience—but the women of Mardi Gras held (and continue to hold) a long-term responsibility as caretakers of memory—concerning origins and segregation. In the coming-out balls of the carnival season, however minutely controlled by men, the wives and especially the daughters of the krewe members become living effigies, the overdressed icons of social continuity. Their performances reveal the high stakes of deep play, marking the boundaries between public and private, timelessness and timeliness, and, as nubile sacrifices to endogamy, between whiteness and everything else (figure 6.9).

Lest the demise of the old-line parades conceal the goings-on of the tableau balls, the society pages of the local paper still report on their symbolism and iconography. In the 1993–94 season, the Harlequins, a youth Mardi Gras affiliate of the old-line krewes, staged a most pointed pageant. On the surface, the film *Jurassic Park* seemed to provide a theme for the preliminary training debut of the Harlequin queen and the maids of her court. Underneath the surface, an explicit restoration of behavior evoked the local creation myths of race and caste:

> As the tableau began, several Jurassic species, including the Comusaurus, the Proteadactyl and Momusraptor, were seen meandering through the primeval forests. They were being watched by

6.9 "Masker and Maid," Mistick Krewe of Comus Ball, 1970.
Photo: Manuel C. Delerno. Courtesy The Historic New Orleans Collection, Museum/Research Center, acc. no. 74.25.19.318

> "modern man," who was confident that his science, his culture, his civilization, were superior to that of these ancient beasts. Man's confidence led him to believe that times were changing, that ancient species should die off and be replaced, and that the dinosaurs must go. Darwin's ghost looked down upon the scene with a wry grin, and the end of the reign of the dinosaurs was proclaimed. But then something went awry. The dinosaurs refused to accept their fate and rose up in rebellion, proclaiming that they too had rights. Modern man was unable to dominate them and in the end, the dinosaurs were left to themselves. ("Primeval Partying")

On the liminal occasion of a rite of passage that serves to mark acceptance of its initiates into society and announce their availability for exchange within its patriarchal kinship network, the soon-to-be marriageable daughters of the krewes performed a most precise embodiment of selective memory. Theirs is a vividly demonstrable genealogy of performance. The Darwinian anxiety about being replaced by another "species" directly quotes the Mistick Krewe of Comus 1873 parade and grand tableau "The Missing Links to Darwin's *Origin of Species*." The "rebellion" of the dinosaurs, justified by a proclamation of their "rights," makes a clear reference to the coup of 1874 and its enactment of "the survival of the fittest" at the expense of the racially mixed Kellogg government.

There are no trivial rituals. In the service of memory, or in its betrayal, performances have powerful, if often unpredictable, consequences. Knowing nothing of the Mistick Krewe of Comus Mardi Gras parade and ball of 1873, historians of constitutional law stress the importance of the almost magical sway of Social Darwinism over the Supreme Court of the United States at the turn of the century (Highshaw, 64–65), particularly in the opinions rendered by Justice Edward Douglas White, Pickwickian, formerly Private White, Company E, Crescent City White League. Many other influences, no doubt, shaped Justice White's reasoning in *Plessy v. Ferguson*, but probably none more exhilarating to one who regarded himself as speaking for the "fittest" than the overthrow of Reconstruction in Louisiana by carnival in New Orleans.

Sovereign Immunity

As white carnivalesque lawlessness evolved incrementally into law, the emerging ordinances regulating Mardi Gras, like *Plessy v. Ferguson* on the national scene, adjusted the boundaries of transgression and immunity in the use of public accommodations. Transgression and immunity, in fact, while they define the carnivalesque in Bakhtin's sense, are eventually written into Louisiana law itself. The antebellum ordinance forbidding masking was still on the books verbatim at century's end (Flynn, 548), but other city ordinances now protected the parade routes of "carnival societies" from obstruction by vehicles, provisions that involved the city police in clearing the streets to make way for the activities that the antimasking ordinance proscribed (Flynn, 1158). The law thus required practical civic assistance to the outlaw practices of the social elite, who could then merrily flaunt their transgressions, making a seasonal public spectacle of their eternally exceptional status (figure 6.10).

In that same spirit, current State of Louisiana statutes regulating carnival masking and throws perpetuate the tradition of making the carnivalesque an elite entitlement under the law. In a state especially celebrated for masquerades, current statutes speak definitively about mask wearing: "No

6.10 Promiscuous maskers, Mardi Gras, 1902.
Louisiana Collection, Howard-Tilton Memorial Library, Tulane University

person shall use or wear in any public place of any character whatsoever, or in any open place in view thereof, a hood or mask, or anything in the nature of either, or any facial disguise of any kind or description, calculated to conceal or hide the identity of the person or to prevent his being readily recognized" (*Louisiana Statutes Annotated*, 14:313). This proscription, however, though descended from earlier antimasking ordinances, has now incorporated certain privileged exceptions as sanctified by custom: children's masks at Halloween, participants in historical pageants, and, significantly, "persons participating in masquerade balls or entertainments, . . . persons participating in carnival parades or exhibitions during the period of Mardi Gras festivities," and, with a most revealing qualifier, "promiscuous masking on Mardi Gras *which are duly authorized by the governing authorities of the municipality*" (*Louisiana Statutes Annotated*, 14:313, emphasis added). This statute recognizes and protects a special class of maskers, who continued even after 1874 to dramatize themselves as the embattled but ultimately triumphant warrior band (figure 6.11).

6.11 Rex parade, "Uneasy Lies the Head that Wears a Crown," 1902. Float #10: armed knights defend a castle besieged by dragons labeled "Socialism."
Louisiana Collection, Howard-Tilton Memorial Library, Tulane University

Other statutes define the privileges of this class while limiting its membership. Processions, marches, and parades in Louisiana require a permit, which in turn requires the posting of an expensive bond and, within Orleans Parish, the payment of fees for police protection. Explicitly exempted is "any procession, march, or parade directly held or sponsored by a bona fide organization specifically for the celebration of Mardi Gras and/or directly related pre-lenten or carnival festivities" (*Louisiana Statutes Annotated*, 14:326). This language excludes the processions of black Second Line organizations and Mardi Gras Indian gangs, though it does extend to Zulu. In his mordant article "New Orleans' Hidden Carnival," Michael P. Smith explains the consequences of such a regressive system: "Black groups . . . are required to pay exorbitant fees, upwards of $4800 per parade, for police monitoring services required by the city—services granted free to clubs parading during the 'official' Carnival season" (6).

In addition, Mardi Gras krewe parades are protected by a special reiteration of the legal doctrine of assumption of risk. By attending a parade, the individual reveler assumes the risk of being run over by a police motorcycle (*Carter v. Travelers, Inc.*, 176 So. 2d 176 [1965]), for instance, or being knocked off a step ladder by a krewe float (*McGinity v. Marquette*, 156 So. 2d 713 [1963]). In one case, however, a Louisiana court made an exception to the assumption of risk: it ruled in favor of a woman attending Zulu who was struck in the head and injured by a flying coconut, the traditional Zulu throw, though the insurer won on appeal (*Schofield v. Continental Ins.*, La. App., 330 So. 2d 376 [1976]). More recently, the state statutes, which had already extended to the Mardi Gras krewes the kind of limitations on tort actions enjoyed by state and municipal governments ("unless the loss or damage was caused by the deliberate and wanton act or gross negligence"), were amended to wrap the krewes' traditional throws specifically in the majestic mantle of Louisiana law: "Any person who is attending or participating in one of the organized parades of floats . . . assumes the risk of being struck by any missile whatsoever which has been traditionally thrown, tossed, or hurled by members of the krewe or organization. The items shall include but are not limited to beads, cups, coconuts, and doubloons unless said loss or damage was caused by deliberate and wanton act or gross negligence of said krewe or organization" (*Louisiana Statutes Annotated*, 9:2796). Once again, carnival infiltrates and expands the law, this time to accommodate the vulnerabilities, however slight, of the privileged to the redress of the injured: deliberate, wanton, and gross negligence requires a high standard of proof. But deeper meaning of such legal protections is clear. The final incorporation of an ancient carnival tradition within the law reinforces the official *public* status of the krewes under the law. This status, an extension of the legal doctrine of sovereign immunity, vitiates any claim to exemption from the law on the basis of privacy, a claim that cannot stand against the import of the regulations guaranteeing the krewes' protection in the public sphere, for the public interest, and at public expense.

As long as the political and social power in the city remained closely aligned, the historic, legitimating reciprocity of carnival and the law in New Orleans could endure. By 1988, however, when debate opened on what became the Mardi Gras Ordinance of 1991, the balance of power in New Orleans's racial politics had shifted to reflect more closely the actual demographics of the city. This pitted the opponents of the ordinance, which passed by a unanimous vote initially, against the authority of the city council and the mayor. It put those who practiced racial discrimination in carnival clubs outside the law. It tore away the mask coded "private" from the public face of Mardi Gras. In other words, it returned white carnival once more to its Bakhtinian category of transgression against the official culture, and, in a way not seen for over a century, the world turned upside down.

Mystic Chords of Memory; or, Stevie Wonder Square

Like *The Octoroon; or, Life in Louisiana*, the hearing held by the Advisory Committee on Human Relations on the Liberty Place Monument played itself out as a mortgage melodrama of entitlement and dispossession. As Michael Kammen points out in *Mystic Chords of Memory: The Transformation of Tradition in American Culture* (1991), there is a perceived struggle at the heart of many American self-conceptions, often melodramatized, between nostalgia and progress (702–3). From where I sat in the hearing room, the melodrama certainly had a villain, one who is too easily hissed and forgotten: David Duke is not to be taken lightly on the subject of the diseases of American memory. Like most skilled performers, he not only embodies an exception to the social norm; he is also and simultaneously a condensation of it. This prolific candidate, who openly celebrated Adolph Hitler's birthday as recently as 1988, came much closer than many people realize to defeating conservative Democrat J. Bennett Johnston for a seat in the United States Senate in 1990: of Louisiana's sixty-four parishes, Duke won twenty-five, polling a statewide total of 59 percent of the white vote, 43.5 percent of all the votes cast (Bridges, 193). As of this writing, with a growing number of mainstream political figures taking up his nativist themes, it is sobering to reflect on Duke's 1990 prediction of a happy resolution to the mortgage melodrama he revived in Louisiana: "We are going to build a political movement in this country to bring back the political rights of the majority" (quoted in Bridges, 193).

Although in such *lieux de mémoire* as the Liberty Place Monument, whiteness and rights reappear as interdependent domains, the self-dramatizing defenders of their contingent frontiers can never allow themselves to forget the obvious: they must always keep alive the specter of the others in opposition to whom they reinvent themselves. At the same time, this necessity means that they cannot erase their fear that their surrogated victims will somehow manage to succeed them after all. Surrendering any bit of their version of the past therefore means somehow losing control over the totality of the future. Thus the past must become the future, a nostalgic fantasy that subdivides into the complementary projects of restitution and revenge. The organizing trope of Richard Verstegen's Anglo-Saxonist *Restitution of Decayed Intelligence* (1605) still resonates in Fred Nash Ogden's language of apocalyptic displacement and return: "Having solely in view the maintenance of our hereditary civilization and Christianity menaced by a stupid Africanization," the *Platform of the Crescent City White League* announced in its 1874 call to arms, "we appeal to the men of our race . . . to re-establish a white man's government in the city and the State." Prior to the Human Relations Committee hearing of 1993, David Duke had already hyperbolized a similar anxiety with regard to the Liberty Place Monument. He did so, predictably, by assigning a performer to the liminal role of effigy and surrogate: "What about Jackson Square?" he asked, referring to the equestrian statue of Andrew Jackson in front of the St. Louis Cathedral, "Do we have to take that down and change the name to Stevie Wonder Square?" (quoted in Powell, 43).

Duke's testimony touched only indirectly on the White League, however, and not at all on the carnival krewes, whose members, in any case, have despised such white-trash opportunists since the days of John Pope's drugstore. Speaking of what he called "the true meaning of the monument," Duke cited the battles of Lexington and Concord as the real precedents invoked by the Battle of Liberty Place and its cenotaph: there the patriotic minutemen had fought and died for their freedom against the occupying forces of "tyranny." Removing the Liberty Monument would be tantamount to desecrating statues of Washington and Jefferson, he continued, which would be defacing public property symbolizing Liberty itself, an act with dire consequences. To remove the monument would be to rewrite history, argued Duke, who believes that the gas Zyklon B was used at Auschwitz only to control lice (Bridges, 116): "Then we don't have a civilization anymore. We have a jungle."

The slippage that conjured the founding fathers out of a self-congratulatory erection honoring silk-stockinged rioters starkly illustrates the mechanisms of dominant circum-Atlantic memory, which struggle to erase the troubling evidence of intervening improvisations by direct appeal to origins. To Duke this distinction suggested a choice between the alternatives of "civilization" and "jungle." Carried away by his defense of American civilization against a rising tide of barbarism, he likened the opponents of the monument to "book-burning Nazis." Rabbi Cohn interrupted the testimony at this point to ask with perfect chairmanly decorum, as if clarifying an obscure phrase for the record, "Nazis, Mr. Duke? Pardon me, but did I hear you say 'Nazis'?" Duke nodded affirmatively but with apparent confusion; then he continued his eulogy, paraphrasing, without attribution and perhaps accidentally, the "mystic chords of memory" passage from Abraham Lincoln's first inaugural address: "Though passion may have strained, it must not break our bonds of affection. The mystic chords of memory, stretching from every battle-field, and patriot grave, to every living heart and hearthstone, all over this broad land, will yet swell the chorus of the Union, when again touched, as surely they will be, by the better angels of our nature" (Lincoln, 224).

A silent witness to the June 15 advisory committee hearing was City Council Member-at-large Dorothy Mae Taylor, who was instrumental in framing and passing the 1991 civil rights ordinance that prompted Comus, Momus, and Proteus to end their Mardi Gras parades, even though the intent of the council's legislation was to end segregation, not celebration. Her silence was eloquent. Taylor's leadership, which was visited by more denunciations and ridicule than support, even from some of the other council members who had voted for the ordinance (Vennman, "Boundary Face-Off"), was forged in the crucible of New Orleans racial politics in the 1960s (Hirsch and Logsdon, 262–319). Taylor's record in this regard seemed to fall prey to a whipsaw of demonization and amnesia. The 1991 ordinance developed logically from the civil rights legislation of the 1960s and indeed from the historic argument of fair and equal access to public accommodations (Rogers). But it was widely characterized as a plot to kill Mardi Gras by attacking freedom of association and the rights of the krewes. Even before the final and softened version of the ordinance had been made law, however, the krewes of Comus and Momus canceled their 1992 parades, and many New Orleanians blamed Taylor for trashing carnival tradition (figure 6.12).

In the mid-1990s, the Mardi Gras festivities of the three old-line krewes continue officially only in private but unofficially here and there in the form of some guerrilla-style street parading lampooning city council members and others. Rex has inducted three members identified as black. Taylor retired from the City Council and was subsequently defeated in her run for a lesser office. The Liberty Place Monument still stands, its future tied up, as they say, in litigation. This empty sarcophagus gives silent testimony to the suppleness of the law in the performance of memory: that it can be stretched even to perpetuate the honor of those who once violently dis-

6.12 Death and Surrogation. “R.I.P. Here lies MARDI GRAS, 1831–1992.”
Signboard carried by promiscuous maskers, Mardi Gras, 1992.
New Orleans City Council member-at-large Dorothy Mae Taylor in effigy, usurping a crown marked “Comus.”
Photo: Barbara Vennman

obeyed it, acting in the avowed cause of disenfranchising forever those who are now charged with enforcing it. If stateways cannot change folkways perhaps it is for the simple reason that stateways *are* folkways.

Jazz Funeral

Surveying the New Orleans urbanscape, anchored on the landmarks provided by its famous Cities of the Dead, the pedestrian thinks more readily of the city as "text," as Roland Barthes did, than as "speech," following the suggestion of Michel de Certeau. Reading the scene as text, the eye takes in a history inscribed by rhetorics of exclusion. For all the evidence that supports such a reading, however, it is nonetheless unsatisfactory. De Certeau's view is also valid, and New Orleans offers a powerful instance of the truth of his insight, nowhere more persuasively than in the mortuary rituals of its community of musicians. Hearing the city as speech (and song), the ear takes in a memory predicated on a rhetoric of inclusion.

In 1992 Joe August, the rhythm and blues pioneer known as "Mr. Google Eyes," or "G" for short, was buried "with music." To be buried with music in New Orleans means that the ordinary service will be followed by what the death notices call a "traditional jazz funeral." However traditional it may be, there is no such thing as a typical jazz funeral: the tradition is that the observances are adapted to suit the occasion. Like the funeral of the old Congo slave observed by Latrobe in 1819, the occasion is likely to call for celebration as well as solemnity, concluding with an up-tempo Second Line parade. Well-known and well-loved local musicians, black or white, will be remembered in this way. Joe August, who recorded "Poppa Stoppa's Be-Bop Blues" for Coleman Records and "No Wine, No Women" and "Rough and Rocky Road" for Columbia, who also wrote one of Johnny Ace's biggest hits, "Please Forgive Me," and who founded the activist agency Blacks That Give a Damn, qualified on both counts of celebrity and affection. In *Under a Hoodoo Moon* (1994), Malcolm Rebennack, better known as Dr. John, the white jazz celebrity, recalls his first meeting with Joe August, who inspired him as a performer and as a personality: "The first time I ever laid eyes on him, he was luxuriating outside his club in a purple Buick with leopard-skin upholstery and leopard skin covering the dash and lining the trunk." Dr. John also remembers that "G played his club with his own badass, low-down, bebop scat-jazz R&B act" (71).

While the mourners, including Dr. John, assembled in the parlor to pay their respects to Joe August, the Olympia Brass Band, consisting of trombones, trumpets, tuba, and drum, waited in the gravel parking lot out front. Inside, friends and relatives heard eulogies addressed to the deceased, as if he were present, spoken on behalf of the community in the first-person plural. Malcolm Rebennack—Dr. John—said: "it is with great pride that we carry the message of the blues that you instilled in us as children." The content of the "message of the blues" remained unspecified, but the auditors voiced their assent. Joe August's parents and grandparents, long since deceased, were remembered by name. Joseph Cool Davis then sang one of Joe's favorite hymns, "Bye and Bye":

> May the circle be unbroken
> Bye and bye, Lord, bye and bye;
> There's a better home a 'waiting
> In the sky, Lord, in the sky.

After a final "Parting View," the undertaker closed the casket and the pallbearers carried it out to the hearse.

Outside, a crowd from the neighborhood had assembled. When the band struck up, following the "Nelson" with a purple sash and baton, the procession began down Claiborne Avenue. The family, holding hands, walked ahead of the hearse. The crowd, six or eight abreast, followed, filling the avenue. The pace was cadenced, neither joyous nor solemn. The marchers spoke, neither loud nor hushed. I heard an old hymn tune I thought I recognized, its meter voicing a solo call and choric response:

> I know moonwise, I know starwise:
> Lay this body down.
> I walk in the moonlight, I walk in the starlight
> To lay this body down.
> I'll walk in the graveyard, I'll walk through the graveyard
> To lay this body down.
> I'll lie in the grave and stretch out my arms:
> Lay this body down.

In earlier days, the procession would have followed the hearse to the gravesite for the interment, but now the old cemeteries are full and the new ones are too far to reach on foot, even with the encouragement of the music. So the family goes its separate way in limos. This moment, when the deceased parts company with the procession in his honor, is called "cutting the body loose," which cues in the festivity. After a respectful silence while the cortege passed from view, the Olympians broke into an up-tempo number and headed back up Claiborne Avenue. The song, addressed with affectionate ribaldry to the memory of the deceased, was "Oh, He Did Ramble." Brown bags opened up and brightly fringed umbrellas popped open, bouncing up and down to the new pulse of the march in the dance style of New Orleans parading known as Second Lining.

The Second Line consists of the marchers following the band, some of whom dance, others of whom add counterryhthmic accompaniment on improvised instruments. Tradition has it that the term "Second Line" comes from Reconstruction days, when black people, new to parliamentary procedure, found themselves jumping up all at once to yell, "I second that!" The band and the Second Liners moved their line of march directly under the Interstate 10 overpass, which runs parallel to Claiborne Avenue, through what was formerly the central tree-lined boulevard of the African-American community in New Orleans. Now the concrete overpass provided a haunting acoustical effect as the layered sounds of brass, percussion, and choric shouts bounced off the reflective surfaces of the highway and its massive supports. The echoes sounded like other bands playing from above (figure 6.13).

The jazz funeral's genius for participation resides in the very expandability of the procession: marchers with very different connections to the deceased (or perhaps no connections at all) join together on the occasion to make connections with one another. Moving along with the packed crowd of the Second Line, which consists of dancers and marchers of different ages and energy levels, requires a high level of cooperation and consideration, not to speak of watching out for equipment-laden members of the Third Line, who sometimes try to run backward while focusing their minicams, with predictable results. Along the line of march of Joe August's funeral procession, an elderly Second Liner politely touched my elbow to draw my attention to my untied shoelaces—a menace amid the flowing mass of dancing bodies, a literal faux pas. In the spin of this musical and kinesthetic vortex, the sounds of the city as participatory speech contradict the city as exclusionary text: as Richard Allen, observing the revelers at a jazz funeral, noted in 1962: "At least two boys and two women danc[ed] with partners of opposite sex and color."

In circum-Atlantic race relations, the production of culture by means of surrogation has traditionally utilized race as the threatening mark of differ-

6.13 Jazz Funeral for Mr. Google Eyes (Joe August), New Orleans, 1992.
Photo: Ed Newman, New Orleans, 1992

ence whereby the effigy is distanced from the community in order to participate sacrificially in its reaffirmation. Miscegenation reenacts the primal scene where that mark of difference becomes affixed. In 1960, after an incident in which he was shot by his white girlfriend Vicki, Joe August was arrested and charged under Louisiana's antimiscegenation law, which the couple had previously tried to evade. Even the precaution of shortening her long blond hair, dyeing the roots jet black, and wearing Man-Tan in public had failed to let Vicki to pass for "Creole" (Hannusch, 89). The couple was first arrested on a charge of loitering, interrogated, and terrorized by the police. After their release, on the day that forced integration began in the New Orleans schools, Miss Vicki, declaring "If I can't have you, nobody can," plugged Joe August in the belly with a shotgun—loving him not wisely but too well. The responding police officers drove the profusely bleeding singer the half mile to Charity Hospital by a leisurely route, stopping off for a beer along the way (Hannusch, 91). Although he survived his wound and the charges of miscegenation were eventually dropped, after this incident, G's career "slowed," as his obituary put it; he cut his last record in 1963, nearly thirty years before his death (obituary, Joseph Charles Augustus, New Orleans *Times-Picayune*, October 12, 1992, B-8).

The state of liminality, like the state of Louisiana, both of which ethnographers find so rich in cultural expressiveness, can be very hard on the people who are actually trying to live there. In relationship to southern protocols of ocular circumspection between the races, the adoption of "Mr. Google Eyes" as a stage name proved a tactless choice. It was a tactlessness manifoldly compounded by the affectation of the purple Buick, not to speak of the white girl. It was also a tactlessness that any performance on the margin makes difficult to avoid. As the ambivalence over the London funeral of Thomas Betterton shows, circum-Atlantic performers act out the anxiety-inducing boundaries between whiteness and blackness on the cusp between life and death.

Effigies, however, are not just for burning. When the mourners at Joe August's jazz funeral cut the body loose, they held open a place for others through the memory of his life in the celebration of his passing. That spirit permeated the laughter evoked by the several pointed verses of "Oh, He Did Ramble." Such obsequies, the suggestive no less than the solemn, reaffirm the existence of a community without sealing it off from the rest of the world—past, present, and future. In the midst of this extraordinary Afrocentric ritual, in the very space it has so generously provided for memory as improvisation, the process of circum-Atlantic surrogation continues to unfold. It unfolded before my eyes in the guise of Mr. Spectator, as it had unfolded before those of Richard Steele, who "look[ed] upon the Distinctions amongst Men to be meerly Scenical" (*Tatler*, 2:424).

Dr. John, Joe August's white eulogist, takes his stage name from the formidable nineteenth-century New Orleans voodoo, alias Bayou John, who intimidated slaves and slaveholders alike. Malcolm Rebennack spoke the eulogy under his own name as a carrier of the "message of the blues" instilled in him by Joe August. He reminded the mourners that neither he nor G was the message; rather, they were both messengers. Malcolm Rebennack, however, records and performs contractually under the assumed name of Dr. John, the original holder of which claimed that he was a Senegalese prince, whose face, like Oroonoko's, was scarified in the African manner, and whose voice, it was said, could be heard from two miles away (Tallant, 33–36). Clearly, in the alchemy of circum-Atlantic memory and surrogation, such a voice can be heard across surprising expanses of time as well.

EPILOGUE: NEW FRONTIERS

Deep down in the deep seam the water's clear
And clean from the black rock of Africa.
There are bards there and craftsmen, heroes, kings,
And dark ecstatic dancers throng the kraals.

– E. M. ROACH

IN THE CLEARNESS OF THE WATERS AT THE SOURCE, THE CARIBBEAN POET'S VERSES imagine purity of origin. While there is every reason to requicken and to celebrate the memory of Africa that these lines evoke, the poet's family name might be thought to muddy the waters a bit. That name points back from the West Indies to County Cork, where the search for roots is arduous, and not only because during the Potato Famine somebody probably ate them. The very language in which Roach writes the poem, called "Fighters," maps a story of memory and forgetting, now ever more widely told, in which both tellers and listeners have found more recoverable meanings in routes than they have in roots.

In the epigraph to the first chapter of *Welcome to the Jungle: New Positions in Black Cultural Studies* (1994), Kobena Mercer cites the prophetic voice of C. L. R. James. Decades ago, the historian of the Caribbean revolution of the 1790s looked ahead to the 1990s and foresaw the impact, as this century nears its end, of millions of black people born in Great Britain as British subjects but not yet, by reason of their blackness, fully a part of it. James saw this divided citizenship, this double consciousness, not as a negation but as a historic opportunity: "What such persons have to say, therefore, will give a new vision, a deeper and stronger insight into both western civilization and the black people in it" (quoted in Mercer, 1). That such persons have called themselves "Settlers" sharpens the ironies of Kobena Mercer's play of geotropes and chronotropes in *Welcome to the Jungle*: "Welcome to Heathrow: you are now entering the labyrinths of a modern Babylon, a green and not-always-so-pleasant Third World Albion" (8). Despite the stubborn and sometimes violent hostility of the supposedly autochthonous population of Britain, Mercer's exhortation to exploration and discovery goes out to "the emerging *cultures of hybridity*, forged among the overlapping African, Asian and Caribbean diasporas" (3). As New Orleans was once poised on the "selvage of civilization," the destiny of London is manifest: it is the New Frontier.

One of the purposes of this book has been to show how specifically that destiny was foreseeable and duly foreseen. In the epic vision of Horace Walpole's prognostication of Mesoamerican sightseers taking in the ruins of St. Paul's Cathedral or in Alexander Pope's prediction of "Feather'd Peoples" sailing up the Thames, rich allusions to the Mediterranean past pointed the way to the Caribbeanized future. The English, however, often imagine the future in and through ruins. This melancholy habit of mind lends a certain logic to their imperial xenophobia. In John Atkins's *Voyage to Guinea, Brasil, and the West-Indies* (1735), for instance, the reader learns that "the Gulph of Mexico . . . may be considered as a little Mediterranean Sea" (232). Such geohistorical homologies plunge Atkins into nostalgic brooding on the fate of cities and empires: "They have a determined Time to flourish, decay, and die in. Corn grows where Troy stood: Carthage is blotted out. Greece and her Republicks (Athens, Sparta, Corinth), with other fam'd Asian and African Cities the Turkish Monarchy has overturned. Their Magnificence, Wealth, Learning, and Worship, is changed into Poverty and Ignorance; and Rome, the Mother of all, overrun with Superstition. Who, on the one hand, but feels an inexplicable Pleasure in treading over that Ground, he supposes such Men inhabited, whose Learning and Virtues have been the Emulation of all succeeding Ages?" In such an evocation of the *lieux de mémoire*, sites lined up along the grand tour, the usurping presence of the speaker as emulator (hence performer) of the past induces his fatalistic prediction of surrogation in the future: "And who again but must mourn such a melancholy Transposition of Scene, and spend a few funereal Reflections over such extraordinary *Exequiae*: Perhaps the Revolution of as many Ages, as has sunk their Glory, may raise it again, or carry it to the Negroes and Hottentots, and the present Possessors be debased" (preface, xvii–xviii). That surrogation is viewed as debasement gives emphasis to the pressure the future exerts on the process of imagining the past. This pressure—of origin, segregation, and destiny—is most excruciating when it is phrased in the present tense and addressed to an imagined community in the first-person plural, such as when Enoch Powell asks, "What sort of people are we?"

As carnival and the law can both be used to affirm, however, surrogation need not be a debasement but an opportunity for renewal: "Festivals are a way of bringing about change. . . . Parades alter truth" (Bunsekei, quoted in Nunley and Bettelheim, 23). The parade, however obdurately resistant to integration it may see itself as being—and many parades have seen themselves in just that way—is nevertheless vulnerable. It is vulnerable because the participants literally succeed themselves before the eyes of the spectators. As the sound of one band dies, another arrives to lift the spirits of the auditors. Generations of marchers seem to arise and pass away. Because it is an additive form, passing by a point of review in succession, its ending is always an anticlimax, a provocation, and an opening.

Viewed as open-ended, like a jazz funeral, the parade of circum-Atlantic identities is itself a kind of orature. As repetition with the inevitability of revision, the parade shares a potentially inclusionary feature with carnival itself: "Carnival," argues Kobena Mercer in his account of London's Notting Hill Carnival, which is now "one of the largest public street events" in Europe, "breaks down the barriers between active performer and passive audience" (9, 59). Carnival is not only an assembly that can be seized on to dramatize the call for redress of grievances—as it was for the White League in New Orleans in 1873 or for black Britons at Notting Hill in 1976—it is also a ghostly double to the law as a technique to remember the past and to reimagine the future. The opening of access to public accommodations to all people, the historic strategy of civil rights legislation and judge-made law in the United States, finds itself performed in the streets during carnival, less so, admittedly, within the traditions of the European carnivalesque but considerably more so within the syncretisms of the African and Caribbean diasporas.

Today the role of performance in voicing the plenitude of circum-Atlantic futures is exemplified by Apache Indian, the East Indian musician who grew up in a Jamaican neighborhood in London, who sings reggae "like a native" but who identifies himself as a Native American. Across the transnational groupings and reinvented affiliations of such an oceanic interculture but within the stubborn eloquence of the intersecting diasporic memories performed within its distinctive urban vortices, the precise location of the New World is no longer clear. Wherever its frontiers might now be provisionally mapped, however, the discursive life of the ancient concept of a "Free-born People" infuses law with the urgency of performance: justice can no longer be imagined as something that merely exists; it is something that must, finally, be done. Only then will the Cities of the Dead be truly free to welcome the new generations of the living.

In *Small Acts: Thoughts on the Politics of Black Cultures* (1993), Paul Gilroy sums up the task facing genealogists of circum-Atlantic performance: "The contemporary musical forms of the African diaspora work within an aesthetic and political framework which demands that they ceaselessly reconstruct their own histories, folding back on themselves time and again to celebrate and validate the simple, unassailable fact of their survival" (37). Genealogists resist histories that attribute purity of origin to any performance. They have to take into account the give and take of joint transmissions, posted in the past, arriving in the present, delivered by living messengers, speaking in tongues not entirely their own. Orature is an art of listening as well as speaking; improvisation is an art of collective memory as well as invention; repetition is an art of re-creation as well as restoration. Texts may obscure what performance tends to reveal: memory challenges history in the construction of circum-Atlantic cultures, and it revises the yet unwritten epic of their fabulous cocreation.

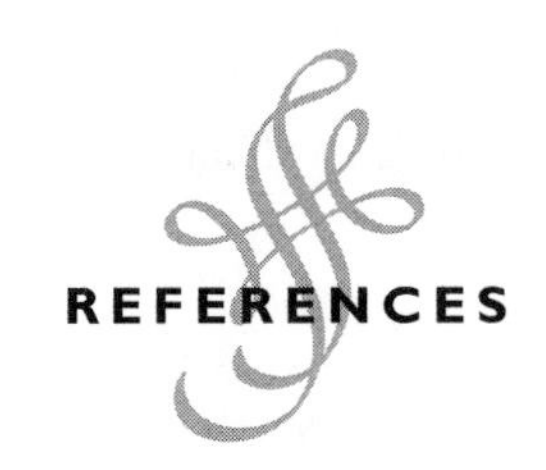

REFERENCES

ABBREVIATIONS

ARC Amistad Research Center, Tulane University.

BDA *Biographical Dictionary of Actors, Actresses, Musicians, Dancers, Managers, and Other Stage Personnel in London, 1660–1800*. Ed. Philip H. Highfill, Jr., Kalman A. Burnim, and Edward A. Langhans. 18 vols. Carbondale: Southern Illinois University Press, 1973–93.

CN Le Code noir; ou, Recueil des reglements rendus jusqu'à present, concernant le gouvernement, l'administration de la justice, la police, la discipline, et le commerce des nègres dans les colonies françaises. Paris: Prault, 1742. Collected in English as "Collection of Regulations, Edicts, Declarations, and Decrees, Concerning the Commerce, Administration of Justice, and the Policing of the French Colonies of America. With the Black Code and Additions to the Said Code." Trans. Olivia Blanchard. Baton Rouge: Survey of Federal Archives in Louisiana, 1940. Louisiana Collection, Howard-Tilton Memorial Library, Tulane University.

HJA William Ransom Hogan Jazz Archive, Tulane University.

LS *The London Stage, 1660–1800*. Part 2, vol. 1, ed. Emmett L. Avery. Carbondale: Southern Illinois University Press, 1960.

PB *Pinacotheca Bettertonaeana; or, A Catalogue of the Books, Prints, Drawings, and Paintings of Mr. Thomas Betterton, That Celebrated Comedian, Lately*

Deceased. I am indebted to Judith Milhous for providing me with this catalogue.

WORKS CITED

Abrahams, Roger D. *The Man-of-Words in the West Indies: Performance and the Emergence of Creole Culture*. Baltimore: Johns Hopkins University Press, 1983.

Abrahams, Roger D., and John F. Szwed, eds. *After Africa: Extracts from British Travel Accounts and Journals of the Seventeenth, Eighteenth, and Nineteenth Centuries Concerning the Slaves, Their Manners, and Customs in the British West Indies*. New Haven: Yale University Press, 1983.

Achebe, Chinua. *Things Fall Apart*. 1958. Oxford: Heinemann, 1986.

Agnew, Jean-Christophe. *Worlds Apart: The Market and the Theater in Anglo-American Thought, 1550–1750*. Cambridge: Cambridge University Press, 1986.

Allen, Richard. File, "Funeral and Music: Local," HJA.

Altick, Richard. *The Shows of London*. Cambridge: Harvard University Press, Belknap, 1978.

Anderson, Benedict. *Imagined Communities: Reflections on the Origin and Spread of Nationalism*. Rev. ed. London: Verso, 1991.

Appadurai, Arjun, ed. *The Social Life of Things: Commodities in Cultural Perspective*. Cambridge: Cambridge University Press, 1986.

Appiah, Kwame Anthony. *In My Father's House: Africa in the Philosophy of Culture*. New York: Oxford University Press, 1992.

Arac, Jonathan. *Critical Genealogies: Historical Situations for Postmodern Literary Studies*. New York: Columbia University Press, 1987.

Ariès, Philippe. *Essais sur l'histoire de la mort*. Paris: Seuil, 1977.

Armstrong, Louis. "Growing Up in New Orleans." In John Miller, ed., *New Orleans Stories*. San Francisco: Chronicle, 1992, 23–38.

Aston, Anthony. *A Brief Supplement to Colley Cibber, Esq.: His Lives of the Late Famous Actors and Actresses*. In Colley Cibber, *An Apology for the Life of Mr. Colley Cibber*, 2:297–318.

Atkins, John. *A Voyage to Guinea, Brasil, and the West-Indies*. London: C. Ward and R. Chandler, 1735.

Axtell, James. *The Invasion Within: The Contest of Cultures in Colonial North America*. New York: Oxford University Press, 1985.

Azim, Firdous. *The Colonial Rise of the Novel*. London: Routledge, 1993.

Backscheider, Paula R. *Spectacular Politics: Theatrical Power and Mass Culture in Early Modern England*. Baltimore: Johns Hopkins University Press, 1993.

Baer, Marc. *Theatre and Disorder in Late Georgian London*. Oxford: Clarendon, 1992.

Bakhtin, Mikhail. *Rabelais and His World*. Trans. Hélène Iswolsky. Bloomington: Indiana University Press, 1984.

———. *Speech Genres*. Ed. Carol Emerson and Michael Holquist. Austin: University of Texas Press, 1986.

Balme, Christopher B. "Cultural Anthropology and Theatre Historiography: Notes on a Methodological Rapprochement." *Theatre Survey* 35 (1994): 33–52.

Bannock, Larry. Personal interview. November 8, 1991.

———. Interview videotaped at New Orleans Jazz and Heritage Festival, 1991. ARC.

Barish, Jonas. *The Antitheatrical Prejudice*. Berkeley: University of California Press, 1981.

Barr, Tony. *Acting for the Camera*. Boston: Allyn and Bacon, 1982.

Barthes, Roland. "Sémiologie et urbanisme." *Architecture d'aujourd'hui* 153 (1971): 11–13.

Bataille, Georges. *The Accursed Share: An Essay on General Economy*. Vol. 1, *Consumption*, trans. Robert Hurley. New York: Zone, 1991.

———. *Erotism: Death and Sensuality*. Trans. Mary Dalwood. San Francisco: City Lights, 1986.

Baudrillard, Jean. *Simulations*. 1975. Trans. Paul Foss, Paul Patton, and Philip Beitchman. New York: Semiotext(e), 1983.

Bauman, Richard. "Performance." In *International Encyclopedia of Communications*. New York: Oxford University Press, 1989, 3:262–66.

Bauman, Richard, and Charles Briggs. "Poetics and Performance as Critical Perspectives on Language and Social Life." *Annual Review of Anthropology* 19 (1990): 59–88.

Beeman, William O. "The Anthropology of Theater and Spectacle." *Annual Review of Anthropology* 22 (1993): 369–93.

Behan, William J. "Pickwick Club Reminiscences." New Orleans: privately printed, 1912. Louisiana Collection, Tulane University Library.

Behn, Aphra. *Oroonoko*. 1688. Ed. Lore Metzger, New York: Norton, 1973.

———. *The Widow Ranter*. In *Oroonoko, The Rover, and Other Works*, ed. Janet Todd. London: Penguin, 1992.

Bennett, Lerone, Jr. *The Shaping of Black America*. Rev. ed. New York: Penguin, 1993.

Bentley, Gerald Eades. *The Jacobean and Caroline Stage*. 7 vols. Oxford: Clarendon, 1941–68.

Berliner, Paul. *Thinking in Jazz: The Infinite Art of Improvisation*. Chicago: University of Chicago Press, 1994.

Bernal, Martin. *Black Athena: The Afroasiatic Roots of Classical Civilization*. 2 vols. New Brunswick, N.J.: Rutgers University Press, 1987–91.

Berry, Jason, Jonathan Foose, and Tad Jones. *Up from the Cradle of Jazz: New Orleans Music Since World War II*. Athens: University of Georgia Press, 1986.

Beverley, Robert. *The History and Present State of Virginia*. 1705. Ed. Louis B. Wright. Chapel Hill: University of North Carolina Press, 1947.

Bhabha, Homi K. *The Location of Culture*. London: Routledge, 1994.

Blackstone, Sarah J. *Buckskins, Bullets, and Business: A History of Buffalo Bill's Wild West*. New York: Greenwood, 1986.

Blake, W. O. *The History of Slavery and the Slave Trade, Ancient and Modern*. 1857. Columbus, Ohio: H. Miller, 1861.

Blassingame, John W. *Black New Orleans, 1860–1880*. Chicago: University of Chicago Press, 1973.

Blau, Herbert. *The Audience*. Baltimore: Johns Hopkins University Press, 1990.

Bloch, Maurice. *Prey into Hunter: The Politics of Religious Experience*. Cambridge: Cambridge University Press, 1992.

Blue Book. Rose Collection, HJA, 606 box 3.

Boime, Albert. *The Art of Exclusion: Representing Blacks in the Nineteenth Century*. Washington: Smithsonian Institution Press, 1990.

Bond, Richmond P. *Queen Anne's American Kings*. Oxford: Clarendon, 1952.

Booth, Michael. *Victorian Spectacular Theatre*. London: Routledge, 1981.

Boucicault, Dion. *The Octoroon; or, Life in Louisiana*. 1861. Rpt., Miami: Mnemosyne, 1969.

Boyarin, Jonathan, ed. *Remapping Memory: The Politics of Timespace*. Minneapolis: University of Minnesota Press, 1994.

Boyer, M. Christine. *The City of Collective Memory: Its Historical Imagery and Architectural Entertainments*. Cambridge, Mass.: MIT Press, 1994.

Brathwait, Richard. *The English Gentleman*. 1630. Rpt., Amsterdam: Theatrum Orbis Terrarum, 1975.

———. *The English Gentlewoman*. 1631. Rpt., Amsterdam: Theatrum Orbis Terrarum, 1970.

Braudel, Fernand. *On History*. Trans. Sarah Mathews. Chicago: University of Chicago Press, 1980.

Braverman, Richard Lewis. *Plots and Counterplots: Sexual Politics and the Body Politic in English Literature, 1660–1730*. Cambridge: Cambridge University Press, 1993.

Bremmer, Jan, and Herman Roodenberg, eds. *A Cultural History of Gesture*. Ithaca, N.Y.: Cornell University Press, 1992.

Bricker, Victoria Reifler. *The Indian Christ, The Indian King: The Historical Substrate of Maya Myth and Ritual*. Austin: University of Texas Press, 1981.

Bridges, Tyler. *The Rise of David Duke*. Jackson: University Press of Mississippi, 1994.

Bromley, J. S., ed. *The New Cambridge Modern History*. Vol. 6, *The Rise of Great Britain and Russia, 1688–1715/25*. Cambridge: Cambridge University Press, 1971.

Brower, Reuben A. *Alexander Pope: The Poetry of Allusion*. Oxford: Clarendon, 1959.

Brown, Dee. *Bury My Heart at Wounded Knee: An Indian History of the American West*. New York: Henry Holt, 1970.

Brown, Laura. *Alexander Pope*. Oxford: Blackwell, 1985.

——. *Ends of Empire: Women and Ideology in Early Eighteenth-Century English Literature*. Ithaca, N.Y.: Cornell University Press, 1993.

Brustein, Robert. *The Theatre of Revolt: An Approach to the Modern Drama*. Boston: Little, Brown, 1964.

Bryan, Violet Harrington. *The Myth of New Orleans in Literature: Dialogues of Race and Gender*. Knoxville: University of Tennessee Press, 1993.

Burford, E. J. *London's Low Life: Covent Garden in the Eighteenth Century*. London: Robert Hale, 1986.

Burke, Peter. *Popular Culture in Early Modern Europe*. New York: Harper and Row, 1978.

Burkert, Walter. *Homo Necans: The Anthropology of Ancient Greek Sacrificial Ritual and Myth*. Trans. Peter Bing. Berkeley: University of California Press, 1983.

Buttrey, John. "[A Cautionary Tale]." In Henry Purcell and Nahum Tate, *Dido and Aeneas*, 228–35.

Calder, Angus. *Revolutionary Empire: The Rise of the English-Speaking Empires from the Fifteenth Century to the 1780s*. New York: Dutton, 1987.

Camden, William. *Brittania; or, A Chorographical Description of Great Britain and Ireland*. 2 vols. 2d ed. London: printed by M. Matthew, for A. Churchill, 1722.

Canfield, J. Douglas, and Deborah C. Payne, eds. *Cultural Readings of Restoration and Eighteenth-Century English Theater*. Athens: University of Georgia Press, 1995.

Carlson, Marvin. *Places of Performance: The Semiotics of Theatre Architecture*. Ithaca, N.Y.: Cornell University Press, 1989.

Carretta, Vincent. "Anne and Elizabeth: The Poet as Historian in *Windsor Forest*." *Studies in English Literature* 21 (1981): 425–37.

Carter, Hodding, ed. *The Past as Prelude: New Orleans, 1718–1968*. New Orleans: Pelican, 1968.

Castle, Terry. *Masquerade and Civilization: The Carnivalesque in Eighteenth-Century English Culture and Fiction*. Stanford, Calif.: Stanford University Press, 1986.

Chandler, James, Arnold I. Davidson, and Harry Harootunian, eds. *Questions of Evidence: Proof, Practice, and Persuasion Across the Disciplines*. Chicago: University of Chicago Press, 1991.

Cibber, Colley. *An Apology for the Life of Mr. Colley Cibber*. Ed. Robert W. Lowe. 2 vols. London: John C. Nimmo, 1889.

Clayson, Hollis. *Painted Love: Prostitution in French Art of the Impressionist Era*. New Haven: Yale University Press, 1991.
Clements, Frances M. "Landsdowne, Pope, and the Unity of *Windsor Forest*." *Modern Language Quarterly* 33 (1972): 44–53.
Clendinnen, Inga. *Aztecs: An Interpretation*. Cambridge: Cambridge University Press, 1991.
Clifford, James. *The Predicament of Culture: Twentieth-Century Ethnography, Literature, and Art*. Cambridge: Harvard University Press, 1988.
Colley, Linda. *Britons: Forging the Nation, 1707–1837*. New Haven: Yale University Press, 1992.
Congreve, William. *Complete Works*. Ed. Montague Summers. 4 vols. 1924. Rpt., New York: Russell and Russell, 1964.
Connerton, Paul. *How Societies Remember*. New York: Cambridge University Press, 1989.
Conquergood, Dwight. "Rethinking Ethnography: Towards a Critical Cultural Politics." *Communication Monographs* 58 (1991): 179–94.
Cowhig, Ruth. "Blacks in English Renaissance Drama and the Role of Shakespeare's Othello." In David Dabydeen, ed., *The Black Presence in English Literature*, 1–25.
Crété, Liliane. *Daily Life in Louisiana, 1815–1830*. Trans. Patrick Gregory. Baton Rouge: Louisiana State University Press, 1981.
Curl, James Stevens. *A Celebration of Death: An Introduction to Some of the Buildings, Monuments, and Settings of Funerary Architecture in the Western European Tradition*. New York: Scribner's, 1980.
Dabydeen, David. *Hogarth's Blacks: Images of Blacks in Eighteenth Century English Art*. Athens: University of Georgia Press, 1987.
——, ed. *The Black Presence in English Literature*. Manchester, UK: Manchester University Press, 1985.
Daily Picayune, February 20, 1853; March 26, 1853; December 20, 1855; December 28, 1855; January 14, 1856; December 24, 1859; December 22 and 24, 1884; January 3, 1885; February 16 and 17, 1885.
Danchin, Pierre, ed. *The Prologues and Epilogues of the Eighteenth Century. First Part: 1701–1720*. Nancy: Presses Universitaires de Nancy, 1990.
[Davenant, Sir William]. *Macbeth, a Tragedy: With All the Alterations, Amendments, Additions, and New Songs. As It Is Now Acted at the Duke's Theatre*. London: A. Clark, 1674.
Davies, Thomas. *Dramatic Miscellanies*. 3 vols. London: Thomas Davies, 1784.
Davis, Susan G. *Parades and Power: Street Theatre in Nineteenth-Century Philadelphia*. Philadelphia: Temple University Press, 1986.
Davis, Tracy C. "The Spectacle of Absent Costume: Nudity on the Victorian Stage." *New Theatre Quarterly* 5 (1989): 321–33.

Deahl, William E., Jr. "Buffalo Bill's Wild West Show in New Orleans." *Louisiana History* 16 (1975): 289–98.

De Caro, Francis A. Review of *The Black Indians of New Orleans*, by Maurice M. Martinez and James E. Hinton. *Journal of American Folklore* 91 (1978): 625–27.

De Certeau, Michel. *The Practice of Everyday Life*. Trans. Steven Rendall. Berkeley: University of California Press, 1984.

——. *The Writing of History*. Trans. Tom Conley. New York: Columbia University Press, 1988.

Defoe, Daniel. *The True-Born English-man*. London: H. Hills, 1708.

Degen, John A. "How to End *The Octoroon*." *Theatre Journal* 27 (1975): 170–78.

Delany, Martin R. *Blake; or, The Huts of America*. 1859–61. Boston: Beacon, 1970.

Deng, Francis M. *The Dinka of the Sudan*. New York: Holt, 1972.

Dennis, Matthew. *Cultivating a Landscape of Peace: Iroquois-European Encounters in Seventeenth-Century America*. Ithaca, N.Y.: Cornell University Press, 1993.

Dent, Tom. *Blue Lights and River Songs*. Detroit: Lotus, 1982.

Derrida, Jacques. *Counterfeit Money*. Given Time, vol. 1. Chicago: University of Chicago Press, 1992.

Detienne, Marcel, and Jean-Pierre Vernaht. *The Cuisine of Sacrifice Among the Greeks*. Trans. Paula Wissing. Chicago: University of Chicago Press, 1989.

Deutsch, Helen. *"Resemblance and Disgrace": Alexander Pope and the Deformation of Culture*. Cambridge: Harvard University Press, forthcoming.

Diderot, Denis. "The Paradox of the Actor." In *Selected Writings on Art and Literature*, trans. Geoffrey Bremer. London: Penguin, 1994, 98–158.

Dobson, Michael. *The Making of the National Poet: Shakespeare, Adaptation, and Authorship, 1660–1769*. New York: Oxford University Press, 1992.

[Doran, John]. "Frozen-Out Actors." *The Cornhill Magazine* 5 (1862): 167–77.

Downes, John. *Roscius Anglicanus; or, An Historical Review of the Stage*. 1706. Ed. Judith Milhous and Robert D. Hume. London: Society for Theatre Research, 1987.

Draper, David Elliot. "Mardi Gras Indians: The Ethnomusicology of Black Association in New Orleans." Ph.D. diss., Tulane University, 1973.

Drewal, Margaret Thompson. "Ritual Performance in Africa Today." *TDR: Journal of Performance Studies* 32, no. 2 (1988): 25–30.

——. *Yoruba Ritual: Performers, Play, Agency*. Bloomington: Indiana University Press, 1992.

Drummond, A. M., and Richard Moody. "Indian Treaties: The First American Dramas." *Quarterly Journal of Speech* 39 (1953): 15–24.

Dryden, John. *The Works of John Dryden*. Vol. 9, *Plays: The Indian Emperour, Secret Love, and Sir Martin Mar-all*, ed. John Loftis. Berkeley: University of California Press, 1966.

——, trans. *Virgil: The Aeneid*. New York: Heritage, 1944.

Du Bois, W. E. B. *The Souls of Black Folk*. 1903. Intro. John Edgar Wideman. New York: Vintage, 1990.

Durham, Weldon, ed. *American Theatre Companies, 1749–1887*. New York: Greenwood, 1986.

Eggler, Bruce. "Barthelemy: Monument Will Be Re-erected." *New Orleans Times-Picayune*, September 22, 1992, B-1–2.

Elias, Norbert. *The Civilizing Process*. Trans. Edmund Jephcott. Vol. 1, *The History of Manners*. New York: Urizen, 1978.

Erdman, Harley. "Caught in the 'Eye of the Eternal': Justice, Race, and the Camera, from *The Octoroon* to Rodney King." *Theatre Journal* 45 (1993): 333–48.

Evans-Pritchard, Edward E. *The Divine Kingship of the Shilluk of the Nilotic Sudan*. Cambridge: Cambridge University Press, 1948.

Fabian, Johannes. *Time and the Other: How Anthropology Makes Its Object*. New York: Columbia University Press, 1983.

Falassi, Alessandro, ed. *Time Out of Time: Essays on the Festival*. Albuquerque: University of New Mexico Press, 1967.

Fanon, Frantz. *Black Skin, White Masks*. Trans. Charles Lam Markmann. New York: Grove Weidenfeld, 1967.

———. *The Wretched of the Earth*. Trans. Constance Farrington. New York: Grove, 1963.

Farquhar, George. *Works*. Ed. Shirley Strum Kenny. 2 vols. Oxford: Clarendon, 1988.

The Female Tatler. Ed. Fidelis Morgan. London: Dent, 1992.

Fenton, William N. "Structure, Continuity, and Change in the Process of Iroquois Treaty Making." In Francis Jennings, ed., *The History and Culture of Iroquois Diplomacy*, 3–36.

Ferguson, Moira. "*Oroonoko*: Birth of a Paradigm." *New Literary History* 23 (1992): 339–59.

Fernandez, James W. *Persuasions and Performances: The Play of Tropes in Culture*. Bloomington: Indiana University Press, 1986.

Fiedler, Leslie A. *Love and Death in the American Novel*. Rev. ed. New York: Dell, 1966.

Fiehrer, Thomas Marc. "The African Presence in Colonial Louisiana: An Essay on the Continuity of Caribbean Culture." In Robert R. MacDonald, John R. Kemp, and Edward F. Haas, eds., *Louisiana's Black Heritage*. New Orleans: Louisiana State Museum, 1979, 3–31.

Finnegan, Ruth. *Oral Poetry: Its Nature, Significance, and Social Context*. Rev. ed. Bloomington: Indiana University Press, 1992.

Flake, Carol. *New Orleans: Behind the Masks of America's Most Exotic City*. New York: Grove, 1994.

Fliegelman, Jay. *Declaring Independence: Jefferson, Natural Language, and the Culture of Performance*. Stanford, Calif.: Stanford University Press, 1993.

Flynn, J. Q. *Digest of the City Ordinances*. New Orleans: L. Graham and Son, 1896.

Foster, Michael K. "Another Look at the Function of Wampum in Iroquois-White Councils." In Francis Jennings, ed., *The History and Culture of Iroquois Diplomacy*, 99–114.

Foster, Susan Leigh. *Storying Bodies: The Choreography of Narrative and Gender in the French Action Ballet*. Bloomington: Indiana University Press, forthcoming.

Foucault, Michel. *Discipline and Punish: The Birth of the Prison*. Trans. Alan Sheridan. New York: Vintage, 1979.

———. "Nietzsche, Genealogy, History." In Donald F. Bouchard, ed., *Language, Counter-Memory, Practice: Selected Essays and Interviews*. Ithaca, N.Y.: Cornell University Press, 1977, 139–64.

Franko, Mark. *Dance as Text: Ideologies of the Baroque Body*. Cambridge: Cambridge University Press, 1993.

Frantzen, Allen J. *Desire for Origins: New Language, Old English, and Teaching the Tradition*. New Brunswick, N.J.: Rutgers University Press, 1990.

Frazer, Sir James. *The Golden Bough: A Study in Magic and Religion*. 1922. New York: Macmillan, 1951.

Gans, Herbert J. "Symbolic Ethnicity: The Future of Ethnic Groups and Cultures in America." In Herbert J. Gans, Nathan Glazer, Joseph R. Gunsfield, and Christopher Jencks, eds., *On the Making of Americans*. Philadelphia: University of Pennsylvania Press, 1979, 193–220.

Ganz, James A. *Fancy Pieces: Genre Mezzotints by Robert Robinson and His Contemporaries*. New Haven: Yale Center for British Art, 1994.

Garber, Marjorie. *Vested Interests: Cross-Dressing and Cultural Anxiety*. 1992. New York: HarperCollins, 1993.

Gates, Henry Louis, Jr. "The Face and Voice of Blackness." In Guy C. McElroy, ed., *Facing History: The Black Image in American Art, 1710–1940*, xxix–xliv.

———. *The Signifying Monkey: A Theory of Afro-American Literary Criticism*. New York: Oxford University Press, 1988.

Geertz, Clifford. *The Interpretation of Cultures*. New York: Basic, 1973.

Genest, John. *Some Account of the English Stage: From the Restoration in 1660 to 1830*. 10 vols. Bath: H. E. Carrington, 1832.

Gennep, Arnold van. *The Rites of Passage*. Chicago: University of Chicago Press, 1960.

Genovese, Eugene D. *Roll, Jordan, Roll: The World the Slaves Made*. New York: Pantheon, 1972.

Giesey, Ralph E. *The Royal Funeral Ceremony in Renaissance France*. Geneva: Droz, 1960.

Gildon, Charles. *The Life of Mr. Thomas Betterton, the Late Eminent Tragedian.* London: printed for Robert Gosling, 1710.

Gilroy, Paul. *The Black Atlantic: Modernity and Double Consciousness.* Cambridge: Harvard University Press, 1993.

———. *Small Acts: Thoughts on the Politics of Black Cultures.* London: Serpent's Tail, 1993.

———. *"There Ain't No Black in the Union Jack": The Cultural Politics of Race and Nation.* Chicago: University of Chicago Press, 1987.

Girard, René. *Violence and the Sacred.* Trans. Patrick Gregory. Baltimore: Johns Hopkins University Press, 1981.

Graff, Gerald. *Professing Literature: An Institutional History.* Chicago: University of Chicago Press, 1987.

Grafton, Anthony, and Ann Blair, eds. *The Transmission of Culture in Early Modern Europe.* Philadelphia: University of Pennsylvania Press, 1990.

Greenblatt, Stephen. *Renaissance Self-Fashioning: From More to Shakespeare.* Chicago: University of Chicago Press, 1980.

Gregory, C. A. *Gifts and Commodities.* London: Academic Press, 1982.

Grimsted, David. *Melodrama Unveiled: American Theater and Culture, 1800–1850.* Chicago: University of Chicago Press, 1968.

Grose, Donald B. "Edwin Forrest, *Metamora*, and the Indian Removal Act of 1830." *Theatre Journal* 37 (1985): 181–91.

Guralnick, Peter. *Last Train to Memphis: The Rise of Elvis Presley.* Boston: Little, Brown, 1994.

Habermas, Jürgen. *Communication and the Evolution of Society.* Boston: Beacon, 1979.

———. *The Structural Transformation of the Public Sphere: An Inquiry into a Category of Bourgeois Society.* Cambridge: MIT Press, 1989.

Halbwachs, Maurice. *On Collective Memory.* Ed. and trans. Lewis A. Coser. University of Chicago Press, 1992.

Hall, Gwendolyn Midlo. *Africans in Colonial Louisiana: The Development of Afro-Creole Culture in the Eighteenth Century.* Baton Rouge: Louisiana State University Press, 1992.

Halttunen, Karen. *Confidence Men and Painted Women: A Study of Middle-Class Culture in America, 1830–1870.* New Haven: Yale University Press, 1982.

Hannusch, Jeff. *I Hear You Knockin': The Sound of New Orleans Rhythm and Blues.* Ville Platte, La.: Swallow, 1985.

Hardy, Arthur. *Mardi Gras Guide: Nineteenth Annual Edition.* New Orleans: Arthur Hardy Enterprises, 1995.

Harper's Weekly, January 21, 1863, and March 29, 1873.

Herndon, Thomas C. "One Hundred Years of Comus: Report of the Historical

Committee of the M. K. C." 1956–57. Rogers Family Papers, Manuscripts Division, Tulane University Library.

Hewitt, Barnard. *Theatre U.S.A., 1668–1957*. New York: McGraw-Hill, 1959.

Hibbitts, Bernard J. " 'Coming to Our Senses': Communication and Legal Expression in Performance Cultures." *Emory Law Journal* 41 (1992): 873–960.

Highshaw, Robert B. *Edward Douglas White: Defender of the Conservative Faith*. Baton Rouge: Louisiana State University Press, 1981.

Hill, Errol. *The Jamaican Stage, 1655–1900: Profile of a Colonial Theatre*. Amherst: University of Massachusetts Press, 1992.

———. *Trinidad Carnival: Mandate for a National Theatre*. Austin: University of Texas Press, 1972.

Hirsch, Arnold, and Joseph Logsdon, eds. *Creole New Orleans: Race and Americanization*. Baton Rouge: Louisiana State University Press, 1992.

Historical Sketch Book and Guide to New Orleans and Environs. New York: Will H. Coleman, 1885.

Hobsbawm, Eric, and Terence Ranger, eds. *The Invention of Tradition*. Cambridge: Cambridge University Press, 1983.

Hofstadter, Richard, and Michael Wallace, eds. *American Violence: A Documentary History*. New York: Knopf, 1970.

Holland, Peter. *The Ornament of Action: Text and Performance in Restoration Comedy*. Cambridge: Cambridge University Press, 1979.

Holloway, Joseph E., ed. *Africanisms in American Culture*. Bloomington: Indiana University Press, 1990.

Holmes, Geoffrey. "The Sacheverell Riots." *Past and Present* 72 (1976): 55–85.

Honour, Hugh. *The Image of the Black in Western Art*. Cambridge: Harvard University Press, 1989.

hooks, bell. *Black Looks: Race and Representation*. Boston: South End, 1993.

Howe, Elizabeth. *The First English Actresses: Women and Drama, 1660–1700*. Cambridge: Cambridge University Press, 1992.

Huber, Leonard V. "New Orleans Cemeteries: A Brief History." In *New Orleans Architecture*. Vol. 3, *The Cemeteries*, ed. Mary Louise Christovich. Gretna, La.: Pelican, 1974, 3–62.

Hulme, Peter. *Colonial Encounters: Europe and the Native Caribbean, 1492–1797*. 1986. London: Routledge, 1992.

Hume, Robert D., ed. *The London Theatre World, 1660–1800*. Carbondale: Southern Illinois University Press, 1980.

Huntington, Richard, and Peter Metcalf. *Celebrations of Death: The Anthropology of Mortuary Ritual*. Cambridge: Cambridge University Press, 1979.

Hutner, Heidi, ed. *Rereading Aphra Behn: History, Theory, and Criticism*. Charlottesville: University Press of Virginia, 1993.

Hyde, Lewis. *The Gift: Imagination and the Erotic Life of Property*. New York: Vintage, 1979.

Hymes, Dell. *Foundations in Sociolinguistics: An Ethnographic Perspective*. Philadelphia: University of Pennsylvania Press, 1975.

James, C. L. R. *The Black Jacobins: Toussaint L'Overture and the San Domingo Revolution*. 1938. 2d ed. New York: Random House, 1989.

Jehlen, Myra. "History Before the Fact; or, Captain John Smith's Unfinished Symphony." *Critical Inquiry* 19 (1993): 677–92.

Jelly Roll Morton. Library of Congress Recordings, vol. 5, 1938; remastered 1970, HJA.

Jennings, Francis. *The Invasion of America: Indians, Colonialism, and the Cant of Conquest*. Chapel Hill: University of North Carolina Press, 1975.

—, ed. *The History and Culture of Iroquois Diplomacy: An Interdisciplinary Guide to the Treaties of the Six Nations and Their League*. Syracuse: Syracuse University Press, 1985.

Johnson, Jerah. "Colonial New Orleans: A Fragment of the Eighteenth-Century French Ethos." In Arnold Hirsch and Joseph Logsdon, eds., *Creole New Orleans*, 12–57.

——. "New Orleans's Congo Square: An Urban Setting for Early Afro-American Culture Formation." *Louisiana History* 32 (1991): 117–57.

Jones, Eugene H. *Native Americans as Shown on the Stage, 1753–1916*. Metuchen, N.J.: Scarecrow, 1988.

Jones, Tom, and Harvey Schmidt. *The Fantasticks*. New York: Avon, 1964.

Kammen, Michael. *Mystic Chords of Memory: The Transformation of Tradition in American Culture*. New York: Knopf, 1991.

Kantorowicz, Ernst. *The King's Two Bodies: A Study in Mediaeval Political Theory*. Princeton: Princeton University Press, 1957.

Keegan, John. *A History of Warfare*. New York: Vintage, 1994.

Kelley, Donald R. " 'Second Nature': The Idea of Custom in European Law, Society, and Culture." In Anthony Grafton and Ann Blair, eds., *The Transmission of Culture in Early Modern Europe*, 131–72.

Kendall, John A. *The Golden Age of New Orleans Theater*. Baton Rouge: Louisiana State University Press, 1952.

——. *History of New Orleans*. 3 vols. Chicago: Lewis, 1922.

Kennedy, Paul. *The Rise and Fall of the Great Powers: Economic Change and Military Conflict, 1500–2000*. New York: Random House, 1987.

Kertzer, David I. *Ritual, Politics, and Power*. New Haven: Yale University Press, 1988.

Ketcham, Michael G. *Transparent Designs: Reading, Performance, and Form in the Spectator Papers*. Athens: University of Georgia Press, 1985.

Kinser, Samuel. *Carnival, American Style: Mardi Gras at New Orleans and Mobile.* Chicago: University of Chicago Press, 1990.

Kirshenblatt-Gimblett, Barbara. "The Future of Folklore Studies in America: The Urban Frontier." *Folklore Forum* 16 (1983): 175–234.

Kmen, Henry A. "The Roots of Jazz in Place Congo: A Re-Appraisal." In *Inter-American Musical Research Yearbook.* Austin: Institute of Latin American Studies, University of Texas at Austin, 1972, 5–16.

Kolb, Carolyn. *New Orleans: An Invitation to Discover One of America's Most Fascinating Cities.* New York: Doubleday, 1972.

Kosok, Heinz. "Dion Boucicault's 'American' Plays: Considerations on Defining National Literatures in English." In Robert Welch and Suheil Badi Bushrui, eds., *Literature and the Art of Creation.* Totowa, N.J.: Barnes and Noble, 1988, 81–97.

Kramer, John Theophilus. *The Slave Auction.* Boston: Robert F. Walcut, 1859.

Kruger, Loren. *The National Stage: Theatre and Cultural Legitimation in England, France, and America.* Chicago: University of Chicago Press, 1992.

Lafitau, Joseph-François. *Customs of the American Indians Compared with the Customs of Primitive Times.* 1724. Ed. and trans. William N. Fenton and Elizabeth L. Moore. 2 vols. Publications of the Champlain Society, 48, 49. Toronto: Champlain Society, 1974–77.

Lamb, Charles. *Works.* 1903. Ed. E. V. Lucas. 5 vols. Rpt. New York: AMS, 1968.

Lamming, George. "Caribbean Literature: The Black Rock of Africa." In Richard Drayton and Andaiye, eds., *Essays, Addresses, and Interviews, 1953–1990.* London: Karia, 1992, 106–25.

Landry, Stuart D. *The Battle of Liberty Place: The Overthrow of Carpet-Bag Rule in New Orleans, September 14, 1874.* New Orleans: Pelican, 1955.

——. *History of the Boston Club, Organized in 1841.* New Orleans: Pelican, 1938.

Las Casas, Bartolomé. *A Short Account of the Destruction of the Indies.* Ed. and trans. Nigel Griffin. Intro. Anthony Pagden. London: Penguin, 1992.

Latrobe, Benjamin Henry. *Journals, 1799–1820: From Philadelphia to New Orleans.* Ed. Edward C. Carter II, John C. Van Horne, and Lee W. Formwalt. New Haven: Yale University Press, 1980.

Laubin, Reginald, and Gladys Laubin. *Indian Dances of North America.* Norman: University of Oklahoma Press, 1977.

Le Goff, Jacques. *History and Memory.* Trans. Steven Rendall and Elizabeth Claman. New York: Columbia University Press, 1992.

Leovy, Henry J. *The Laws and General Ordinances of the City of New Orleans.* New Orleans: E. C. Wharton, 1857.

Le Roy Ladurie, Emmanuel. *Carnival in Romans.* Trans. Mary Feeney. New York: Braziller, 1979.

——. *Montaillou: The Promised Land of Error*. Trans. Barbara Bray. New York: Vintage, 1979.

Levine, Lawrence W. *Black Culture and Black Consciousness: Afro-American Folk Thought from Slavery to Freedom*. New York: Oxford University Press, 1977.

——. *Highbrow/Lowbrow: The Emergence of Cultural Hierarchy in America*. Cambridge: Harvard University Press, 1988.

Lincoln, Abraham. *Speeches and Writings, 1859–1865*. Ed. Don E. Fehrenbacher. N.p.: Library of America, 1989.

Lipsitz, George. *Dangerous Crossroads: Popular Music, Postmodernism, and the Politics of Place*. London: Verso, 1994.

——. *Time Passages: Collective Memory and American Popular Culture*. Minneapolis: University of Minnesota Press, 1990.

Lislet, L. Moreau. *A General Digest of the Acts of the Legislature of Louisiana, 1804–1827*. New Orleans: Benjamin Levy, 1828.

Lofgren, Charles A. *The Plessy Case: A Legal-Historical Interpretation*. New York: Oxford University Press, 1987.

Lomax, Alan. *Mister Jelly Roll: The Fortunes of Jelly Roll Morton, New Orleans Creole and "Inventor of Jazz."* New York: Duell, Sloan, and Pearce, 1950.

Longfellow, Henry Wadsworth. "The Quadroon Girl." In *The Complete Poetical Works*. Boston: Houghton Mifflin, 1902, 28.

Lott, Eric. *Love and Theft: Blackface Minstrelsy and the American Working Class*. New York: Oxford University Press, 1993.

Louisiana Statutes Annotated. St. Paul, Minn.: West, 1991.

Lowe, Robert W. *Thomas Betterton*. London: Kegan Paul, 1891.

Luttrell, Narcissus. *A Brief Historical Relation of State Affairs from September 1678 to April 1714*. 6 vols. Oxford: Oxford University Press, 1857.

MacAloon, John J. *Rite, Drama, Festival, Spectacle: Rehearsals Toward a Theory of Cultural Performance*. Philadelphia: Institute for the Study of Human Issues, 1984.

McClary, Susan. "Music, Pythagoreans, and the Body." In Susan Foster, ed. *Choreographing History*. Bloomington: Indiana University Press, 1995, 82–104.

McConachie, Bruce A. *Melodramatic Formations: American Theatre and Society, 1820–1870*. Iowa City: University of Iowa Press, 1992.

McCrea, Brian. *Addison and Steele Are Dead: The English Department, Its Canon, and the Professionalization of Literary Criticism*. Newark: University of Delaware Press, 1990.

MacDougall, Hugh A. *Racial Myth in English History: Trojans, Teutons, and Anglo-Saxons*. Hanover: University Press of New England, 1982.

Mack, Maynard. *Alexander Pope: A Life*. New York: Norton, 1985.

MacNamara, Brooks. "Invisible Theatre: Folk and Festival Tradition in America." In C. J. Stevens and Joseph Aurbach, eds., *Theatre Byways: Essays in Honor of Claude L. Shaver*. New Orleans: Polyanthos, 1978, 6–16.

Mahan, Alfred Thayer. *The Influence of Sea Power Upon History, 1660–1783*. 1890. Rpt., New York: Dover, 1987.

Markley, Robert. *Two-Edg'd Weapons: Style and Ideology in the Comedies of Etherege, Wycherley, and Congreve*. Oxford: Clarendon, 1988.

Marx, Karl. *Capital*. Trans. Ben Fowkes. Vol. 1. New York: Random House, 1977.

Mason, Jeffrey D. *Melodrama and the Myth of America*. Bloomington: Indiana University Press, 1993.

Mauss, Marcel. *The Gift: Forms and Functions of Exchange in Archaic Societies*. New York: Norton, 1967.

McElroy, Guy C., ed. *Facing History: The Black Image in American Art, 1710–1940*. Washington, D.C.: Corcoran Gallery of Art, 1990.

Meisel, Martin. *Realizations: Narrative, Pictorial, and Theatrical Arts in Nineteenth-Century England*. Princeton: Princeton University Press, 1983.

Meller, Hugh. *London Cemeteries*. 3d ed. Aldershot, England: Scolar, 1994.

Mellers, Wilfrid. *Harmonious Meeting: A Study of the Relationship Between English Music, Poetry and Theatre*. London: Dennis Dobson, 1965.

Mellon, James, ed. *Bullwhip Days: The Slaves Remember, An Oral History*. New York: Avon, 1988.

Mercer, Kobena. *Welcome to the Jungle: New Positions in Black Cultural Studies*. New York: Routledge, 1994.

Meserve, Walter J. *An Emerging Entertainment: The Drama of the American People to 1828*. Bloomington: Indiana University Press, 1977.

Miceli, Augusto P. *The Pickwick Club of New Orleans*. New Orleans: Pickwick, 1964.

Michals, Teresa. " 'That Sole and Despotic Dominion': Slaves, Wives, and Game in Blackstone's *Commentaries*." *Eighteenth-Century Studies* 27 (1993–94): 195–216.

Michie, Helena. *Sororophobia: Differences Among Women in Literature and Culture*. New York: Oxford University Press, 1992.

Milhous, Judith. "An Annotated Census of Thomas Betterton's Roles, 1659–1710." *Theatre Notebook* 29 (1975): 33–45 (part 1); 85–94 (part 2).

Mintz, Sidney W. *Sweetness and Power: The Place of Sugar in Modern History*. New York: Viking-Penguin, 1985.

Mintz, Sidney W., and Richard Price. *The Birth of African-American Culture: An Anthropological Perspective*. 1976. Rpt., Boston: Beacon, 1992.

Mitchell, Reid. *All on a Mardi Gras Day: Episodes in the History of New Orleans Carnival*. Cambridge: Harvard University Press, 1995.

Mitford, Jessica. *The American Way of Death*. New York: Simon and Schuster, 1963.

Morris, David B. *Alexander Pope: The Genius of Sense*. Cambridge: Harvard University Press, 1984.

Morrison, Toni. *Playing in the Dark: Whiteness and the Literary Imagination*. New York: Vintage, 1992.

Mudimbe, V. Y. *The Invention of Africa: Gnosis, Philosophy, and the Order of Knowledge*. Bloomington: Indiana University Press, 1988.

Mulira, Jessie Gaston. "The Case of Voodoo in New Orleans." In Joseph E. Holloway, ed., *Africanisms in American Culture*, 34–68.

Mullaney, Steven. *The Place of the Stage: License, Play, and Power in Renaissance England*. Chicago: University of Chicago Press, 1988.

Myerhoff, Barbara. "The Transformation of Consciousness in Ritual Performance: Some Thoughts and Questions." In Richard Schechner and Willa Appel, eds., *By Means of Performance*, 245–49.

Nair, Sypriya. *Making History: Social Revolution in the Novels of George Lamming*. Ann Arbor: University of Michigan Press, forthcoming.

Nash, Gary B. *Red, White, and Black: The Peoples of Early America*. Englewood Cliffs, N.J.: Prentice-Hall, 1974.

Ngugi wa Thiong'o. Interview with Bettye J. Parker. In G. D. Killam, ed., *Critical Perspectives on Ngugi wa Thiong'o*. Washington, D.C.: Three Continents, 1984, 58–66.

Nora, Pierre. "Between Memory and History: *Les Lieux de Mémoire*." *Representations* 26 (spring 1989): 7–25.

Nunley, John W., and Judith Bettelheim, eds. *Caribbean Festival Arts: Each and Every Bit of Difference*. Seattle: University of Washington Press, 1988.

O'Brien, Rosary Hartel. "The New Orleans Carnival Organizations: Theatre of Prestige." Ph.D. diss., UCLA, 1973.

Okpewho, Isidore. *African Oral Literature: Backgrounds, Character, and Continuity*. Bloomington: Indiana University Press, 1992.

[Oldmixon, John]. *The British Empire in America, Containing the History of the Discovery, Settlement, Progress, and State of the British Colonies on the Continent and Islands of America*. 2d ed. 2 vols. London: J. Brotherton, J. Clarke, 1741.

Olsen, Otto H., ed. *The Thin Disguise: Turning Point in Negro History. Plessy v. Ferguson. A Documentary Presentation, 1864–1896*. New York: Humanities, 1967.

One Hundred Years of Comus. New Orleans: privately printed, 1957. The Rogers Family Papers, Special Collections, Howard Tilton Memorial Library, Tulane University.

Pagden, Anthony. *The Fall of Natural Man: The American Indian and the Origins of Comparative Ethnology*. Cambridge: Cambridge University Press, 1982.

Pajaud, Willie. File, "Funeral and Music General," HJA.

Patterson, Orlando. *Slavery and Social Death: A Comparative Study*. Cambridge: Harvard University Press, 1982.

Paulson, Ronald. *Hogarth*. Vol. 2, *High Art and Low*. New Brunswick, N.J.: Rutgers University Press, 1992.

Peters, Julie Stone. *Congreve, the Drama, and the Printed Word*. Stanford, Calif.: Stanford University Press, 1990.

Phelan, Peggy. *Unmarked: The Politics of Performance*. London: Routledge, 1993.

The Pickwick Club: Historical Summary, Act of Incorporation, By-Laws, and Roster of Membership. New Orleans: privately printed, 1929. Churchill Family Papers, Manuscripts Division, Tulane University Library.

Pinnock, Andrew. "Play into Opera: Purcell's *The Indian Queen*." *Early Music* 18 (1990): 3–21.

Plank, Stephen E. " 'And Now About the Cauldron Sing': Music and the Supernatural on the Restoration Stage." *Early Music* 18 (1990): 393–407.

Platform of the Crescent City White League. New Orleans, June 27, 1874. Fred Nash Ogden Papers, Special Collections, Howard Tilton Memorial Library, Tulane University.

Pope, Alexander. *The Poems of Alexander Pope*. Vol. 1, *Pastoral Poetry and an Essay on Criticism*, ed. E. Audra and Aubrey Williams. New Haven: Yale University Press, 1961.

———. *The Poems of Alexander Pope*. Vol. 2, *The Rape of the Lock and Other Poems*, ed. Geoffrey Tillotson. 2d ed., rev. New Haven: Yale University Press, 1954.

———. *The Poems of Alexander Pope*. Vol. 3.2, *Epistles to Several Persons*, ed. F. W. Bateson. New Haven: Yale University Press, 1951.

———. *The Correspondence of Alexander Pope*. Ed. George Sherburn. Vol. 1. Oxford: Clarendon, 1956.

Porcupine. "Account of the Messiah." In *The Ghost-Dance Religion and Wounded Knee*. 1896. Ed. James Mooney. New York: Dover Publications, 1973, 793–96.

Postlewait, Thomas. "Historiography and the Theatrical Event: A Primer and Twelve Cruxes." *Theatre Journal* 43 (1991): 157–78.

Powell, Lawrence N. "A Concrete Symbol." *Southern Exposure* 18, no. 1 (1990): 40–43.

Prescott, W. H. *History of the Conquest of Mexico*. 1843. New York: Random House, n.d.

Price, Curtis. "*Dido and Aeneas* in Context." In Henry Purcell and Nahum Tate, *Dido and Aeneas: An Opera*, 3–41.

"Primeval Partying for Harlequins." *New Orleans Times-Picayune*, December 29, 1993, E-3.

Purcell, Henry, and Nahum Tate. *Dido and Aeneas: An Opera*. Ed. Curtis Price. New York: Norton, 1986.

Quint, David. *Epic and Empire: Politics and Generic Form from Virgil to Milton.* Princeton: Princeton University Press, 1993.

Quintero, Ruben. *Literate Cultures: Pope's Rhetorical Art.* Newark: University of Delaware Press, 1992.

Radcliffe-Brown, Alfred R. *Method in Social Anthropology: Selected Essays.* Chicago: University of Chicago Press, 1958.

Ragon, Michel. *Space of Death: A Study of Funerary Architecture, Decoration, and Urbanism.* Trans. Alan Sheridan. Charlottesville: University Press of Virginia, 1983.

Rebennack, Malcolm [Dr. John], with Jack Rummel. *Under a Hoodoo Moon: The Life of Dr. John the Night Tripper.* New York: St. Martin's, 1994.

Reid, Mayne. *The Quadroon; or, A Lover's Adventures in Louisiana.* New York: Robert M. De Witt, 1856.

Richardson, Gary A. "Boucicault's *The Octoroon* and American Law." *Theatre Journal* 34 (1982): 155–64.

Richardson, Ruth. *Death, Dissection, and the Destitute.* London: Penguin, 1988.

Richter, Daniel K. *The Ordeal of the Long-House: The Peoples of the Iroquois League in the Era of European Colonization.* Chapel Hill: University of North Carolina Press, 1992.

Rightor, Henry. *Standard History of New Orleans, Louisiana.* Chicago: Lewis, 1900.

Roach, Joseph R. *The Player's Passion: Studies in the Science of Acting.* 1985. Rpt., Ann Arbor: University of Michigan Press, 1993.

Robin, C. C. *Voyage to Louisiana, 1803–1805.* Trans. Stuart O. Landry. New Orleans: Pelican, 1966.

Robinson, Amy. "Forms of Appearance of Value: Homer Plessy and the Politics of Privacy." In Elin Diamond, ed., *Performance and Cultural Politics.* London: Routledge, forthcoming.

Rogers, Kim Lacy. *Righteous Lives: Narratives of the New Orleans Civil Rights Movement.* New York: New York University Press, 1993.

Rohrer, John H., and Munro S. Edmondson. *The Eighth Generation Grows Up: Cultures and Personalities of New Orleans Negroes.* New York: Harper and Row, 1960.

Rosaldo, Renato. *Culture and Truth: The Remaking of Social Analysis.* 1989. Boston: Beacon, 1993.

Rose, Al. *Storyville, New Orleans.* Tuscaloosa: University of Alabama Press, 1974.

Rowe, Nicholas. *The Works of Mr. William Shakespear.* 6 vols. London: Jacob Tonson, 1709.

Rubin, Gayle. "The Traffic in Women: Notes on the 'Political Economy' of Sex." In Rayna Reiter, ed., *Toward an Anthropology of Women.* New York: Monthly Review Press, 1975, 157–210.

Ryan, Mary P. "The American Parade: Representations of the Nineteenth-Century Social Order." In Lynn Hunt, ed., *The New Cultural History*. Berkeley: University of California Press, 1989, 131–53.

——. *Women in Public: Between Banners and Ballots, 1825–1880*. Baltimore: Johns Hopkins University Press, 1990.

Said, Edward W. *Orientalism*. New York: Vintage, 1979.

Sands, Rosita M. "Carnival Celebrations in Africa and the New World: Junkanoo and the Black Indians of Mardi Gras." *Black Music Research Journal* 11 (1991): 75–92.

Savage, Roger. "Producing *Dido and Aeneas*." In Henry Purcell and Nahum Tate, *Dido and Aeneas*. New York: Norton, 1986, 255–77.

Saxon, Lyle, Edward Dreyer, and Robert Tallant. *Gumbo Ya-Ya: A Collection of Louisiana Folk Tales*. 1945. Rpt., Gretna, La.: Pelican, 1988.

Schafer, Judith Kelleher. *Slavery, the Civil Law, and the Supreme Court of Louisiana*. Baton Rouge: Louisiana State University Press, 1994.

Schechner, Richard. *Between Theater and Anthropology*. Philadelphia: University of Pennsylvania Press, 1985.

——. *The Future of Ritual: Writings on Culture and Performance*. London: Routledge, 1993.

Schechner, Richard, and Willa Appel, eds. *By Means of Performance: Intercultural Studies of Theatre and Ritual*. Cambridge: Cambridge University Press, 1990.

Schlesinger, Arthur. *The Disuniting of America*. New York: Norton, 1992.

"Scope of the HRC 'Liberty Monument' Hearings." Human Relations Commission, Advisory Committee on Human Relations, City of New Orleans, June 15, 1993.

Scott, Dennis. *An Echo in the Bone* In *Plays for Today*. Ed. Errol Hill. Harlow, Essex, U.K.: Longman, 1985.

Scott, James C. *Domination and the Arts of Resistance: Hidden Transcripts*. New Haven: Yale University Press, 1990.

Senelick, Laurence. "The Erotic Bondage of Serf Theatre." *The Russian Review* 50 (1991): 24–34.

——, ed. *National Theatre in Northern and Eastern Europe, 1746–1900*. Theatre in Europe: A Documentary History. Cambridge: Cambridge University Press, 1991.

Simmons, William S. "Culture Theory in Contemporary Ethnohistory." *Ethnohistory* 35 (1988): 1–14.

Slotkin, Richard. *Regeneration Through Violence: The Mythology of the American Frontier, 1600-1860*. Middletown, Conn.: Wesleyan University Press, 1973.

Smith, Charles W. *Auctions: The Social Construction of Value*. Berkeley: University of California Press, 1989.

Smith, Michael P. *Mardi Gras Indians*. Gretna, La.: Pelican, 1994.

———. "New Orleans' Hidden Carnival: Traditional African-American Freedom Celebrations in Urban New Orleans." *Cultural Vistas* 1, no. 2 (1990): 5 ff.

———. *Spirit World: Pattern in the Expressive Folk Culture of Afro-American New Orleans*. New Orleans: Urban Folklife Society, 1984.

Solow, Barbara L., ed. *Slavery and the Rise of the Atlantic System*. Cambridge: Cambridge University Press, 1991.

Southern Reporter, 2nd Series. Vols. 156, 176, 330. St. Paul, Minn.: West, 1965–76.

Southerne, Thomas. *Oroonoko*. Ed. Maximillian E. Novak and David Stuart Rodes. Lincoln: University of Nebraska Press, 1976.

The Spectator. Ed. Donald F. Bond. 5 vols. Oxford: Clarendon, 1965.

Spencer, Christopher, ed. *Davenant's Macbeth from the Yale Manuscript: An Edition, with a Discussion of the Relation of Davenant's Text to Shakespeare's*. New Haven: Yale University Press, 1961.

Soyinka, Wole. *The Strong Breed*. In *Wole Soyinka: Collected Plays*. Oxford: Oxford University Press, 1973.

Stallybrass, Peter, and Allon White. *The Politics and Poetics of Transgression*. Ithaca, N.Y.: Cornell University Press, 1986.

Stanley, Arthur Penryhn. *Historical Memorials of Westminster Abbey*. London: Murray, 1886.

Stannard, David E. *American Holocaust: Columbus and the Conquest of the New World*. New York: Oxford University Press, 1992.

States, Bert O. *Great Reckonings in Little Rooms: On the Phenomenology of Theater*. Berkeley: University of California Press, 1985.

Staves, Susan. *Players' Scepters: Fictions of Authority in the Restoration*. Lincoln: University of Nebraska Press, 1979.

Stone, George Winchester, Jr. "The Making of the Repertory." In Robert D. Hume, ed., *The London Theatre World, 1660–1800*, 181–209.

Stone, John Augustus. *Metamora; or, The Last of the Wampanoags*. Ed. Eugene R. Page. Vol. 14 of *America's Lost Plays*, ed. Barrett H. Clark. Princeton: Princeton University Press, 1941.

Straub, Kristina. *Sexual Suspects: Eighteenth-Century Players and Sexual Ideology*. Princeton: Princeton University Press, 1992.

Sundquist, Eric J. *To Wake the Nations: Race in the Making of American Literature*. Cambridge: Harvard University Press, Belknap, 1993.

Survey of London. Vol. 35, *The Theatre Royal, Drury Lane, and the Royal Opera House, Covent Garden*. London: Athlone, 1970.

Sussman, Charlotte. "The Other Problem with Women: Reproduction and Slave Culture in Aphra Behn's *Oroonoko*." In Heidi Hutner, ed., *Rereading Aphra Behn*, 212–33.

Sypher, Wylie. *Guinea's Captive Kings: British Anti-Slavery Literature of the Eighteenth Century*. 1942. Rpt. New York: Octagon, 1969.

Tallant, Robert. *Voodoo in New Orleans*. 1946. Rpt., Gretna, La.: Pelican, 1983.

Tate, Nahum. *Brutus of Alba; or, The Enchanted Lovers*. London: Jacob Tonson, 1678.

The Tatler. Ed. Donald F. Bond. 3 vols. Oxford: Clarendon, 1987.

Taussig, Michael T. *The Devil and Commodity Fetishism in South America*. Chapel Hill: University of North Carolina Press, 1980.

Taylor, Diana. *Theatre of Crisis: Drama and Politics in Latin America*. Lexington: University of Kentucky Press, 1991.

Taylor, Gary. *Reinventing Shakespeare: A Cultural History, From the Restoration to the Present*. New York: Weidenfeld and Nicholson, 1989.

Taylor, Joe Gray. *Louisiana Reconstructed, 1863–1877*. Baton Rouge: Louisiana State University Press, 1974.

Thompson, E. P. "The Moral Economy of the English Crowd in the Eighteenth Century." In *Customs in Common*. New York: New Press, 1993, 185–258.

Times-Picayune, October 4, 1991; February 26, 1992; September 22, 1992; October 12, 1992.

Todd, Janet. *Gender, Art, and Death*. New York: Continuum, 1993.

Todorov, Tzvetan. *The Conquest of America: The Question of the Other*. Trans. Richard Howard. New York: HarperCollins, 1984.

Trevelyan, George Macaulay. *England Under Queen Anne*. 3 vols. London: Longmans, Green, 1930–34.

Truettner, William H. *The West as America: Reinterpreting Images of the Frontier*. Washington, D.C.: Smithsonian Institution Press, for the National Museum of Art, 1991.

Turner, Victor. *The Forest of Symbols: Aspects of Ndembu Ritual*. Ithaca, N.Y.: Cornell University Press, 1967.

———. *From Ritual to Theatre: The Human Seriousness of Play*. New York: PAJ, 1982.

———. *Schism and Continuity: A Study of Ndembu Village Life*. Manchester, U.K.: Manchester University Press, 1957.

—, ed. *Celebration: Studies in Festivity and Ritual*. Washington, D.C.: Smithsonian Institution Press, 1982.

Uffenbach, Zacharias Conrad von. *London in 1710*. Trans. and ed. W. H. Quarrel and Margaret Mare. London: Faber and Faber, 1934.

United States Postal Service. *The Postal Service Guide to U.S. Stamps*. 20th ed. Washington, D.C.: U.S. Postal Service, 1993.

Vanbrugh, John. "Vanbrugh's Proposals for the Fifty Churches (1711)." In Laurence Whistler, *The Imagination of Vanbrugh and His Fellow Artists*, appendix 2. London: B. T. Batsford, 1954, 247–52.

Van Creveld, Martin L. *Technology and War: From 2000 B.C. to the Present*. New York: Free Press; London: Collier Macmillan, 1989.

Vansina, Jan. *Oral Tradition as History*. Madison: University of Wisconsin Press, 1985.

Veblen, Thorstein. *The Theory of the Leisure Class: An Economic Study of Institutions*. New York: Vanguard, 1927.

Vennman, Barbara. "Boundary Face-Off: New Orleans Civil Rights Law and Carnival Tradition." *The Drama Review: A Journal of Performance Studies* 37, no. 3 (1993): 76–109.

———. "New Orleans 1993 Carnival: Tradition at Play in *Papier-Mâché* and Stone." *Theatre Insight* 5, no. 1 (1993): 5–12.

Versényi, Adam. *Theatre in Latin America: Religion, Politics, and Culture from Cortés to the 1980s*. Cambridge: Cambridge University Press, 1993.

Verstegen, Richard. *Restitution of Decayed Intelligence in Antiquities Concerning the Most Noble and Renowned English Nation*. 1605. London: T. Newcomb, for Josuah Kirton, 1653.

Voltaire. *Letters Concerning the English Nation*. 1733. Rpt., New York: Burt Franklin Reprints, 1974.

———. *The Selected Letters of Voltaire*. Trans. Richard A. Brooks. New York: New York University Press, 1973.

Wade, Les. "New Orleans French Theatre and Its Cultural Containment: The Origins of Bourbon Street Burlesque." *L'Annuaire théâtral: Revue québécoise d'études théâtrales* 12 (1992): 7–30.

Waith, Eugene M. *The Herculean Hero in Marlowe, Chapman, Shakespeare, and Dryden*. New York: Columbia University Press, 1962.

Waldo, J. Curtis. *Hand-Book of Carnival, Containing Mardi Gras, Its Ancient and Modern Observance, History of the Mistick Krewe of Comus, Twelfth Night Revelers and Knights of Momus, with Annals of the Reign of His Majesty, the King of Carnival in New Orleans*. New Orleans: W. E. Seebold, 1873.

———. *History of the Carnival in New Orleans, 1857–1882*. New Orleans: L. Graham and Son, 1882.

———. *The Roll of Honor: Roster of the Citizen Soldiery Who Saved Louisiana*. Revised and Complete. New Orleans: privately printed, 1877. Louisiana Collection, Tulane University Library.

Walker, Thomas. "Ciaccona and Passacaglia: Remarks on Their Origin and History." *Journal of the American Musicological Society* 21 (1968): 300–320.

Walpole, Horace. *Correspondence*. Ed. W. S. Lewis. 48 vols. New Haven: Yale University Press; Oxford: Oxford University Press, 1937–83.

Warner, Michael. *The Letters of the Republic: Publication and the Public Sphere in Eighteenth-Century America*. Cambridge: Harvard University Press, 1990.

Wasserman, Earl R. *The Subtler Language: Critical Readings of Neoclassical and Romantic Poems*. Baltimore: Johns Hopkins University Press, 1959.

Weekly Budget, March 6, 1878.

Weimann, Robert. "Shakespeare (De)Canonized: Conflicting Uses of 'Authority' and 'Representation.' " *New Literary History* 20 (1988): 65–81.

Wendorf, Richard. *Sir Joshua Reynolds: The Painter in Society*. Cambridge: Harvard University Press, forthcoming.

Werlein Memorandum. Unsigned letter to Philip Werlein, president, Pickwick Club, from the daughter of Charles H. Churchill, founding president, June 18, 1915. Churchill Family Papers, Manuscripts Division, Tulane University Library.

Whitehorse, David. *Pow-Wow: The Contemporary Pan-Indian Celebration*. Publications in American Indian Studies 5. San Diego: San Diego State University, 1988.

Williams, Patricia J. *The Alchemy of Race and Rights: Diary of a Law Professor*. Cambridge: Harvard University Press, 1991.

Wilmeth, Don. "Noble or Ruthless Savage?: The American Indian On Stage and in the Drama." *Journal of American Drama and Theatre* 1, no. 1 (1989):39–78.

———. "Tentative Checklist of Indian Plays." *Journal of American Drama and Theatre* 1, no. 2 (1989):34–54.

Winton, Calhoun. *John Gay and the London Theatre*. Lexington: University of Kentucky Press, 1993.

Wright, James. *Historia Histrionica: An Historical Account of the English Stage*. 1699. In Colley Cibber, *An Apology for the Life of Mr. Colley Cibber*, 1:xxi–li.

Young, Perry. *Carnival and Mardi-Gras in New Orleans*. New Orleans: Harmanson's, 1939.

———. *The Mistick Krewe: Chronicles of Comus and His Kin*. 1931. Rpt., New Orleans: Louisiana Heritage Press, 1969.

Young, William. *An Account of the Black Charaibs in the Island of St. Vincent's*. 1795. Rpt., London: Frank Cass, 1971.

Zanger, Jules. "The 'Tragic Octoroon' in Pre-Civil War Fiction." *American Quarterly* 18 (1966): 63–70.

Zumthor, Paul. *Oral Poetry: An Introduction*. Trans. Kathryn Murphy-Judy. Minneapolis: University of Minnesota Press, 1990.

INDEX

Designer: Linda Secondari
Text: Fournier
Compositor: Columbia University Press
Printer: Edwards Brothers
Binder: Edwards Brothers